Himalayan Voices

VOICES FROM ASIA

1. Of Women, Outcastes, Peasants, and Rebels: A Selection of Bengali Short Stories. *Translated and edited by Kalpana Bardhan.*
2. Himalayan Voices: An Introduction to Modern Nepali Literature. *Translated and edited by Michael James Hutt.*

Himalayan Voices

An Introduction to Modern Nepali Literature

TRANSLATED AND EDITED BY

Michael James Hutt

UNIVERSITY OF CALIFORNIA PRESS
Berkeley Los Angeles Oxford

University of California Press
Berkeley and Los Angeles, California

University of California Press, Ltd.
Oxford, England

Library of Congress Cataloging-in-Publication Data

Himalayan voices : an introduction to modern Nepali literature / translated and edited by Michael James Hutt.
p. cm. — (Voices from Asia ; 2)
Translated from Nepali.
Includes bibliographical references (p.) and index.
ISBN 0-520-07046-1 (cloth). — ISBN 0-520-07048-8 (paper)
1. Nepali poetry—20th century—Translations into English. 2. English poetry—Translations from Nepali. 3. Short stories, Nepali—Translations into English. 4. Short stories, English—Translations from Nepali. 5. Authors, Nepali—20th century—Biography. I. Hutt, Michael. II. Series.
PK2598.Z95E5 1990
891′.49—dc20 90-11145
CIP

Printed in the United States of America
9 8 7 6 5 4 3 2 1

The paper used in this publication meets the minimum requirements of American National Standard for Information Sciences—Permanence of Paper for Printed Library Materials, ANSI Z39.48-1984. ♾

CONTENTS

PREFACE

The compiler of any literary anthology is always liable to be accused of sins of omission and commission, and I do not expect to be spared. I began work on this project with the idea of producing two separate books: a much larger and more comprehensive selection of poems in English translation, including works by as many as forty poets, and an anthology of some thirty short stories. These objectives were modified for a number of reasons. It gradually became clear to me that the poetry of another culture can rarely be appreciated or understood fully if its authors are not properly introduced or presented in the context of their own historical and literary traditions. The approach I subsequently adopted was to provide an introduction to the works of a fairly limited number of important Nepali poets. At a later stage it dawned on me that although Nepali short stories contain a wealth of interesting material, many are simply less compelling in a strictly literary sense than are the more highly developed poetic genres.

Each poet who is the subject of a separate chapter in Part One of this book has been chosen for reasons of significance, and the importance of the contribution each has made to Nepali poetry is explained in an introductory preamble to the selection of translated poems. The farther back into the historical past one ventures, the easier it becomes to assess the importance of individual poets. Thus, it is unlikely that any Nepali will wish to quarrel with my choice of the first six poets. It is inevitably more difficult to predict who will come to be regarded in future years as the most important Nepali poets of the more recent past. In general, however, I have relied on the assessments of Nepali critics and anthologists in my choice of both poets and poems. If a poet appears regularly in the four anthologies published by the Royal Nepal Academy and Sājhā

Prakāshan, it seems safe to assume that he or she is considered significant. I have adopted a similar rule with regard to the selection of poems for translation, although it must be admitted that personal taste and the extent to which I have felt satisfied with my translations have also played a part in this process. Thus, some poems are translated here because Nepali critics agree that they are important; others appear simply because I have enjoyed them.

My aim in Part Two has been to present translations of some of the most interesting and best-known examples of the short story in Nepali, to demonstrate the extent to which they describe life in Nepal, and to give some indication of the way in which the genre has developed. This selection has been "boiled down" from my original collection of more than thirty translated stories and is presented as far as possible in order of first publication. Obviously, each story was originally written by a Nepali for a Nepali readership. It should also be borne in mind that the authors are from a particular section of Nepali society—the educated urban middle class—and that these stories therefore inevitably reflect the prejudices, perceptions, and preoccupations of members of that class. It is part of a translator's duty to explain and interpret, and I have tried to do this as unobtrusively as possible with a fairly brief introduction to the genre and its themes and with an explanation of Nepali terms and cultural references in brief footnotes to the texts. A number of Nepali words have been retained in these translations because no single English word could adequately translate them. More detailed explanations of such terms may be found in the glossary at the end of the book.

In selecting these stories for translation, I consulted with a number of scholars, critics, and authors in Kathmandu in the summer of 1988 and compiled a list of more than fifty important Nepali short story writers. Obviously, this list had to be shortened because the inclusion of one story by each writer would have produced a book of unmanageable and unpublishable proportions. It soon became clear that certain writers could be represented adequately by one story apiece but that justice would not be done to others if only one story of theirs was translated. Thus, an initial selection was made of thirty stories by twenty-two authors, of whom six were represented by two stories and one (Bishweshwar Prasād Koirālā) by three. Once the authors had been selected, the problem of which stories to translate was solved with reference to critical opinion in Kathmandu and to the choices of the editors of the five important Nepali anthologies. These are *Kathā Kusum* (Story Flower, 1938), the first anthology of short stories ever published in Nepali; *Jhyālbāṭa* (From a Window, 1949), an anthology of twenty-five stories; *Sājhā Kathā* (Sājhā Stories, 1968), which includes twenty-six of the most famous Nepali stories; *Pachhīs Varshakā Nepālī Kathā* (25 Years of Nepali Stories,

1983), a collection of thirty-five of the best stories published between the establishment of the Royal Nepal Academy in 1957 and 1983; and *Samsāmayik Sājhā Kathā* (Contemporary Sājhā Stories, 1984), a supplement to *Sājhā Kathā* that contains thirty-seven more recent stories. My original intention had been to publish all thirty stories as a separate anthology, but, as I have explained, I later cut down the number of stories to what I consider an irreducible minimum. I hope that those that remain will serve to give a flavor of modern Nepali fiction.

I regret that stories by such noted Nepali authors as Pushkar Shamsher, Govindabahādur Malla Goṭhālé, Shankar Koirālā, Shailendra Sākār, Dhruba Sāpkoṭā, Pushkar Lohanī, Jainendra Jīvan, Jagdīsh Ghimiré, Kumār Nepāl, Keshavrāj Piṇḍālī, Ishwar Ballabh, Somadhwaja Bishṭa, Bhāupanthī, Devkumārī Thāpā, Anitā Tulādhar, and Bhīmnidhi Tiwārī have not found their way into this collection. Some readers may also be surprised by the absence of two of Nepal's greatest writers—Lakshmīprasād Devkoṭā and Bālkrishna Sama—who both wrote a number of short stories. My opinion, shared by many Nepalis, is that Devkoṭā's and Sama's greatest contributions were to the fields of poetry and drama in Nepali, not to fiction. This book might also be accused of ignoring to some extent the enormous contribution made by Nepali writers from India because most of the research on which the book is based was conducted in Nepal. Such, however, are the limitations inherent in a work of this nature. Let me conclude by saying that I hope that others will continue to investigate and translate Nepali literature, so that the gaps I have left may be filled and Nepal's rich literary heritage may be appreciated more fully in the world beyond the hills.

ACKNOWLEDGMENTS

It is difficult to state with any certainty when it was that I actually began work on this book because I first read and translated some of these poems and stories as long ago as 1980 while conducting research for a doctoral thesis. The project might well have taken another eight years to reach fruition had the British Academy not granted me a three-year research fellowship in Nepali in 1987. It is to that illustrious body that I am most deeply indebted.

I must also record my gratitude to innumerable members of staff at the School of Oriental and African Studies (SOAS) in London and particularly to Dr. David Matthews, who first taught me Nepali; to Professor Christopher Shackle, who encouraged me to maintain my involvement in this field; and to Dr. Ian Raeside, present head of the Department of Indology, who kindly agreed to host my fellowship.

The British Council and the Research Committee of the School were extremely generous in their support of visits to Nepal in 1987 and 1988. My thanks also to Dr. Nicholas Allen of Oxford University; to Professor J. C. Wright and Professor Lionel Caplan of SOAS for their help with some obscure mythological references; and to Dr. John Whelpton for helping me to unravel some of the historical background to these texts.

I have of course received an enormous amount of help from friends and colleagues in Nepal. Chief among these has been Mr. Abhi Subedī, who helped me to make many invaluable contacts in Kathmandu; spent long hours reading through the translations, often in consort with the authors themselves; and showed me great-hearted kindness in Nepal—earthquakes and monsoons notwithstanding. The assistance and hospitality of Mr. Peter Moss, the British Council's Representative in Nepal, are also gratefully acknowledged. The enthusiasm for this project expressed by Mohan Koirālā, Bānīrā Giri, Kedār Mān Vyathit, Pārijāt, Siddhicharaṇ Shreshṭha, Bishwabimohan Shreshṭha, Chūḍā Maṇi Bandhu, Ballabh Maṇi Dāhāl, Krishna Bhakta Shreshṭha, Dayārām Sambhava, Bijay Malla, Krishna Chandra Singh Pradhān, Achyūtaraman Adhikārī, and many other members of Kathmandu's literary community has been the single greatest spur to its completion. They are, after all, the true authors of this book.

My sincere thanks to Lynne Withey and Betsey Scheiner at the University of California Press and copyeditor Jan Kristiansson for the meticulous way in which they prepared this book for publication.

Finally, I must record my greatest debt of all: that which I owe to my dear Lucy, who has given me love and support and acquiesced gracefully to my long absences. To her I dedicate this book.

NOTE ON TRANSLITERATION

Because this book is intended primarily for the reader who knows no Nepali, I have not gone to great extremes to represent the exact Devanāgarī spellings of Nepali names and terms; I have sought instead to provide an adequate representation of their pronunciation. Any reader who is familiar with the Devanāgarī script, however, should have little difficulty in reconstructing original spellings. Differences in vowel length and between retroflex and dental consonants are indicated, but distinctions such as those that Devanāgarī makes between ś and ṣ, which are unimportant for the purposes of pronunciation, are glossed by presented both as sh. The temptation to follow the practice of spelling words such as Lakshmī *Laxmī*, or Bhūpi *Bhoopi* has been resisted on aesthetic grounds. Nevertheless, some single consonants, such as *v*, may be pronounced in various ways: v, w, or b. In each case, the transliteration follows the most likely pronunciation. *Vishvavimohan* Shreshṭha's first name is pronounced *Bishwabimohan*, and the poet actually spells it like this when required to do so. It would seem pedantic, not to say arrogant, to differ with a man over the spelling of his own name.

Long vowels are distinguished from short vowels by the addition of a macron: *a*/*ā*, *u*/*ū*, *i*/*ī*. *A* is pronounced like the "a" in southern English "bus," whereas *ā* is like "a" in English "father" or "bath," or occasionally harder, as in "hat." *I* is like the "i" in "hit," whereas *ī* is like the "ee" in "week." *U* is like the "u" in "put," whereas *ū* is like the "oo" in "moon." Most Devanāgarī consonants have aspirated, or "breathy," forms, represented here by the addition of an "h." Ordinary dental consonants are pronounced with the tongue against the back of the front teeth; retroflex consonants, indicated here by the addition of a dot beneath the dental form (*ṭ*, *ḍ*, *ṇ*, and so on) are pronounced with the tongue pressed up into the palate.

INTRODUCTION

NEPAL AND ITS ENVIRONMENT

Nepal is a Hindu kingdom, approximately equal in size to England with Wales, that lies along a 500-mile stretch of the eastern Himalaya between India and Tibet. The most striking feature of the country is its spectacular landscape, and the region's dramatic topography has been a crucial factor in its historical and cultural development since the most ancient times. From a strip of fertile lowland known as the Tarāī in the south, Nepal rises in range after range of hills to the snow-covered crest of the main Himalayan range. Nepal's location between two great cultures and its previous isolation from the outside world have produced a rich and variegated mixture of ethnic groups, languages, and cultures. Because communication and travel in such mountainous country present enormous problems, the region remained politically fragmented until the recent historical past. In the south, the jungles and malarial swamps of the Tarāī prevented both settlement and foreign military incursions, whereas the far north was cold, lofty, and inhospitable. The heartlands of Nepal have therefore always been the hill areas between these two extremes and, more particularly, the intermontane valleys with their fertile soils and equable climate.

Since the early medieval period, the Kathmandu Valley (often still known simply as Nepāl) has been the most prosperous and sophisticated part of this region, and it is still famous for the distinctive arts and architecture of its most ancient inhabitants, the Newārs. The hill regions are the home of an enormous variety of different ethnic groups, each with its own language. Although Hinduism predominates, Buddhism and minor local cults are strong. A large number of petty states existed within the present-day borders of Nepal until the mid-eighteenth century (within the central valley alone, there were three separate Newār kingdoms); but all of these were overcome by the tiny principality of Gorkhā within only a few decades. Gorkhā's campaign of conquest and unification was inspired and led by the remarkable king, Prithvīnārāyaṇ Shāh, whose forces finally took the Kathmandu Valley in 1769. Prithvīnārāyaṇ is now revered as the father of the modern nation-state. Nepal assumed its present proportions early in the nineteenth century after a series of battles with the British East India Company in 1815 and 1816. A treaty imposed on the Nepalis and signed at Sagaulī, now in Bihar, India, was a severe blow to national pride.

MODERN HISTORY

As a Hindu kingdom, Nepal has been ruled since its "unification" by a series of Gorkhālī monarchs—the Shāh dynasty—who claim a lineage that stretches back to ancient origins in the Rājput states of western India. For most of the time between the conquest of Kathmandu, the new nation's capital, and the mid-nineteenth century, however, a minor occupied the throne. This led to an almost continual and often bloody struggle for power among a number of rival families. An abrupt end was brought to this period of political chaos in 1846, when Jang Bahādur, head of the powerful Kunwar family, contrived to have most of his rivals killed off in an event now known as the *Koṭ* Massacre, the *koṭ* being a courtyard of the royal palace in which it took place. He subsequently became a virtual dictator, and the massacre inaugurated more than a century of rule by a succession of "prime ministers" who styled themselves *Rāṇā*.

Jang Bahādur laid down the foundations of the Rāṇā regime during his thirty-one years in power: the Rāṇās' primary concern was political stability, and they were generally supported by the British in India. Foreigners were barred almost totally during the nineteenth century, the kings were made virtual prisoners in their palaces, the office of prime minister became hereditary, and all foreign ideologies were viewed with considerable suspicion. Although it can be argued that the Rāṇā governments saved Nepal from the threat of annexation to British India, it is quite evident that their conservative policies severely retarded the development of the kingdom. Educational policy is an important case in point. Until after World War I, education was provided only for the children of the elite in Kathmandu, and the national literacy rate remained abysmally low. The sons of high-caste families followed traditional modes of education: they studied the Hindu scriptures and the Sanskrit language and often traveled to the ancient centers of learning in India for their studies. For most of the people, however, social and educational advancement remained an impossibility, and subsistence farming was the only means of support.

After each world war, thousands of young men returned to Nepal from the British and Indian armies, bringing with them a much wider perspective on the world. Throughout the nineteenth and twentieth centuries, Nepal lagged behind even India in every aspect of development; roads, hospitals, schools, and industries were conspicuous by their absence. The nation's backward condition was readily apparent to the returnees, and the Rāṇās' hold on power became vulnerable to criticism from a growing class of educated and disaffected Nepalis. Despite a number of palliative measures taken to assuage political opposition, and despite periods of harsh repression exemplified by the 1941 execution of members of an illegal political organization, the Prajā Parishad, the government's position became precarious after the departure of the British from India. By 1950 the main opposition group, the Nepali Congress, had begun to mount an armed insurrection, and early in 1951 the king, Tribhuvan, was restored to power in a series of events now called the "revolution" of 1950–1951. These events marked the advent of democracy in Nepal, and most Nepali historians regard 1950 as the beginning of the modern period of their history.

Since this revolution, Nepal has sought to enhance its national unity and identity and to establish viable political institutions and processes. The first decade of Nepali democracy was a troubled period characterized by vacillatory policies, the collapse of several short-lived administrations, and obstructive factionalism. In 1959 the Nepali Congress achieved a sweeping victory in the nation's first ever general election, but the Congress's program of radical reforms met with stiff opposition. In 1960 King Mahendra revoked the constitution, dismissed the government, and imprisoned its leaders, alleging that the Congress had failed to provide national leadership or maintain law and order. King Mahendra and his supporters also argued that the country's recent political instability had proved that parliamentary democracy was an alien system unsuited to Nepal. After 1960 Mahendra and his son and successor, Birendra, developed and refined a new system of *Panchāyat* democracy based on a formal structure of representation from the "grass roots" up to national level. For most of this time all political parties were banned. Muted dissent flared up into student riots in the late 1970s, and a national referendum was conducted in 1980 to ascertain the people's will with regard to the national political system. The *Panchāyat* system was vindicated by a slim majority in this referendum, but rumbles of unrest continued to recur from time to time.

Toward the end of 1989 the banned Nepali Congress Party joined with other opposition groupings to launch the Movement for the Restoration of Democracy (MRD). The situation seemed ripe for change. A dispute with India concerning trade and transit agreements had caused severe shortages of basic commodities in Nepal. The continued ban on political parties meant that opposition activists faced increasingly harsh repression. Educated Nepalis found the pace of development frustratingly slow, particularly in view of the massive sums of foreign aid that they knew had poured into Nepal since the 1950s. Strong rumors circulated of corruption in high places, and many of these rumors implicated members of the royal family. Initially, the government responded harshly to the strikes and demonstrations the MRD had organized. Thousands were arrested and many newspapers were censored or banned. Dozens of demonstrators died in police actions during February and March 1990. On April 6, police fired on a large crowd of unarmed demonstrators who were marching on the royal palace in Kathmandu, and scores of marchers died. After this tragedy, the government capitulated. A curfew was declared to restore public order, the ban on political parties was lifted for the first time in thirty years, and a general amnesty was declared. After a brief period of intense negotiation, the king accepted a constitutional role, and an interim government was set up to redraft the country's constitution and to supervise elections in 1991.

After 1951 Nepal "opened up" to the outside world, becoming an active member of the international community, a popular tourist destination, and a major recipient of foreign aid. Massive schemes of road construction, health care, educational provision, power generation, and so on have been in progress throughout this period, and despite the unpopularity of the Panchāyat system and of certain members of the royal family, King Birendra himself has always been considered an essential symbol of national identity and unity. Nevertheless, Nepal's future remains uncertain. It is still one of the world's ten poorest countries and faces such problems as the rapid growth of a population almost entirely dependent on land, severe ecological decline and consequent landlessness, and the growth of a class of educated but underemployed young whose thirst for change can only have increased during the early months of 1990. The events of recent history are referred to regularly in Nepali literature, and writers have not shied away from addressing current issues with insight and vigor. Because most of the research for this book was completed in 1988, the poems and stories translated here make no reference to the momentous events that occurred only two years later, although some contain hints of the circumstances that produced the "revolution."

NEPALI LITERATURE: ANTECEDENTS

Nepali is an Indo-European language that is closely related to the other major languages of northern India, such as Hindi and Bengali. Approximately 17 million people speak Nepali, of whom perhaps one-third have acquired the language in addition to the mother tongue of their own ethnic group. The great majority of Nepali speakers, of course, live within the borders of modern Nepal, but Nepali is also the dominant language of the Darjeeling district of West Bengal, Sikkim, and parts of southern Bhutan and Assam. Substantial Nepali communities have grown up in north Indian cities such as Patna, New Delhi, and Banāras. For at least three centuries, Nepali has fulfilled the need for a "link language" or lingua franca among the various communities of the eastern Himalaya, a region of extraordinary linguistic diversity. During the past few decades, Nepali's prestige as a major language of South Asia has also grown considerably. In 1958 it was formally declared to be the national language of Nepal and was thus invested with an important role in the promotion of national unity. More recently, it was recognized as a major Indian literary language by the Sāhitya Akādemī in New Delhi, India's foremost institution for the promotion of vernacular literatures.

The oldest specimens of written Nepali extant are royal edicts from western Nepal, inscribed on stelae and copperplates, that date from the thirteenth century. Other than epigraphic material, however, very little Nepali literature has been discovered that dates back further than the seventeenth century. Nepali literature is therefore a much newer phenomenon than is literature in certain other languages of the region; Newārī, for instance, has a rich literary tradition that dates back at least five hundred years. The translations into Nepali from Sanskrit scripture, royal biographies, and medicinal treatises that emanate from the seventeenth century possess very little literary merit, and the first Nepali poet of any real stature was Suvānand Dās, who composed panegyric verse in praise of the king of Gorkhā, Prithvīnārāyaṇ Shāh. Although the works of several other quite interesting eighteenth-century Nepali poets have been preserved and published, it is to a Brāhmaṇ named Bhānubhakta Āchārya (1814–1868) that Nepali literature really owes its first major work.

Bhānubhakta Āchārya played a fundamental role in the development of Nepali as a literary language and is therefore honored as its "founder poet" (*ādi-kavi*).[1] Obviously, he was by no means the first person ever to compose Nepali verse, but his rendering of the Rāmāyaṇa epic into simple, idiomatic, rhyming Nepali was entirely without known precedent in the language. Until Bhānubhakta,[2] few Nepali writers had been able to shake off the influence of the more sophisticated Indian literatures. As a consequence, their literary language was heavily larded with Sanskrit philosophical terms, or else it borrowed extensively from the languages of adjacent regions of India that possessed more developed literatures. Hindi devotional verse was an obvious source for such borrowings. Nowadays, Nepali writers come from various strata of society and strive to distance their language from Hindi, to which Nepali is quite closely related and with which it shares much of its word stock. These efforts are inspired partly by a nationalism that was largely invisible among the high-caste Nepali elites that monopolized the literary culture of Nepal in earlier centuries. Bhānubhakta's Rāmāyaṇa was the first example of a Hindu epic that had not merely been translated into the Nepali language but had been "Nepali-ised" in every other aspect as well. It is still among the most important and best-loved works of Nepali literature, and along with Bhānubhakta's other works it became a model for subsequent writers.

The second great writer in the history of Nepali literature, Motīrām Bhaṭṭa (1866–1896), was an enthusiastic literary activist inspired by the example of the Indian writers who were organizing themselves in Banāras, where Motīrām spent about twenty years of his short life. Bhaṭṭa was the first to recognize the significance of Bhānubhakta's Rāmāyaṇa, and it was due to Bhaṭṭa's efforts that the poem was first published in 1887, some forty years after its composition. The Rāmāyaṇa was followed four years later by Bhaṭṭa's biography of Bhānubhakta (M. Bhaṭṭa [1891] 1964). This is a delightful narrative interspersed with poems, but its historical authenticity is open to question. Bhaṭṭa subsequently became concerned about increasing the prestige of Nepali literature: he gathered groups of contemporaries about him in both Banāras and Kathmandu, encouraging literary debate and undertaking publishing projects. Through his own writings, he also attempted to broaden the scope of Nepali poetry, which was still largely confined to devotional verse, by developing interest in other genres such as the Urdu lyric known as the *gazal* (a Persian meter used in popular love songs) and the "erotic" style

1. The term *ādi-kavi* translates literally as "first" or "prime" poet.

2. Nepali writers do not necessarily refer to people by the names that a Western reader might assume to be surnames because these are often impersonal titles (*Āchārya*, for instance, translates as preceptor) or exceedingly common caste designations. I have followed the Nepali practice: because Nepalis do not refer to their "founder poet" as *Āchārya*, or their "laureate" as *Pauḍyāl*, there seems no need for us to do so either.

of *shringār* poetry. This latter genre, which celebrates the beauty of the female form in heavily stylized and allegorical language, is now generally considered decadent and indulgent, but it retains a few exponents among older poets. Kedār Mān Vyathit's "*Woman: Flavor, Sweetness, Brightness*" (*Nārī: Rasa, Mādhurya, Āloka*) is an example of modern *shringār* poetry.

Bhaṭṭa and his contemporaries prepared the ground for the growth of a body of creative literature in the Nepali language that would eventually enhance its prestige beyond measure. At the turn of the century, however, this process had barely begun. There were very few printing presses in Nepal and even fewer commercial publishers. The grammar and spelling of written Nepali remained completely unstandardized. The almost total absence of facilities offering public education meant that literacy was still the exclusive preserve of the powerful elites. The scope of existing Nepali literature was governed and limited by traditional convention and the somewhat decadent tastes of a tiny readership. The development and enrichment of Nepali literature that have taken place since the early twentieth century can only be described as remarkable.

The first signs of a literary awakening are actually to be found in a number of important government initiatives. A tradition of formal journalism was established in 1901 when the unusually liberal Rāṇā ruler Deva Shamsher established the *Gorkhāpatra* (Gorkhā Paper). This newspaper, which is now published daily, is the official organ of the government of Nepal, and during the first thirty years of its existence it was the only periodical publication to be produced within the kingdom. It therefore provided a much-needed forum for the publication of poems, stories, and articles. The Rāṇā administration headed by Chandra Shamsher (r. 1901–1929) also sought to promote Nepali literature by establishing the Gorkhā (later Nepālī) Bhāshā Prakāshinī Samiti (Gorkhā Language Publication Committee) in 1913. Chandra Shamsher is reputed to have declared, "There aren't even any books in Nepali! Just reading the Krishnacharitra and the Rāmāyaṇa is not enough!" (Ḍhungānā 1972, 29).[3] The committee had a dual role, however: as well as publishing books that met with its approval, it also operated a strong code of censorship:

> If anyone wishes to publish a book, he must first bring it to the committee for inspection. No book may be published without the stamp of the committee's approval. . . . If a book is published without the committee's ap-

3. The *Krishnacharitra* is a poem of 169 verses by Vasant Sharmā (1803–1890) that narrates the legends of Krishna and enjoyed some popularity in Nepal during the nineteenth century.

> proval, its publisher will be fined 50 rupees. If the contents of this book are deemed to be improper, all copies will be seized and punishment proclaimed and meted out. (Bhaṭṭaraī 1976, 30)

Although this law was not enforced very consistently, there were periods during which offending writers were punished with extreme severity. The committee therefore came to be regarded with suspicion, and because it maintained an effective monopoly over Nepali publishing inside Nepal until the 1930s, poets and writers who wished to escape the overbearing censorship of their work had to publish, and even live, in Indian towns, most notably Banāras and Darjeeling. The relative conservatism of early works by poets such as Lekhnāth Pauḍyāl and Lakshmīprasād Devkoṭā is explained partially by the fact that they resided in Kathmandu and therefore had to exercise extreme caution. Periodical publications, such as *Sundarī* (The Beautiful, established 1906), *Mādhavī* (1908), *Gorkhālī* (1916), and the *Nepālī Sāhitya Sammelan Patrikā* (Nepali Literature Association Journal, 1932),[4] that emanated from Nepali communities in India played a crucial role in the development of Nepali literature during the first few decades of the century. Indeed, Bālkrishna Sama is quoted as once having said, "What Darjeeling thinks today, Nepal thinks tomorrow" (Giri & Pariyār 1977, 5).

In my discussion of Nepali literature I have avoided as far as possible the question of modernity because any division of literature into the categories "modern" and "premodern" is inevitably contentious. Nevertheless, the concept of modernity is of central concern to Nepali writers and critics when they consider the development of their literature. Some consider Bhaṭṭa, Lekhnāth, or Guruprasād Mainālī to be the founders of the modern era; others regard the political changes of 1950 as a watershed. These assessments are based upon a number of assumptions. It is held to be axiomatic, for instance, that religious or devotional literature is "old-fashioned" and that the modern writer should concentrate on secular themes. Time-honored forms and conventions inherited from Sanskrit literature have come to be considered restrictive; the abandonment by many poets of metrical forms and the development of prose genres are therefore regarded as major steps forward. In fiction, social realism came to be highly prized, and Western genres such as the novel and the short story were adopted and developed. This impulse to modernize Nepali literature was closely linked to a widespread desire for greater freedom of thought and expression and a growing interest in, and exposure to, the world outside Nepal.

4. This was the journal of the Nepālī Sāhitya Sammelan (Nepali Literature Association), founded in Darjeeling in 1924. The association is still active today and produces a journal, *Diyālo* (The Lamp).

Perhaps the most important event in this process was the appearance of Kathmandu's first literary journal, the monthly *Shāradā*, in 1934. *Shāradā*, named after the goddess of the arts, Saraswatī, was published with the help of a government subsidy under a regime headed by Juddha Shamsher that initially gave ground to demands for reform and liberalization. Described by Yadunāth Khanāl as "a product of an unwritten, silent compromise, allowed and accepted as an experiment, between the authorities and the rising impatient intellectuals" (1977, 236), *Shāradā* provided a vital forum for Nepalis to publish their works within the kingdom itself. In a sense, this journal also gave birth to some of Nepal's first "modern" writers. Between 1936 and 1963, when its publication ceased, *Shāradā* published nearly two hundred poems by Siddhicharaṇ, Lekhnāth, Rimāl, Sama, and Devkoṭā alone, as well as innumerable stories by Sama, Bishweshwar Prasād Koirālā, Bhavānī Bhikshu, and others (Subedī 1978, 7–9). It is therefore from the *Shāradā* era and the years that followed that most of the works translated here emanate.

PART ONE

The Poets of Nepal

Nepali Poetry

Poetry is the richest genre of twentieth-century Nepali literature. Although the short story has developed strongly, the drama holds its ground in the face of fierce competition from the cinema, and the novel is increasingly popular, almost every Nepali writer composes poetry. Since the appearance of *Shāradā*, Nepali poetry has become diverse and sophisticated. The poets I have selected for inclusion represent different stages and strands of this development, and I have attempted to present them in an order that reflects the chronology of literary change. The direction that this process of evolution has taken should be clear from the introduction to individual poets and the translations of their poems. Here, a few general comments are offered by way of introduction.

Lekhnāth Pauḍyāl, Bālkrishna Sama, and Lakshmīprasād Devkoṭā were undoubtedly the founders of twentieth-century Nepali poetry, and each was a distinctly different poet. Lekhnāth was the supreme exponent of meter, alliteration, and melody and the first to perfect the art of formal composition in Nepali. His impact on poets contemporary with him was powerful, eventually producing a kind of "school." Although his influence has waned, this school retains some notable members.[1] Sama was primarily a dramatist, but his poems were also important. He began as a disciple of Lekhnāth but later rebelled against the restraints of conventional forms with the same vigor that he brought to his opposition to Rāṇā autocracy. Sama's compositions are colored by sensitivity, intellectualism, and clarity, and because of his role as a social reformer and the accessibility of his work, he is still highly respected. Both Lekhnāth

1. These include Mādhav Prasād Ghimire (b. 1919), whose long lyric poem on the loss of his wife, *Gaurī* (1947), remains extremely popular.

and Sama were deliberate, methodical craftsmen and masters of particular modes of poetic composition, but the erratic genius of Lakshmīprasād Devkoṭā brought an entirely new tone and spirit to Nepali poetry. Early in his career, he took the revolutionary step of using folk meters in the long narrative poems that are now among the most popular works of Nepali literature. Later, he produced the greatest epics of his language and finally, adopting free-verse forms, he composed some of its most eloquent poems. It would be difficult to overstate Devkoṭā's importance in the modern literature of Nepal: his appearance on the scene has been compared to that of a meteor in the sky or as Nepali poetry reaching full maturity "with a kind of explosion" (Rubin 1980, 4).

The *Shāradā* era produced poets who were influenced by their three great contemporaries, but also made their own distinctive contributions to the development of the genre. In his early years, Siddhicharaṇ was obviously a disciple of Devkoṭā, but his poems are calmer, clearer, and less rhapsodic. Vyathit also had much in common with Lekhnāth, but he differed in his obvious social concern and his gift for composing short epigrammatic poems. Rimāl was motivated principally by his political views, but he also did much to establish free verse and the prose poem in Nepali. His influence is more apparent in the work of young poets today than is that of most of his contemporaries. The *Shāradā* poets were men who were in their prime during the 1940s and 1950s, although both Siddhicharaṇ and Vyathit remain active today. The revolution of 1950–1951 certainly brought an atmosphere of greater freedom to Nepal, and a large number of works were published that had been withheld for fear of censorship. Few immediate changes took place in the Nepali literary scene, however, and the prerevolutionary poets continued to occupy a preeminent position until the following decade.

During the 1960s, Nepali poetry departed quite radically from the norms of the preceding twenty-five years, which was a result of the unprecedented changes that occurred in Nepali society in general and in intellectual circles in particular. After 1960, a new literary journal, *Rūprekhā* (Outline) quickly became Nepal's major organ for aspiring new writers. Among these was Mohan Koirālā, arguably the most significant poet to have emerged in Nepal since Devkoṭā. The philosophical outlook of the generation of poets who emerged after 1960 differed from that of its predecessors in many respects. The immense expansion of education spread literacy throughout Nepal and produced a generation of graduates who were familiar with philosophies and literatures other than their own. The initial effects of this intellectual opening out in Nepal could be seen clearly in the poetry of the Third Dimension movement and particularly in the work of Bairāgī Kāinlā and Ìshwar Ballabh. The new poetry of the 1960s was full of obscure mythological references and apparently meaningless imagery; this "cult of obscurantism" also influenced later poets, such as Bānīrā Giri. It was coupled with a sense of pessimism and social alienation engendered by lack of opportunity in Nepal, which is expressed poignantly by the novelist and poet Pārijāt and angrily by Haribhakta Kaṭuvāl.

The emergence of Bhūpi Sherchan brought about further changes in the language and tone of Nepali poetry as well as in its purpose. His satire, humor, and anger were expressed in rhythmic free-verse forms, and the simplicity of his diction signified an urge to speak to a mass readership, not just to the members of the intellectual elite. During the 1960s, Nepali poetry seemed divorced from the realities of the society that produced it, but in the decade that followed it again addressed social and political issues in a language stripped of earlier pretensions. Poetry reassumed the role it had played during the *Shāradā* era, once again becoming a medium for the expression of social criticism and political dissent. This trend reached a kind of climax in the "street poetry revolution" of 1979–1980, and Nepali writers played an important role in the political upheavals of February–April 1990 (Hutt 1990). This would surely have been a source of satisfaction to the *mahākavi* (great poet) Lakshmīprasād Devkoṭā, who once wrote:

> Our social and political contexts demand a revision in spirit and in style. We must speak to our times. The politicians and demagogues do it the wrong way, through mechanical loudspeakers. Ours should be the still, small voice of the quick, knowing heart. We are too poor to educate the nation to high standards all at one jump. Nor is it possible to kill the time factor. But there is a greater thing we can do and must do for the present day and the living generation. We can make the masses read us if we read their innermost visions first. (1981, 3)

Almost every educated Nepali turns his or her hand to the composition of poetry at some stage of life. In previous centuries, poetic composition was considered a scholarly and quasi-religious exercise that was closely linked to scriptural learning. It therefore remained the almost exclusive preserve of the Brāhmaṇ male. Today, however, Nepali poets come from a variety of ethnic groups. Among those whose poems are translated here, there are not only Brāhmaṇs but also Newārs, a Limbū, a Thākālī, and a Tāmāng, and although it is still rather more usual for a poet to be male, the number of highly regarded women poets is growing steadily. Even members of Nepal's royal family have published poetry: the late king Mahendra (M. B. B. Shāh) wrote some very popular romantic poems, and the present queen, writing as Chāndanī Shāh, has recently published a collection of songs.

The Nepali literary world is centered in two Himalayan towns: Kathmandu, the capital of Nepal, and Darjeeling, in the Himalayan foothills of the Indian state of West Bengal. Other cities, notably Banāras, served as publishing centers during the period of Rāṇā rule in Nepal, but their importance has diminished in recent years. Until the fall of the Rāṇās, some of the most innovative Nepali writers were active in Darjeeling (the novelist Lainsingh Bāngdel and the poet Agam Singh Giri are especially worthy of note), and fundamental work was also done by people such as Pāras Maṇi Pradhān to reform and standardize the literary language. In more recent years, Darjeeling Nepalis have been concerned with establishing their identity as a distinct ethnic and linguistic group within India and with distancing themselves from Nepal. Thus, the links between the two towns have weakened to the extent that writers are sometimes described as a "Darjeeling poet" or a "Kathmandu poet" as if the two categories were in some way exclusive. This difference is also underscored by minor differences in dialect between the two centers.

It has always been well-nigh impossible for a Nepali writer to earn a livelihood from literary work alone. All poets therefore support themselves with income from other sources. Lekhnāth was a family priest and teacher of Sanskrit; Devkoṭā supported his family with private tutorial work and occasionally held posts in government institutions. Nowadays, poets may be college lecturers (Bānīrā Giri), or they may be employed in biscuit factories (Bishwabimohan Shreshṭha). Many are also involved in the production of literary journals or in the activities of governmental and voluntary literary organizations. Devkoṭā, for instance, edited the influential journal *Indreṇī* (Rainbow) and was also employed by the Nepālī Bhāshānuvād Parishad (Nepali Translation Council) from 1943 to 1946. Sama became vice-chancellor of the Royal Nepal Academy, as did Vyathit. Both Rimāl and Siddhicharaṇ were for some time editors of *Shāradā*, and nowadays many younger poets are active in associations such as the Sāhityik Patrakār Sangha (Literary Writers' Association) or the Sirjanshīl Sāhityik Samāj (Creative Literature Society), which organize readings, publish journals, and attempt to claim a wider audience for Nepali literature.

There are various ways in which Nepal rewards its most accomplished poets. Rājakīya Pragyā Pratishṭhān (the Royal Nepal Academy), Nepal's foremost institution for the promotion of the kingdom's arts and culture, was founded in 1957 and now grants salaried memberships to leading writers and scholars for periods of five years. Academy members are thereby enabled to devote themselves to creative and scholarly work without the need for a subsidiary income. The period during which Kedār Mān Vyathit was in charge of the academy is remembered as a golden age for Nepali poetry, but in general the scale of the academy's activities is limited by budgetary constraints. Nevertheless, the academy is a major poetry publisher and has produced many of the anthologies and collections upon which I have drawn for the purpose of this book. The academy also produces a monthly poetry journal, *Kavitā* (Poetry), edited until his recent demise by Bhūpi Sherchan, and awards annual prizes to prominent writers; these include the Tribhuvan Puraskār, a sum of money equivalent to two or three years of a professional salary.

Another important institution is the Madan Puraskār Guṭhī (Madan Prize Guild), founded in 1955 and based in the city of Pāṭan (Lalitpur). The Guṭhī maintains the single largest library of Nepali books, produces the scholarly literary journal *Nepālī*, and awards two annual prizes (Madan Puraskār) to the year's best literary book and nonliterary book in Nepali.

Sājhā Prakāshan (Sājhā Publishers) is the largest commercial publisher of Nepali books, with a list of nearly six hundred titles. It assumed the publishing role of the Nepālī Bhāshā Prakāshinī Samiti (Nepali Language Publications Committee) in 1964 and established an annual literary prize, the Sājhā Puraskār, in 1967. Since 1982 Sājhā Prakāshan has also produced another important literary journal, *Garimā* (Dignity). The Gorkhāpatra Sansthān (Gorkhāpatra Corporation) produces the daily newspaper *Gorkhāpatra* and the literary monthly *Madhupark* (Libation). The latter publication has become the kingdom's most sophisticated periodical under the editorship of Krishnabhakta Shreshṭha, who is himself a poet of some renown. With *Garimā, Bagar* (The Shore, an independently produced poetry journal), and the academy's *Kavitā* (Poetry), *Madhupark* is now among the leading journals for the promotion of modern Nepali poetry. The monthly appearance of each of these journals is eagerly awaited by the literary community of Kathmandu, many of whose members congregate each evening around the old *pīpal* tree on New Road. *Madhupark* in particular has a wide circulation outside the capital. In India, too, institutions such as Darjeeling's Nepālī Sāhitya Sammelan (Nepali Literature Association) and the West Bengal government's Nepali Academy produce noted journals and award annual literary prizes.

Despite the limited nature of official support for publishing and literary ventures in Nepal, the literary scene is vibrant. The days when Nepali poets had to undertake long periods of exile to escape censorship, fines, and imprisonment have passed, but until April 1990 the strictures of various laws regarding public security, national unity, party political activity, and defamation of the royal family still made writers cautious. With increasing frequency during the 1980s, writers were detained, newspapers and journals were banned, and editors were fined.

But poetry remained the most vital and innovative genre and the medium through which sentiments and opinions on contemporary social and political issues were most frequently expressed. In Nepal, poets gather regularly for *kavi-sammelan* (reading sessions), and the status of "published poet" is eagerly sought. Most collections and anthologies produced by the major publishers have first editions of 1,000 copies—a fairly substantial quantity by most standards. Literary communities exist in both Kathmandu and Darjeeling, with the inevitable loyalties, factions, and critics. Books and articles on Nepali poetry abound, and critics such as Tārānāth Sharmā (formerly known as Tānāsarmā), Ishwar Barāl, and Abhi Subedī are highly respected.

FEATURES OF NEPALI POETRY

The last eighty years have seen a gradual drift away from traditional forms in Nepali verse, although a few poets do still employ classical meters. Until the late nineteenth century, however, almost all Nepali poetry fulfilled the requirements of Sanskrit prosody and was usually composed to capture and convey one of the nine *rasa*. *Rasa* literally means "juice," but in the context of the arts it has the sense of "aesthetic quality" or "mood." The concept of *rasa* tended to dictate and limit the number of themes and topics deemed appropriate for poetry.

Classical Sanskrit meters, many of which are derived from ancient Vedic forms, are based on quantity and are extremely strict. A syllable with a long vowel is considered long, or "heavy," whereas a syllable is short, or "light," when it contains only a short vowel. Whether a syllable is followed by a single consonant or a conjunct consonant also affects its metrical length. The simplest classical meter, and consequently one of the most commonly used, is the *anushṭubh* (or *anushṭup*), often referred to simply as *shloka*, "stanza." This allows nine of the sixteen syllables of each line to be either long or short and therefore provides an unusual degree of flexibility. In most other meters, however, the quantity of each syllable is rigidly determined. The *shārdūla-vikrīḍita* that Bhānubhakta adopted in his Rāmāyaṇa epic is a typical example. Each line of verse in this meter must contain nineteen syllables with a caesura after the twelfth, and the value of each and every syllable is dictated with no scope for adaptation or compromise.

Evidently, the ability to compose metrical verse that retains a sense of freshness and spontaneity is a skill that can be acquired only through diligent study and has therefore remained the preserve of the more erudite, high-caste sections of society. Most Nepali poets now regard these rules and conventions as restrictive, outdated, and elitist, especially because they also extend to considerations of theme and structure. Yet it is significant that the skill to compose poetry in a classical mode was considered an important part of a poet's repertoire until quite recently. Bālkrishna Sama used Vedic meters even in some of his later poems, and Devkoṭā gave a dazzling display of his virtuosity in the *Shākuntala Mahākāvya* (The Epic of Shakuntalā) by employing no less than twenty different meters.

The first attempts to break the stranglehold of classical conventions were made during the 1920s and 1930s when poets such as Devkoṭā began to use meters and rhythms taken from Nepali folk songs. The musical *jhyāure* became especially popular and retains some currency today. Such developments were part of a more general trend toward the definition of a specifically Nepali identity distinct from pan-Indian cultural and literary traditions. These changes could also be regarded as a literary manifestation of the Nepali nationalism that eventually toppled the Rāṇā autocracy.

In the years that followed, many poets abandoned meter altogether. Nonmetrical Nepali verse is termed *gadya-kavitā*, literally "prose poetry." Most nonmetrical poems can be described as free verse, but a few works do exist, such as Sama's "Sight of the Incarnation" (*Avatār-Darshan*), that seem to be conscious efforts to compose genuine prose poems. As Nepali poetry departed from the conventions of its Sanskrit antecedents, its language also changed. The arcane Sanskrit vocabulary required by classical formulas was no longer relevant. When poets began to address contemporary issues and to dispense with traditional forms, they also strove to make their works more readily comprehensible. The vocabulary of the "old" poetry was therefore rapidly discarded.

Nepali poetry is composed in several distinct generic forms. The most common is, of course, the simple "poem" (*kavitā*) written in metrical or free-verse form. A *khaṇḍa-kāvya*, "episodic poem," is longer and is usually published as a book in its own right. It consists of either a description or a narrative divided into chapters of equal length. Devkoṭā's narrative poem *Munā-Madan* (Munā and Madan) and Lekhnāth's description of the seasons, *Ritu-Vichāra* (Reflections on the Seasons), are two famous examples. Because the *khaṇḍa-kāvya* is a form with classical antecedents, it is invariably composed in metrical verse. The *lāmo kavitā*, or "long poem," however, is a modern free-verse form that is not divided into chapters and that can address any topic or theme. The longest poetic genre is the *mahākāvya*, the "epic poem," another classical form that must be composed in metrical verse. The importance and popularity of the *khaṇḍa-kāvya* and the *mahākāvya* have diminished significantly in the years since 1950.

SOME PROBLEMS OF TRANSLATION

All translation involves a loss, whether it be of music and rhythm or subtle nuances of meaning. To translate from one European language into another is no easy task, but when the cultural milieus of the two languages concerned are as different from each other as those of Nepali and English are, the problems can sometimes seem insurmountable. The first priority in translating these poems has been to convey their meaning, tone, and emotional impact. On numerous occasions, I have begun to translate poems that seemed especially important or interesting only to realize that justice simply could not be done to the original and that the task had best be abandoned. Lekhnāth's poems in particular, with their dependence on alliteration and meter, are inhospitable territory for the translator: to render them into rhyming couplets would be to trivialize and detract from their seriousness, but a free-verse translation that lacked a distinctive rhythm would be dishonest. For these reasons, Lekhnāth is represented here by only a few of his shorter poems: to appreciate fully the elegance of a work such as *Reflections on the Seasons*, a knowledge of Nepali is essential. In contrast, some of Bhūpi Sherchan's compositions lend themselves particularly well to translation, especially to an admirer of Philip Larkin's poems. (See, for example, "A Cruel Blow at Dawn" [*Prāta: Ek Āghāt*].) In every case, I have attempted to produce an English translation that can pass as poetry, without taking too many liberties with the sense of the original poem. I cannot claim perfection for these translations, and it would of course be possible to continue tinkering with them and redrafting them for years to come. Eventually, however, one must decide that few major improvements can be made and that the time has come to publish, although, one hopes, not to await damnation.

The intrinsic difficulty of translating Nepali poetry into English stems partly from some important differences between the two languages. The nature of the Nepali language provides poets with great scope for omitting grammatically dispensable pronouns and suffixes and for devising convoluted syntactic patterns. In some poems, it is impossible for any single line to be translated in isolation: the meaning of each stanza must be rendered prosaically and then reconstituted in a versified form that comes as close as possible to that of the original Nepali. This is partly because Nepali follows the pattern of subject-object-verb and possesses participles and adjectival verb forms for which English has no real equivalents. But the untranslatable character of some Nepali poetry can also be explained in terms of poetic license. Nepali is also capable of extreme brevity: to convey accurately the meaning of a line of only three or four words, a much longer English translation may be necessary.

The translator is often torn between considerations of semantic exactitude and literary elegance. For example, how should one translate the title of Pārijāt's "Sohorera Jāu"? *Jāu* is a simple imperative meaning "go" or "go away," but *sohorera* is a conjunctive participle that could be translated as "sweeping," "while sweeping," "having swept," or even "sweepingly," none of which lends itself particularly well to a poetic rendering. "Sweep Away" is the closest I have come to a compromise between the exact meaning and the requirements of poetic language. Problems can also arise when poets refer to specific species of animals or plants. This causes no difficulty when such references are to owls or to pine trees, but in many instances one can find no commonly known English name. A botanically correct translation of a verse from Mohan Koirālā's "It's a Mineral, the Mind" (*Khanij Ho Man*) would read as follows:

> I am a Himalayan pencil cedar with countless boughs,
> the *sayapatrī* flower which hides a thousand petals,
> a pointed branch of the scented *Ficus hirta* . . .

Clearly, such a pedantic rendering would do little justice to the original Nepali poem.

A further problem is caused by the abundance of adjectival synonyms in Nepali, which English cannot reflect. The translator must therefore despair of conveying the textural richness that this abundance of choice imparts to the poetry in its original language. As John Brough points out, Sanskrit has some fifty words for "lotus," but "the English translator has only 'lotus,' and he must make the best of it" (1968, 31). Nepali poets also make innumerable references to characters and events from Hindu, and occasionally Buddhist, mythology and from their own historical past. Nepali folklore and the great Mahābhārata epic are inexhaustible sources of stories and parables with which most Nepalis are familiar. A non-Nepali reader will require some explanation of these references if the meaning of the poem is to be comprehended, and brief notes are therefore supplied wherever necessary.

Lekhnāth Pauḍyāl (1885–1966)

Lekhnāth Pauḍyāl was the founding father of twentieth-century Nepali poetry, but his most important contribution was to the enrichment and refinement of its language rather than to its philosophical breadth. His poems possessed a formal dignity that had been lacking in most earlier works in Nepali; many of them conformed in their outlook with the philosophy of orthodox Vedānta, although others were essentially original in their tone and inspiration. The best of Lekhnāth's poems adhered to the old-fashioned conventions of Sanskrit poetics (*kāvya*) but also hinted at a more spontaneous and emotional spirit. Although often regarded as the first modern Nepali poet, Lekhnāth is probably more accurately described as a traditionalist who perfected a classical style of Nepali verse. Note, however, that his poems occasionally made reference to contemporary social and political issues; these were the first glimmerings of the poetic spirit that was to come after him.

Lekhnāth was born into a Brāhmaṇ family in western Nepal in 1885 and received his first lessons from his father. Around the turn of the century, he was sent to the capital to attend a Sanskrit school and thence to the holy city of Banāras, as was customary, to continue his higher education. During his stay in India, his young wife died, and he met with little academic success. Penniless, he embarked on a search for his father's old estate in the Nepalese lowlands, which was ultimately fruitless, and he therefore spent the next few years of his life seeking work in India. In 1909 he returned to Kathmandu, where he entered the employ of Bhīm Shamsher, an important member of the ruling Rāṇā family, as priest and tutor. He retained this post for twenty-five years.

As an educated Brāhmaṇ, Lekhnāth was well acquainted with the classics of Sanskrit literature, from which he drew great inspiration. From an early age, he composed pedantic "riddle-solving" (*samasyā-pūrti*) verses, a popular genre adapted from an earlier Sanskrit tradition, and his first published poems appeared in 1904. Two poems published in an Indian Nepali journal, *Sundarī*, in 1906 greatly impressed Rām Maṇi Āchārya Dīkshit, the editor of the journal *Mādhavī*, who became the first chair of the Gorkhā Bhāshā Prakāshiṇī Samiti (Gorkha Language Publication Committee) in 1913 and did much to help Lekhnāth to establish his reputation as a poet. His first major composition was "Reflections on the Rains" (*Varshā Vichāra*) and it was first published in *Mādhavī* in 1909. This poem was later expanded and incorporated into *Reflections on the Seasons* (*Ritu Vichāra*), completed in 1916 but not published until 1934. More of his early poems also appeared in a collection published in Bombay in 1912.

One of Lekhnāth's most popular poems, "A Parrot in a Cage" (*Pinjarāko Sugā*) is usually interpreted as an allegory with a dual meaning: on one level of interpretation, it describes the condition of the soul trapped in the body, a common theme in Hindu devotional verse, but it also bewails the poet's lot as an employee of Bhīm Shamsher. Here the parrot, which has to make profound utterances according to its master's whim, is actually the poet himself. This particular poem is extremely famous in Nepal because it is one of the earliest examples of a writer criticizing the Rāṇā families who ruled the country at the time. In terms of literary merit, however, it does not rank especially highly in comparison with Lekhnāth's other verse because it suffers from excessive length and frequent repetition. Indeed, some critics regard it as a poem originally written for children.

Lekhnāth produced one of his most important contributions to Nepali poetry at quite an early stage of his career: his first *khaṇḍa-kāvya* (episodic poem), *Reflections on the Seasons*, demonstrated a maturity that was without precedent in Nepali poetry. Indeed, it is largely to Lekhnāth Pauḍyāl that this genre owes its prestige in Nepali literature. The primary inspiration for this work was probably *The Chain of the Seasons* (*Ritu-Saṃhāra*) by the great fifth-century Sanskrit poet Kālīdāsa. Each of the six "episodes" of Lekhnāth's poem comprises one hundred couplets in the classical *anushṭup* meter and describes one of the six seasons of the Indian year. Most of the metaphors and similes employed in the poem were borrowed directly from Sanskrit conventions for the description of nature (*prakriti-varṇana*), but a few were unusual for their apparent reference to contemporary political issues:

> In the forest depths stands a bare poinsettia
> Like India bereft of her strength and wisdom . . .

Soon the flowers seem tired and wan,
  sucked dry of all their nectar,
As pale as a backward land

The poem is also often praised for the subtlety of its alliterations and for the dexterity with which Lekhnāth constructed internal rhymes:

divya ānandako *ranga* divya-kānti-*taranga* cha
divya unnatiko *ḍhanga* divya sārā *prasanga* cha

Divine the *colors* of bliss,
  divine the *ripples* of light,
Divine the *manner* of their progress,
  divine the whole *occasion*

Lekhnāth did not develop the great promise of these early episodic poems further until much later in his life, but a large number of his shorter poems continued to appear in a variety of literary journals in both India and Nepal. Many poems were probably never published and may now be lost. A two-volume collection, *Delicacy* (*Lālitya*) was published in 1967–1968 and contained one hundred poems. Lekhnāth's shorter works covered a wide variety of topics and conveyed all of the nine *rasa*. Although many are plainly moralistic, some have a whimsical charm and are often couched in uncharacteristically simple language. One such is "The Chirruping of a Swallow" (*Gaunthalīko Chiribiri*), first published in 1935, in which a swallow explains the transient nature of existence to the poet:

You say this house is yours,
I say that it is mine,
To whom in fact does it belong?
Turn your mind to that!

His devotional poems are more formal and are admired for their beauty and for the sincerity of the emotions they express. "Remembering Saraswatī" (*Saraswatī-Smriti*) is the prime illustration of this feature of Lekhnāth's poetry. Other compositions, such as "Dawn" (*Aruṇodaya*, 1935), represent obscure philosophical abstractions:

Inside the ear, a mellifluous sound
is drawn out in the fifth note,
the more I submerge to look within,
the more I feel a holy mood

Poems such as "Himalaya" (*Himāl*) are probably intended to arouse patriotic feeling. Lekhnāth approached all his work in the deliberate manner of a craftsman, paying meticulous attention to meter, vocabulary, and alliteration. His primary concern was to create "sweetness" in the language of his poems, and many were rewritten several times before the poet was content with them.

In 1951, Lekhnāth was invested by King Tribhuvan with the title of *kavi shiromaṇi*, which literally means "crest-jewel poet" but is generally translated as "poet laureate." Since his death in 1966, no other poet has been similarly honored, so the title would seem to be his in perpetuity. His first composition after 1950 was a long poem entitled "Remembering the Truth of Undying Light" (*Amar Jyotiko Satya-Smriti*), which expressed grief over the death of Mahātmā Gāndhī. Under the censorious rule of the Rāṇā regime, this would probably have been interpreted as an expression of support for the Nepali Congress Party.

The work that is now regarded as Lekhnāth's magnum opus is "The Young Ascetic" (*Taruṇa Tapasī*), published in 1953. "The Young Ascetic" is a lengthy narrative poem concerning a poet stricken by grief at the death of his wife, who sits beneath a tree by the wayside. As he mourns alone, a renunciant sādhu appears before him; this man later turns out to be the spirit of the tree beneath which the poet sits. The sādhu delivers a long homily to the mourning poet: as a tree, rooted to one spot, the sādhu has experienced many hardships and has learned much from his observation of the people who have rested in his shade. Thus, after long years of watchfulness and contemplation, he has achieved spiritual enlightenment. The poem contains much that can readily be construed as symbolism, allegory, and even autobiography. The poet probably represents Lekhnāth himself, and the descriptions of the changing seasons are said to represent the advent and departure of the various ruling families of Nepal.

Lekhnāth was honored by the Nepali literary world on his seventieth birthday in 1955 when he became the focal point of a procession around the streets of Kathmandu. The procession was probably modeled on the old-age initiation ceremony practiced by the Newārs of Kathmandu Valley. The old poet was seated in a ceremonial carriage and paraded through the city, pulled by most of the better known poets of the time and even by the prime minister. In 1957, he was awarded membership in the newly founded Royal Nepal Academy, and in 1969 he was honored posthumously with the prestigious Tribhuvan Puraskār prize. These honors are a mark of the peculiar reverence felt by members of the cultural establishment of Nepal for the man whose poems represent the "classical" aspect of their modern literature. He can no longer escape the scorn of the young, however, and he is rarely imitated by aspiring poets. In an essay published in 1945, Devkoṭā defended the "laureate" from his critics:

> Whether poetry should be composed in colloquial language or not is still a matter for dispute: we praise the attempts that are made to utilize the melodiousness of rural or mountain dialects, but this, after all, is not our only resort. Even if one agrees that meter can fragment the flow of poetry, it remains true that less criticism can be made of the poet whose feelings emerge in rounded, smooth, illuminated forms than of the poet who expresses himself in an undeveloped torrent of primitivism. (1945, 223)

Surprisingly little is known about the personal life of the man whose poems are now read and learned by every Nepali schoolchild. In the few portraits that exist, Lekhnāth, an old man with a long white beard, peers inquisitively at the camera from behind a pair of cheap wire-framed spectacles. Born into a tradition of conservative and priestly scholasticism, he was innovative enough to compose poems in his mother tongue that dared to make occasional references to contemporary social realities, and he also brought the discipline and refinement of ancient Sanskrit conventions to the development of Nepali poetry.

The essential quality of much of Lekhnāth's poetry derives mainly from his choice of vocabulary and his use of meter and alliteration; it is therefore rather less amenable to effective translation than the works of most later poets, a fact reflected by the small number of poems translated here. Of these, "A Parrot in a Cage" has been slightly abridged: the Nepali poem contains 25 verses. A translation of *Reflections on the Spring*, completed some years ago, has with some regrets been deleted from this selection. Many of the one hundred couplets that make up this famous poem are merely exercises in alliteration and rhyme, and as a whole *Reflections on the Spring* tends to defy translation.

Most of Lekhnāth Pauḍyāl's shorter poems are collected in *Lālitya* (Delicacy), published in two volumes in 1967 and 1968. His longer works —*khaṇḍa-kāvya* and *mahākāvya*—are (with dates of first publication) *Ritu Vichāra* (Contemplation of the Seasons, 1916), *Buddhi Vinoda* (Enjoyments of Wisdom, 1916), *Satya-Kali-Samvāda* (A Dialogue Between the Degenerate Age and the Age of Truth, 1919), *Amar Jyotiko Satya-Smriti* (Remembering the Truth of Undying Light, 1951), *Taruṇa Tapasī* (The Young Ascetic, 1953), and *Mero Rāma* (My God, 1954). Another epic poem, entitled *Gangā-Gaurī* (Goddess of the Ganges), remains unfinished.

A PARROT IN A CAGE (*PINJARĀKO SUGĀ*)

A pitiful, twice-born[1] child called parrot,
I have been trapped in a cage,

1. *Dvija* means "twice born" and therefore of Brāhmaṇ, or possibly Vaishya, caste.

Even in my dreams, Lord Shiva,
I find not a grain of peace or rest.

My brothers, my mother and father,
Dwell in a far forest corner,
To whom can I pour out my anguish,
Lamenting from this cage?

Sometimes I weep and shed my tears,
Sometimes I am like a corpse,
Sometimes I leap about, insane,
Remembering forest joys.

This poor thing which wandered the glades
And ate wild fruits of daily delight
Has been thrust by Fate into a cage;
Destiny, Lord, is strange!

All about me I see only foes,
Nowhere can I find a friend,
What can I do, how shall I escape,
To whom can I unburden my heart?

Sometimes it's cold, sometimes the sun shines,
Sometimes I prattle, sometimes I am still,
I am ruled by the fancies of children,
My fortune is constant change.

For my food I have only third-class rice,
And that does not fill me by half,
I cast a glance at my water pot:
Such comforts! That, too, is dry!

Hoarse my voice, tiresome these bonds,
To have to speak is further torment,
But if I refuse to utter a word,
A stick is brandished, ready to beat me.

One says, "It is a stupid ass!"
Another cries, "See, it refuses to speak!"
A third wants me to utter God's name:
"Ātmā Rām, speak, speak, say the name!"

Fate, you gave my life to this constraint,
You gave me a voice I am forced to use,
But you gave me only half my needs;
Fate, you are all compassion!

And you gave me faculties both
Of melodious speech and discerning taste,
But what do these obtain for me, save
Confinement, abuse, constant threats?

Jailing me, distressing me,
Are the curious sports Man plays,
What heinous crimes these are,
Deliver me, thou God of pity.

Humanity is all virtue's foe,
Exploiting the good till their hearts are dry,
Why should Man ever be content
Till wingèd breath itself is snatched away?

While a single man on this earth remains,
Until all men have vanished,
Do not let poor parrots be born,
Oh Lord, please hear my prayer!

(1914/17; from *Ādhunik Nepālī Kavitā* 1971)

HIMALAYA (*HIMĀL*)

A scarf of pure white snow
Hangs down from its head to its feet,
Cascades like strings of pearls
Glisten on its breast,
A net of drizzling cloud
Encircles its waist like a gray woolen shawl:
An astounding sight, still and bright,
Our blessed Himalaya.

Yaks graze fine grass on its steepest slopes,
And muskdeer spread their scent divine,
Each day it receives the sun's first embrace:
A pillar of fortune, deep and still,
Our blessed Himalaya.

It endures the blows of tempest and storm,
And bears the tumult of the rains;
Onto its head it takes the burning sun's harsh fire,
For ages past it has watched over Creation,
And now it stands smiling, an enlightened ascetic,
Our blessed Himalaya.

Land of the Gangā's birth,
Holy Shiva's place of rest,
Gaurī's jeweled palace of play,[2]
Cruel black Death cannot enter
This still, celestial column,
Our blessed Himalaya.

It nurtures mines of precious gems,
And gives pure water, sweet as nectar,

2. Gaurī is a name of Pārvatī, spouse of Shiva.

And they say it still contains
Alakā, the Yaksha's capital;[3]
Climbing to its peak, one's heart
Is full of thoughts of heaven,
Thus bright with light and wealth,
Our blessed Himalaya.

(from *Ādhunik Nepālī Kavitā* 1971; also
included in *Nepālī Kavitā Sangraha*
[1973] 1988, vol. 1)

REMEMBERING SARASWATĪ (*SARASWATĪ-SMRITI*)

She plays the lute of the tender soul,
Plucking thousands of sweet sounds
With the gentle nails of the mind,
As she sits upon the heart's opened lotus:
May I never forget, for the whole of my life,
The goddess Saraswatī.[4]

She wears a crystal necklace
Of clear and lovely shapes,
It refines the practical arts of this world,
And my heart ever fills with her waves of light:
May I never forget, through the whole of my life,
The goddess Saraswatī.

She keeps the great book of remembrance,
Recording all things seen, heard, and felt,
All are entered in their fullness,
And nothing is omitted:
May I never forget, through the whole of my life,
The goddess Saraswatī.

She rides the quick and magical swan[5]
Which dives and plays in our hearts' deep lake,
And she brings to life the world's games and their glory:
May I never forget, through the whole of my life,
The goddess Saraswatī.

"When you come to comprehend
The world-pervading sweetness
Of this my art of living,
Your fear and ignorance must surely end."
With this she gestures reassurance:

3. The Yakshas are attendants to the god of wealth, Kubera, who dwells in the fabulous city of Alakā.
4. Saraswatī, consort of the god Brahmā, is patron of the arts and literature.
5. Each Hindu deity has his or her own "vehicle"; Saraswatī is borne by a swan.

May I never forget, through the whole of my life,
The goddess Saraswatī.

(from *Ādhunik Nepālī Kavitā* 1971)

AN ODE TO DEATH (*KĀL MAHIMĀ*)

It knows naught of mercy, forgiveness, love,
It makes neither promises nor mistakes,
And never is it content,
Indra himself may bow down at its feet,[6]
But it heeds not Indra's plea,
It does not pick through the pile,
Dividing sweet from sour,
But checks through all our records;
It never strikes in error.

Kings and paupers are all alike,
It picks them up and bears them away,
Never put off till its stomach is filled;
Medicine's cures present no threat,
Like an undying hunter, it moves unseen.

It bathes in pools of tears,
It dislikes all cool waters,
Without a dry old skeleton
It cannot make its bed,
It wears no more than ashes,
Sings naught but lamentation.

Everything is gulped straight down,
To pause and chew would mean starvation,
All that is swallowed is spewed straight out,
Nothing is digested, through long ages,
Death's hunger never sated.

(from *Ādhunik Nepālī Kavitā* 1971)

LAST POEM (*ĀKHIRĪ KAVITĀ*)

God Himself endures this pain,
This body is where He dwells,
By its fall He is surely saddened,
He quietly picks up His things, and goes.

(1965?; from *Ādhunik Nepālī Kavitā* 1971)

6. Indra is the mighty Hindu god of war and of the rains.

Bālkrishna Sama (1903–1981)

Lekhnāth Pauḍyāl, Bālkrishna Sama, and Lakshmīprasād Devkoṭā were the three most important Nepali writers of the first half of this century, and their influence is still felt today. Lekhnāth strove for classical precision in traditional poetic genres; Devkoṭā's effusive and emotional works provoked a redefinition of the art of poetic composition in Nepali. In contrast to both of these, Bālkrishna Sama was essentially an intellectual whose personal values and knowledge of world culture brought austerity and eclecticism to his work. He was also regarded highly for his efforts to simplify and colloquialize the language of Nepali verse.

Sama was born Bālkrishna Shamsher Jang Bahādur Rāṇā in 1903. As a member of the ruling family, he naturally enjoyed many privileges: his formative years were spent in sumptuous surroundings, and he received the best education available in Nepal at that time. In 1923 he became a high-ranking army officer, as was customary for the sons of Rāṇā families, but from 1933 onward he was able to dedicate himself wholly to literature because he was made chair of the kingdom's main publishing body, the Nepali Language Publication Committee. He changed his name to *Sama*, "equal," in 1948 after spending several months in prison for his association with political forces inimical to his family's regime. It is by this pseudonym that he is now usually known. Sama is universally regarded as the greatest Nepali playwright, and it was primarily to drama that he devoted his efforts during the first half of his life. In recognition of his enormous contribution to the enrichment of Nepali literature, he was made a member of the Royal Nepal Academy in 1957, its vice-chancellor in 1968, and a life member after his retirement in 1971.

The young Bālkrishna seems to have been unusually gifted because he began to compose metrical verses before he was eight years old, imitating those of his father and his tutor, the father of Lakshmīprasād Devkoṭā. Bālkrishna conceived an affection for music and art and developed a sense of reverence for sacred literature, particularly the Rāmāyaṇa of Bhānubhakta: "Up until then, it had never occurred to me that the Rāmāyaṇa was the work of a human being. When I watched my sister bowing down before the book, I thought it had been created by one of the gods!" (Sama 1966, 14).

At school, he read William Wordsworth and other English poets and even translated the poem "Lucy Gray" into Nepali in 1914. He was also impressed by Lekhnāth Pauḍyāl's "*Ritu Vichāra*," and Lekhnāth's influence is clearly discernible in Bālkrishna's earliest compositions. His first play, *Tānsenko Jharī* (Rain at Tānsen), which he wrote in 1921, used the classical *anushṭup* meter, and he wrote most subsequent dramas in verse forms. These included the classic works of Nepali theater: *Muṭuko Vyathā* (Heart's Anguish, 1929), *Mukunda-Indirā* (Mukunda and Indirā, 1937), and *Prahlād* (1938). Sama was undoubtedly influenced by Shakespeare's use of verse in drama and experimented with unorthodox metrical combinations, showing scant regard for the rules of Sanskrit prosody.

Sama was also an accomplished painter and story writer, as well as the author of a speculative philosophical treatise, *Regulated Randomness* (*Niyamit Ākasamiktā*). His poetry represented the second facet of his literary personality, although it was certainly no less important to him than his plays. All of his poems were published as a single collection in 1981, with the exception of two long works that appeared separately. It is clear from this volume that Sama produced far more poetry in his later years than in his youth: less than forty poems were published before 1950, but more than one hundred and fifty appeared between 1950 and 1979. T. Sharmā (1982, 92) believes that Sama's poems fall into four categories. The earliest were fairly conventional compositions in Sanskrit meters and were followed by the many songlike poems that are sprinkled throughout Sama's first verse dramas. After 1950, he produced poems that dealt with philosophical themes in ancient Vedic meters, as well as thematically similar poems written in free verse. The earlier compositions were more formulaic than later works, although Sama's interest in experimentation was clearly evident at an early stage. In "Broken Vase" (*Phuṭeko Phūldān*, 1935), for instance, the opening verse is symbolically shattered and fragmented:

oh the vase . . . from my hand . . .
slipped . . . fell to the floor . . . broke with a crack
. . . water spilled . . . flowers, too,
. . . smashed . . . to smithereens!

His most famous nonmetrical poems are praised for the sweetness and simplicity of their language and often have a strong didactic tone. If they have a fault, it is their tendency to become long-winded and humorless. Sama was a rationalist and an agnostic, which made him highly suspect in the eyes of the rulers. His personal beliefs were set forth in poems such as "Man Is God Himself" (*Mānis Svayaṃ Devatā Huncha*), translated here, and a longer poem, "I, Too, Believe in God" (*Ma Pani Dyautā Mānchu*):

I, too, believe, holy man,
I, too, believe in God,
but between your God and mine
there is the difference of earth and sky.
Him you see when you close your eyes
in meditation's abstract clouds,
Him I see with my eyes wide open
in the dear sight of every man.

The subject of many poems was poetry itself: one of his longest works, "Sight of the Incarnation" (Avatār-Darshan, 1973) is a seventeen-page prose poem that describes a dream in which Sama encountered the goddess of poetry, presumably Saraswatī. Extracts from this poem are presented here. Sama's incomplete autobiography is entitled *My Worship of Poetry* (*Mero Kavitāko Ārādhana*), and the composition of poetry evidently meant far more to Sama than a mere literary pursuit. This attitude to poetry, common to all South Asian poets of earlier generations, is derived from ancient classical traditions, as expounded by the tenth-century poet Rājashekhara in his *Kāvya-Mīmāṃsā* (Treatise on Poetry). This attitude continued to influence Nepali poets well into the present century. Sama's literary perspective was far broader than that of thoroughly traditional poets such as Lekhnāth, however, and his exposure to Western literatures and knowledge of world affairs led him to conduct a number of unusual experiments.

Among the most ambitious of these was a long poem in free verse entitled *Fire and Water* (*Āgo ra Pānī*), which was published in book form in 1954. In *Fire and Water*, Sama attempted to describe the whole history of humankind as a struggle between the forces of good (water) and evil (fire):

Golden fire, silver water,
ruby spark and diamond snow,
their confrontation is not new,
their lack of concord, constant conflict,
struggle, tangle, war and scrabble,
slaughter, murder: these all began in long ages past.

Certain passages of *Fire and Water* are remarkable, but the work as a whole is somewhat overcontrived, and its concluding chapters, which describe a utopia governed by "regulated randomness," are unconvincing. Despite these shortcomings, *Fire and Water* is considered, with some justification, to have been a bold and significant new venture in Nepali literature.

Sama's second major poetic work was a full-blown epic (*mahākāvya*) entitled *Cold Hearth* (*Chīso Chūhlo*), published in 1958. Its theme was a tragic love affair between two young people divided by a difference in caste. Part of the epic's novelty lay in the fact that its various characters spoke in a diction that imitated that of other Nepali poets. *Cold Hearth* also demonstrated Sama's erudition and represented his humanistic rejection of the Sanskrit convention that holds that the hero of an epic must be a character of high birth and nobility: the central character of the story was Sante Damāī, a low-caste tailor. Critics generally agree that *Cold Hearth* is diffuse and overextended and that it ranks somewhat lower than *Fire and Water* and "Sight of the Incarnation" among Sama's major poetic works.

All of Sama's shorter poems (including "Sight of the Incarnation") are collected in *Bālkrishna Samakā Kavitā* (The Poems of Bālkrishna Sama, 1981), and some appeared in English translation in *Expression after Death* (1972). The two long works *Āgo ra Pānī* (Fire and Water) and *Chīso Chūhlo* (Cold Hearth) were published in 1954 and 1958 respectively.

MAN IS GOD HIMSELF (*MĀNIS SVAYAṂ DEVATĀ HUNCHA*)

He who loves flowers has a tender heart,
he who cannot pluck their blooms
has a heart that's noble.

He who likes birds has a gentle soul,
he who cannot eat their flesh
has feelings that are sacred.

He who loves his family
has the loftiest desires,
he who loves all of Mankind
has the greatest mind.

He who lives austerely has the purest thoughts,
he who makes life serve him well
has the greatest soul.

He who sees that Man is Man
is the best of men,
he who sees that Man is God,
he is God himself

(1968; from Sama 1981)

I HATE (*MA GHRIṆĀ GARCHU*)

I hate the loveliest star-studded silks,
I hate the scent of the prettiest flower,
I hate the moonlight's thin, lacy veil,
I hate your sweetest love song,
because, because,
they come between your lips and mine.

(1968; from Sama, 1981)

ALL-PERVADING POETRY (*KAVITĀKO VYĀPTI*)

Picking up a huge basket, a holy man
ventured out to the forest to gather poetry.
Through hills and streams, pastures and fields,
he searched every waterfall, fruit and bush,
but nowhere could he find it,
so he decided such things were out of season,
at a loss he had set off home
when he came upon an aesthete.

To his enquiry this man replied,
"Is poetry not everywhere?
If you look at those falls through prosaic eyes,
even they will be dry, just declaring the void
left by the hair which falls out as youth passes;
but what could dry up these waters,
or make this hillside bald?

"Holy man, look with redoubled love
at the heart's smooth surface
where foaming blood gathers;
gather up all this sad world's blows,
attack with a powerful breath;
lift waves of experience to your head,
scatter pure drops till your eyes are wet,
make your vision subtle with sympathy,

look closely: you will see the blood
which runs through the veins of these rocks,
you will touch the hearts of stones,
the cliffs will shower nectar,
you will have poetry to drink!"

With this the aesthete faded away,
melting like beeswax in the sun,
and the holy man's eyes softened too.
The trees melted like resin, the fruits like honey,
the green fields dissolved into lakes,
the whole world thawed like snow,

the sky dissolved to become the Gangā,
the stars were all droplets of water.

And then the holy man knew
he meant no more than a teardrop;
throughout the world, in each atom's womb,
pervading destruction's terrible sound,
he found poetry surging forth.

(1972; from Sama 1981; also included in
Pachhīs Varshakā Nepālī Kavitā 1982)

FROM *SIGHT OF THE INCARNATION* (*AVATĀR-DARSHAN*)

She came before me incarnate,
the mother of the universe, beautiful verse,
snatching sun-flowers, scattering star-leaves,
streaks of dark cloud her agile pen,
their rain her ink,
the poems she wrote were lines
of heavenly lightning-letters,
making the moon sing softly,
making the thunder echo a song
that only the moonbird could hear.

She came dancing, her slim body of spotless crystal,
and as she spread her veil of delusion I doubted
that I had truly seen.
She came like my mind's reflection,
she surely came,
but what of this watcher's reform?

On trembling elbows, my head bowed low,
I try to crawl on four limbs of rhyme
toward poetry's tempting light,
but into a trap I tumble
to struggle there like a four-legged beast,
with no prospect of further progress:
my weight makes me sink ever deeper.
Or maybe I am a black insect,
tumbling onto the wrong path,
prostrate in despair on a slippery rock,
waving four legs at the empty sky.

I saw Poetry's tangible image,
the speech of the cosmos incarnate,
beauty and joy I witnessed,
but what could I do? I could not touch her feet,
I could not bow low with a change in my heart,

no words of strong love could I find,
I could not fly, could not dissolve in the Goddess.

Poetry, Poetry, was it an illusion,
that sight of your lovely incarnation? If so,
whence came such joy? I could not guess
at such joy in the world,
except the bliss which springs from your touch.

I write, remembering things from my past,
but most I forget—all that remain are the dregs
which cling in an emptied jug.
Yesterday is met by today,
today obscured by tomorrow,
tomorrow wiped out by the following day,
each second erases our footprints,
wandering around, awaiting death,
one sleep shatters scores of resolutions.
Death closes our eyes and makes us forget
the things we aimed for in life. I write what I remember,
but Great Death tells me, if my heart should stop
as the morning sun climbs high tomorrow,
I would go to embrace the fire,
forgetting my resolves,
forgetting that fire can burn. But still
I begin to relate the events I recall,
I cannot account for all the blows inflicted,
but write all I can of important times.
I remember him who caused me pain,
but forget the one who wiped my tears,
I remember him who wounded me,
he who healed me I forget,
I remember the man who brought me fear
but forget the one who always consoled,
I remember the ones I have loved,
forgetting those who loved me.
Though I am a sinner, ungainly and unvirtuous,
I will never forget that sacred vision,
I feel you came just now: still I see you,
all before me fades away
as your feet approach with the sound
of ringing anklet bells . . .

Where have they gone, those lovely childhood hours,
when I lived through each day and night
as if they were my body?
All that once was has passed away,
all that was not has come to pass,
the future holds all that the present lacks.

Still the days are fine, sun and moon undiminished,
Dasāin and Tihār come adorned as before,[1]
Dasāin comes anointing foreheads with red,
making the rupees ring, then comes Tihār,
applying strokes of sandalwood paste,
adding dashes of color in lines,
filling mouths with fruits, piling garlands high,
cracking chestnuts with the teeth.
But now such lovely feasts bring dreams,
dreams from the past which tell only of death,
and that high peak of festivals melts,
springs of tears burst from the eyes,
pools of water collect and soon
the dam is breached and they fall.
Garlands, anointments, are all washed away,
the heart is uneasy, the mouth is dry,
unswallowed fruits stick in the throat.

Where has that burning childhood fled?
What of the golden sun, the silvery moonlight?
What of the gilded finial set by the sun
on silver mountains made by the moon?
They are no longer seen,
now only cold snow is heaped on the mountains,
their peaks always bear fresh wounds,
inflicted by dark ignorance, by insane selfishness,
whose hunger gnaws ever deeper:
that time is gone like the sky itself.

I remember that day of my vision,
I was nine years old, new things fell to new eyes
all around, the sky was as clear
as an ideal, I thought it would reflect the earth,
all upside-down. There was sweet new sunshine,
transparent and soft, a display of colors
surrounded me with grandeur. Tall trees danced
with classical gestures, bending from the waist,
whispering their songs, lifting their hands
to stir the white clouds with brushes,
weaving poetry, poetry! In this movement I felt
I might clearly see you take shape;
the air was ringing with bird song
as if your voice would burst out—then it flared!

1. Dasāin is an important festival celebrated in honor of the fearsome goddess Durgā during the month of Ashwin (September–October). It is part of a long national holiday in Nepal that involves the slaughter of buffalo and other livestock and the anointing of foreheads with their blood. Tihār is a name for the Diwālī festival of lights.

You appeared, I saw you! In your face
I found such joy that now I know
no other happiness in this life.
This is no fulfillment,
it is a lifelong thirst,
a hope which will last until the pyre
raises its last flag of flame.

(1973; from Sama 1981)

Lakshmīprasād Devkoṭā (1909–1959)

When a truly great poet appears during an important phase in the development of a particular literature, the fortunes of that literature are changed forever. All poets who follow are bound to the traditions that their great predecessor has established, even if it is only in the sense that these become the conventions against which they rebel, the norms from which they make their departures. The contributions made to the development of Nepali poetry by Bhānubhakta, Bhaṭṭa, Lekhnāth, and Sama have been fundamental, yet Devkoṭā stands head and shoulders above all of these. An American scholar of comparative literature has written, "In Devkoṭā we see the entire Romantic era of Nepali literature" (Rubin 1980, 5), but this is an oversimplification or even an understatement. In Nepali, Devkoṭā's works have formed a colossal touchstone and are the undisputed classics of his language.

In the short space of twenty-five years Devkoṭā produced more than forty books, and his works included plays, stories, essays, translations from world literature, a novel, and poems that ranged in length from a 4-line rhyme to an epic of 1,754 verses. His writings were certainly extraordinarily profuse, but they were also remarkable for their intellectual and creative intensity. Devkoṭā rarely returned to a poem to revise or edit, being in too great a hurry to commence his next composition, nor was he averse to using little-known dialect words to enrich his vocabulary. As a result, some poems suffer from obscurities that puzzle even the most scholarly Nepali reader. Nevertheless, little that Devkoṭā wrote would now be considered dispensable.

Born into a Brāhmaṇ family in Kathmandu in 1909, Devkoṭā was educated at the Durbār High School and Trichandra College in the capital and received a B.A. in 1930. Married at sixteen years of age, he became a father at nineteen, and most of the rest of his life was a struggle to support his family, usually by teaching, although he briefly held governmental posts in later years. He often complained bitterly that it was impossible for him to earn a living from writing alone. A prey to deep depressions, Devkoṭā was confined to an Indian mental home in 1939 and was almost suicidal after the death of his son in 1952. His life was a series of financial problems and personal sorrows, but through them all shone a personality of humor, warmth, and deep humanity. These personal ups and downs never retarded the growth of his genius; in fact, some of his best humorous poetry was written in the most tragic circumstances. Certain events in Devkoṭā's life, such as his pilgrimages to the mountain lakes north of Kathmandu in the 1930s, the time he spent in a mental hospital, his employment as a writer and translator from 1943 to 1946, and his subsequent political exile in Banāras can be identified as definite influences on his work. To some extent, however, Devkoṭā's poetry often seems to have been a kind of "inner life" in which he found solace and optimism despite the trials of everyday life.

The life and works of Lakshmīprasād Devkoṭā have been described and analyzed at length in scholarly works in Nepali (see, for instance, Paṇḍé 1960; K. Joshī 1974; and Bandhu 1979) and in a recent study published in English to which readers are referred for more detailed biographical information (Rubin 1980). Because Devkoṭā's oeuvre is so immense, and because his greatest achievements are to be found in epics such as *Shākuntala Mahākāvya, Sulochanā,* and *Prometheus,* the introduction and translations presented here offer only a glimpse of a talent that was unprecedented in Nepali poetry.

Devkoṭā's earliest poems reveal the powerful influence of English Romantic verse. Many of the poems collected in *The Beggar* (*Bhikhārī*) celebrate the fundamental goodness of humble people, as typified by "Sleeping Porter" (*Nidrit Bhariyā*), or look back with longing to the innocence of childhood:

> We opened our eyes to a glimmering world,
> in wonder we wandered freely,
> playing games celestial,
> running in bliss and ignorance

Soon, however, Devkoṭā began to spice his poetry with a flavor that was essentially Nepali, and *Munā and Madan* (*Munā-Madan*) marked an important stage in this development. *Munā and Madan* is based on an old Newār folktale (D. Shreshṭha 1976) and derives much of its considerable charm from its simple language and musical meter. Devkoṭā broke new ground by becoming the first Nepali poet to employ the *jhyāure* meter of the folk song, despised by earlier poets as vulgar and unfitting for serious poetry. He defended this novel move with an appeal to patriotic sentiment:

Nepali seed, Nepali grain, the sweetest song,
watered with the flavor of Nepal;
which Nepali would close his eyes to it?
If the fountain springs from the spirit,
will it not touch the heart?

The plot of *Munā and Madan* can be summarized as follows: Madan, a trader, resolves to go to Tibet to seek his fortune. He intends to spend only a few weeks in Lhasa and then to return to Kathmandu to grant his aging mother her final wishes. Munā, his wife, is sure that he will never return and begs him not to go. Madan ignores her pleas, and once he has arrived in Lhasa, he becomes entranced by the city's beauty. Suddenly he realizes that he has stayed too long in Tibet, and he sets off home but falls sick with cholera on the way. In Kathmandu, a suitor tells Munā that her husband has perished. But in fact, he has been rescued by a Tibetan, who nurses him back to health. By the time Madan returns home, both his mother and his wife have died, one of old age and the other of a broken heart. Madan decides that he will follow them, and he also passes away at the end of the poem.

Although it is primarily a romantic tragedy designed to tug at the heartstrings, *Munā and Madan* contains a number of moral statements and comments on the Nepali society of its time. The melodramatic climax of the tale makes its principal message clear: loved ones are far more precious than material wealth. Certain passages from *Munā and Madan* have the quality of proverbs and are often quoted by ordinary Nepalis in the course of their everyday lives:

hātakā mailā sunakā thailā ke garnu dhanale?
sāga ra sisnu khāeko bes ānandī manale!

Purses of gold
are like the dirt on your hands,
what can be done with wealth?
Better to eat only nettles and greens
with happiness in your heart.

The most progressive element of the poem is its implicit rejection of the importance of caste: Madan is saved by a Tibetan, a meat-eating Buddhist, described by Rubin (1980, 31) as a "Himalayan Samaritan," whom an orthodox Hindu would regard as untouchable. Here, the poem proclaims a belief in the goodness of humble people:

This son of a Chetrī touches your feet,
but he touches them not with contempt,

a man must be judged by the size of his heart,
not by his name or his caste.

Munā and Madan was Devkoṭā's most beloved composition: on his deathbed he made the famous remark that even though all of his works might perish after his demise, *Munā and Madan* should be saved. It is also the most popular work in the whole of Nepali literature: in 1936, only 200 copies were printed, but by 1986 it had entered an eighteenth edition, for which 25,000 copies were produced. In 1983 alone, more than 7,000 copies were sold.[1]

Munā and Madan represented something of a watershed in the development of Nepali literature, but it was a minor work in comparison with the great flood of poetry that Devkoṭā unleashed in subsequent years. Between 1936 and his death in 1959, Devkoṭā produced many works on a far more grandiose scale, as well as a wealth of shorter poems that now fill nearly thirty volumes. The five poems presented here in translation shed light upon separate facets of Devkoṭā's poetic personality: "Sleeping Porter" is typical of his early period, during which, as I have noted, his tone and philosophical stance were strongly reminiscent of English poets such as Wordsworth. *Munā and Madan* was his first great success, a romance written in a melodic meter and simple language that struck a chord in the minds of ordinary Nepali readers. "Prayer on a Clearing Morning in the Month of Māgh" (*Māghko Khuleko Bihānko Jap*) is an entirely different composition because it weaves together references to Hindu mythology and descriptions of natural beauty to offer an insight which is deeply personal but also resounds with a profundity which is universal. "Mad" (*Pāgal*), on the other hand, is a poetic expression of the personal philosophy that Devkoṭā developed in his essays (1945) and was clearly inspired by his experiences of the asylum at Rānchī:

When I saw the first frosts of Time
on the hair of a beautiful woman,
I wept for three days:
the Buddha was touching my soul,
but they said that I was raving!

"Mad" also communicates a political message that can be described as revolutionary:

Look at the whorish dance
of shameless leadership's tasteless tongues,
watch them break the back of the people's rights.

1. This statistic was reported in the English language daily *The Rising Nepal*, January 17, 1984. Nepali literary publications are usually printed in editions of 1,000 copies.

For Lekhnāth and Sama, poetry was ultimately a discipline that had to be painstakingly acquired and cultivated. For Devkoṭā, however, and particularly in his later years, poetry was "a hill stream in flood" or "a spontaneous overflow of powerful feelings." Devkoṭā died while he was still developing his craft and entering new fields of endeavor. Indeed, as the deathbed poem "Like Nothing into Nothing" (*Shūnyamā Shūnyasari*) demonstrates, he continued to compose until hours before his demise. His death was Nepal's eternal loss: despite the poems' flaws and inconsistencies, it seems extremely unlikely that his poems will ever come to be considered wholly "outdated" or that his genius will ever be deemed unworthy of emulation.

Much of Devkoṭā's poetry was not published until after his death in 1959. In the following titles, arranged in approximate order of composition, dates given are of first publication.

Devkoṭā's shorter poems are collected in *Bhikhārī* (The Beggar, 1953), *Putalī* (The Butterfly, 1952), *Gāine Gīt* (Minstrel Songs, 1967), *Bhāvanāgāngeya* (The Ganges of Emotion, 1967), *Ākāsh Bolcha* (The Sky Speaks, 1968), *Sunko Bihāna* (Golden Morning, 1953), *Manoranjana* (Enjoyments, 1967), *Janmotsava Muṭuko Thopā* (Tears of a Birthday Heart, 1958), *Chaharā* (Cascade, 1959), *Chillā Pātaharū* (Smooth Leaves, 1964), *Kaṭak* (The War, 1969), *Chāngāsanga Kurā* (Conversations with a Waterfall, 1966), *Lakshmī-Kavitā-Sangraha* (Collection of "Lakshmī's" Poems, 1976), and *Mrityushayyābāṭa* (*From the Deathbed*, 1959).

The shorter narrative poems, *khaṇḍa-kāvya*, and verse-dramas are *Munā-Madan* (Munā and Madan, 1936), *Sāvitrī-Satyavān* (Sāvitrī and Satyavān, 1940), *Rājakumār Prabhākar* (Prince Prabhākar, 1940), *Mhendū* (The Flower, 1958), *Krishibālā* (The Peasant Girl, 1964), *Sītāharaṇa* (The Abduction of Sītā, 1968), *Dushyanta-Shakuntalābheṭa* (The Meeting of Dushyanta and Shakuntalā, 1968), *Lūnī* (Lūnī [a woman's name], 1966), *Kunjinī* (Girl of the Groves, 1945); *Rāvaṇa-Jatāyu-Yuddha* (The Battle of Rāvaṇa and Jatāyu, 1958), *Pahāḍī Pukār* (Mountain Cry, 1948), *Navarasa* (The Nine Sentiments, 1968), *Māyāvinī Sarsī* (Circe the Enchantress, 1967), *Vasantī* (Girl of the Spring, 1952), *Mainā* (Mainā [a woman's name], 1952), and *Sundarī Projarpinā* (The Fair Prosperina, 1952).

Devkoṭā's epic poems (*mahākāvya*) are *Van-Kusum* (Forest Flower, 1968); *Shākuntala Mahākāvya* (The Epic of Shakuntalā, 1945), *Sulochanā* (Sulochanā [a woman's name], 1946), *Mahārāṇā Pratāp* (King Pratāp, 1967), and *Pramithas* (Prometheus, 1971).

SLEEPING PORTER (*NIDRIT BHARIYĀ*)

On his back a fifty-pound load,
his spine bent double,

six miles sheer in the winter snows;
naked bones;
with two rupees of life in his body
to challenge the mountain.

He wears a cloth cap, black and sweaty,
a ragged garment;
lousy, flea-ridden clothes are on his body,
his mind is dulled.
It's like sulphur, but how great
this human frame!

The bird of his heart twitters and pants;
sweat and breath;
in his hut on the cliffside, children shiver:
hungry woes.
His wife like a flower
searches the forest for nettles and vines.

Beneath this great hero's snow peak,
the conqueror of Nature is wealthy
with pearls of sweat on his brow.
Above, there is only the lid of night,
studded with stars,
and in this night he is rich with sleep.

(1958; from Devkoṭā 1976)

FROM *MUNĀ AND MADAN* (*MUNĀ-MADAN*)

MUNĀ PLEADS WITH MADAN

Madan:

I have only my mother, my one lamp of good auspice,
do not desert her, do not make her an orphan,
she has endured nigh sixty winters,
let her take comfort from your moonlight face.

Munā:

Shame! For your love of your mother
could not hold you here,
not even your love for your mother!
Her hair is white and hoary with age,
her body is weak and fragile.
You go now as a merchant
to a strange and savage land,
what's to be gained, leaving us for Lhasa?

Purses of gold
are like the dirt on your hands,
what can be done with wealth?
Better to eat only nettles and greens
with happiness in your heart.

MADAN GOES TO TIBET

Hills and mountains, steep and sheer,
rivers to ford by the thousand:
the road to Tibet, deserted and bare,
rocks and earth and poison drizzle,
full of mists and laden with rain,
the wandering wind as cold as ice.

Monks with heads round and shaven,
temples and cremation pillars,
hands and feet grow numb on the road
and are later revived by the fire,
wet leafy boughs make the finest quilts
when the teeth are ringing with cold,
even when boiled, it's inedible:
the rawest, roughest rice.

At last, roofs of gold
grace the evening view:
at the Potālā's foot, on the valley's edge,
Lhasa herself was smiling,
like a mountain the Potālā[2] touched the sky,
a filigreed mountain of copper and gold.

The travelers saw the golden roof
of the Dalai Lama's vast palace,
where golden Buddhas hid behind yak-hair awnings,
graven rocks of every color, embroidered like fairy dresses,
snowcapped peaks, waters cool,
the leaves so green, mimosa flowers
blooming white on budding trees.

MUNĀ IN HER SOLITUDE

Munā alone, as beautiful as the flowering lotus,
like moonlight touching the clouds' silver shore,
her gentle lips smile, a shower of pearls,
but she wilts like a flower as winter draws near,
and soon her tears rain down.

2. The Potālā is the magnificent palace-cum-monastery that dominates the Tibetan capital, Lhasa, and was the winter residence of the Dalai Lama.

Wiping wide eyes, she tends Madan's mother,
but when she sleeps in her lonely room
her pillow is soaked by a thousand cares.

She hides her sorrow in her heart,
concealing it in silence,
like a bird which hides with its wing
the arrow which pierces its heart.
She is only bright by the flickering lamp
when the day draws to its close.

A wilting flower's beauty grows
while Autumn is approaching,
when the clouds' dark edges are silver
and the moon shines ever brighter.
Sadness glares in her heart,
recalling his face at their parting,
wintry tears fall on the flower,
starlight, the night's tears
drip down onto the earth.

A rose grows from the sweetest roots,
but roots are consumed by worms;
the bud which blooms in the city
is the prey of evil men;
pure water is sullied
by dirt from a human hand;
men sow thorns in the paths of men.

Most lovely our Munā at her window,
a city rascal saw her, a fallen fairy,
making a lamp for goddess Bhavānī,
oblivious to all.
He saw the tender lobes of her ears,
saw her hair in disarray,
and with this heavenly vision
he rose like a madman and staggered away.

You see the rose is beautiful,
but brother do not touch it!
You look with desire, entranced,
but be not like a savage!
The things of Creation are precious gems,
a flower contains the laughter of God,
do not kill it with your touch!

MADAN TARRIES IN LHASA

Six months had passed, then seven,
suddenly Madan was startled,

remembering his Munā, his mother:
a wave of water rushed through his heart.

A dove flew over the city,
it crossed the river near the ford,
Madan's mind took wing, flew home,
as he sat he imagined returning,
and Munā's eyes were wide with sorrow,
her wide almond eyes.

"Dong" rang the monastery bell,
the clouds all gathered together,
mountain shadows grew long with evening.
Chilled by the wind in sad meditation,
Madan rose up, saw the moon wrapped in wool,
his mother, his Munā, danced in his eyes,
it became clear to him that night,
his pillow was wet with tears.

His heart oppressed by the reddening sky,
he packed his purses of gold away,
he gathered up his bags of musk,
then took his leave of Lhasa,
calling out to the Lord.

MADAN FALLS SICK ON HIS JOURNEY HOME

Here in the pitiless hills and forests,
the stars, the whole world seemed cruel,
he turned over slowly to moan in the grass . . .
some stranger approached, a torch in his hand,
a robber, a ghost, a bad forest spirit?
Should he hope or should he fear?
His breath hung suspended, but in an instant
the torch was beside him before he knew.

A Tibetan looks to see who is weeping,
he seeks the sick man there,
"Your friends were worthless, but my house is near,
you will not die, I shall carry you home."

Poor Madan falls at his feet,
"At home, I've my white-haired mother
and my wife who shines like a lamp,
save me now and the Lord will see,
he who helps his fellow man
cannot help but go to heaven.
This son of a Chetrī touches your feet,[3]

3. Chetrī is the second Hindu caste in Nepal, roughly equivalent to the Indian Kshatriya.

but he touches them not with contempt,
a man must be judged by the size of his heart,
not by his name or his caste."

MADAN DEPARTS FOR NEPAL

Far away lies shining Nepal,
where cocks are crowing to summon the light,
as morning opens to smile down from the mountains.
The city of Nepal wears a garland of blue hills,
with trees like earrings on the valley peaks,
the eastern ridges bear rosy clouds,
the fields are bright and dappled with shadows,
water falls like milk from distant hills.

Madan recalls the carved windows and doors,
the *pīpal* tree loud in the rising wind,
the little house where Munā sits,
his Munā, his mother, the world of his heart.

"Your kindness has been unbounded,
for you restored my life to me,
a deed I cannot repay.
Two purses of gold I have buried,
now one is mine, the other is yours,
take it and bid me farewell,
I must depart for my home,
as I go forth I remember your charity."

The Tibetan protests,
"What can I do with this yellow gold?
Does gold grow up if you plant it?
You are kind, but we have no use for it,
here are my children, left by their mother,
what use is gold, is wealth,
when Fate has plucked her away?
These children cannot eat gold,
these children do not wear trinkets,
and my wife is above the sky,
the clouds are her only jewels."

THE PASSING OF MADAN'S MOTHER

No tears in her eyes now, pervaded by peace,
day's final radiance in pale evening waters,
mainstay of her life, her bar against death: her son far away,
she thinks she sees him, wishfully thinking,
hot with fever, her thin hand is burning
as it lovingly clasps her daughter-in-law's hand.

"My time is near, I must cross to the other world,
no point in weeping, wife of my son.
This is everyone's road, little one,
the road of rich and poor,
this clay turns to clay
and is lost on the shores of sorrow,
and this you must bear:
be not trapped by the snares of grief,
practice devotion which illumines the final path.
I have seen the world's flower garden blooming and wilting,
and in my sorrow, daughter, I have recognized the Lord;
the seeds sown on earth bear their fruit in heaven,
my deeds I take with me, but what goes with me, in truth?
The wealth you acquire in this dream
is in your hands when you wake."

MADAN LEARNS OF MUNĀ'S DEATH

"My poor brother," says Madan's sister,
"wipe your tears with the edge of my shawl,
be patient, my brother, do not act in this way,
know that we all must go at last,
just a few short days for this sinful body, this dirty pride,
in the end the wind scatters them, a handful of ash,
the flower of the flesh withers away
and mixes once more with the soil,
but a second flower blooms beyond this earth
to sway forever in a heavenly breeze.
We were born to bear sorrow,
to be made pure by suffering;
on our way to the heavenly mansions
we bathe in rivers of tears."

"Do not look down," cries Madan,
"Munā, I come to join you now,
you left a diamond of love here below,
and I shall return it to you . . .
I am veiled, obstructed by the curtain of Death,
I shall not weep, I shall set out tomorrow,
lift the curtain, oh Fate,
quickly now, and you will be blessed."

The clouds parted, a lovely moon smiled down,
it peered with the stars through the clear glass pane,
the clouds drew together, Madan slept forever,
next day, the sun rose in the clearest of skies.

CLOSING VERSE

Have you washed the dust from your eyes, brother and sister?
We must understand this world, we must not be cowards,
look the world in the face and muster our courage,
stretch our wings to the sky while we still live on earth.
If life were just eating and drinking, Lord,
what would living mean?
If Man did not hope for an afterlife, Lord,
then what would Man be?
Here on earth, we shall turn our eyes to Heaven,
don't look down at the ground, lamenting!
The mind is our lamp, the body our offering,
and Heaven the grace which rewards them.
Our deeds are our worship of God,
so says Lakshmīprasād.[4]

(from Devkoṭā [1936] 1986)

PRAYER ON A CLEAR MORNING IN THE MONTH OF MĀGH[5]
(*MĀGHKO KHULEKO BIHĀNKO JAP*)

How clear this morning is!
The blueness has cast off her lacy veil.

The sky is as pure as Vālmīkī's heart,
how lovely this is, Rām's dawning.
The crane's blood briefly speckled the sky,[6]
and kindness was born in the heavens;
compassionate verse came in a wave of golden light.
Celestial gods appear to those
who long with shrinking hearts to see them:
the sun climbs up.

A bird flies in the ashen day: it turns to gold
and sings new songs of the human future,
unmoving, a tree raises one finger:
it points to immortal sunbeams
which have attained their own enlightenment,
and are flung out now for the world.

4. It is an old convention in Indian poetry for a poet to include his or her name in the final verse of a poem as a kind of signature.

5. The month of Māgh corresponds to late January and early February in the Western calendar.

6. Vālmīkī, a legendary sage and the author of the original Sanskrit Rāmāyaṇa, is said to have discovered the art of poetry when he saw a hunter kill a crane. His compassion for the bird moved him to speak in spontaneous metrical verse.

With these rays I weave a net
of emotion in my heart.

The morning star which disappears
is Brahmā, who envisaged all Creation,
a flock of pure cranes swims in the brightness,
moving living wings of joy to life's rhythm,
the quest begins, the world is moving,
its feet climb onto the street.

A bird of lustrous beauty came first to the treetop,
it sang a secret rainbow of music, and slipped away.
Within me, a bird cried out, moving its wings.

Heaven descends and Earth flies up
to meet on a mountain peak:
they embrace and kiss with red lips of pleasure;
now see them more composed,
sitting smiling together,
telling the tale of morning,
casting forth warm colors.

Creation dons a lovely garment,
she deludes with her gentle intoxication
and moves with a fickle temper.
The flow of dawn's music comes in through five doors[7]
and the bird thinks its cage is freedom,
so it sings all those songs once again.

The poet lies exhausted on a mat,
the net of straw is ragged,
he's a lame dog with a one-horned cow.[8]
We say this life is joy when we feel
the sun's warmth on our bodies.

Death is cold, so they say,
but the sun's ageless dish is hot.
The grasses chant their morning prayer;
rooted in soil, they rise up for the sunbeams.
Oh precious glory, oh Sun!
In your presence I mumble a prayer,
great plate of radiance, I bow my head.

Teach me, God,
to win through the net of Death.

(1956; from Devkoṭā 1976)

7. The "five doors" represent the five human senses, and the bird in its cage is a metaphor for the human spirit trapped inside the body.

8. This appears to be one of Devkoṭā's characteristically cryptic references to himself.

MAD (*PĀGAL*)

Surely, my friend, I am mad,
that's exactly what I am!

I see sounds,
hear sights,
taste smells,
I touch things thinner than air,
things whose existence the world denies,
things whose shapes the world does not know.
Stones I see as flowers,
pebbles have soft shapes,
water-smoothed at the water's edge
in the moonlight;
as heaven's sorceress smiles at me,
they put out leaves, they soften, they glimmer
and pulse, rising up like mute maniacs,
like flowers—a kind of moonbird flower.
I speak to them just as they speak to me,
in a language, my friend,
unwritten, unprinted, unspoken,
uncomprehended, unheard.
Their speech comes in ripples, my friend,
to the moonlit Gangā's shore.
Surely, my friend, I am mad,
that's exactly what I am!

You are clever, and wordy,
your calculations exact and correct forever,
but take one from one in my arithmetic,
and you are still left with one.
You use five senses, but I have six,
you have a brain, my friend,
but I have a heart.
To you a rose is a rose, and nothing more,
but I see Helen and Padmiṇī,
you are forceful prose,
I am liquid poetry;
you freeze as I am melting,
you clear as I cloud over,
and then it's the other way around;
your world is solid, mine vapor,
your world is gross, mine subtle,
you consider a stone an object,
material hardness is your reality,
but I try to grasp hold of dreams,

just as you try to catch the rounded truths
of cold, sweet, graven coins.
My passion is that of a thorn, my friend,
yours is for gold and diamonds,
you say that the hills are deaf and dumb,
I say that they are eloquent.
Surely, my friend,
mine is a loose inebriation,
that's exactly how I am.

In the cold of the month of Māgh I sat,
enjoying the first white warmth of the star:
the world called me a drifter.
When they saw me staring blankly for seven days
after my return from the cremation *ghāṭ*s,[9]
they said I was possessed.
When I saw the first frosts of Time
on the hair of a beautiful woman,
I wept for three days:
the Buddha was touching my soul,
but they said that I was raving!
When they saw me dance
on hearing the first cuckoo of Spring,
they called me a madman.
A silent, moonless night once made me breathless,
the agony of destruction made me jump,
and on that day the fools put me in the stocks!
One day I began to sing with the storm,
the wise old men sent me off to Rānchī.[10]
One day I thought I was dead,
I lay down flat, a friend pinched me hard,
and said, "Hey, madman, you're not dead yet!"
These things went on, year upon year,
I am mad, my friend,
that's exactly what I am!

I have called the ruler's wine blood,
the local whore a corpse,
and the king a pauper.
I have abused Alexander the Great,
poured scorn on so-called great souls,
but the lowly I have raised
to the seventh heaven on a bridge of praise.
Your great scholar is my great fool,

9. A *ghāṭ* is a stepped platform beside a river where Hindus take their daily baths and where the bodies of the dead are cremated.

10. Rānchī is the mental asylum in Bihār, northern India.

your heaven my hell,
your gold my iron, my friend,
your righteousness my crime.
Where you see yourself as clever,
I see you to be an absolute dolt,
your progress, my friend, is my decline,
that's how our values contradict.
Your universe is as a single hair to me,
certainly, my friend, I'm moonstruck,
completely moonstruck, that's what I am!

I think the blind man is the leader of the world,
the ascetic in his cave is a back-sliding deserter;
those who walk the stage of falsehood
I see as dark buffoons,
those who fail I consider successful,
progress for me is stagnation:
I must be either cockeyed or mad—
I am mad, my friend, I am mad.

Look at the whorish dance
of shameless leadership's tasteless tongues,
watch them break the back of the people's rights.
When the black lies of sparrow-headed newsprint
challenge Reason, the hero within me,
with their webs of falsehood,
then my cheeks grow red, my friend,
as red as glowing charcoal.
When voiceless people drink black poison,
right before my eyes,
and drink it through their ears,
thinking that it's nectar,
then every hair on my body stands up,
like the Gorgon's serpent hair.
When I see the tiger resolve to eat the deer,
or the big fish the little one,
then into even my rotten bones there comes
the fearsome strength of Dadhīchī's soul,[11]
and it tries to speak out, my friend,
like a stormy day which falls with a crash from Heaven.
When Man does not regard his fellow as human,
all my teeth grind together like Bhīmsen's,[12]
red with fury, my eyeballs roll round

11. According to the Mahābhārata, the magical "diamond-weapon" of Indra, the god of war, was made from a bone of the legendary sage Dadhīchī. Dowson [1879] 1968, 191.

12. Bhīmsen "the terrible" was the second of the five Pāṇḍava princes and was described in the Mahābhārata as an enormous man of fierce and wrathful disposition.

like a half-penny coin, and I stare
at this inhuman world of Man
with a look of lashing flame.
My organs leap from their frame,
there is tumult, tumult!
My breath is a storm, my face is distorted,
my brain burns, my friend, like a submarine fire,
a submarine fire! I'm insane like a forest ablaze,
a lunatic, my friend,
I would swallow the whole universe raw.
I am a moonbird for the beautiful,
a destroyer of the ugly,
tender and cruel,
the bird that steals the fire of Heaven,
a son of the storm thrown up
by an insane volcano, terror incarnate,
surely, my friend, my brain is whirling, whirling,
that's exactly how I am!

(1953; from Devkoṭā 1976; also included in *Ādhunik Nepālī Kavitā* 1971 and *Sājhā Kavitā* 1967)

LIKE NOTHING INTO NOTHING (*SHŪNYAMĀ SHŪNYASARI*)

In this heaven I knew earthly joy,
taking the picture within,
but it all became a cremation ground.
As night falls, at last I know.
This world is like the night,
I did not know this while I lived,
in the end, there is only Lord Krishna:
no devotion, no knowledge, no mind.

Like a grain of desert sand, I am hot,
burning, dying, a fool without hope,
as empty as a dried-out tree.
I warm myself on the funeral pyre,
forfeiting all my sacraments
while trying to put it out,
and now I go like nothing into nothing.

I was born, I grew strong in this heaven,
in the end I am ash and I vanish.

(1959; from Devkoṭā 1976; also included in *Nepālī Kavitā Sangraha* [1973] 1988, vol. 1)

Siddhicharaṇ Shreshṭha (b. 1912)

Siddhicharaṇ Shreshṭha, who was born in Okhalḍhungā in eastern Nepal in 1912, comes from a prosperous landowning Newār family. He has lived most of his life in Kathmandu but has responsibilities for an estate in the Tarāī. Siddhicharaṇ is a member of the influential first generation of modern Nepali poets who grew up under the autocratic Rāṇā government, and his poetry reflects the turbulent period through which he has lived. At various times, he has worked as editor of the important literary journal *Shāradā* and of Nepal's daily newspaper, the *Gorkhāpatra*. He was granted membership of the Royal Nepal Academy in 1957 and is now a life member.

Although he has much in common with Devkoṭā, Siddhicharaṇ is less versatile as a writer and has been described as "the most subjective of all Nepali poets" (Khanāl 1977, 264). It is true that most of his better known poems are focused inwardly, but this does not mean that he has not addressed himself with vigor on many occasions to the social and political issues of his day.

Siddhicharaṇ's first published poem, "Earthquake" (*Bhuinchālo*), was written after the great Kathmandu earthquake of 1934 and appeared in the *Gorkhāpatra*. Most of his early compositions were rhapsodic or contemplative poems concerned primarily with the beauties of nature. He admits to having imitated Lekhnāth Pauḍyāl and to having been influenced in his early years by the great Indian poet Sumitranandan Pant (Kunwar 1966, 25). Siddhicharaṇ became known in the literary circles of Kathmandu during the 1930s, when a respected scholar, Sūryavikram Gyavālī, published a laudatory essay about Devkoṭā and Siddhicharaṇ entitled "Two Stars in Nepal's Literary Sky" (*Nepālī Sāhityākāshkā Duī Tārā*). One of his most famous early poems was "My Beloved Okhalḍhungā" (*Mero Pyāro Okhalḍhungā*), a somewhat formulaic and over-praised poem that looks back with longing to childhood:[1]

In the beauty of your verdant green,
in the coolness of your heart,
this poet spent his childhood,
laughing, playing, wandering the glades,
my beloved Okhalḍhungā

Because this poem was widely interpreted as the expression of a desire to be free of the Rāṇā regime, its author became the subject of much discussion.

Siddhicharaṇ Shreshṭha was clearly not from the same mould as firebrands such as Gopālprasād Rimāl, but Siddhicharaṇ's view of human affairs and the social order in Nepal did undergo a fairly radical change during the 1930s and 1940s. Some critics regard his "revolutionary" poems to be his most important works and argue that the romantic mysticism and pathos he often expresses are secondary aspects of his poetry (A. Bhaṭṭa [1968] 1977, 179). In 1940, he was imprisoned for publishing a poem that began, "There can be no peace without revolution," and he was not released until 1944. In jail, he wrote an episodic poem, *Urvashī*, that was based on a theme from the Mahābhārata. A later foray into Hindu mythology produced *The Sacrifice of Bālī* (*Bālībadha*). Yet it is upon his shorter poems that his reputation now rests. Most of these first appeared in *Shāradā* and are now available in three collections entitled *The Bud* (*Kopilā*), *My Reflection* (*Mero Pratibimba*), and *Mist and Sunlight* (*Kuhiro ra Ghām*).

The poems presented here in translation reflect themes that are typical of Siddhicharaṇ's poetry. The acclaimed poem "A Suffering World" (*Vishva-Vyathā*), which was published in the year of his imprisonment, is basically an expression of personal sorrow expanded to encompass the suffering of the whole world. The poem, which clearly has sociopolitical undertones, voices the speaker's wish to be conscious of the sorrow of the world:

May my heart always churn with longing,
may my tears never cease,
may I stay here above,
bringing the world storms of sorrow.

The speaker hints at the action he might take to remedy the situation—the Bhairava is a fearsome aspect of the god Shiva.

1. T. Sharmā (1982, 110) dismisses "My Beloved Okhalḍhungā" as a poem of little literary merit or importance.

Run far from me all people,
or come together and kill me now,
lest I become the Bhairava
and dance with a garland of skulls.

"My Reflection" (*Mero Pratibimba*), a poem in a similar vein, caused something of a stir when first published. In this poem Siddhicharaṇ focuses attention on what he feels to be a general decline in human values. The language of this particular poem is extremely simple, which increases its effectiveness. "Untouchable" (*Achūt*) attacks a specific social evil: the speaker in the poem is evidently intended to be the deity of a temple.

Siddhicharaṇ's revolutionary poems are exemplified here by "No Smoke from the Chimneys" (*Dhuvāṃ Niskandaina*) and "*Father Has Not Come Home*" (*Bā Āunu Bhaeko Chaina*). The first of these expresses the poet's solidarity with and enthusiasm for the political struggle of the 1940s that eventually removed the Rāṇās from government. The latter poem sums up the general disillusionment of the Nepali elite with the factional and vacillatory administrations of the 1950s. "My Son" (*Mero Choro*), a purely personal poem, demonstrates the beauty and profundity of the finest of Siddhicharaṇ's mystical verse. Finally, "To the Poet Devkoṭā" (*Kavi Devkoṭālāī*) shows signs of a revolutionary spirit, as Siddhicharaṇ consoles his illustrious contemporary after the death of his son and exhorts him to

Go, make proclamations
to put a stop to tears and sighs . . .
you have sons throughout this land.

Siddhicharaṇ Shreshṭha's shorter poems are collected in *Kopilā* (The Bud, 1964), *Mero Pratibimba* (My Reflection, 1964), and *Kuhiro ra Ghām* (Mist and Sunlight, 1988). There are also two *khaṇḍa-kāvya: Urvashī* (Urvashī [a woman's name], 1960), and *Bālībadha* (The Sacrifice of Bālī, no date).

A SUFFERING WORLD (*VISHVA-VYATHĀ*)

Life is a length of printed cloth,
wet with resolutions.
Birth and death stand at each end,
drying it in the sunshine of Truth,
hanging it from the tree of this world,
sheltering it from the showers of Hope.

While one man's cloth is drying,
another's is soaked even more.

My cold life was drenched by hopes,
but a parched soul and the heart's fire
dried up all my support.
The storms of a suffering world are raging
high above us today,
birth and death stand and stare, open-mouthed,
and the sentimental declare, oh poet,
lament is the essence of life.

I shed a stream of hot tears each day,
while oblivion's ghost is woken
on the topmost layer of Time;
may it never find my consciousness,
burning in this world's pain,
may my heart always churn with longing,
may my tears never cease,
may I stay here above,
bringing the world storms of sorrow.

The sun is spat out by an agonized day,
I watch it run to and fro like a dark cloud,
black warring tusks, sharp fangs of envy,
are trying to swallow me: I mock them.

It is useless to call this a world of action,
this dark burning ground of deeds,[2]
it is a blessing for those who live
to be offered up to fire.

Anxiety ripens, wells up as hot tears,
the world has wept a river
at the parting of ways, through long ages past.
Demonic valleys, wretched hills,
sad and lonely river shores,
all of them spew forth venom,
dawn and dusk fall as swords on my head.

Can I survive on this earth,
living and dying as other men do?
Run far from me all people,
or come together and kill me now,
lest I become the Bhairava[3]
and dance with a garland of skulls.

(1940; from *Sājhā Kavitā* 1967; also included in
Nepālī Kavitā Sangraha [1973] 1988, vol. 2, and
Ādhunik Nepālī Kavitā 1971)

2. The word translated as both "action" and "deeds" is karma, which has a wealth of connotations. Principal among these is the notion of accumulated merit, or guilt, which determines one's fate in subsequent incarnations.

3. Bhairava is a fearsome aspect of the Hindu god Shiva, often depicted dancing upon the corpses of demons and wearing a necklace of human heads.

NO SMOKE FROM THE CHIMNEYS (*DHUVĀṂ NISKANDAINA*)

I don't have time,
Death, do not call me,
I don't have time to mop up
the blood from a broken head.

Lady, do not detain my advancing feet,
I have no time for your blandishments.
The people of my country
have canceled their meals,
and are struggling: look!

No smoke comes from their chimneys.

(c. 1948; from S. Shreshṭha [1964] 1978)

MY REFLECTION (*MERO PRATIBIMBA*)

Who is this coming down the path,
somewhat defeated, somewhat forgetful,
walking meekly like a dog,
redeeming pain with weakness,
who is this coming down the path?

Like a boulder on two sticks,
with a pumpkin placed on top,
pulled along by children
who say that it is Man;
who is this coming down the path?

Oblivious to Truth,
embracing only Falsehood,
he falls ever deeper, but thinks he ascends,
looking around him, unable to see,
polluting the very air,
who is this coming down the path?

This is a form devoid of beauty,
this is a language empty of feeling,
this is a man who has no soul,
where thought is shut out on all sides,
this, my reflection walking!

(1948; from S. Shreshṭha [1964] 1978; also included in *Sājhā Kavitā* 1967 and *Ādhunik Nepālī Kavitā* 1971)

UNTOUCHABLE (*ACHŪT*)

What is this you have brought me,
untouched by your brothers and sisters?

Take it back, I do not want such things,
you cannot worship while hating yourselves,
you may not enter my temple
if you shut its door to others.

Go away, oh sinners,
go away, fools and savages,
your offerings I reject.
Do not bow down at my feet,
my body is burning, burning.
The waters you bring are defiled,
far worse than pus or mucus.
If you truly wish to worship,
bring before me the man
whose rights you've usurped through all ages,
touch first his feet against whom you have sinned,
him you have called untouchable.

Only then may you come to my temple,
only then are you blessed as men,
only then will you cease being thorns
preventing our nation's progress,
only then will you be straight.

(1955; from S. Shreshṭha [1964] 1978)

FATHER HAS NOT COME HOME (*BĀ ĀUNU BHAEKO CHAINA*)

The rain is falling, the wind is blowing,
Time has donned her garb of lateness,
the lamps are lit, a meal is cooked.
A woman is crying out,
"Father has not come home."

Times have changed,
the Rāṇās have sunk,
they say our chains are broken,
but freedom, progress, democracy,
none of these has come.
A woman is crying out,
"Father has not come home."

The slings of our thought,
the thunderbolts of our dream,
have smashed the skull of darkness,
but a new dawn, a new age, a new day,
none of these has dawned.
A woman is crying out,
"Father has not come home."

(1952; from S. Shreshṭha [1964] 1978)

MY SON (*MERO CHORO*)

This is my son:
Infinity disappears
into the mouth of Great Time,
and only its tail protrudes;
one end of a long series,
its first part unfathomed,
which moves in great heavens;
the uppermost layer of generations uncounted:
the final edition of the Mystery emerges.

Destruction, whirlwind, thunder and threat,
the vast overturning,
baked in the kiln of Death;
these have created a soft and lovely image:
this is my son.

All over our hearts' lake
we sowed the seeds of dreams,
my wife and I together,
and a young plant was born
to grow from the void:
this is my son.

Into his pocket he puts
a piece of golden bangle,
and he's rich!
He bends a feather for his royal plume,
he mounts a horse of reeds,
he wins a glorious battle,
he awards us medals of flowers;
in his laughter and lightness
he flows on unhindered.

Though life's trees are often felled,
pushed out into a sea of sorrow,
though dark, despairing storms may blow,
he is shielded by a wisdom
called innocence, and he goes laughing on:
this is my son.

Young master, the world is not like that!
It is full of distrust, and grief, and strife,
full of hypocrisy, worry and loss!
He mocks my dullness, and I angrily say,
"Can you not see the world, you fool?"
But he weeps at my blindness until,
restored by the nectar of mother's arms,
he laughs in the sunshine of joy
like a rose just after the rain has ceased:
this is my son.

As he laughs he sheds flowers,
as he cries he sheds pearls,
creating beauty as he goes.
He walks on, leading true bliss,
the supreme soul, behind him:
this is my son.

(1948; from S. Shreshṭha [1964] 1978;
also included in *Sājhā Kavitā* 1967 and
Ādhunik Nepālī Kavitā 1971)

TO THE POET DEVKOṬĀ (*KAVI DEVKOṬĀLĀĪ*)

You are a wounded bird,
what can I say as your injuries grow?
Perhaps this world still needs to snatch your very soul.
Your songs you have sung,
squeezing your heart, shedding your blood,
does this world heed only ambition?

Tell me what your singing gained you
as it sapped your life away?
Did you see this dry earth melting
to life as it still lived?
If you spread your hands and weep and wail,
this world is not your friend,
it does you no good to gather
deceit disguised as sympathy.

Turn it round, turn back that horror
which bore off your son at a tender age,[4]
which inspired that gross violation
and caused you your fire sacrifice.
Sing songs of fire,
before a thousand more sons are lost,
sing a song to dispel the faint of aeons,
to raise the corpses of our countless sons.

Life's ship sails a vast sea of sorrow.
Your beloved son has died—shed no tears.
Consider this world's anguish:
so many pass their lives
with nothing to eat, and nothing to wear:
weep into their sea of sorrow,
sail your ship on their sea.

4. Devkoṭā's second son, Krishna Prasād, died of typhoid in 1946 at the age of eleven and his eldest son, Prakāsh, died in 1952, age eighteen. It is not clear to which bereavement Shreshṭha refers.

Dance, and tread down the ashes
of burned-out dreams and rotten hopes,
bring thousands to life, create thousands more,
survive even sorrow.
Create a new world without such outrage,
endure and save others, defeat even Death,
spread freedom from sickness here.
May this world's children not all die young.

Go, make proclamations
to put a stop to tears and sighs,
nation-maker, poet,
you have sons throughout this land.
Go now, arise, for others may die,
alas, how can they live?

(1953; from S. Shreshṭha [1964] 1978; also included in *Sājhā Kavitā* 1967)

Kedār Mān "Vyathit" (b. 1914)

Kedār Mān "Vyathit"[1] is one of Nepali literature's grand old men. A close contemporary of Devkoṭā, Sama, Rimāl, and many other influential Nepali poets, Vyathit has made the greatest contribution of all his peers to the development of Nepal's literary institutions during a long career of more than a half century.

Vyathit was born in 1914 to a Newār family of Bānsbārī in the Sindhupālchok district to the east of the Kathmandu Valley. He found his first gainful employment as an accounts clerk in the household of the Rāṇā prime minister Juddha Shamsher in 1930. By 1940, however, Vyathit had become fiercely opposed to the regime, and from 1948 onward he was active in the banned Nepali Congress Party. For this reason, he suffered years of imprisonment in Nepal (from 1940 to 1945) and in India and a long period in exile. After the revolution of 1950–1951, he was rehabilitated and his political career reached its climax in 1962 when he was made minister for transport and communications. Vyathit's literary activities had commenced much earlier, however: inspired by Siddhicharaṇ Shreshṭa and Chittadhar Hridaya, both fellow Newārs, Vyathit began writing poems in jail. In 1945 he convened Nepal's first ever literary conference, and in 1962 he founded the kingdom's first literary institution, the Nepālī Sāhitya Sansthān (Nepali Literature Institute). Seven years later he became chancellor of the Royal Nepal Academy, the country's most prestigious cultural institution. Vyathit now lives in retirement in central Kathmandu, in a house he calls *kavi kuṭir*, "poet's cottage."

Vyathit is a prolific writer. Twenty-three volumes of his poems have

1. *Vyathit*, meaning "distressed," is a pseudonym resembling those adopted by many Hindi poets of the mid-twentieth century, such as *Nirālā*, "strange," or *Dinkar*, "sun."

been published in all: sixteen in Nepali, four in Newārī, and three in Hindi. No two Nepali critics seem able to agree on a categorization of his poetry: he has been called a romantic, a didacticist, a mystic, a socialist, and even an anarchist. A number of specific themes do recur frequently in his poetry, however, and it is fair to say that his style is generally consistent and readily identifiable. As a poet, Vyathit has attracted both praise and criticism, but as Khanāl has written, "The significance of his poetry is unmistakeable" (1977, 243).

Almost all of Vyathit's poems are written in metrical verse (Abhi Subedī [1978, 61] describes rhythm as their main characteristic), and most are very brief, rarely exceeding one page in length. The earliest were written in jail during the 1940s and are melancholy, pessimistic, or revolutionary by turns. The revolutionary poems are exemplified here by "Fragment from the Year '09" (*09 Sālko Kavitā 1*) and "The Storm" (*Āndhi*). In the latter poem, Vyathit looks back with relish to the political upheavals of 1950. A recurrent theme in his work is the description of human love and natural beauty. "A Glimpse" (*Ek Jhalko*) presents a charming cameo from rural life, and other poems invest the beauty of the natural world with a mystical significance. Vyathit does not shrink from eroticism in his frequent descriptions of women, as in the long poem, published in book form, *Woman: Flavor, Sweetness, Brightness* (*Nārī: Rasa, Mādhurya, Āloka*):

> You, wholly revealed,
> how lovely,
> moonlight is poured out
> to fill your naked body

Vyathit's concern for the modern human condition is expressed in many poems, such as "War" (*Raṇa*), translated here, and he can often be extremely pessimistic. Two of his most famous poems, "Ants" (*Kamilā*) and "The Practice of Sculpture" (*Shilpa-Sādhanā*), describe the futility of human activity and the basic hypocrisy of the world using original allegorical devices. In "The Practice of Sculpture" the artist is aware of the events taking place outside but ignores them, engrossed in work. The human world may speak of peace, but it continues its conflicts unabated; it is only in the arts that words and deeds coincide.

One of the most common criticisms leveled at Vyathit's poetry is that it is influenced excessively by the mystical *chāyāvādī* (shadowist or reflectionist) poets of Hindi literature with whom Vyathit became acquainted during the 1940s and 1950s.[2] Indeed, his revolutionary poems

2. T. Sharmā (1982, 111) particularly critical of Vyathit because of this feature of his poetry.

have been compared to those of the Hindi poet Dinkar (Rākesh 1987, 53), and many critics complain that Vyathit's style is imitative of this tradition and that his language is too full of Sanskrit vocabulary. It is true that Vyathit has made little effort to distance the language and symbolism of his poetry from the clichés of mid-twentieth century Hindi verse because it is from this literature that he has drawn much of his inspiration. Although this fact dismays many Nepali critics, who heap their highest praise upon literature from which all traces of "foreign" influence are absent, it need not detract from an objective assessment of Vyathit's work. The careful tapping of the sculptor's chisel described in "The Practice of Sculpture" resembles Vyathit's art: he has produced a constant stream of small, polished poems for more than forty years, and although these have not been greeted by universal acclaim, their value and merit are considerable.

Vyathit's Nepali poems are collected in *Sangam* (Confluence, 1952), *Praṇava* (Obeisance, 1957), *Ek Din* (One Day, 1958), *Sanchayitā* (The Hoarder, 1958), *Triveṇī* (Three Rivers, 1958), *Junelī* (Moonlight, 1962), *Nārī: Rasa, Mādhurya, Āloka* (Woman: Flavor, Sweetness, Brightness, 1968), *Sapta Parṇa* (Seven Feathers, 1967), *Āvāj* (The Voice, 1974), *Badalirahne Bādalkā Ākriti* (The Ever-changing Shapes of Clouds, 1976), *Mero Sapnāmā Hāmro Desh ra Hāmī* (Us and Our Country in My Dreams, 1977), *Ras Triphalā* (*Three Fruits of Flavor*, 1981), and *Agni-Shringār* (Fire-Decoration, 1982).

FRAGMENT FROM THE YEAR '09[3] (*09 SĀLKO KAVITĀ 1*)

The waywardness of snow,
havoc's cruelest dance,
the naked helplessness of trees,
and darkness circling over them.
But my heart still tells me:
have faith, the day will come.

And then the people's roads grow wide,
from whistling rivers, singing spreads,
sudden music in the desert:
a fruitful dream springs up.

And suddenly they draw nearer:
joyous Spring and sunshine warm.

(1952; from Vyathit [1952] 1962)

3. The political upheavals that removed the Rāṇā regime began in 1950, the year 2007 in the *Vikram* calendar commonly observed in Nepal. Thus, the year '09 equates with 1952, two years after this revolution.

ANTS (*KAMILĀ*)

Coming from a dark hole,
a comet in the night sky,
singing, anxious for drops of water,
in a straw-filled yard of thirst:
a line of ants, confused, confused,
running through the garden.

Like men, they think they travel
the path which leads to virtue,
weak, they descend to a pit of sin,
bearing their sick, and a traveler's needs:
a line of ants, confused, confused,
running through the garden.

Time and again they hide beneath straw,
fearing the threats of Death,
who stages a show of lightning
on the path which leads back home:
a line of ants, confused, confused,
running through the garden.

Bodies tiny, thirst enormous,
eyes filled with darkness on an endless road,
they run with the restlessness of the clouds,
taking their limited means with them:
a line of ants, confused, confused,
running through the garden.

As they ascend a bent old tree,
it's as if the world's defined
in the scribbled language of their line,
the poetry of termites:
a line of ants, confused, confused,
running through the garden.

(1954; from Vyathit [1958] 1968; also included in *Sājhā Kavitā* 1967 and *Ādhunik Nepālī Kavitā* 1971)

A GLIMPSE (*EK JHALKO*)

Fickle as a mountain stream,
affectionate as the earth,
lovely like ripened crops,
shy like bending straw,
a girl with a basket
climbs up the hill.

A young man snakes down the mountain trail,
regarding her with the handsome eyes
of a young bull,
watching her and smiling,
as cheerful as a bouquet.

Suddenly two pairs of eyes
meet by chance on the path,
they look down at the ground
as if perplexed or ashamed,
and after a moment they part,
like the ways of a crossroad.

The stream which tumbles merrily down
says to thc youth, "I shall join with the river,
and wander the deserts, singing
the song of your sweet encounter."
But the youth ploughs his love
into the fields of his heart,
and his eyes are a channel
to water love's harvest.

He heaves a long sigh and counts
the furrows made by the plough.

(1954; from *Sājhā Kavitā* 1967)

THE STORM (*ĀNDHĪ*)

The black cloud sang,
spreading the voice of thunder
to the horizon's end,
and the crazy storm danced
like a destructive god.

Earth and sky were dust,
blow, counterblow, struggle and thunder,
cracking and crackling, terrible rain,
all around fearsome lightning flashed.

But next morning I heard,
great trees had fallen,
the streets were washed clean,
the crops were flourishing!

And I was eager to see
a revolution in this land.

(1956; from Vyathit [1958] 1971; also
included in *Ādhunik Nepālī Kavitā* 1971)

THE END (*ANTA*)

The new-moon sky was rich
with the glory of the pyre;
the night was nonplussed
by its exaltation of darkness,
a nightmare mocked me, a dream
of days burned up by care,
weary eyes blinked,
and slept for an instant.

As soon as I woke I saw
golden sunlight from my window,
kissing, enriching my head:
I remembered the meaning
of dawn; beloved, they say
that our end will not be dark.

(1957; from Vyathit [1958]
1971)

WAR (*RAṆA*)

I saw a bomber attacking,
like an eagle swooping down on a chick,
I saw Creation tremble with fear,
wounded, bloodied, disrupted.
Flames of cosmic dissolution
blazed all over the earth,
the culture preserved for aeons past
reduced to ash in a second.

Love lies down and weeps,
a load set down by the wayside,
containing humanity's smouldering corpse.
And yet they say
this war is fought for justice,
it is waged for peace and progress.

(1958; from Vyathit [1958] 1971)

THE PRACTICE OF SCULPTURE (*SHILPA-SĀDHANĀ*)

Slowly striking the chisel,
tap, tap, tap,
the sculptor steps back from time to time
to regard the image he carves,
pleased, grave, discontented by turn.

On this the fifteenth of Chaitra
a great procession passes by,[4]
at Pashupati the Gītā sings
the glory of action's way,
in every quarter the Pāṇḍava roars,[5]
clamoring for his rights.

At half-past one the radio gives out
the program for Buddha Jayantī,
at Ānandakuṭi the sermons run on,[6]
but still it does not cease:
the sculptor's tap, tap, tap.

Though the Pope may send from Rome
a message of Christmas greeting,
some Asian lands still bathe in blood:
it is only on paper pages
that the Bible goes abroad.

But Buddha, Jesus, Krishna give
their blessings to the tapping sound,
and a statue of Gāndhī, smiling down,
pronounces his "Amen."

(no date; from Vyathit [1958] 1968;
also included in *Ādhunik Nepālī Kavitā*
1971)

4. This is a reference to a public protest that occurred in Kathmandu when the Rāṇā government banned the populace from greeting political detainees as they emerged from the courts after trial. Chaitra corresponds to late March and early April in the Western calendar.

5. The Pāṇḍavas were one of the two great families who fought one another in the Mahābhārata wars. Vyathit perhaps intends to convey the beginning of a titanic struggle.

6. Buddha Jayantī is an annual festival to celebrate the birthday of the Buddha Shākyamuṇi; Ānandakuṭi is a Buddhist sanctuary near Kathmandu.

Gopālprasād Rimāl (1918–1973)

Gopālprasād Rimāl was born in Kathmandu in 1918. He is remembered as the first "revolutionary" Nepali poet and the first to reject the use of meter. He was one of the group of influential writers, including Bijay Malla, Siddhicharaṇ Shreshṭa, and Govind Bahādur Goṭhāle, who produced and contributed to *Shāradā*, the journal that played a most crucial role in the development of Nepali literature during the late Rāṇā period. Rimāl was the most overtly political of all Nepali poets at a time when most writers were addressing social and political issues in their work. Indeed, he was too controversial for his political masters, who removed him from his post as editor of *Shāradā* after only two months and later imprisoned him on several occasions. In an innovative form of blank verse, he railed against the injustices and inadequacies of the Rāṇā government and longed for a social awakening, which was symbolized in his poems as a new birth.

Nor did Rimāl shrink from taking political action; in 1941, for instance, after the execution of a number of political agitators, he gathered his peers around him to protest. Each morning the group of young poets visited the temple of Pashupatināth, and each evening they gathered at the shrine of Shobhā Bhagavatī to sing hymns such as the following:

> I serve the country, give me strength,
> may I bring happiness and welfare to all,
> to you we cry in supplication,
> we are free, all slavery is abolished,
> oh Shiva, give me strength,
> I serve the country, give me strength.[1]

1. Tānāsarmā (1970, 115).

Rimāl's first published composition was a metrical piece, the first of two poems simply entitled "To—" (*—Prati*), and it appeared in the *Gorkhāpatra* in 1935. He also employed the *jhyāure* folk meter, which Devkoṭā had popularized with his *Munā-Madan*, in poems such as "To the Madman" (*Bolāhāsita*, 1937) and "Cloud" (*Bādal*, 1938). His "Poet's Song" (*Kaviko Gān*), which appeared in the *Gorkhāpatra* in 1935, was acclaimed as the first Nepali poem in free verse, and by the late 1930s he had become the first Nepali poet to abandon meter altogether.[2]

The Nepali poetry of the 1940s and early 1950s was filled with expressions of hope for the future, although writers who wished to express controversial views had to do so obliquely if they wished to avoid imprisonment or censorship. Many of Rimāl's poems were therefore phrased as pleas to a mother from her suffering children. He refrained from identifying this mother with Nepal or from naming her children's oppressors, and most of these poems could be interpreted as expressions of the angst that grips the world during the *kali yuga*, the age of universal degeneration, or as general depictions of the human condition. In the context of Nepal at the time, however, Rimāl's message was abundantly clear: the mother was Nepal; her oppressors were the Rāṇās.

The poem that made Rimāl's radicalism most plainly apparent was the second of his poems entitled "To—," published in 1960. At first glance, it appears to be merely a short poem addressed to an anonymous lover, albeit in unorthodox terms, but its startling political message soon becomes clear:

> Here we should give birth to Buddha,
> here we should give birth to Lenin,
> here we need self-knowledge:
> is there a better mirror than the face of a child
> for us to see ourselves?

Rimāl's most famous poem is "A Mother's Dream" (*Āmāko Sapnā*), an allegory that expressed his firm conviction that change would come soon to Nepal. As in many subsequent poems, Nepal was symbolized by a mother who dreamed of bearing the son who would combat evil and inaugurate a future full of hope. The poem consists of a dialogue between a mother and her son: she assures him that "he" will surely come to fight against injustice:

> At first you will think him a dream,
> you will grope with your hands to touch him,
> but he will surely come,
> more tangible than fire or snow.

2. Ibid., p. 116. Subedī (1981, 15) states that this poem first appeared in *Shāradā*. Tānāsarmā ([1977] 1979), meanwhile, devotes a whole chapter of a book to a discussion of the question "Who first experimented with prose-poetry in Nepali?"

The mother (Nepal) concludes by telling her son (the people of Nepal) that she had dreamed in her youth that he would be her liberator. A critic, Madhusudan Thākur, penned a tribute to Rimāl shortly after his death, and described "A Mother's Dream" as "a great dream, rising out of great depths, and nothing could suppress the cry with which this memorable poem closes . . . simply because it is an eternal cry that Rimāl voices, not merely a political one. . . . The betrayal has passed; the faith endures" (1975, 64).

Several of Rimāl's other poems, such as "Consolation" (*Sāntvanā*) and "A Mother's Pain" (*Āmāko Vedanā*), return to this theme. Naturally, Rimāl was exhilarated by the fulfillment of his dream when the Rāṇā regime was overthrown in the revolution of 1950–1951, and his delight was expressed in the poem "A Change" (*Parivartan*). The new political order, however, failed to live up to his expectations, and he felt betrayed by the factional strife that bedevilled the several administrations set up between 1950 and 1960, as is clear from his poem "Who Are You?" (*Timī Ko?*). This disillusionment may well have contributed in part to Rimāl's clinical depression and subsequent mental derangement. Like Devkoṭā, Rimāl spend a long period in the asylum at Rānchī and later took to roaming the streets of Kathmandu at night (Upādhyāya [1968] 1977, 119). Thus, one of Nepali poetry's most distinctive voices fell silent after 1960, and Rimāl died in 1973.

Rimāl was a major formative influence on the development of Nepali poetry, despite the fact that he produced only one collection of poems, *Āmāko Sapnā* (a number of poems remain uncollected). Although this received the Madan Puraskār in 1962, the quality of his work was rather inconsistent. Yet his best compositions were "symbolic yet simple, simple yet lyrical, lyrical yet progressive" (Tānāsarmā 1970, 115) and are deservedly recognized as an important aspect of Nepal's poetic heritage. His dramas, too, particularly *Cremation Ground* (*Masān*, 1946), have achieved a certain renown. The figure of Gopālprasād Rimāl inspires affection and respect. He did not hesitate to use poetry as a medium for the expression of political dissent, although he rarely descended to the level of sloganeering, and his experiments with new forms of verse marked the beginning of a new era. For these two facets of his poetry he is justly remembered.

A MOTHER'S DREAM (*ĀMĀKO SAPNĀ*)

Mother, will he come?

Yes son, he will come,
come spreading light like the morning sun;
at his waist you will see a weapon,

for his fight against injustice,
shining like the dew.
At first you will think him a dream,
you will grope with your hands to touch him,
but he will surely come,
more tangible than fire or snow.

Are you sure, mother?

When you were born,
I hoped to find his shadow in your soft face,
his beauty in your lovesome smile,
his soft voice in your baby talk,
but that sweet song has not made you its flute,
though in my youth I had dreamt
that you yourself would be him.
But he will come, whatever befalls us,
a mother speaks for all Creation,
I know this is no idle dream.

When he comes, you will lift your face from my lap,
cease listening to truth like some fantastic tale;
you will be able to see it,
to bear it and grasp it yourself.
Instead of drawing courage from me,
you will go to war alone,
consoling a mother's inconsolable heart,
and I shall no longer stroke your hair
as if you were a sickly child.

You will see him come as a storm,
follow him like a leaf in the wind,
see, he comes falling down from life's sphere,
pouring forth like moonlight,
our lifeless inertia squirms like a snake;
my son, rise up when he comes.

Will he come like dawn's softness to the throats of birds?
My heart trembles with hope.

Yes, son, he will surely come,
come spreading light like the morning sun,
but that you yourself would be him:
this was the dream of my youth.

(1943; from Rimāl [1962] 1983; also included in *Ādhunik Nepālī Kavitā* 1971 and *Nepālī Kavitā Sangraha* [1973] 1988, vol. 1)

CONSOLATION (*SĀNTVANĀ*)

Do not weep, just wait a while,
your warrior drives the world forward,

he will come to your small room at dusk.
He will come to fill your arms,
his bright, shining face will appear
in the soft light of your lamp.
Do not weep, just wait a while.

Yes, he has become quite strange to you,
he has toughened his loving heart,
his light, musical voice is harsh and heavy,
his dreamy gaze sharp and abrasive,
his soft hair is matted
with the dust of a yogi's ashes,
he has found that the world needs overturning,
so now he is a warrior;
he girds up his loins to fight.

But no, he has not become cruel,
he has not killed off his love for you,
just wait a while, and he will come
to your loving lap for rest,
he will come to fill your arms;
your warrior drives the world forward,
he will come to your small room at dusk.

Be not distressed, be happy, be bright,
you may not fear for yourself,
but he cares only for you.
On he fights, oblivious
to news of all but you,
so you must shine bright,
the source of his power.
Do not fear, he is not out of reach,
the warrior who battles far away
will return to play in your lap at dusk.

He has made up his mind, so be resolved,
his life he offers for life, do not fail him,
if he returned as evening fell,
saying, "I melt in your love,
beloved, I return,"
to hide his dark face in your skirts,
would you not die?

Say firmly, "I look upon no defeated face,
the door of my home is shut
to one who flees from battle,
the wreath of my arms
is not for the vanquished,
my garland is for victors alone."
Speak out without fear
against the tyranny which bows our heads,

against the poverty which keeps us silent,
against the poverty which keeps us from living,
against the ignorance which stops us knowing.

He girds up his loins, resolving to fight,
victory will be his.
Speak out, for you are his power,
victory will be his.

And he will return soon,
you will see his bright shining face
in the soft light of your lamp.
Your warrior is fighting far away,
your warrior drives the world onward,
he will come to your small room at dusk.

(1946–1950; from Rimāl [1962] 1983; also included in *Ādhunik Nepālī Kavitā* 1971 and *Nepālī Kavitā Sangraha* [1973] 1988, vol. 2)

A MOTHER'S PAIN (*ĀMĀKO VEDANĀ*)

The night was as dark as unknowing,
the storm winds as cold as selfishness,
like arrogance the storm clouds roared.
It crouched in my heart, and suddenly flashed:
a fire! Like lightning,
was it the dawning of the light
which makes this darkness bright?

And in the paleness of dawn,
before the sun had even shot
its first golden barb at the dark,
I made a sweet discovery.
A fire was born within me,
and was slowly taking form.
From this knowledge a Springtime
of dreams fell into my mind,
it poured out a Summer flood of hopes,
my feet would not stay on the ground,
and since I was fuel for that flame
I was seen one instant, and vanished the next,
like lightning in the world.

He began to take shape;
sun and moon,
earth and water,
wind and sky,
all helped to foster him,

and often I knew my heart was beating
in time with Creation's pulse.

He was born.
I discovered why flowers bloom in this world.
My love for him grew tenfold,
the stars taught me the cradle songs
with which they wake the sleeping earth.
He grew up.

A mother's blessing is as vast as the sky,
that flash of fire I imagined,
playing in the ripples of my mind
on life's new-moon day,
now grows like the waxing moon,
and the pain I suffered, bearing and rearing him,
lies down now to sleep in my heart.
but he, will he be as we hoped?

(1947–1950; from Rimāl [1962] 1983)

A CHANGE (*PARIVARTAN*)

They had always lived in misery,
today they would gladly pledge their lives.
Their voices were empty, till yesterday,
not even the echoes of their minds,
unlike human speech, till yesterday,
just words without meaning, till yesterday;
but now there is life in their voices,
anguish, appeal, madness, attraction,
today their very silence speaks out.
They had always lived in misery,
today they would gladly pledge their lives.

He who held out his hands to beg
now clasps them together in prayer,
inspired to offer his life to a dream;
charity's impulse had never dawned
in the man who ends his helpless days,
days of immobile cowardice:
today all are braced to take life in their hands.
They had always lived in misery,
today they would gladly pledge their lives.

He had no friend to love him,
he had no foe to hate him,
such was the depth of his poverty,
his meanness and baseness were his all,
he walked with a shield of cowardice.

But now he has friends who would lay down their lives,
foes who would take his life, too:
such are his greatness and wealth.
Today he is shielded by his chest,
puffed out with glorious pride.

They had always lived in misery,
today they would gladly pledge their lives.

(1949; from Rimāl [1962] 1983)

WHO ARE YOU? (*TIMĪ KO?*)

Here we are fond of our needs,
the vanity which hides them
is dear to us:
who are you to expose them?

Here we cling to our complexes,
fond of this weak lassitude,
we do not want to give it a name.
Who are you to name it?

And who are you to try to bring order?
We love this necklace of defeat,
soon to be our victory garland:
who are you to tell us
that we have not won,
that others will triumph?

We love our lethargy,
we love this predicament,
if we prefer to lie down,
who are you to raise us?

We do not need to reform ourselves,
we need no revolution,
that someone will lend us virtue,
the semblance of change:
this is our prayer.
Who are you to tell us
to do it now, ourselves?

We merely need some vessel
to fill with our need, our lazy malice,
although we have killed our kindness,
we claim that we have not.

So who are you to stand in our way
if we wish to prove our valor?

(1950; from Rimāl [1962] 1983; also
included in *Sājhā Kavitā* 1967)

TO— (—*PRATI*)

Oh young woman, lovely young woman,
my meeting you was just rain falling in sunlight.
You probably remember: we were wrapped up together
like a cloud, with rainbows, showers and storms,
and like the sky we cleared.

By your depth and your gravity
my hasty eminence confounded,
we wept and we laughed, but today
our return to consciousness
makes that all seem insipid,
for in our passion there should be awareness
that will help me to say not "I love you,"
but "I shall make you conceive."

Oh young woman, lovely young woman,
there is even love in the jungle,
but for this whole village, this whole town,
love alone is not nearly enough.

We need healthy, blatant pregnancy.

Here we should give birth to Buddha,
here we should give birth to Lenin,
here we need self-knowledge:
is there a better mirror than the face of a child
for us to see ourselves?

Oh young woman, lovely young woman,
if we meet again, I will simply say,
"I shall make you conceive."
If we never meet, I shall find
another young woman,
a lovely young woman who attracts my heart,
as rash and as jaded as you.
And I will have the strength to say,
"I shall make you conceive."

(1960; from Rimāl [1962] 1983; also included in *Sājhā Kavitā* 1967 and *Ādhunik Nepālī Kavitā* 1971)

Mohan Koirālā (b. 1926)

As one of Nepali literature's most respected and enduring poets, Koirālā has been writing for more than forty years, but his poetry continues to evolve and change, adopting new styles and addressing new themes. He has wielded considerable influence over poets contemporary with him and is revered by younger writers. Yet it is extremely difficult to identify him with any particular school of modern Nepali literature, be it romanticism, dimensionalism, or the "contemporary" movement. Although Koirālā has made his own important contribution to each of these and has been influenced by them in turn, Subedī's comment remains true: "Koirālā is of his own kind" (Subedī 1970, 68).

Mohan Koirālā was born in 1926 into a comparatively prosperous Kathmandu family. His father fell on hard times, however, and because college fees could no longer be afforded, Koirālā was obliged to break off his college education before it was complete. As a young man, he took up a variety of jobs in various areas of Nepal, working for some time as a schoolmaster in the town of Hetauḍā and latterly for the Transport Corporation in Kathmandu. In 1974, in recognition of his contribution to Nepali literature, he was made a member of the Royal Nepal Academy, a post that reached the end of its five-year term in 1979 and was not subsequently renewed. Since then, Koirālā has lived with his family (he has five children) in their simple home in a quarter of Kathmandu known as Dillī Bazaar.

The first poem Mohan Koirālā admits to having written[1] is "Remembering as I Go" (*Jāndā-Jāndai Samjhera*), composed in 1946 when he was

1. Koirālā has hinted at the existence of a few early metrical poems. These are unpublished and are likely to remain so.

twenty years old and published in 1953. According to Ìshwar Barāl, the editor of Koirālā's first volume of collected verse, Koirālā was first persuaded to try his hand at writing by his younger brother, Shankar, now a well-known novelist. Mohan, however, preferred to compose poetry, considering himself a poor storyteller (M. Koirālā 1973, i). It is generally accepted, and acknowledged by the poet himself, that his early compositions were inspired by the example set by Devkoṭā and by contemporaries such as Siddhicharaṇ Shreshṭha, and Bālkrishna Sama. Indeed, Koirālā grew up at a time when these poets were household names, at least among the educated class of the capital. Inspired by men who are still regarded as monumental figures in the history of Nepali literature, Mohan Koirālā began to write, and his poems appeared alongside theirs in journals such as *Shāradā, Indreṇī* (Rainbow), and *Pragati* (Progress).

From the beginning, it was clear that his poetry possessed its own unique qualities. Although "Remembering as I Go" is quite obviously a nostalgic evocation of youth, an echo of Wordsworthian sentiments similar to Devkoṭā's "Childhood," its theme is actually less personal than it seems. The poem's nostalgic sentiments seem to articulate the consciousness that many Kathmandu residents retain of their families' origins in the rural hill regions. Other early poems address similar themes in a tone that is essentially romantic, but many convey an additional message. "I Remember" (*Ma Samjhanchu*) contains references to a desire for political change (which was an increasingly powerful force during Koirālā's youth). Similarly, "An Introduction to the Land" (*Deshko Parichaya*) describes Nepal on the eve of the Rāṇās' downfall. Barāl (in M. Koirālā 1973, i) also discerns the influence of Rimāl's "A Mother's Dream" in "I Love Your Daughter" (*Ma Timro Chorīlāī Prem Garchu*) because both poems share the theme of awaiting the arrival of a person who will in some way improve the quality of life.

All of Koirālā's published works are written in free verse. He explained his preference for this genre, which has predominated in Nepali verse since the 1950s, to Uttam Kunwar:

> Although it appears to be small, a cup of water can contain the whole of the sky. This is the capacity of prose poetry. . . . It can reflect the most subtle human feelings. People do not converse in meter, or in verse, so why should we make our literature artificial and contrived by introducing meter into it? (Kunwar, 1966, 110)

Comment on social or political issues, an important element of Koirālā's poetry, is overt in his early poems but less so in his later works. "The Martyrs" (*Shahīd*) looks back in anger at the execution of three political agitators ordered by Prime Minister Juddha Shamsher in 1941. The poem also seems to urge the nation to look to its future and to the problems of the present, however, and not to dwell for too long on the sad events of the past:

> But they have died already.
> I make the picture clear,
> I wash the dusty ground with water . . .
> and I turn the page to another history.

"The Fiddle" (*Sārangī*) is probably Koirālā's most famous poem, quoted in most analyses of his work. The minstrel (*gāine*) is a well-known figure in rural Nepal, where he travels from village to village singing songs that often satirize contemporary political events (Macdonald 1975, 169–174). The sorry fate of Koirālā's young minstrel reflects the lot of the poor and lowly majority of Nepal for whose sake, in the poet's view, the political revolution of 1950–1951 had taken place. The poem ends with a protest at the fact that none of the promised changes had come to be. The minstrel quotes the mantras of social reformers ironically in Sanskrit:

> Where are those rotten wise men who said,
> "May all beings be happy"?
> Where are the men who said,
> "Truth, not Falsehood, shall triumph"?

Despite such statements, Koirālā is extremely wary of political ideologies (vād). To Uttam Kunwar, he explained:

> Is it not Man who writes? Poetry must benefit Man; it must exert an influence in language that is artistically pure. Although there are many "isms" or ideologies, I do not adhere to any of them. Once poetry has been infiltrated by an ideology, it is no longer literature, but simply sloganeering to support some partisan view or another. (Kunwar 1966, 109)

Koirālā is even dubious of the relevance or validity of such concepts as modernity; when we first met in 1987, he told me, "Our modernity is the dust on our streets."

The Poems of Mohan Koirālā (*Mohan Koirālākā Kavitā*) contains all of the poems published in various journals between 1953 and 1971 and thus represents the first half of Koirālā's literary career. Two lengthy poems appended to the collection contain signs of the way in which his poetry was to develop in subsequent years. These are "Mountain" (*Lek*) and "Gift of the Sun" (*Sūrya Dān*). The first fills nearly sixty pages, the second thirty-four. Both poems make great use of abstract symbols, many of them personal and therefore difficult to comprehend. This tendency toward obscurity becomes more marked in Koirālā's later poems, as should be evident from a reading of two of the poems translated here, "The Snow Peak's Blood-Red" (*Himchuli Raktim Cha*) and "It's a Mineral, the Mind" (*Khanij Ho Man*). Nepali critics often claim that Koirālā has been influenced by T. S. Eliot or even by Gertrude Stein.[2] In view of the poet's limited knowledge of English, however, this seems unlikely in any immediate sense and is perhaps more true of the dimensionalist poets. Such influences are no doubt discernible in the works of Hindi poets such as Agyey, with whom Koirālā is familiar, and so if any similarity truly exists between poems such as Koirālā's "Toward the Last Day of Bhīmsen Thāpā" ('*Bhīmsenthāpāko Antim Dintira*') and Eliot's "Gerontion," as Barāl has argued (M. Koirālā 1973, xv), it may be something less than a total coincidence. Nevertheless, a trend toward modernist innovation in Nepali poetry that in some way resembles an earlier trend in English poetry does not automatically imply that one tradition is consciously emulating the other.

Koirālā is a prolific writer. His six volumes of collected verse contain 121 poems, of which many are extremely long; quite a number of other poems remain uncollected. The first collection is considered by critics to be his most important, but Koirālā continues to experiment. His *Fishermen on the Riverbank* (*Nadīkinārākā Mājhī*) received the Madan Puraskār literary prize in 1981, and together with his most recent volumes, *Invitation of the Seasons* (*Ritu-Nimantraṇa*) and *Blue Honey* (*Nīlo Maha*), it marks a return to a syntax and general style that are simpler than those in *The Snow Peak's Blood-Red*. But the poet still ranges widely over his immense vocabulary. Koirālā himself admits quite frankly that his poetry is often difficult and that it is criticized for this, but he makes no apology: "I might claim to have served Nepali literature in some small way. I would venture to say that I have tried to elevate the style of modern poetry and to introduce a new flavor to the flow of old poetry. Only time will tell whether or not I have been successful" (Kunwar 1966, 114).

Since the publication of the 1978 collection, Koirālā has made strenuous efforts to develop the genre of the long poem (*lāmo kavitā*) in Nepali. *Invitation of the Seasons* and *Blue Honey* are both poems of considerable length, and *Fishermen on the Riverbank* contains six poems of between twenty-seven and ninety pages in length. For obvious reasons, it has not been possible to include translations of these later works in this book, which concentrates on Koirālā's poetry prior to 1978. The long poems, which perhaps represent the third phase of Koirālā's development, are equally worthy of translation.

Koirālā is clearly unique in the field of Nepali poetry, and his personal charm and simplicity ensure that he is greatly respected by other writers. In early 1987 he fell ill with what appeared to be a kidney complaint,

2. Subedī (1978, 72) comments, "It has become a cliché to compare Mohan Koirālā with T. S. Eliot."

and poets, publishers, and students pooled their resources to defray his medical expenses, just as they had done for Devkoṭā when he was dying in 1959. Many feel that Koirālā has not received the credit from the authorities that he deserves and question the nonrenewal of his academy membership. Between 1960 and 1990, Koirālā was perhaps less than wholehearted in his support for the prevailing political order in his land, and there are suspicions that this may have been a factor in the decision. He is, however, an essentially apolitical man, and his tremendous contribution to the literature of Nepal deserves greater recognition both in his homeland and in the world outside.

Earlier drafts of the translations of "An Introduction to the Land," "I Love Your Daughter," "The Martyrs," and "I Remember" appeared in the *Himalayan Research Bulletin* (Hutt 1988b).

Koirālā's poems are collected in *Mohan Koirālākā Kavitā* (The Poems of Mohan Koirālā, 1973), *Sārangī Bokeko Samudra* (An Ocean Bearing a Violin, 1977), *Himchuli Raktim Cha* (The Snow Peak's Blood-Red, 1978), *Nadīkinārākā Mājhī* (The Fishermen on the Riverbank, 1981), *Ritu-Nimantraṇa* (Invitation of the Seasons, 1983), and *Nilo Maha* (Blue Honey, 1984).

Postscript. After the political changes of spring 1990, almost all of the members of the Royal Nepal Academy offered their resignations. The academy was subsequently reconstituted under a new vice-chancellor, Ishwar Barāl. As this book went to press, I learned that Mohan Koirālā had been reinstated in the academy, along with Bairāgī Kāinlā and several other poets translated here.

REMEMBERING AS I GO (*JĀNDĀ-JĀNDAI SAMJHERA*)

To the meadows which spread their laps
by our villages in the high hills,
where our children were given their place
in love and affection: my kiss of love.

The great old rock where we laugh and mock
is wrinkled with moss, white with flowering grass;
it digested our forefathers,
stood firm through flood and storm,
and responds with a roar to even an echo;
to those grinning white jaws: my kiss of love.

And to the unchecked song of the free-falling stream
which flows nearby, mocking our love,
(beloved, you are mine!)
to your modest smile which laughs and brings cheer

at every moment of pain or sorrow:
my kiss of love.

To the budlike eyes of cheap little girls,
dragged down by tears,
by seasons which fled before their time:
my kiss of love.

The sweet wind whispers,
unobstructed, trouble-free,
in the place where I drew warm breath,
and a child was filled with laughter.
In this corner of the world
is the courtyard where I once crawled,
here are the cold stones, the warm graves
of my loved ones who have died.

So, numbed by the chill gusts and white frosts,
by the cold, the sorrow, the shame, death and famine,
to this hearth that warms me
I offer my kiss of love.

(1946; from M. Koirālā 1973; also included in *Ādhunik Nepālī Kavitā* 1971)

AN INTRODUCTION TO THE LAND (*DESHKO PARICHAYA*)

This is the first bell, and this the first voice,
to our duties we are called
as the orchids flower on the precipice;
once the *kumārī* has shared out the garlands,
every day will be the auspicious time:[3]
very soon the light will come
on a golden morning.

When the sun has rubbed vermilion[4]
into the blessed mountains' hair,
Springtime hills delight in their scent;
eyes drink in the scene to the music of bird song,
every day there is a wedding:

3. "Auspicious time" is my translation of the Nepali word *sāit*. Strictly, *sāit* is the time fixed by astrologers for a bride to leave her parents' home on the day of her wedding. Here, *sāit* also represents the auspicious time for democracy to be established in Nepal. The *kumārī* is the so-called living goddess of Kathmandu, who presents a garland of flowers to the king during the annual festival of Indrajātrā. In 1950, this festival presaged the series of events that toppled the Rāṇā regime.

4. Vermilion (*sindūr, abir*) is worn in the parting of the hair by married Hindu women. It symbolizes the happy state of a woman who enjoys a husband's protection.

very soon the light will come
on a golden morning.

Oh night-extinguishing light!
In night's dark obscurity
birds have pecked up their food
from the pavements of Asan market,[5]
and now dawn's sun is rising
from a new day's wings,
washing the dirty streets clean:
very soon the light will come
on a golden morning.

Rising from the northern sea,
the moon swells over a crooked hill,
dressed in her widow's attire;[6]
bushes and trees sway in the wind,
light and shade are playing, dancing,
river shores glisten, the whole night is still:
very soon the light will come
on a golden morning.

An owl is weeping with open wings
from its roost behind the cremation ground,
another adds its song in fragments:
"In what soil grows the lotus now?
From which bough sings the nightingale?
In which forest do the peacocks dance?
On what green plain will those eyes open,
which sleep now in deep emotion?"

Twisting its body, night attacks me,
black fangs glistening, it readies itself,
its arms are outstretched: I beat a drum,
to declare that the world still meditates
and has yet to wake from its trance.
I picked up a firefly, held it up to the stars:
"It fears no one, it glows and dims,
it dims and glows, of its own accord,
Light, oh Light!" I cried,
and the eastern sky reddens:
very soon the light will come
on a golden morning.

5. Asan is the central marketplace of old Kathmandu.

6. In Hindu tradition, white is the color of mourning, and for this reason women who are widowed, and may therefore not remarry, often dress in white for the rest of their lives.

The moonbird calls out to make me restless,[7]
I stride out—the sound of voices is far away,
and the river sleeps between us;
it has rushed and roared,
washing vermilion from the Himalaya's hair.
Without the human hustle and bustle
which drag me along with this country's dreams
or knock me up with its awakened martyrs,
my country grows cold
in a shroud of clouds.

The sun hides under my pillow
and appears around midday,
when sunshine melts into the snow,
warming the hillsides, reopening every door:
very soon the light will come
on a golden morning.

(1951?; from M. Koirālā 1973)

I LOVE YOUR DAUGHTER
(*MA TIMRO CHORĪLĀĪ PREM GARCHU*)

Oh blue reflection on an unstained rock,
you do not know how I love your daughter,
who darts behind green shrubs when she sees you,
who is startled when you find her alone.

When I love your daughter,
it is a sweat stain, a smile, that I love,
and cheeks that are colored by toil,
I love the girl weary from breaking clods,
tired from working on the soil,
who stands now in the neem tree's shade,
coming into the first shadows of youth;
I love your budding flower,
I love that girl.

I am setting out with ax and sickle,
seeking wood for a boat,
with hammer and chisel to look for a millstone,
with a bough and some pegs to divert a stream,
you will see me nearby, scraping a plough,
carving an image,

7. The *chakor* bird plays an important role in the poetic tradition of northern India and Nepal. Fabled to subsist on moonbeams, its longing for the moon is a metaphor for the separation of human lovers or of the soul from God.

digging a channel;
I am proud, I stroke my mustache.

Oh Man, the first to plough the deserts,
the first to adorn its furrows with green;
if shoots should wither, we revive them with sweat,
if stones block soft roots, we remove them with hoes,
if wounds strike our crops, we heal them with kisses,
if pests eat soft buds, we crush them with tongs;
with one ear of corn we will build the whole field,
then we will embrace this world!

We have a boon for our untiring souls,
before us the seasons bow their heads,
and we are fortunate:
the clods of our soil are safer
than a soul wrapped in cotton-wool.
Oh Man, I am he
who makes Fate himself with his ax,
then cleans and carves and paints it,
who creates his own fortune himself:
how we long for sturdy arms,
a pure, sweet manner,
and sweet, fat bread,
how fervently we desire
dominion over free soil.

Is it a sin to love?
We love each other,
we sow love in the soil,
and make it grow in our hearts,
we raise up our children from the ground,
we dust them down and kiss them;
I love your daughter.

(1954; from M. Koirālā 1973)

THE MARTYRS (*SHAHĪD*)

A January night—
footprints deserted on an empty street,
a vulture is perched on top of a tree,
tightly folding its wings,
and a demoness opens the gates of the jail.
The Bishṇumati[8] waits, its bosom swells,
a fainting engine disturbs the air,

8. The Bishṇumati River flows through the western quarter of Kathmandu.

jackals dig into the earth,
and at Pachalī Bhairava[9] a corpse is burning.

I saw them there,
pointing a gun at the martyrs,
pulling them round with a rope
on the orders of demoness Darkness
who has shaken the hearts of this land and its mothers;
I watch from eyes like two imminent bullets.

We cried out: "Stop, you butchers!
They have not stolen your shame and servitude,
they have not taken your malice and envy,
they have not robbed you of hunger and hate,
they have tried to fill your eyes with joy;
such great men of the future
must not set like the sun tonight,
stop, you butchers, stop!"

The martyrs were speaking
to beloved friends, who had forgotten
their pleasant words and noble ways.

The martyrs were speaking.
But they have died already.
I make the picture clear,
I wash the dusty ground with water,
with pain in my heart I show you a picture
drawn with the blood of the sun's red light:
a picture of leaves kissing the sun's rays,
and eyes kissing the moon,
and I turn the page to another history.

Bloodied martyrs are still in that cell:
the picture has an ancient frame,
made from the soft bones of Jang Bahādur's massacres;[10]
the horse received a lovely statue,
the warrior a well-trained horse;
when he spurred it on and tightened its reins,
he crushed the heart of many a woman,
trampled the playground of many a child,
he washed the vermilion from their hair.[11]

9. This is a temple in Kathmandu.

10. Jang Bahādur, the founder of the Rāṇā regime, achieved his preeminent position in the famous massacre of 1846. The two final verses of this poem refer to a statue of Jang Bahādur on the Tuṇḍikhel parade ground in Kathmandu: he is shown mounted on a rearing horse and looking back in an imperious manner. Koirālā compares Jang Bahādur's steed to the people of Nepal.

11. That is, he made them widows or robbed them of their loved ones.

He who turned back to look down
made the whips fly through the air;
he crossed both rivers and flames
and now fills the land with corpses
and the stench of dead memories.
There we find the rising walls of a funeral ground,
a pyre burning down to its ashes,
someone killing,
someone dying.

(1955; from M. Koirālā 1973)

I REMEMBER (*MA SAMJHANCHU*)

Spring wakes up in secret
to kiss the malodorous soil
on the sturdy hills of this land
and on its strong, white islands;
winter had just undone their belts,
winter had just laid bare their bodices;
and on the ochre cliffs
and the rush of blue rivers
it seems a snail is trying to climb
up into another hemisphere;
as a caterpillar lopes down a bough,
I remember, I was born just now.

The sky was always vast and fearsome,
the horizon always grand and broad;
I peered out from my mother's breast,
travelers whistled from the near river shore,
travelers whistled from the far river shore;
fishermen came out with their oars,
fisherwomen came out with their oars;
travelers whistled from this side and that
and in the middle a boulder
was toppling in the waves:
I feel I was born just now.

As gifts on the day of my birth,
my loving mother gave out (and all to me)
teeth to the toothless, claws to the weak,
bones to the maimed, limbs to the crippled,
fingers to duty and roads to my legs.
There I clenched my fists and made my choice,
there I clenched my fists and made my resolution,
I feel I was born just now.

My mother's eyes lustrous and brightened by love,
her puckered lips, her kisses and smiles,
cheeks wrinkled by health and the rush of her love;
I gamboled in rags like a small unwise lord
on the soil of the serpent's coils.[12]
My delicate bud of desire was drenched
by the sweet sherbet of an ocean of milk,
my breast by the sweat of unfathomed love.
When I cried out, striking and rocking
the earth which was my cradle,
my mother came rushing with wings,
like the sky swooping down with eagles,
and I feel I was born just now.

(1956; from M. Koirālā 1973; also included in
Ādhunik Nepālī Kavitā 1971)

A FLOWER AMID THE MOUNTAIN ROCKS (*PAHARĀKO PHŪL*)

Untroubled by dust and its location,
unborne, unsapped by tenderness, harshness,
a bud bursts open unseen,
unseen in a lonely place.

The smile on its soft, silken skin
is stolen away by the emptiness,
its beauty is lost before it arrives,
unknown hands rip out
the season's joy:
a bud bursts open unseen,
unseen in a lonely place.

(1956; from M. Koirālā 1973; also included in
Ādhunik Nepālī Kavitā 1971)

THE FIDDLE (*SĀRANGĪ*)

Now brother minstrel is utterly cold:
he's had no chance to play his fiddle[13]
and so his hands are numb.

Without men all around to abuse him
he is desolate now, for their taunts had warmed him,

12. Serpent's coils are a reference to the famous image of Vishṇu at Budhānīlkaṇṭha near Kathmandu, where the god rests on the coils of the cosmic serpent Shesha Nāga after completing the creation of the universe.

13. A *sārangī* is a simple stringed instrument played with a bow that is commonly used by Nepalese folk musicians.

made his ears as hot as if wrapped in a scarf,
now his bow has withered like his veins.

His fiddle's as hollow as his smooth, greasy skull,
and all his body pains him,
because no one is throwing stones,
so he carries on, singing from time to time,
why would anyone not think him mad?

He does not beg,
in case it is said that he cries out in hunger;
if he goes about with an earthen pot,
people he knows call him minstrel,
but still if he goes out with his fiddle,
people will call him a beggar.
Songs fill his heart to its brim
like layers of dark, fertile soil;
they have spilled out, burning,
and layers of age-old convention
have been rubbed by the bow in his hand.

His lips twitch, uneasy on the asphalt road,
like fragments of gramophone records,
spurned by our ears, cast out by our hands.
In this breeze, neither warm nor chill,
brother minstrel is utterly cold.

His songs are famous,
thundering like the laughter of Chandra Shamsher,[14]
his songs are young and winsome
like the girls at the Hotel Royal,
his songs are boozy and jealous,
like a *kirāta* woman deprived of her beer,[15]
his songs are hunched up and bent,
like a harem matron who has retired;
songs unwritten by pencil on paper,
songs stored away in an unlocked heart,
but he'll be the prey of these songs undigested,
he'll die here like this, a helpless criminal,
a broken-down gramophone
in a mechanic's workshop.

If he survives he will be just a leaky canister,
badly repaired by an unskilled blacksmith.
So now brother minstrel is utterly cold,

14. Chandra Shamsher Jang Bahādur Rāṇā was prime minister of Nepal from 1901 to 1929.

15. *Kirāta* is a general ethnic designation applied to the varied groups of eastern Nepal who speak Tibeto-Burman languages and is applied particularly to the Rāī tribes and the Limbū. Many caste Hindus take a rather dim view of *kirāta* social customs.

perhaps his life will pass in coldness
until the day he dies.

Arriving home, he lies awake until midnight,
then in his dream his dead wife appears,
bringing the child he once had.
The child comes wailing to its father's lap,
like a hopeless glimpse of money
changing hands in Indrachowk square.[16]
Briefly, a lovely lamp brightens his hovel,
and it becomes a palace.

When he awakes, for brother minstrel it's hard
to distinguish dreams from reality;
he plucks the fiddle of his heart alone,
as if to decide if he's mad or he's sane;
those who hear him think it's a song,
but brother minstrel has never called it that;
he broods, merely recalling a heart
cooked in the oil of his tears;
he never unleashes that song for money,
it is deep inside the folds of his soul.

There it stays, crammed inside,
if you seek his purpose,
you will find he is mad,
if you look for his knowledge,
he is a renunciant,
if it's power that you search for,
his songs are Creation,
but if you seek wisdom,
brother minstrel is merely a wooden butterpot
compared to the common man.
Surrounded by landslides on every side,
men can live lives without purpose:
he has become their metaphor.

I wake with a start: he is moving on,
planting his feet on the street,
those feet of his are naked and cold,
unfettered by shoes since they left the womb,
thus he walks heavily down a road without end,
from bright sunlight to dusk.

I say, "Why does the blind man sing
when he sees the world as nothing

16. Indrachowk is the main intersection at the center of Asan market in Kathmandu. When Koirālā was young, shoppers could exchange large denomination notes or coins for small change at a dais in this crossroad (personal communication, 1987).

but the ashes of burned meadows?"
And he asks me, "Where are the trees?
Where are the bushes, green shade for the traveler?
Where is the high land, the low land,
rent-free for the hoe?
The rivers and streams for my thirst,
the glass of water for my labors?
Where are those rotten wise men who said,
'May all beings be happy'?
Where are the men who said,
'Truth, not Falsehood, shall triumph' "?[17]

(1961; from M. Koirālā 1973; also included in *Sājhā Kavitā* 1967, *Ādhunik Nepālī Kavitā* 1971, and *Nepālī Kavitā Sangraha* [1973] 1988, vol. 2)

THE SNOW PEAK'S BLOOD-RED (*HIMCHULI RAKTIM CHA*)

The earth is sturdy, I am young,
my face is eager, the snow peak's blood-red,
my strong arms are holy juniper,
replete with strength and wealth,
I hope my midday smile
will not grow stale or doze
in rhododendron boughs.
I hope the river gorge
will not fail or be slow
to quote my summons.

Thus my desires are joy and sorrow;
from the mocking laughter of a national peak
comes the people's misty song, just begun,
perplexed and startled
in the eaves of an atrophied barn.
Thus there is one word
which turns me back in despair each moment
and pours forth distress:
it is Truth.

Another word which often tempts and beguiles
is Untruth,
and this perplexity, from the throat of hill and valley,
is now me:
I ponder the future's writing board,[18]

17. These two mantras are quoted in their original Sanskrit in the Nepali poem.
18. The writing board (*dhulauṭo*) is a board sprinkled with powder on which children learn to write in remote regions of Nepal.

I remember and write,
forget and erase.

An epic play was staged in that theater
where Kālīdāsa wrote without success;[19]
the great music of that stage
where Shakespeare sang despairing,
joyous stories amid a sea of sorrow,
the stage where Vedavyāsa aimlessly[20]
laid a foundation stone,
and where a novice now sings
with busy, fresh desire,
playing the violin of Gaṇḍak and Koshī.[21]

Now I am beneath some arena of that future,
writing, erasing, pondering my board.
Oh Himalaya, King of Mountains,
hiding in a fringe of clouds,
oh frost-singing lands, abode of snow,
where our emotions and pleas are numbed
by cold love in the musk deer chase,
where we have consumed the useless with relish,
and found the tasteless delicious.

For hours the debate can be heard:
casting meaning on meaning,
dividing reason from reason,
they have pondered the cause.

(1966; from M. Koirālā 1978a)

IT'S A MINERAL, THE MIND (*KHANIJ HO MAN*)

Velvet the Himalayan poinsettia in bloom,
silver the scabbard of thrusting power,
the mind is a clear scent,
the pen a new ridge of hills.

I am a tree with countless boughs,
a flower which hides a thousand petals,
a juniper, a pointed branch of the scented fig,
its rough, misshapen fruit.

19. Kālīdāsa lived around A.D. 400 and was the author of *Shākuntala Mahākāvya* (The Epic of Shakuntalā) and *Meghadūta* (Cloud Messenger). He is regarded as the most outstanding writer of classical Sanskrit.

20. Vyāsa was the author of the great Sanskrit epic, the Mahābhārata. This is either a reference to him or to "the Vyāsa of the Vedas," the unknown author or authors of the most ancient Hindu scriptures.

21. The Gaṇḍak (or Gaṇḍakī) and the Koshī are two of Nepal's greatest rivers.

In my belief I am Nepali,
my faith the highest Himalaya,
my favorite season is the one
when leather jackets are donned,
my clothes are only freedom.

The Himalayan lights my touching place,[22]
equality spread on the ground where I stand.

(1974; from M. Koirālā 1978a)

YOU WHO REMEMBER (*SAMJHANEHARŪ*)

Oh you who remember, remember,
remember me in a thousand years,
I shall be fossils by then,
I shall not even be in the air,
you will not see me in melted water,
nor seek me out in the moss.

For those who try to know me then,
wandering away from Man,
I shall be some tea leaves,
a few sugar grains,
flakes of calcium in a laboratory,
some dust in a coffee shop,
some ice cream licked from plates by children.

Believers, aesthetes of poetry,
if you seek me in poetic styles,
you will find me in coffee and juniper roots,
not in any face,
ploughed-up, dust-blown soil,
all joy and sorrow in the form
of earth dug up in past and future,
those who address one, those who do not.

Who knows, after a thousand years,
these poems may be pastures of grass,
and I a clod of earth,
sprouting roots of gourd, and pumpkins.

(1975; from M. Koirālā 1978a)

22. *Ājju* is a children's game similar to tag or musical chairs; "my touching place" is a reference to ājju.

Bairāgī Kāinlā (b. 1939)

In May 1963, an unusual literary journal appeared on the Darjeeling bookstalls. The publication of a new Nepali periodical was not a remarkable event in itself because short-lived magazines and papers had proliferated since the 1950s. This slim periodical, entitled *Tesro Āyām* (Third Dimension), was of greater significance than most, however, because it represented the first effort by a group of Nepali writers to formulate a coherent theory regarding the nature and function of the literature they produced. Indeed, one might even go so far as to describe this new movement, of which *Tesro Āyām* was the principal organ, as the first articulation of self-conscious modernism in Nepali literature. Although most Nepali writers aimed to produce literature that conformed with their own conceptions of modernity, none had yet begun to propound a philosophy that would define the attitudes and values of modern Nepali literature.

Tesro Āyām was published and edited by three young writers with common ideals: Bairāgī Kāinlā, Ìshwar Ballabh, and Indra Bahādur Rāī. Their contention, set forth in Kāinlā's editorials and Rāī's essays, was that conventional Nepali literature was "two-dimensional," or "flat," and that it had to acquire a "third dimension" if it was to approach life as an indivisible whole to be apprehended objectively. In the editorial statement of the second edition of *Tesro Āyām*, Kāinlā criticized the old style of Nepali literature:

> The bland sentimentalism (of earlier writers) is not simply drivel; it is also an escape from a sense of responsibility and therefore an escape from the realities of life. In dimensional terms, this kind of writing is "flat" because it lacks a third dimension (depth, and thought or vision) and has no faith in life. Such literature cannot satisfy the needs of the modern intellect. (Quoted in Tānāsarma [1977] 1979, 201)

The distinctive features of dimensionalist (*āyāmelī*) literature are most clearly apparent in its poetry. Most of the clichéd allegories, metaphors, and vocabulary of the "old school" were discarded, as was the use of meter. Poets began to borrow heavily from psychological theory and world mythology. Kāinlā and Rāī urged writers to adopt a moral dimension of their own and to embark upon a fresh exploration of their language. This led to genuine originality and innovation, but also on occasions to "literary obscurantism at its worst" (Subedī 1970, 67). Opinions vary with regard to the value of the movement and to the validity of its arguments. Yadu Nāth Khanāl, for instance, writes that the dimensionalist school "has not gone much further than to suggest that modern sensibility must find a more complex form than traditionally available to express itself fully" and argues that Mohan Koirālā has been more successful in this endeavor (Khanāl 1977, 245). The overtly intellectual tone of much dimensionalist poetry, exemplified by the eclecticism of its references to obscure myths and its use of abstruse symbolism, means that some works cannot be comprehended fully without extensive recourse to the few commentaries that have been produced (see, for instance, Subedī 1981, 178–188). Several poems have come to be regarded as minor classics, however, and the finest of these were the work of the poet Bairāgī Kāinlā.

Kāinlā, whose real name is Tilvikram Nembāng, is a Limbū who was born in the Pānchthar district of eastern Nepal in 1940 and educated across the Indian border in Darjeeling. Very little information is available regarding Kāinlā's life prior to 1960, and he has published nothing since returning to his home in 1966 after a period of residence in Kathmandu. His appearance on the Nepali literary scene was therefore brief, but his contribution has had a lasting effect. The following comments are restricted to an examination of the three poems presented here in translation.

"The Corpse of a Dream" (*Sapnāko Lās*) appears to have been written some time before the philosophy of third dimensionalism was first formulated, when Kāinlā's first poems appeared in a collection entitled *Flower, Leaf, and Autumn* (*Phūl-Pāt-Patjhar*), edited by Ìshwar Ballabh and published around 1960. This is a poem about unrequited love; references to "that love I gave up for mother and father" and to the "ritual of living" that "requires the sacrifice of a life" suggest that the love affair that the poem describes was aborted because of a difference in caste between the lovers. Thus, the poem concludes,

> Man must walk on feet of convention
> over the corpse of a dream,
> trampling life's every morning.

The resentment of social and moral conventions implicit in this early poem is expressed more overtly in "A Drunk Man's Speech to the Street After Midnight" (*Māteko Māncheko Bhāshaṇ: Madhyarātpachiko Saḍaksita*) and "People Shopping at a Weekly Market" (*Hāṭ Bharne Mānis*), the two most famous poems of the dimensionalist movement. The first of these is an obvious summons to rebel against accepted values and practices. Tānāsarmā explains that "the drunk man . . . is a symbol of the modern progressive intellectual: the freedom he craves is the freedom to build a new life and to establish a new set of values" ([1977] 1979, 201). The narrowing streets clearly represent the constraints and strictures of social (and perhaps political) convention, but although the drunkard cries out against the "cramped and crumbling houses," the "self-defeated men, / tangled together like worms," and even against the history of Nepal and life itself, he does not evince a lack of faith in the future. Thus, the poem ends on a note of optimism:

> . . . look with me for the first time:
> as far as we can see, all around,
> there is a battleground for victory
> and a radiant light for life.

"People Shopping at a Weekly Market" is altogether more abstruse. Kāinlā often took months to complete a poem, and the unspontaneous and painstaking manner in which he composed, piling up layer upon layer of symbols and meanings, often made his works inaccessible. The central theme of "People Shopping at a Weekly Market" is reasonably clear, however: it concerns the imbecility and materialism of modern humanity, whose members sell "blood at the bloodbank nearby / to pay for rotting potatoes" but remain oblivious to the presence and proximity of death. The response of the poem's speaker is an angry one, a desire to smash through the emptiness of those around him, but he also admits his own collusion in the situation against which he rages. At various points, however, the poem seems to wander off on strange tangents, and its message becomes unclear. The poem's penultimate verse, in which the line "Oh death went empty-handed from the market today" is repeated three times, is surely imitative of Eliot's "The Hollow Men" (This is the way the world ends / Not with a bang but a whimper).

There is indeed clear evidence in Kāinlā's poems of the influence of the earlier phenomenon of English modernism, a movement that was also regarded as revolutionary in its time. The main fault of both dimensionalist and modernist poetry is its introversion and density: unlike Bhūpi Sherchan, the greatest single influence upon young poets in recent years, Kāinlā made little effort to speak with simplicity or clarity to his times. The significance of Kāinlā, and of contemporaries such as

Ìshwar Ballabh, who continues to write today, is that they orchestrated the most overt rejection of previous tradition that Nepali literature has ever experienced.

Most of Bairāgī Kāinlā's poems are collected in *Bairāgī Kāinlāka Kavitāharū* (The Poems of Bairāgī Kāinlā, 1974).

THE CORPSE OF A DREAM (*SAPNĀKO LĀS*)

My love,
a dream should last the whole night long.[1]
My breast is where I sleep at nights,
covered by vest and blouse,
like an old man's cave inside a village
where only the jackal and the fox
call out their evil omens.
Ruthlessly it is beaten
by bundles of office files
which must be revealed to others,
by crises of convention,
the absence of choice.

When he looks at his face,
primordial, unwashed,
in a mirror on a table,
a man has to say to himself—

a dream should last the whole night long,
as long as sleep goes undisturbed.
As soon as you wake from dark oblivion,
at dawn in the temple of the sun,
with flowers offered up by maidens:
these you must pluck yourself.
(Just like today, when I buried
the love I said I had for you
over there in the bank of the field;
that love I gave up for mother and father
I hear has sprung up, a jasmine tree;
so often these days I dream
of yellow flowers.)

This life must be lived
less for yourself, more for others.
In history, this great ritual of living
requires the sacrifice of a life.

1. The speaker in this poem is a woman, who addresses her lover as *mero hajur*, "my lord." It is not especially unusual for a male Nepali poet to write a female persona poem: see, for instance, Rimāl's "A Mother's Dream" and "A Mother's Pain."

Our unfulfilled souls
will frighten us all our lives,
all through each night in our beds,
in the mornings they will weep
tears of blood onto arum leaves:
young doves sacrificed
by soft, soft dreams.

But life is a ritual,
we must be honest with life,
we must live with fists unclenched.
Emptying ash from pillows and quilts,
we find the remains of scattered dreams,
some burned right up, some broken:
the wings of moths
which flocked all night round the lamp.

Watching in silence, compelled,
from a half-veiled window,
as the sun lifts its head,
belching and dipping its hands in blood,
over there, beyond the mountain.

Man must walk on feet of convention
over the corpse of a dream,
trampling life's every morning,
each man a solitary mourner,
each must mourn the corpse of his dream.

When the dream tumbles down,
like a bee's lifeless body into a lake,
cruel darkness of love and compulsion,
as soon as life rises, rubbing its eyes,
Man must bear sorrow on earth.

Man must walk on feet of convention
over the corpse of a dream,
trampling life's every morning.

My love,
a dream should last the whole night long.

(c. 1960; from Kāinlā 1974)

A DRUNK MAN'S SPEECH TO THE STREET AFTER MIDNIGHT (*MĀTEKO MĀNCHEKO BHĀSHAṆ: MADHYARĀTPACHIKO SAḌAKSITA*)

When I emerge from the wine shop,
long after midnight has passed,
cockerels crow their welcome
from every coop and perch,

flapping their wings in rebellion.
My very breath, drenched in alcohol fumes,
is a great storm in this atmosphere,
this lifelessness, this system.
Grand mansions line the street,
weakness hides in their foundations:
now now now—they will soon collapse!

All my steps are earthquakes today,
volcanoes erupt in each sensation;
how have I lived to such an age
in these cramped and crumbling houses,
too small for a single stride?
I am saddened:
even now they sleep, self-defeated men,
tangled together like worms
in the pestilent houses of the earth,
and do they sleep so late?

Today I am more immense than the world,
my breath is shut in by the ground of this street,
I stamp all over the road.
People say I am drunk—"Keep left"—
people say we should keep to the verge,
but people should walk all over this street,
as many as it can contain,
the police pick up all who keep to the verge,
saying, "This one's drunk, and that one, too!"[2]

At the head of each bed in the rooms
of sky-kissing mansion and tower,
all through each night they burn:
blue, blue bulbs, the eyes of owls.
Here the owls' eyes watch through the night:
who are they waiting for, who will be ambushed?

Faceless men drag by
on legs of darkness,
all night long they walk this street,
their heads hanging low from their shoulders,
their heads full of letters and papers,
their hearts full of the office clock's hands,
their lives machine parts, soon obsolete.

And so the street is shrunken today:
who steals its corners and verges?

2. Under the Rāṇās, Nepali society was rigidly stratified along lines of caste to the extent that a person's caste dictated which side of a city street he or she could walk on. This rule was enforced by police officers in Kathmandu.

Who tears life in chunks from its sides?
Why is the street more narrow each night?
"Tear up this road and widen it! . . . "
The witless policeman stands on the curb,
prepared to arrest me for these words,
for I am drunk!
But when the wine pervades my heart,
I feel I am full of such vastness,
the street is too narrow for me.

May the engineers hear me,
the leaders, the teachers, the poets,
may each second of history attend
to my speech, broadcast from the pavement
beside the main post office:
Streets!
A man walks upon you,
he is too great for you, he commands you:
crack and split and widen yourselves,
rupture and tear down those buildings
which encroach upon your borders,
further, further with each historic moment,
rend and crack the pavements:
they are like history's naked pages,
inscribed with flattering lineages
of the *Koṭparva*'s victors and the ruling family;[3]
split them from head to heart.
We should be allowed to stand here
on the feet of Columbus,
a revolution should walk here,
its head held high.
So I order you: Streets!
Crack and tear yourselves apart,
if potholes appear, I will fill them
with goodwill soaked in wine,
I will cover them with my immensity.
For otherwise I will not fit in,
otherwise, at nine 'o'clock, when it's time for school,
how will the little boy's mother and I
send him to school from this place
if the road cannot hold the sole of one foot?

Oh life, already flat on your back,
constantly trampled by hundreds of boots,
continually tortured by the wheels of cars,

3. The *Koṭparva* was the massacre of 1846 that is now considered to mark the beginning of Rāṇā rule in Nepal.

oh streets, confined by the mists of inertia,
bounded by signboards and poles,
fragmented and fractured by turnings and bends
—a thousand splinters of the valor
of the universal emperor.

Oh sixty thousand cursed sons of Sagar,[4]
advancing to conquer the world,
driving a horse to sacrifice,
I pour the heavenly Gangā's waters
from the firmament of a bottle,
down over you with the faith of Bhagirath,[5]
onto your foreheads, eyes and chests.
Drink this wine which I pour on the street,
bottle by bottle, drop after drop,
revive and arise, my fathers,
you sixty thousand cursed sons of Sagar!

And now wipe the mist with a Himalayan fist,
from the horizon's gummy eyes,
and look with me for the first time:
as far as we can see, all around,
there is a battleground for victory
and a radiant light for life.

(c. 1963; from Kāinlā 1974; also included in
Sājhā Kavitā 1967, *Ādhunik Nepālī Kavitā* 1971,
and *Nepālī Kavitā Sangraha* [1973] 1988, vol. 2)

PEOPLE SHOPPING AT A WEEKLY MARKET
(*HĀṬ BHARNE MĀNIS*)

Naked hills are licked clean
by a locust swarm which hides the sky,
Mikjiri flowers borne by the hills
wilt on the century's breast,
crawled upon, half-burned.
Clumsily flowing, overturning,
in laces and buttonholes,
in the market's bounds,
in a crowd of countless shadows,

4. According to Hindu mythology, Sagar once ruled over the celebrated kingdom of Ayodhyā. One of his two wives bore him 60,000 sons, who outraged the gods by their impious behavior. Sagar therefore engaged in the sacrifice of a horse to assuage the anger of the gods, but the horse escaped and was pursued to the infernal regions by Sagar's sons. Dowson [1879] 1968, 271–272.

5. Bhagirath was the sage whose devotions brought the celestial Gangā River down from heaven in order to cleanse Sagar's accursed sons. Dowson [1879] 1968, 272.

in mist, the gunsmoke of a great war,
in a storm, their eyes are wheeling.

A void, the beginning
to which life has returned in pieces,
each eye has its own void,
a great lake of emptiness
filling their eyes.

I feel impelled
to smash the lake asunder
at Chobhār, with Manjushrī's sword's sharp fingers,[6]
to make flourishing harvests of each fleeing moment,
drenching life with the Bāgmatī's waters,
raising humanity, wounded and torn,
from its grave (on the third day),
with the land which revives with the sun
. . . but it is only an impulse.

History drags along
until shirts are torn in its pages,
a map is etched onto bare, bloodied bodies,
signs declaring the fall of Hiroshima,
this drop of blood,
a moment in my hand,
a rock at this bend of Time
by the riverside.

Upon my brow I bear the blood
of the chicken the shaman killed[7]
to ward off the future:
two or three drops from a martyr
(yes, death is an honor indeed).

This is an oasis with one sapling green,
it grew with the sands, and drank
only reflected light,
but it is kicked out without an heir,
free and aimless in Time's dry desert.

Cobwebs strung up to fill window frames,
blown out from their own horizons,
reaching the lintel over the door;
how sadly, sadly they live,

6. Kathmandu Valley was once filled by a lake. According to the Buddhist Svayambhū Purāṇa, the valley was made habitable by the Bodhisattva Manjushrī, who cleaved its rim of hills at Chobhār, to the south of the city, in order to release the Bāgmatī River.

7. The word translated here as "shaman" is *phaidangbā*, a tribal priest of the Limbū people of eastern Nepal.

even deliverance is insipid and sad,
this aimless freedom, this lonely freedom,
imprisoned in the pointlessness
of a struggle for derelict hopes,
ah, even deliverance is insipid and sad.

These eyes are raised up to the sky,
they collide with wall after wall,
in disappointment and ignominy
they fail to find the sky,
exhausted they fall to a dark pit of void,
another century of indecision.
And yes I must tear out my heart
with the hand of Prometheus,
a vulture on my shoulder,
deprived of the natural feeling of pain.
Within me in folds of wrinkled skin
there lies interned
a rebellion already suppressed
a rebellion already suppressed
a rebellion already suppressed.

Although I send myself to war
in inner conflict, mere inner conflict,
I make Vesuvius and Bali erupt;
to leaping floods of flame I offer
the parallel lines of harrowing evil
from the maps of life
which cause the fever and giddiness,
the angering dullness of impotence,
in the eyes of these people filling the market,
the brown sea of their eyes.
With a touch of ice they dry up the Nile
in the palm of the hand,
they accumulate time in a clod of being.

This ocean of countless cursed eyes,
I feel impelled to smash it to ripples,
to set fire to flame with fragments of waves,
fire and conflagration!
To offer up life at life's demand,
then once more, to life, to life.

But the guilty are mired in damp shadows
in this small yard, feet bound by compromise,
their eyes poured out into footprints,
their lives emptied out down both sides of New Road,
empty pots lie still here and there,
the market of people held tight in their eyes,

picking a fight, the blows of the Gītā,
Arjuṇ's star lit in every eye,
halting the sun for an instant,
on the canvas reversed, at Kurukshetra, in life.[8]

Attack every valley, uproot from all eyes
the border posts of apathy which exile me,
I lack the courage, I erase the blade
with a layer of rust, I kill the senses,
I grow the mosses of death,
oh such an ordinary death!

The serpent cannot find
the bullets in Gāndhī's breast,
the *kharī* tree on the Tuṇḍikhel,[9]
the nails in the lanes of Jerusalem,
again it wanders in suicide,
thin at each end, checkered and damp,
disclosing a plot, the death of the ear.

Dodging the eyes of the guardians of faith,
who move to and fro by the main gate with music,
kindling a smile round the closed sight of Buddha,
on the face of a Japanese shrine,
hastening past necks beyond number,
I walk flat out . . .

With the black car that almost touched me,
the car that is already far away,
death passed by close to life today,
this life which cannot be bought
with the small change of accident:
death left the market empty-handed today.

These people filling the marketplace,
selling blood at the blood bank nearby
to pay for rotting potatoes,
gathering up pieces of their will to live,
packing their being into a bag of shrouds,
they are quite unaware that death left today,
knowing the price of life.

Oh death went empty-handed from the market today
oh death went empty-handed from the market today
oh death went empty-handed from the market today.

8. These are references to the famous battle recounted in the Mahābhārata. The Bhagavad Gītā, one part of the epic, records a sermon given by Lord Krishna to the warrior Arjuṇ on the battlefield at Kurukshetra regarding the nature of dharma, or "duty."

9. The *kharī* tree marks the site in Kathmandu of the notorious political executions, referred to in many other poems, that took place in 1941.

With the black car that almost touched me,
the car that is already far away,
death passed by close to life today.

(c. 1964; from Kāinlā 1974; also included in *Sājhā Kavitā* 1967 and *Ādhunik Nepālī Kavitā* 1971)

Pārijāt (b. 1937)

Pārijāt, the Nepali name for a species of jasmine with a special religious significance, is the pen name adopted by Bishṇukumārī Wāibā, a Tāmāng woman now resident in Kathmandu who has been hailed as one of the most innovative Nepali writers of recent years. The themes and philosophical outlook of her poems, novels, and stories are influenced by her Marxist and feminist views and her own personal circumstances: Pārijāt has suffered from a partial paralysis since her youth and has ventured from her home only rarely during the past twenty years. She is unmarried and childless, a status that is not usual for a woman in Nepalese society and that is due partly to her illness and partly, it seems, to personal preference. Despite her disability, Pārijāt is a formidable force in Nepali literature, and her flower-filled room in a house near Bālāju has become a kind of shrine for progressive Nepali writers.

Pārijāt was born in Darjeeling in 1937, and her childhood was deeply unhappy. Her mother died while Pārijāt was still young, and an elder brother drowned shortly afterward. At the age of about thirteen, it seems that she became passionately involved in a love affair that ended in heartbreak and a period of intense depression. Pārijāt herself has described this as a "self-inflicted wound." In 1954, the family moved to Kathmandu, where Pārijāt completed a B.A. in 1958 and later completed an M.A. in English literature. Her father subsequently became mentally ill. Pārijāt's memoirs, which Subedī describes as "confessional and intimate" (1978, 213), were serialized in *Rūprekhā* (Outline) and a volume of reminiscences have recently appeared (Pārijāt 1988). In view of this background of tragedy and hardship, it is not surprising that most of Pārijāt's writings evince an attitude of alienation, pessimism, and atheism.

Pārijāt's first poem, entitled "Aspirations" (*Akānkshā*), was published in 1953; a collection of poems with this title appeared some years later. In 1970, she announced that she would no longer write poetry,[1] and a second collection of poems from before 1970 appeared in 1987. During the 1970s, Pārijāt became better known as a novelist: her first novel, *Shirishko Phūl* (*The Mimosa Flower*)[2] had already won the Madan Puraskār prize for fiction in 1965 and was wholly without precedent in Nepali literature. It tells the story of a retired soldier in middle age whose life is empty and lacking in purpose. Gradually, he develops a desperate infatuation with the sister of a drinking companion. This woman is the complete antithesis of the traditional Nepali heroine: she is cynical and sometimes cruel, she wears her hair cropped short, and she smokes continually. The psychological background to the story is the soldier's memory of his sexual exploitation of Burmese women during his military service. On only one occasion does he attempt to reveal his feelings to the woman, and shortly afterward she dies. The novel caused great controversy: some thought it decadent and vulgar; others praised it for its modernity. Pārijāt has published five novels since *The Mimosa Flower*, and since 1980 she has also written several new poems. These differ from her earlier poetry in that they are less personal and address social issues.

Pārijāt's second collection of poems, the source of the selection translated here, is very highly regarded, although it does perhaps represent an earlier phase in her development as a writer. All these poems are written in the first person and are deeply subjective. Some of the earliest compositions, exemplified here by "Sweep Away" (*Sohorera Jāu*), are simple lyrics tinged with a mysticism similar to that of the *chhāyāvād* school of Hindi verse. Others, such as "To Gopālprasād Rimāl's 'To—' ", (*Gopālprasād Rimālko "—Prati" Prati*), have political undertones (this particular poem should be read in conjunction with the poem referred to in its title, which also appears in this book). Pārijāt's political views are overtly leftist: in the early 1970s, she attempted (unsuccessfully, it turned out) to initiate a literary movement dubbed *Rālphā* (an apparently meaningless term) that would combine ideas drawn from existentialist thought with the values of Marxism.

About her role as a writer, however, she is self-effacing:

> I consider literature to be the most important part of civilization. Without literary development there can be no national development because literature is an inalienable part of the nation. . . . No, I do not believe that

1. Barāl in Pārijāt (1987, 2). In 1966, however, she had declared that she preferred writing poetry to prose. Kunwar (1966, 237).

2. *Blue Mimosa* was the title given to a translation of this novel by Tanka Vilas Varya and Sondra Zeidenstein, published in 1972.

> the development of literature depends in any way upon my own writing. I write; the readers read: that is the only constraint I put upon my compositions. (Kunwar 1966, 234)

The majority of Pārijāt's poems spring from her physical condition and from a profound atheism and moral despair. "In the Arms of Death" (*Mrityukā Angālāmā*) expresses a hope that the doctrine of reincarnation is not true and that death will be a final release:

> How eager this flower is to fall,
> how it longs to cut short the winter day,
> to pass in a half-conscious night;
> Death returns, defeated,
> from the hands of Life—
> alas, Man does not die.

Pārijāt's most famous poem, "A Sick Lover's Letter to Her Soldier" (*Lāhurelāī Ek Rogī Premikāko Patra*), contains the line "Love does not die, you have to kill it," which sums up very well the antisentimental view she holds of human life.

Pārijāt's poems from the years before 1970 are collected in *Ākānkshā* (Aspirations, 1960) and in *Pārijātkā Kavitā* (The Poems of Pārijāt, 1987).

SWEEP AWAY (*SOHORERA JĀU*)

Sweep away, red glow of evening,
dawn may not come here again,
my sky may not redden again,
sweep down, oh red glow of evening.

This Gangā, this Jamunā, may not flow again,
Nature may no longer weep
on the leaves of this *sungābhā*[3] flower;
come today and bring me
beauty to soak my eyes;
sweep away, red glow of evening.

Go, and ignore the paths which have passed,
no traveler may ever come there again,
do not disturb those nights of sleep past,
that dream may never recur.

If you cannot leave, come, recalling
the lament which is played on a flute,
remembering the song that I sing,

3. The *sungābhā* is a yellow orchid.

remembering the widow who burns
in the eyes of desire and attraction;
sweep down, oh red glow of evening.

(1959; from Pārijāt 1987)

TO GOPĀLPRASĀD RIMĀL'S "TO—"[4]
(*GOPĀLPRASĀD RIMĀLKO "—PRATI" PRATI*)

Truly, love is not nearly enough,
the statement "I love you" is vague;
surely Truth should be plainly seen
in the culmination of love.
It is I who must truly conceive
the tangible fruits of love:
in my sons I must see
the face of my soul.

Yes, it is I who must bear them,
the effigies of reality:
Buddha, Lenin, Gāndhī,
but to actual love I cannot give
the ideal of motherhood;
I cannot pour out peace of heart
to the old man born in a cellar
who fights for stale rice with the scurvy dogs.

My aged son, gutter born;
you may spew out hope for his salvation;
my love, you make conception
the manifestation of Truth,
my Lenin, even as you are born,
you anoint the sick and the stained.
I see only the face of self-reproach,
I cannot console anything which is mine;
it is over! I save Truth's fragments,
poor Lenin, Buddha, Gāndhī,
I save them from calumny,
these I cannot sacrifice
in gutters of filthy water.

And so I formulate vague ideals
instead of love's clear reality.

(1960; from Pārijāt 1987)

4. See page 81 for a translation of Rimāl's poem "To—."

A SICK LOVER'S LETTER TO HER SOLDIER
(*LĀHURELĀĪ EK ROGĪ PREMIKĀKO PATRA*)

Life companion, much, much love;
I feel I might send you a heart,
I feel I might send you a love letter,
tied round the necks of these free-flying pigeons,
repeating the sentiment of last century's love,
but what free bird could fly
across today's lines and borders,
with what sighs could this withered existence
lay down to rest in the winds of this world?

My love, I cannot raise you in my mind,
you are far away and hidden from me,
I cannot speak to you, I cannot see you,
I do not even try to cross the seven seas to you,
and so I simply watch for you
as I sit here all alone,
my brain as limited as my body,
Gautamī turned to stone.[5]

Love,
love is a mirage,
love is the greed of a goose,
love is a lifeless truth,
the thirst of a *kākākul* bird[6]
which loves the sun and blocks its setting;
an ephemeral body, an endless desire,
but love is the union of bodies,
me in your arms, each night,
a row of desires set out to block death—
I am dreaming and burning my sweet dreams.

Beloved, you wrote to ask me
if I smiled in your billet picture,
you said you did not want to lose me,
you said my letter woke you up like a phoenix.
This is all just history now,
how I have survived I do not know,
I have waited long, you will surely come
to this phoenix in her ashes,
not rising to health once more,

5. In the Rāmāyaṇa, Rāma releases the wife of the sage Gautam from a curse that had turned her to stone as a punishment for her infidelity.

6. The *kākākul* bird is a symbol of thirst because it is fated to drink only the water that falls from the sky and therefore spends its life crying to heaven for rain.

but deep in eternal sleep
leaving unspoken the things in her mind.

My love, I have already died,
your love burned with me on my pyre.
I am buried, I sleep the endless sleep,
you must live on, waking tomorrow
to new sunshine: do not cry,
do not make a mockery of conflict.

Do you know the power of my ending?
A part of finality was smashed;
do you know that my death was strong?
It left immortality itself half-dead.

Love does not die, you have to kill it,
you must begin with the strength of my end.
Now here is the rest of my letter,
now here is the rest of your phoenix,
life companion, here for you
is the remnant of all my love.

(1964; from Pārijāt 1987; also included in *Sājhā Kavitā* 1967)

IN THE ARMS OF DEATH (*MRITYUKĀ ANGĀLĀMĀ*)

At midnight the moonlight comes in by a window,
it melts all over the quilt on my bed;
I am already wrapped in my shroud,
my bed is already my tomb.

Something within me is trying to vanish,
someone inside me is trying to leave,
but these are not my remains,
night after night I am living and dying;
I set my own corpse before me.

I lie on my back and I weep,
I mourn at my own funeral rite,
I am my own undying ghost,
I have roamed through half the graveyard,
each night I return from the pointless journey,
feet soaked by stygian waters.

But Death does not speak like this
from the pages of the Upanishads,[7]
there, Death is a mother's welcome
to a child returning from play.

7. The Upanishads are commentorial texts on the Vedas dating from the sixth century B.C. onward; they contain many of the most important writings of Hindu philosophy.

The end is no intermission,
let me leave it once and for all,
I will play for so long before I return,
I will be so tired when I set down my load,
come, let us not regard this world
so darkly, just for a moment,
I have endured this life quietly,
suffering like a dumb beast.

How eager this flower is to fall,
how it longs to cut short the winter day,
to pass in a half-conscious night;
Death returns, defeated,
from the hands of Life—
alas, Man does not die.

This is the twentieth century,
death is not easy or hard,
and so my eyes are eager
to open in pale morning light,
to crawl through life's listless day,
a day where no hope has its home.

The new age is lost on its way,
Time comes but makes all newness a void
before it can reach my door,
so Time passes through me as before,
it saddens all those who are happy,
it cheers all those who are sad,
but my indifference is a full stop
to the desires of life:
it strikes all changes dumb.

It is laughable:
as if governed by regular rules,
lizards continue to run to and fro
with regiments of ants
on the four walls of this room;
each plank of the floor is wondering why
this burden upon it never gets up or goes,
it lives, but it is lifeless,
it hardly moves;
this irritation should be thrown out.

A snail can feed without reaching its goal,
but I cannot; so when I am gone,
do not think that anything great is lost:
the warmth of the small space I filled
will simply cool as I grow cold.

A part of my blanket, the edge of my quilt,
will know that a lightweight existence,
a living helplessness, have fled away;
I shall come to my end before dying,
so many have died, but not ended:
but I wish for no preservation:
although the Himāl ever melts at Gangotrī,[8]
and never ceases to be,
I must die, and see myself ended.

What claim can I make to be human?
A fistful of weary flesh,
a little bundle of tired bones:
that is all, and what of it?

(1964; from Pārijāt 1987)

8. Gangotrī is the source of the holy Ganges River (Gangā) in the Himalaya mountains of India.

Bhūpi Sherchan (1936–1989)

Bhūpi Sherchan, who died in 1989, was probably the most popular and widely read Nepali poet of the previous twenty years. The reasons for his popularity are easily identified: his poems are written in simple Nepali; they address issues crucial to all Nepalis, not just to the educated elite; and they are distinctive for their humor and anger.

Bhūpendramān Sherchand was born in 1936 into a wealthy Thākālī family of Tukuche, a settlement on the banks of the Kālī Gaṇḍakī River in the remote district of Mustāng. The Thākālī are a distinct ethnic group in Nepal, and their cultural orientation is basically Tibetan. Because their main towns and villages are all situated on an historically important trade route leading to Tibet, they have become one of Nepal's most enterprising and prosperous communities and in recent years have sought to distance themselves from Tibetan culture and to identify more closely with the mainstream of Hindu Nepal.

Initially, Bhūpi seems to have rebelled against the commercial traditions of his family and community. It may be that he felt some sense of rejection when his mother died in 1941, a feeling that could only have been heightened when he was sent to Banāras in India to begin his college education before he reached his teens. In 1956, when still a student in Banāras, he published a book of songs in the *jhyāure* meter of Nepali folk songs. This collection expressed views that reflected Bhūpi's conversion to communism, a fact also evinced by his adoption of the pen name *Sarvahārā*, "Proletariate."[1] Some four years later, he came to live in Kathmandu, where he was subsequently jailed for his activities in an obscure political group, the Bhadra Avagyā Āndolan (Civil Resis-

1. Tānāsarmā (1970, 192) sums up the tone of this book with a slogan: "*materialism is yours, socialism is ours, one day we will compare them*" (italics added).

tance Movement). In jail, he developed colitis and several other related complaints and was never completely healthy again. At about this time his second book, *Nirjhar* (*Waterfall*), described by Subedī as a "collection of lyrical poems" (1978, 73), was published.

Neither of Bhūpi's early collections seems to be at all well regarded; both are unobtainable, and none of the poems they contain has been reprinted elsewhere. Bhūpi did not make any real impact on Nepali poetry until he dropped his pseudonym, shortened his name to Bhūpi Sherchan, and began to submit his startling poems to literary journals, notably *Rūprekhā*. As he explained to Uttam Kunwar, "I used to give importance to an '-ism' when I wrote, but later I began to write about whatever theme attracted me—although I must say that I still do not believe in 'art for art's sake' " (Kunwar 1966, 93).

A collection of forty-two prose poems entitled *A Blind Man on a Revolving Chair* (*Ghumne Mechmāthi Andho Mānche*) was first published in 1969 and was awarded the Sājhā Puraskār. *A Blind Man on a Revolving Chair* has since become one of the most influential and acclaimed collections of Nepali poetry and is already in a fourth edition of 2,100 copies. Despite the fact that no subsequent volume of his poems was published, *A Blind Man* established beyond dispute Sherchan's reputation as one of the most important Nepali poets. The poems translated here are all drawn from this collection.

Sherchan was a man tormented by the great questions of his age and by the contradiction between his family's wealth and his own strongly held socialist beliefs. Comparing the poetry published under the pen name to Bhūpi's more recent work, Khanāl observes, "Gone is the easy and confident feeling . . . of having found answers to the questions that he asked as a teenager. The question returns and continues to plague him" (Khanāl 1977, 272). Kunwar (1966, 96) claims that Sherchan often felt suicidal. Whatever the truth of this suggestion, his addiction to tobacco and overindulgence in alcohol became almost legendary during the last years of his life.

Sherchan worked for most of his active years in the family business and as a building contractor. His duties took him to various parts of the country, particularly Pokhara, Kathmandu, and Bhairahavā. His intense dislike for Bhairahavā was expressed in the poem "Bhairahavā," which sums up like no other the hillman's contempt for the plains:

> You can hear only transistor radios,
> Swimming on the air,
> The cough of bronchitic trucks,
> The revving of ancient buses . . .
> Dry, disgusting Bhairahavā,
> Bellowing like a buffalo emerging from its wallow.

He also seemed to find Kathmandu decadent and oppressive and so he resided mainly in Pokhara until he was awarded membership of the Royal Nepal Academy in 1979. This perhaps ameliorated to some degree the frustration he expressed in his interview with Uttam Kunwar about the fact that his writing could not support him financially and that he was obliged to rely upon his family's wealth.

Sherchan's poetry, like that of Rimāl and Koirālā before him, was largely without precedent in Nepali. As Khanāl points out, the poet's philosophical vantage point was unusual: he came from a minority ethnic group of a fairly remote region, whereas most of the better known Nepali poets before him had been upper-caste Hindus from central Nepal or Darjeeling. This fact lent him a certain detachment from the Kathmandu elite that he satirized with such success and set him apart from the intrigues that pervaded the atmosphere of the capital city.

The prevailing tone of this poetry is ironic, although Sherchan was often passionately angry. His irony is expressed most clearly here in "A Poem" (*Ek Kavitā*), in which the speaker contemplates the sleeping body of a beggar boy on a Kathmandu pavement, and in his most famous poem, "A Blind Man in a Revolving Chair" (*Ghumne Mechmāthi Andho Mānche*), a cruelly satirical depiction of a man in a position of authority who is corrupt, narrowminded, and insensitive. Bhūpi's anger bursts out almost uncontrollably in "This Is a Land of Uproar and Rumor" (*Yo Hallai-Hallāko Desh Ho*), a long cry of patriotic rage against the corruption and lack of intellect he considered to be his country's most crippling weaknesses. His anger over the low status of poets and writers in Nepal is expressed in a reference to Devkoṭā, Rimāl, and Pārijāt:

> where the great poet must die an early death to pay his debts
> and a poet, driven mad by the pain of his land,
> must take refuge in a foreign hospice;
> where Saraswatī's lonely daughter
> must live her whole life shriveled
> by a sickness untreated in her youth

Sherchan repeated his criticism of Nepal as a country of "gullible fools" in a long poem entitled "We" (*Hāmī*) in which the fable of Droṇāchārya and his disciples from the Mahābhārata epic was reinterpreted to argue that a disciple should not accede to his guru's every demand without question. This reinterpretation was in direct contradiction to the intended moral of the original tale:

> We practice our archery constantly,
> developing skills far greater than the guru's own disciples,
> but Droṇāchārya comes to each generation,
> surprised and alarmed by our expertise,

demanding his guru's fee.
Joyfully we cut off our thumbs and present them to him,
erase our existence and surrender to him,
then we rejoice at our devotion and our self-sacrifice.
So we are brave, no doubt, but we are gullible fools.

"We" is considered an important poem by Nepali critics, but it is somewhat repetitive and does not compare especially well with the poems translated here. Many of Sherchan's shorter poems are explicitly personal and express a profound disappointment with life, but in general he believed in poetry as a medium that should be used to convey a social or political message. So that his poems could be readily understood, he developed a style of Nepali almost totally devoid of the Sanskrit-derived vocabulary that filled the poetry of earlier writers, such as Lekhnāth and Devkoṭā. Sherchan also rejected the idea of metrical verse out of hand: "meter is an artificial thing, and any attempt to systematize the tears and laughter of mankind is an even more artificial thing" (Kunwar 1966, 92).

Although he was not the first Nepali poet to try dispensing with Sanskrit vocabulary (the trend dates back at least as far as Sama), Sherchan was probably the most successful and influential purifier of the language of Nepali poetry. "In Bhūpi's poetry," writes Khanāl, "Nepali has been restored to its pristine glory" (Khanāl 1977, 268). Despite the admiration and respect accorded to Mohan Koirālā, it is Sherchan's language that is emulated by the majority of younger poets today.

Bhūpi Sherchan's poems are collected in *Nayāṃ Jhyāure* (New Songs, 1956), *Nirjhar* (Waterfall, 1958), and *Ghumne Mechmāthi Andho Mānche* (A Blind Mind on a Revolving Chair, 1969).

ALWAYS ALWAYS IN MY DREAM (*SADHAIṂ-SADHAIṂ MERO SAPNĀMĀ*)

Always always in my dream
countless young mothers come before me
and sing this song as if insane:
"Now my milk is worthless,
my motherhood has no meaning,"
then they show me dirty piglets
suckling at breasts tight with milk,
and all at once they beat their breasts
and tear their hair
and beg me for all the sons they have lost.

Always always in my dream,
countless old men come with timeworn bodies,

countless old women with minds torn asunder,
they all collapse before me,
kicked down by life, unredeemed by Death;
they beg for the thread of the unfathomed future,
beg for their lost and only son.

Always always in my dream,
countless young widows come before me
and strip themselves quite naked,
showing me black blisters
where the world's salacious eyes
have burned their snow-white bodies;
they beg me for some support for their lives,
they beg me for some end to their journey.

Always always in my dream,
consumptive orphans come before me;
they beg me for school fees, money for books,
cricket bats, and a father's kiss;
they ask for protection
and a night of sweet sleep.

So always always in my dream
a great ocean forms:
the tears of the men in Malaya;[2]
a corpse rises up and a corpse sinks down
in every ocean wave,
regarding me with hatred.

Ah in my dreams I am loathed
by the history of my awakening.

(1959; from Sherchan [1969] 1984; also included
in *Nepālī Kavitā Sangraha* [1973] 1988, vol. 1)

MIDDAY AND THE COLD SLEEP
(*MADHYĀHN DIN RA CHĪSO NIDRA*)

In the newspaper's "wanted" column,
I seek the face of my future,
I search for a foothold in every procession,
every assembly, every speech,
I look through the files of each new plan.[3]
On the lips of the new budget
I seek some reassurance,

2. This is a reference to the heavy casualties incurred by British Gurkha troops during the Malaya campaign of the 1950s.

3. The plan is the five-year plan for national development drawn up by the government of Nepal.

from radio announcements I beg
two words of consolation;
my family's age I measure
with a new pay scale, made young again
by the news of each vacant post;
each time I hear from my interviews,
life stinks like sweat in an armpit.

Somebody is mixing despair
into even my mother's love,
even in my father's encouraging words
a cold, impatient sigh can be heard.
It is as if vermilion fears
the parting of my daughter's hair,[4]
and my wife is always serving up
satire on my plate.
An age has passed:
with a face like an application letter,
I have wandered from door to door,
I have called from house to house.

A cold sleep always tries to engulf me,
I know that if I sleep this time
I shall never wake again.
Oh you who form lines like caterpillars,
chant more slogans, chant them loud;
I do not want to sleep today.
Wake me up! Wake me up!

(1960; from Sherchan [1969] 1984)

I THINK MY COUNTRY'S HISTORY IS A LIE (*GALAT LĀGCHA MALĀĪ MERO DESHKO ITIHĀS*)

When I pause for a few days
to look at these squares steeped in hunger,
these streets like withered flowers,
I think my country's history is a lie.

These gods, dug in all down the street,
these knowing men who are deaf and dumb,
these temples ravaged by earthquakes,
these leaning pinnacles,
these statues of great men at the crossroads:
when I see all these, ever present,
never changing, all alike,

4. Vermilion paste is applied to the parting of a woman's hair when she is married. The speaker means that he cannot arrange his daughter's marriage because he has no income.

then I think it is a lie,
the history of these men who share my table.

When I constantly see young Sītās[5]
in the streets, the alleys, the markets,
in my country and in foreign lands,
stripped bare like eucalyptus trees,
when I see countless Bhīmsen Thāpās,[6]
standing still and silent,
shedding the songs of their souls,
like *kalkī* trees[7] with their hands hanging down,
I really feel like mocking my blood.

I hear that Amarsingh[8] extended the kingdom to Kangra,
I hear that Tenzing climbed Sagarmāthā,[9]
I hear that the Buddha[10] sowed the seeds of peace,
I hear that Arniko's[11] art astounded the world;
I hear, but I do not believe it.

For when I pause for a few days
to look at these squares steeped in hunger,
these streets like withered flowers,
I know that this is the truth of my past,
and I think our history is a lie.

(1960; from Sherchan [1969] 1984)

A BLIND MAN ON A REVOLVING CHAIR
(*GHUMNE MECHMĀTHI ANDHO MĀNCHE*)

Dozing and regretting all day long,
like a withered bamboo lamenting its hollowness,
opening wounds all day long,
like a sick dove which pecks at its breast;

5. Sītā is the consort of Lord Rāma, the princely incarnation of Vishṇu, and the epitome of female chastity and fidelity.

6. Bhīmsen Thāpā dominated Nepalese politics from about 1804 until 1837 and is given especial credit for building up the military strength and prestige of Nepal. See M. S. Jain (1972, 4–13).

7. A *kalkī* is a flower or the plume on the Rāṇās' ceremonial helmet. The ambiguity is almost certainly intentional.

8. Amarsingh Thāpā was the commander in chief of the Nepalese army who pushed the borders of the kingdom westward as far as Kangra, in modern Himachal Pradesh, during the early nineteenth century.

9. Sagarmāthā is the Nepali name for Mount Everest.

10. Because Lumbinī, the birthplace of Shākyamuṇi, is now within the borders of modern Nepal, the Buddha is sometimes claimed to have been a Nepali.

11. Arniko (1244–1306), a Newār craftsman, was taken to the court of Kubilai Khan by a powerful Tibetan lama in 1265. The khan was overwhelmed by Arniko's skills and assigned him a number of major projects, including the building of several famous temples.

weeping softly all day long,
over sorrows which are unspoken,
like a pine forest in its solitude,
my feet are set in a tiny space,
sheltered by a mushroom umbrella,
far from the vastness of earth and sky.

In the evening,
when Nepal shrinks down to Kathmandu,
and Kathmandu shrinks to New Road,[12]
which breaks up, trampled by countless feet,
to newspapers, tea shops, paan shops,
various rumors come and go,
each in a different guise,
newspapers pass by, clucking like hens,
and here and there the darkness
climbs onto the sidewalk, terrified
by the headlights of the cars.

The hive in my brain collapses,
I stand up, alarmed
by stinging, buzzing bees beyond number;
I rise like a soul on Judgment Day,
but I do not find the Lethe,[13] river of oblivion,
so I slide down into some wine to forget
the past, my previous lives and deaths.

The sun always rises from the kettle,
and sets in an empty glass,
the earth I inhabit goes on turning,
I am the only one who cannot see
the changes all around me,
the only one who is unaware
of all this world's beauty and pleasure,
like a blind man at an exhibition,
forced to sit on a revolving chair.

(1961; from Sherchan [1969] 1984; also
included in *Ādhunik Nepālī Kavitā* 1971)

By 1273, Arniko was the supervisor of all the craftsmen in China and was granted the hand of a descendant of the Sung royal family in marriage. Rossabi 1988: 171.

12. Originally known as Juddha Saḍak, one of the main commercial streets of Kathmandu which was reconstructed after the 1934 earthquake. New Road is a popular evening meeting-place for the young intellectuals of the city, who gather to buy newspapers and literary journals.

13. A reference to Greek mythology. The Lethe river flowed through the underworld and those who drank from its waters forgot their past completely. *Larousse* ([1959] 1983, 165).

THIS IS A LAND OF UPROAR AND RUMOR
(*YO HALLAI-HALLĀKO DESH HO*)

This is a land of uproar and rumor,
where deaf men wearing hearing aids[14]
are judges at musical contests;
and those whose souls are full of stones
are connoisseurs of poetry;
where wooden legs win races, and bayonets of defense
are held by plastered hands;
where, basket upon basket,
truckload after truckload,
souls are offered for sale
along the roads, in front of doors;
where the leaders are those who can trade in souls,
like shares on a stock exchange;
where the men who presume to lead our youth on
have faces wrinkled like roofing steel;
where the "wash and wear" creases of honor
are never spoiled by any malpractice,
and even the prostitute's terylene skin
cannot crease, whatever her crime;
where seeds which double production
are displayed at farmers' fairs
which fill with news of drought and famine;
where beer and whisky flow instead of sacred rivers[15]
and people come to our holiest shrines
less to receive the food of the gods,
more to consume the forbidden fruits
of Adam and Eve in the gardens behind;
where the sugar factory makes booze, not sugar,
and mothers of freedom give birth to soldiers instead of sons;
where the great poet must die an early death to pay his debts
and a poet, driven mad by the pain of his land,
must take refuge in a foreign hospice;
where Saraswatī's lonely daughter
must live her whole life shriveled
by a sickness untreated in her youth;[16]
where a guide describes to a tourist
Nepal's contributions to other lands,

14. The English words "ear phone" are used in the Nepali original.

15. The original Nepali poem refers to the Bishṇumatī and the Bāgmatī, the two sacred rivers of the Kathmandu Valley. Similarly, the following line names the temples of Swyambhū and Pashupati.

16. The "great poet" referred to here is Lakshmīprasād Devkoṭā, the poet who is driven mad is Gopālprasād Rimāl, and "Saraswatī's lonely daughter" is Pārijāt.

then departs, demanding his camera,
where young men sing the songs
of forts and foreign conquests,
marching in parades . . .

In this land I am forced to say,
clipping a *khukurī* to my tie and lapel,[17]
tearing open my heart:
compatriots, nation-poets of this land,
who sing the songs of my country's awakening,
respected leaders of my people:
if you wish, you may call me a slanderer, a traitor,
but this land is mine as well as yours,
my hut will stand on a piece of this land,
my pyre will burn beside one of our rivers;
I am forced to say, made bold by this feeling,
this is a land of uproar and rumor,
dig deep, and you find hearsay
heaped up beneath every home,
so this is a land of tumult and gossip,
a country supported by rumors,
a country standing on uproar:
this is a land of uproar and rumor.

(1967; from Sherchan [1969] 1984)

NEW YEAR (*NAYĀṂ VARSHA*)

Like a postman newly transferred,
who carries a parcel of sun in his sack,
Baisākh[18] is walking on the roof,
moving with slow heavy steps,
making the walls swing like a pendulum.

The sun grows dark
and lies down to rest with a despairing face:
a downpour of bad weather,
a constant rumbling from the clouds,
the sky has diarrhea; it must have drunk
the Bishṇumatī's choleric waters.
From the *shehnai*[19] there comes a tuneless sound;
cholera germs are coming, unseen and countless,

17. The *khukurī* is the ubiquitous Nepali knife that has become a military emblem and almost a national symbol. Sherchan perhaps intends to show that he does not lack patriotic feeling.

18. Baisākh is the first month of the Hindu year in Nepal.

19. The *shehnai* is a type of South Asian wind instrument.

at midday, fierce sunshine,
all the trees scratching their limbs.

So once more
New Year has come,
so once more
I must hang my life's visa
in a new calendar on the wall,
so once more
I must draw up a list of my friends,
once more, sitting beneath rockets
and airplanes bearing horrific bombs,
I must write my dear ones letters
wishing them success,
peace,
long lives.

(no date; from Sherchan [1969] 1984; also included in *Sājhā Kavitā* 1967)

A POEM (*EK KAVITĀ*)

For the lad who says "I am hungry"
there is neither a meal nor a home,
but even so he lives, he grows up,
this beggarly youth on a New Road pavement,
trampled beneath many feet.

This boy was shot into outer space,
an unknown, uncertain future,
in the speeding rocket of someone's carnal pleasure,
no space suit, no oxygen,
no guide or direction;
but he came down safely from his brief experience
of irresponsibility, unburdened freedom,
onto the New Road pavement,
wrapped in a dirty parachute.

This child was born
like Jesus,
from a virgin mother's womb,
and now he sits by the wayside,
supporting a lamppost: his cross.

On a night so cold the hair stands on end,
he sleeps tucked into a bend on a sad, empty footpath,
wrapped in a dirty sack, an old newspaper;
on his breast in huge letters lies the news of Children's Day:
a minister's official address,

the presentation of sweets and prizes,
announcements of progress for boys and girls.

Sleep, little boy,
sleep, wise child,
sleep, little king,
sleep like this, carefree,
the day will come when your clothes,
your dirty sack and newspaper,
will hang in a museum like Kālū Pāṇḍe's.[20]

And then historians will write,
"At that time in Nepal
there were two kinds of men:
one rested on newspaper headlines,
he was important news,
the other wrapped himself in them to keep warm,
surviving the winter oblivious . . .
. . . then Nepal was like an old paper:
completely out of date."

(no date; from Sherchan [1969] 1984)

A DOVE OF TWO DELICATE WHITE HANDS: YOUR GREETING (*DUĪ SETĀ KALILĀ HATKELĀKO PAREVĀ: TIMRO NAMASTE*)

You were standing on a rooftop,
your head bowed demurely,
in blushing haste you tossed
a dove, two delicate white hands,
into the air toward me:
your greeting.

All day it flies
through the skies of my eyes
on the white wings of your purity.
In the evening your youth
spreads across my heart's horizon,
in the night, the seven colors of your bracelets
are set into the rafters of my sleep.

And from now on your laughter,
your solitude's silent entreaty,
will always fill my heart, my eyes.

You were standing on a rooftop,
your head bowed demurely,

20. Kālū Pāṇḍe was the commander in chief of the Nepalese army during the reign of the great unifier of the kingdom, Prithvīnārāyaṇ Shāh.

in blushing haste you tossed
a dove, two delicate white hands,
into the air toward me:
your greeting . . .

(no date; from Sherchan [1969] 1984; also included in *Sājhā Kavitā* 1967 and *Ādhunik Nepālī Kavitā* 1971)

COLD ASHTRAY (*CHĪSO AISHṬRE*)

Those who come
come with hearts full of fire,
with flames on their lips,
but those who live here
live with hands full of ash
and eyes full of smoke.
Those who leave take with them
a bundle of extinguished beliefs,
the stub-ends of their dreams.
Such is this Valley of Four Passes,[21]
it's a cold ashtray,
this Valley of Four Passes.

(no date; from Sherchan [1969] 1984)

A CRUEL BLOW AT DAWN (*PRĀTA: EK ĀGHĀT*)

Every day,
dawn comes secretly like a thief,
and it squeezes me a little.
I am woken by the touch of sunbeams,
I see the bright, white teeth of the east,
scrubbed regularly clean;
there falls upon some corner of my heart
a light but penetrating blow:
ah, my life is going toward its end;
a certain amount passes each day,
squeezed out like toothpaste.

(no date; from Sherchan [1969] 1984)

21. *Chār Bhānjyāng* (Valley of Four Passes) is an epithet for the Kathmandu Valley.

Bānīrā Giri (b. 1946)

Born in the town of Kurseong, near Darjeeling in the Himalayan foothills of West Bengal, Bānīrā Giri is one of the very few Nepali women writers to have established any reputation outside the kingdom. She moved to Kathmandu with her parents when still a young girl, and most of her writing therefore refers to the environment and society of her adopted home, rather than to her birthplace. The poem "Kathmandu" (*Kāthmāṇḍū*), for instance, expresses a mixture of affection and contempt for the city:

> Kathmandu makes my poor, dear son
> cry out in his dreams every night . . .
> I have come to live in Kathmandu,
> but Kathmandu does not live in me.

Bānīrā was educated at Tribhuvan University during the 1960s, and her philosophical and intellectual stance is typical of the generation that grew up in Nepal while its age-old cultural isolation was rapidly coming to an end. The same generation has produced several other notable women poets, such as Premā Shāh, Toyā Gurung, and Kundana Sharmā.[1] Having completed an M.A. and an M.Ed., Bānīrā became the first woman to be awarded a Ph.D. by Tribhuvan University, for her thesis on the poetry of Gopālprasād Rimāl. She is an ambitious and energetic writer with several literary awards to her credit and a teaching post at Padma Kanyā Campus, a women's college in Kathmandu. She participates regularly in literary conferences at home and abroad, having traveled to Tashkent for the Young Afro-Asian Writers' Conference and to New

1. Nepali preserves a distinction between a male poet (*kavi*) and a female poet (*kavayitrī*).

Delhi for the International Writers' Seminar in 1976 and to Bhopāl for the Kavitā Asia Festival in 1988.

Bānīrā's voice emanates from the new urban professional classes of Kathmandu. Her poems first appeared in *Rūprekhā* and are now published regularly in various journals and newspapers. Their tone is generally cerebral, and many adopt a feminist viewpoint, employing metaphors drawn from the experiences of Nepali women. Bānīrā's best poems are her earlier compositions; these are articulate, terse, and beautifully constructed. Some of her more recent poems have been criticized as contrived or pretentious, and Bānīrā has begun to diversify by writing novels and publishing acutely observed essays on contemporary social issues in *Madhupark*.

In "Time, You Are Always the Winner" (*Samay Timī Sadhaiṃko Vijetā*), one of Bānīrā's finest poems, references to Paurāṇic mythology mingle with symbols that are unmistakably modern in their description of the transience of human life. The nature of time and history are common themes in Bānīrā's poems, and her symbolic representations of time are often extremely well conceived. Like the dimensionalist poets, she makes frequent reference to mythological figures but restricts herself to the Hindu myths of her own tradition. Although these require explanatory footnotes when presented to a Western audience, most would be readily comprehensible to Bānīrā's own readership. Her femininism is expressed more overtly in a simple poem such as "Woman" (*Āimāī*), based on the story of the blind men and the elephant. This was published to mark International Women's Day in 1986 and caused both controversy and delight.

Bānīrā Giri has published three volumes of poems and two novels, *The Prison* (*Kārāgār*, 1985) and *Unbound* (*Nirbandh*, 1986). Her works are now included in the postgraduate curriculum of Tribhuvan University. Her latest poetic work, *My Discovery* (*Mero Āvishkār*, 1985) is a series of fragments based on subjective experience. Many poems have been translated into Hindi for publication in India, and a slim volume of poems "adapted" by the Indian poet Yuyutsu R. D. into English with a most laudatory introduction was published in Jaipur, India, in 1987.

Most of Bānīrā Giri's earlier poems are collected in *Euṭā Euṭā Jiundo Jang Bahādur* (Each One a Living Jang Bahādur, 1974), *Jīvan Thāyamarū* (Life: No Place, 1978), and *Mero Avishkār* (My Discovery, 1984).

TIME, YOU ARE ALWAYS THE WINNER
(*SAMAY TIMĪ SADHAIṂKO VIJETĀ*)

Snatch me up like an eagle
swooping down on a chicken,

wash me away like a flood destroying the fields,
fling me from the door
like my daughter carelessly sweeping out dirt.

In infinite wilds I lead
a solitary life,
just a naming ceremony,
set aside, forgotten;
even in the Rāmāyaṇa, Lakshmaṇ's line
had first to be drawn
before Sītā could cross it.[2]

Time, you are always the winner,
I bent my knee before you
like Bārbarik faced by compulsion,[3]
like King Yāyati faced by old age,[4]
I fell prostrate like grandfather Bhīshma
before the arrows from your arms.[5]

Touch my defeated existence just once
with your hands of ironwood;
how numb I am,
how hard to grasp, how lifeless
in the presence of your strength and power.

You spread out forever like the seas,
I rippled like the foaming waves,
you blazed up fiercely like a volcano,
I smouldered, slow as a forest fire.
You are power, wholly embodied,
ready to drink even poison,
we follow—my fellows and I a party,
we descend on a wheel of birth and death,
bearing bags full of gifts,
gifts of alcohol and oxygen,

2. This is a reference to an event in the Rāmāyaṇa epic.

3. Bārbarik is mentioned in Hindu scriptures such as the Skanda Purāṇa. He lived his whole life under a curse, inherited from a previous life, that he would be killed by Vishṇu. He was therefore compelled to worship various deities to preserve his life (Vettam Mani 1975, 107).

4. Different versions of the story of King Yāyati are told in the Padma Purāṇa and the Vishṇu Purāṇa. Both, however, agree that his amorous disposition and infidelity to his first wife brought upon him the curse of eternal old age and infirmity from his father-in-law. Dowson [1879] 1968, 376.

5. In the Mahābhārata wars, Bhīshma took the side of the Kauravas on the condition that he should not be called upon to fight against the warrior Arjuṇ. Goaded on by another warrior, however, Bhīshma attacked Arjuṇ and was pierced by innumerable arrows. When he fell, mortally wounded, from his chariot, the arrows that filled his body held him above the ground. Dowson [1879] 1968, 52–53.

blood and cancer,
tumors and polio.

My grandson will be born
with sleeping pills in his eyes,
his potency already dead,
needing no vasectomy.

Perhaps he will be born as a war,
embracing every cripple,
perhaps he will be born as a void,
to replace the meaningless babble
of revolt, lack of faith, and being.

Perhaps he will even refuse to be born
from a natural mother's womb;
Time, you are always the winner:
revealed like a crazy Bhairava,[6]
keep burning like the sun,
keep flowing like a river,
keep rustling like the bamboo leaves.

Upon your victory,
I will let loose the calves from the tethering post,
fling open the doors of grain stores and barns,
hand over my jewels to my daughter-in-law,
and lay out green dung, neatly,
around the *tulsī* shrine.[7]

So snatch me up like an eagle
swooping down on a chicken,
wash me away like a flood destroying the fields,
and, like my daughter carelessly sweeping out dirt,
sweep me from the threshold with a single stroke,
sweep me from the threshold with a single stroke.

(no date; from Giri 1974)

I AM A TORN POSTER (*MA EUṬĀ CHYĀTIEKO POSHṬAR*)

Man, do not vary the meanings you give
to pieces of splintered sentences,
I have forgotten my story.

Beside the fireplace in the dead of winter,
an old man tells the children a tale:

6. The Bhairava is a fearsome emanation of the god Shiva who figures prominently in the religious iconography of the Kathmandu Valley.

7. The *tulsī*, or sacred basil tree, is often grown in special shrines in front of Hindu homes or in domestic courtyards.

Pārohāng and Lempuhāng descend,[8]
and from the old man's eyes it seems
he is the Shiva of some era, who has lost
the goddess Satī in Daksha's sacrifice.[9]

He tells the story of Lāl and Hīrā;[10]
he chases Lāl away on the white horse
of centuries ago, whose hooves still issue
their orders to the ears of Time.
How helpless, those men, we men,
that old man telling stories.

Has he contrived to cut loose
from the pulling of Time, the commands of Time?
Has he managed to break
Time's heedlessness and deceits?
How did Moses cut through the ocean?
How could he part the seas?
Yes, here I discuss matters of faith,
of belief and the lack of belief.

My truths, my faith, they are sold off,
auctioned at the Harishchandra Ghāṭ,[11]
even my beliefs walk fearfully now,
like a scavenging dog in the midden.

I am cursed
by this womb, these flowers,
like a broken pot, thrown away, useless,
like a grape with no juice,
dried up, inedible.

After centuries I stand, a folktale,
upon a bank of Time,
my Time is ragged and thin,
it feels its scars and its wounds.
Our feet leave only prints,
soon erased from the desert's breast,
the cold mountain breeze, like drunkenness,
adds more pain as it leaves next day,

8. Lempuhāng and Pārohāng are legendary kings from the folklore of the Limbū people of eastern Nepal.

9. Daksha once incurred Shiva's wrath by failing to invite him to partake of an offering he had made to the gods. Satī was the daughter of Daksha and the wife of Shiva. Unable to endure the quarrel between these two, or to take sides, she took her own life by entering the sacrificial fire. Dowson ([1879] 1968, 76–78, 287).

10. This is a popular Nepali folktale that relates the love of Lāl for the princess Hīrā. A white horse is traditionally regarded as an especially auspicious animal.

11. Harishchandra Ghāṭ is the platform beside the Bāgmatī River at Pashupatināth temple where the Hindu dead of Kathmandu are cremated.

lightening by a miscarriage
of belief and dreams, security, rights.

We walk boldly upon corpses,
the earth itself stands over a grave,
we build our homes, we eat our feasts,
we live our lives upon a grave,
we summon our corpses from the grave.

Now betrothals are all decided
by Shiva's bow at King Janak's court,[12]
nowadays even Lord Rāma's sons
flow past in the muddy Tukuchā;[13]
Man's faith needs somewhere firm to stand,
a resting place to lay down its load,
some attachment if it is to love—
if it is to love its death.

A life of more than one hundred years!
Life is an invalid, the very thought is madness;
this is no commentary on an epic,
nor the start of an autobiography,
nor an edition of my own works,
I puff out this life from a chimney,
and boil a pot of rice,
onto a mirror I breathe out one life,
and see my own face dimly.

I am a torn poster on the wall of Time,
Man, do not vary the meanings you give
to pieces of splintered sentences:
I have forgotten my story.

(no date; from *Sājhā Kavitā* 1967)

KATHMANDU (*KĀTHMĀṆḌŪ*)

Kathmandu is a heater inflamed
by one hundred thousand volts;
this capital's orphan girls sit waiting,
like Sītā[14] on her pyre of fire,

12. This is a reference to the betrothal of Sītā, daughter of King Janak, to Lord Rāma. Rāma gave evidence of his divinity by breaking the mighty bow of Shiva.

13. The Tukuchā is a stream that runs through the center of Kathmandu. There is a popular belief, to which the poem refers, that women often dispose of babies born of illicit unions in this stream.

14. Sītā, the spouse of Lord Rāma, was obliged to undergo a rite of purification by fire to prove that her chastity had not been besmirched while she was held captive by Rāvaṇa, the demon-king of Lankā.

ready to brand their bodies of gold,
snared by the noose of its love.

Snow-white doves fly the endless blue sky,
there's a prison in each citizen's eye,
as Rānī Pokharī[15] floods with color,
there come dark smugglers and sneaks,
fat hypocrites and backbiters,
and all are made pure.
Pīpal trees, comb trees, mimosa,
kalkī and juniper in rows wave their fans
at inhabitants pure and foul,
but Kathmandu is not just cool calm,
Kathmandu is hocus-pocus, too.

And isn't it also that white-wheeled Toyota
which gulps down its petrol,
never satisfied?
And isn't it also Nānichā's wine store
where young men come in swarms each day:
Gunjamāns, Rām Bahādurs,[16] heads held high,
who go home to beat their wives?
A Toyota's tire marks deep on the street,
green bruises covering women:
samples perhaps of each Kathmandu day.

Kathmandu makes my poor, dear son
cry out in his dreams every night;
half I understand, half I do not,
but still I wish to hear,
hemmed in and oppressed
by past attractions, repulsions,
I find that many will curse me,
I find there are few who like me:
I have come to live in Kathmandu,
but Kathmandu does not live in me.

The countless processions of these city streets
pour forth each night in my dreams,
my nights are weighed down by uproar,
they belong to Kathmandu,
covered entirely by mist.
How silent my cold mornings,
as if the city's dead have waited all night,
and are rotted completely away.

It is an interesting epic, beloved Kathmandu,
full of stories, sweet and bitter:

15. Rānī Pokharī, the "Queen's Lake," is near the center of modern Kathmandu.
16. These are common Nepali male names.

the opening verses of tremendous speeches,
the communal song of wants and needs;
wages—the happy chance of increase,
prices—the miserable rise,
an unremitting struggle of loss and gain:
oil for the lamp, and sugar,
everything is here.

Wretched Kathmandu,
dear to everyone, abused by all,
its people narrators of *Satyanārāyaṇ*,[17]
forever repeating the ancient tales,
of Līlāvatī and Kalāvatī,[18]
always singing the same forest creeper,
always walking the same back streets,
always keeping the same feasts,
always observing the same holidays,
always celebrating the same occasions;
ceaselessly they chant, like *kākākul* birds,
Kathmandu, Kathmandu,
Kathmandu, Kathmandu.

(1979; from *Pachhīs Varshakā Nepālī Kavitā* 1982)

WOMAN (*ĀIMĀĪ*)

Unclothed, unrestricted,
undoubting, unhesitant,
a woman stands at the crossroad
in her pure primordial form.

A crowd of blind men are eager
to discover the nature of woman;
the first strokes her smooth, flowing hair
and mutters, "Woman is a waterfall, she is the Gangā,
flowing down from Shiva's head."[19]

A second feels her arm, her fingers,
and happily declares,
"Woman is the lotus of Saraswatī's hand."[20]
A third grasps her shapely thigh and jabbers,
"Woman is the soft bamboo of the marriage pavilion."
A fourth feels her lips,

17. The *Satyanārāyaṇ pūjā* is a ritual that is frequently performed in Brāhmaṇ and Chetrī households to dispel evil and bring good luck.
18. This is a popular Nepali romantic folktale.
19. This is a reference to the mythological origin of the Ganges River.
20. Saraswatī is the goddess of the arts.

which hum the sweet song of Creation:
"Woman is a ripened raspberry."
A fifth strokes her breasts,
motherhood's undying boon:
"Woman is a pot filled with Lakshmī's gifts."[21]
The sixth discovers the half-secret
of the inaccessible place of Creation:
he leaps up and cries out,
"Woman is just a contemptible hole!"

Her eyes grow wet
at the blind man's revelation;
a seventh feels her tear-filled eyes:
"You evil fools! Woman is not just a hole!
She is also Gosāinkuṇḍa,
She is also Mānasārovar!"[22]

(from *Samīkshā* weekly, March 7, 1986)

21. Lakshmī is the goddess of wealth and prosperity.
22. These sacred lakes are important pilgrimage sites in the Himalayas.

New Trends in Nepali Poetry

This chapter presents some Nepali poetry that reflects the predominant trends of the past twenty years or so. I have resisted attaching the label *contemporary* to this poetry, partly because it is difficult to decide a specific date from which contemporary literature should be deemed to have commenced and partly because all literature is by its very nature contemporary when it is written. Qualities such as "modernity," "contemporaneity," and so on can be assessed only subjectively, and assessments change with the passage of time. Of course, this fact has not prevented most Nepali critics from debating ceaselessly about what is, and what is not, modern.

The majority of these poems are drawn from an anthology entitled *Samsāmayik Sājhā Kavitā* (Contemporary Sājhā Poetry) published in 1983 as a supplement to the important *Sājhā Kavitā* anthology of 1967. Because the youngest poet to appear in this latter volume was Bānīrā Giri (born in 1946), it was originally supposed by the publishers that the new anthology would be restricted to works by poets born after this date. The editor of *Samsāmayik Sājhā Kavitā*, Tārānāth Sharmā, argued that this was not an appropriate criterion for selection. Many poets born before 1946 began to write rather later in life. He also pointed out that poets who were included in the earlier volume, such as Mohan Koirālā and Ìshwar Ballabh, could not be regarded as uncontemporary because their poetry had continued to evolve. In an interesting postscript to the anthology, Sharmā described the features of the Nepali poetry he considered to be truly contemporary.

After about 1965, Nepali poetry entered a period during which its accessibility and popularity seriously declined. The new class of intellectuals wrote in language that was pedantic and abstruse and made references to mythologies and concepts that were alien to ordinary Nepalis. The old school continued to publish verse in time-honored metrical forms that imparted traditional values. Thus, the new poetry became innovatory and experimental to the extent that it was incomprehensible to all but a small intellectual elite, whereas the old style of poetry reworked well-worn themes and formulas, offering little that was new.

Both of these styles retain some currency today, and the poems by Ìshwar Ballabh and Avināsh Shreshṭha demonstrate that abstraction is alive and well. This style of poetry has been eclipsed in more recent years by a new and most welcome development. The distinctive features of the most recent poetry are linguistic simplicity, the complete absence of metrical forms, the use of symbols drawn from everyday life, and frequent references to present-day social and political issues. It therefore exhibits more than anything else the influence of Nepali poets such as Rimāl and Sherchan and is deserving of the title contemporary poetry in the sense that it is clearly intended to speak to its times.

During the early 1970s, and to some extent during the previous decade, too, most modern poetry was pessimistic and gloomy and gave evidence of a growing sense of social alienation among the educated urban young. Such tendencies are clearly apparent in the poems of Bhairava Aryāl and Haribhakta Kaṭuvāl. In 1979, however, changing political circumstances brought about some significant new developments in Nepali poetry.

Since 1960, Nepal had been governed by a pyramidal system of *Panchāyat* councils at local and national levels, headed by the monarch. Although all political parties were banned, dissatisfaction with the political status quo became increasingly apparent and eventually led to the national referendum of 1980. During the twelve months leading to this referendum, strenuous efforts to influence public opinion were made by both supporters and opponents of the *Panchāyat* system. In the capital, a new atmosphere of political freedom produced the *saḍak kavitā krānti* (street poetry revolution). Young poets recited their poems on street corners, and people gathered on New Road each evening to purchase collections of political verse all supporting the alternative "multiparty" option. These collections were printed and sold in large numbers and were typified by the short-lived journal *Swatantratā* (Freedom). The August 1979 issue of *Swatantratā*, a "Street Poetry Revolution Special," included political poems by young writers such as Ashesh Malla, Bimal Nibhā, and Mīn Bahādur Bishṭa, who are now among the leading exponents of the "new" poetry. Nepali poetry had once again descended from its ivory tower to become a medium for the expression of popular sentiment. As a consequence, its language regained its former simplicity, and its references and allegories were readily comprehensible. Although these poets' aspirations were not fulfilled by the outcome of the referendum, the legacy of this brief but important period is still clearly apparent in more recent poetry.

As this book goes to press in July 1990, conditions in Nepal are changing once more. The *Panchāyat* system has been dismantled, Nepal's constitution is being redrafted, and political parties are operating freely. One hopes that all of these changes will produce an atmosphere that is more conducive to free expression than has been the case hitherto and that Nepali literature will thrive as a result.

The selection of poems that follows is arranged as far as possible in an order that reflects the process of change. Dates of first publication are given, when known. Ìshwar Ballabh and Avināsh Shreshṭha are both important present-day poets, but the ways in which their poems contrast with the rest of this selection should perhaps serve as a warning to those of us who seek to identify simple and consistent patterns in the process of literary and cultural change.

BHAIRAVA ARYĀL (1936–1976)

Bhairava Aryāl was well known for his humorous and satirical essays, which have been published in four volumes. He was also a poet of some importance. "A Leaf in a Storm" (*Hurīko Patkar*) expresses a sense of alienation and pessimism that was common in the Nepali poetry of the late 1960s and early 1970s, and this poem may shed some light on the aspect of Aryāl's character that contributed to his suicide in 1976.

A LEAF IN A STORM (*HURĪKO PATKAR*)

He frightens himself, defeats himself,
this consumptive man, this man of today,
this man who is called Man.
Every night when he goes to sleep,
he puts his death warrant under his bed,
every day as he rises at dawn
he winds on a heavy turban of rags.

Yes, through each day I walk,
selling my moments, selling my days,
as if to bargain for a night with my wife,
for some nights with life and the world.
These are this century's terms:
from Creation I must rent each day,

to buy myself I must sell myself here.
My days transport the paralyzed sun
in a cranky ambulance,
I stand at the junction of listless eyes,
amazed and astonished:
my day comes empty-handed without gifts,
my day goes back gloomy without news.

(c. 1966; from *Sājhā Kavitā* 1967)

HARIBHAKTA KAṬUVĀL (1935–1980)

Kaṭuvāl was born in the northeast Indian state of Assam in 1935 and was also known by the pseudonym *Pravāsī*, "exile." He was one of the most popular Indian Nepali poets, and unusually for an India-based Nepali writer, he was also well known in Kathmandu. His poems describe the meaninglessness and futility of modern life, a common theme in the Nepali poetry of the late 1960s and early 1970s. Kaṭuvāl died in 1980.

Haribhakta Kaṭuvāl's poems and songs are collected in *Samjhanā* (Remembrance, 1959), *Bhitrī Mānche Bolna Khojcha* (The Inner Man Tries to Speak, 1961), *Sudhā* (Nectar, 1964), *Yo Jindagī Khai Ke Jindagī*! (This Life, What Life Is This? 1972), and *Badnām Merā Yī Ānkhāharū* (Infamous These Eyes of Mine, 1987).

A WISH (*RAHAR*)

Father, I will not go to school,
there they teach the history of days long dead.

Math's formulas are old,
the rusted components of a machine,
I refuse to live in history's pages,
I must live in days still to come,
I must overtake history, become something more.

So father, I will not go to school,
there they teach the history of days long dead.

I prefer ideals I can feel
to ideals which are locked in a frame,
I prefer building my road as I travel
to walking a ready-made road,
my muscular arms need a hoe, not a tome,
and plans are not for me.

My feet must traverse each lofty peak
to pay off the debt of this earth.

Father, I will not go to school,
there they teach the history of days long dead.

(no date; from Kaṭuvāl 1972)

THIS LIFE, WHAT LIFE IS THIS?
(*YO JINDAGĪ KHAI KE JINDAGĪ?*)

This life, what life is this?

Hollow within, alive from without,
sucked by the atomic dread,
harassed by the spirits of problems,
this life, what life is this?

Here you must sleep with your head on a gun,
here you must live on the edge of a knife,
afraid to open or close your eyes:
this life, what life is this?

Like a bangle made of glass
adorning a trader's showcase,
it can break at once on a maiden's wrist.
Like cheap sandals made of rubber,
it can suddenly break as you walk.

This life might suddenly break:
this life, what life is this?

(no date; from Kaṭuvāl 1972)

ÌSHWAR BALLABH (B. 1937)

Ìshwar Ballabh was one of the trio of writers who initiated the *Tesro Āyām* movement from Darjeeling in the early 1960s. Unlike Bairāgī Kāinlā, however, Ìshwar Ballabh continues to publish poems today. Many of these are apparently intended to do little more than to convey a series of abstracted images, and in a poem such as "The Shadows of Superfluous Songs" (*Anāvashyak Gītkā Chāyāharū*) language often seems to be an end in itself. Thus, the legacy of the dimensionalists is clearly apparent in many of Ìshwar Ballabh's works. In others, however, there is evidence of a concern with the realities of human society. "Where Is the Voice?" (*Āvāj Kahāṃ Cha?*) is the expression of an overtly humanistic poet who is contemptuous of the hold religious tradition still has on the ordinary people of Nepal.

Ìshwar Ballabh's poems are collected in *Āgokā Phūlharū Hun, Āgokā Phūlharū Hoinan* (These Are Flowers of Fire, These Are Not Flowers of Fire, 1972), *Samāntara* (Parallels, 1981), and *Kasmai Devāya* (Oath of the Gods, 1985).

THE SHADOWS OF SUPERFLUOUS SONGS
(*ANĀVASHYAK GĪTKĀ CHĀYĀHARŪ*)

All of a sudden I sit down to write
the lines of songs which no one needs;
I always attempt such pointless sorcery,
feeling perhaps they will vanish within me,
running away like water,
their forms turning dark and vague.

Once I would say, "Do not make me write songs,
my songs are all lost, they make my flesh ache,"
but I was afraid when I heard someone say,
"No song is lost"—so I write.

This is a thousand-year process, my love,
my songs are formed and they vanish,
disappearing into dark backgrounds,
like my skylines, my countless dreams.

"Be not a mirage," said I, and I heard,
"This is a path which must go on."
"Remembering the endless," I say, then I hear,
"Continue it must, like these strange voices"
—and then a song is made.

Sometimes I suddenly try to be
like the juniper trees which no one needs,
like these tall mountain peaks:
I have found them standing like evening,
ruminating in solitude,
I have touched them deepening like the sky.
I am surprised—why is the evening not faith?
Why is it not the flowers
offered up in temples?

So I refuse to write more songs
for which there is no need,
the far shores are not illusions, my love,
"They are illusions which nobody needs."

Climbing stairs which must be climbed,
I am up on Olympus, the pagan god's peak,
far below I see waters and shores;
my desires a river seen from a mountain,
my strange urges a city seen from a mountain,
the communal life of strangers:
a bond of chance seen from a mountain;
the lines of my song are those images,
for as long as they may last,
these forms always busy with shadows,

these distances, too, are my kin,
desolate places always busy with light.

I am asked, "What is this shadow?"
It is the superfluous songs I write.

(no date; from Ballabh 1981)

WHERE IS THE VOICE? (*ĀVĀJ KAHĀṂ CHA?*)

We had watched the festival of flowers,
we had seen them in their rows,
even as we spoke another folktale formed;
tales of Sunkesharī and Dīkpāl disappear,
Dīkpāl is lost, of the demons there's no sign[1]
in the festival of flowers.

Unfamiliar faces are walking by
with paper flowers for the Gāī Jātrā,[2]
their lines are dark smoke, dark words,
they walk with dark conduct.
I asked—where is this procession going?
but received no reply:
we always want an answer,
but no procession ever gave one.
We asked, what are these eyes and masks?
Just their festival, they replied.

Just a procession that has not set out,
just lines all ready which have not moved.
Those shapes and horizons,
those skies and patterns!

How distant it is, unreachable,
however far the procession goes,
tramping mountain paths,
up hill and down dale, however long we walked,
that unreachable world was nowhere,
nowhere to be found.
Why can't we arrive there today?

With our feast of flowers
we have made flowers grow in the gardens.

Here one must not mention it;
it could be a song,

1. Princess Sunkesharī and Prince Dīkpāl are the central characters of one of the most popular Nepali folktales. Dīkpāl rescued the princess from the clutches of some demons (*daitya*) who had devoured all the inhabitants of her father's kingdom and kept her under a spell.

2. This is the annual "cow festival" celebrated by the Newārs of the Kathmandu Valley.

it could be a god,
it could even be this Kāl Bhairava.
To the dumb Kāl Bhairava by the Hanumān Gate[3]
we said, get up and walk,
why do you squat on a rock?
But he did not walk; he is afraid,
he would melt if he walked the roads of Man.
We are quite different:
he is the Bhairava, we are men:
such valorous men, defeated by a stone Bhairava.
Multilingual men defeated by a Tantric rock:
the history of this day.
Come, you rocks,
soften and melt and run:
this is the world of Man.

Whoever tells a story here
just watches a flower blooming;
a few pretty blossoms, and Man melts away.
Come, oh dreams, tell the tale of Dīkpāl,
sing the song Sunkesharī sang.
The sky and the earth have died without songs,
the rocks are dead,
they have hardened, hardened,
even God has died and turned to stone;
flow now, rocks, come and save
the thing we once called life.

But far away there was nothing,
no breeze, no sky, not even those houses.
Apprehensive, we watch the god of faith,
we watch Gaṇesh and Bhairava,
we watch even the stairs.

At such a time,
why does no voice reassure us?
Where is the voice?
Where is the voice?

(1981; from Ballabh 1985)

HEM HAMĀL (B. 1941)

Hem Hamāl is a popular modern poet who writes gently satirical poems in simple, musical language. His work is typical of a recent trend of "softness" in Nepali poetry, which is also evident in the poems of Mohan Himānshu Thāpā (b. 1936) and Shailendra Sākār (b. 1946).

3. Kāl Bhairava is a famous statue of the fearsome aspect of Shiva situated near the Hanumān Ḍhokā entrance to the old royal palace in central Kathmandu.

VILLAGE AND TOWN (*SAHAR RA GĀUṂ*)

If the town prospers
the country progresses,
so say the men of the town.
If it rains this year
the village will prosper,
so say the village men.

A man from the town
stops his car on the road
and asks, "How are the crops
in the village this year?"
A farmer comes forward to answer:
"The farming is not so bad,
but can the sweat of our labors
fill your motor car's stomach?"

(no date; from *Samsāmayik Sājhā Kavitā* 1983)

CHILDREN GOING TO SCHOOL (*PĀṬHSHĀLĀ JĀNA LĀGEKĀ NĀNĪHARŪ*)

Do not ask these little children,
coming toward you all in a line,
do not ask them where they are going.
They have their own roads to travel,
their own tools for creating themselves.

They have feet you cannot see,
do not ask about when and where,
these children are their own open sky,
their wings they make themselves.

Their language is different, meanings diverge,
if they are noisy, it does not matter.
Do not try to understand what they say:
these are the books of tomorrow's Nepal.

(no date; from *Samsāmayik Sājhā Kavitā* 1983)

BEFORE THE DAWN (*BIHĀNA HUNUBHANDĀ PAHILE*)

The sweepers have not risen
to come and sweep our floors,
no tinkling is heard from bangles
on arms unlocking doors,
no one has begun to daub

the yard below the stairs,[4]
drops of dew have still to fall
from the petals of the flowers,
the birds have not yet stretched their wings,
they have not begun to sing.
Still there is no one about,
in the east no hint of light,
no cock has yet been heard to crow:
sleep, Nepali, sleep,
it is not yet time to rise.

(no date; from *Samsāmayik Sājhā Kavitā* 1983)

KRISHNABHŪSHAN BAL (B. 1947)

Krishnabhūshan Bal is one of the most powerful poets of recent times. All of his poems comment forcefully on contemporary social and political issues. "April Wind" (*Chaitko Hāvā*) is an unambiguous call for radical change in Nepali society and something of a prophecy, too, because the political upheaval of 1990 reached its climax in April of that year; "Historical Matters" (*Itihāskā Kurā*) bewails the "backwardness" of the kingdom.

APRIL WIND (*CHAITKO HĀVĀ*)

April has come to these lowlands,[5]
the wind strips bare the trees
like a mad, demented elephant.
This is no breeze to merely grasp
the gentle scent of flowers:
it sweeps away the dust of ages,
fells ancient trees with ease.

This wind made most of the history we read,
this wind makes most of the history we write,
I may fear for my house of confidence,
but it blows down not only weak buildings,
it uproots not only frail voices;
it can blow away the ocean's waters,
and drive the rain from the sky.

4. It is traditional for Hindu householders to smear their courtyards and so on with fresh mud or cow dung early each morning. This hardens to provide a clean, smooth floor surface.

5. The month of Chait, or Chaitra, corresponds to the second half of March and the first half of April in the Western calendar.

And can I omit to say,
it dispels the clouds which cover this land,
it rips up the leaves of our incongruous history,
sounding the bugles of revolution.

Today it is filling the skies
with the whirlwind of a tree's old leaves:
contractors' houses, founded on profit,
cannot stand for long,
the clouds can no longer keep the sun
from warming people's backs.

A prayer flag flutters before my house,
furious in the wind,
the *pīpal* tree sounds loud and free.
The wind has bypassed truth and peace,
rashly deciding to bring in the Spring.

If hindered, if blocked by a mountain,
who knows what might not happen?
May it not destroy the prayer flag,
may it not bring down the *pīpal* tree
which gives us all cool shade.

April has come to the lowlands
with a wind like a crazy elephant.
Oh cooks with ladles and spoons in your hands,
beware of the fire!
Oh you who try to act as a father,
grabbing your whole family by its hair,
beware of the fire!
Beware of the wind!

(no date; from *Samsāmayik Sājhā Kavitā* 1983)

HISTORICAL MATTERS (*ITIHĀSKĀ KURĀ*)

A moon of creation set foot here among us
and has only just gone on its way,
to the riverside steps, taking an air of excitement,
there to make it cold.
The city carries a great crush of dead bodies,
frightened like a kitten,
the streets are dumb amid dull footsteps.

There history stayed, and there we stayed, too.

To find out whether the rivers were sleeping,
we immersed the wood for our fires,
to discover whether the hills still slumbered,
we wandered from town to town.

When we found out these things for certain,
we were already washed away,
when we discovered these things for sure,
we had subsided with the land.

There history stayed, and we moved far behind,
branded by the Sagaulī Treaty,
cursed by Satī,
we who saw Bhīmsen uncremated.[6]

How long can the lamp go on burning,
wrapped in a sky of coldness?
How will the fallen trees stride out
from the banks of the Aruṇ River?
The cock which just summoned the morning
is already plucked bare by a jackal,
a cloud has already hidden the sun
which glimmered just now on the hill.

Geography has cheated us both,
but we have defrauded history.

(no date; from *Samsāmayik Sājhā Kavitā* 1983)

BIMAL NIBHĀ (B. 1952)

Like Hem Hamāl, Bimal Nibhā is a poet of gentle satire, and this poem mocks the escapism of the romantic nature-poetry that is still popular in Nepal.

ARE YOU QUITE WELL, OH POET?
(*KE TAPĀĪṂLĀĪ SANCHAI CHA KAVIJĪ?*)

. . . flowers of many colors bloom,
bees are buzzing, birds are singing,
the sky is clear and spotless,
the river flows by swiftly . . .
. . . but pardon me please, oh poet,
I break the flow of your poem,
to ask you—are you quite well?

6. The Treaty of Sagaulī (1816) ended a series of military clashes between the Nepalese and the forces of the British East India Company. Because the treaty deprived Nepal of some of its most fertile territories, many felt it to have been a humiliation. Bhīmsen Thāpā was the commander in chief of the Nepalese army, and therefore the most powerful man in Nepal, from 1804 until his assassination in 1837. For the Nepali belief that Nepal was cursed by a *satī* as she mounted her husband's funeral pyre, so that altruism would never be rewarded in Nepal, see Raj (1979, 29).

. . . the mountains stand with heads held high,
the cascades tumble, melodious sound,
the kites are wheeling in the sky,
a flute sounds sweetly from afar,
the breeze is whispering soft . . .
but pardon me please, oh poet,
I must ask you this in your poem—
have you had enough to eat?

. . . the moon is spreading its coolness,
the night is fragrant, the body light,
the heart is overjoyed . . .
. . . but pardon me please, oh poet,
again I interrupt—
Is rice very cheap in the marketplace?
Is rice very cheap in the marketplace?
Have you had enough to eat today?
Are you quite well, oh poet?

(no date; from *Samsāmayik Sājhā Kavitā* 1983)

ASHESH MALLA (B. 1954)

Malla was born in Dhankuṭā, in eastern Nepal, and is also known as a successful playwright. He continues a style of verse that was first made popular by Gopālprasād Rimāl. In both of the poems translated here, concern is expressed for the exodus of hill Nepalis to the cities and lowlands in search of land and employment.

TO THE CHILDREN (*TINĪHARŪLĀĪ*)

Little children should gambol and play,
cheerfully, clutching books,
carefree in the streets and fields,
beneath the piece of the sky they choose,
playing any game they please,
their lips all filled with Autumn.

Why do these strange children
bear the silence of pain in their eyes?
Why do their minds' dumb voices cry
that the wounds on their feet have not healed,
that their mothers and fathers who left seeking faith
have not returned from other towns?

These children's lips should bear smiles,
new buds should bloom in their cheeks,

why do they try to hide their hands,
wearing on one side a shower of rain,
on the other a slap of wind?

Books should be tucked under their arms,
but now they can go nowhere, they cannot rise
above the town which fills their eyes.
All they need is a mind,
to be able to see,
a warm human embrace,
a father's sweet kiss,
and a breast of mother's milk.

(no date; from *Samsāmayik Sājhā Kavitā* 1983)

NONE RETURNED FROM THE CAPITAL (*RĀJDHĀNĪBĀṬA PHARKE PHARKENAN UNĪHARŪ*)

Munching *chiurā*[7] the old faiths came
to attend the capital's festive day;
they never returned from Pashupati's bare slopes,
from the softness of dawn sleeping wrapped in frost,
perhaps even now they are sipping the dew,
chanting God's name on some temple steps,
or moving dumb lips in the crowds and the noise,
their walking sticks lost on the streets,
feeling the void with trembling hands,
wrongly attired at pedestrian crossings.

They came to the capital seeking their country,
they entered the city they knew as Nepal,[8]
freed, they will run to the streets
already auctioned in their name:
these are not the bare mountain valleys,
these are not the lowlands' tax-free dusts[9]
(in short, I call the capital
the headline of a newspaper).

Old fathers, come to the festival,
know nothing of its glorious tales;
perhaps they have listened to Scripture
and imagine entering Swasthānī's palace.[10]

7. *Chiurā* is parched rice, a common staple among the poorer sections of Nepali society.

8. Kathmandu is still often referred to as "Nepal" by people from outside the valley.

9. This reference is to recent government policies that encourage landless people from the hills to settle in the lowland Tarāī.

10. Swasthānī is a goddess of prosperity and fertility to whom women who wish to bear children often make a vow.

I fear they did not return,
waking cold perhaps beneath some statue;
so many gathered,
sucking *chiurā* in toothless mouths.

Somewhere, small children await old fathers,
watching from walls in hill villages,
expecting blessed food and sweet stories.
They do not know of the few scraps of *chiurā*
which now remain in the bag,
no one knows if they have returned;
where can they be?
There is no hint of them anywhere.

(no date; from *Samsāmayik Sājhā Kavitā* 1983)

MĪNBAHĀDUR BISHṬA (B. 1954)

Bishṭa is a resourceful poet who criticizes political and economic conditions in Nepal with great verve. "What's in the Bastard Hills?" (*Sālā Pahāḍmeṃ Kyā Hai?*) mourns the environmental decay that is gathering pace in the hills of western Nepal and forcing farmers to abandon their ancestral lands. "Thus a Nation Pretends to Live" (*Yasarī Euṭā Rāshṭra Bānchne Bahānā Garcha*) is a satire on Nepal's dependence upon foreign aid donors.

WHAT'S IN THE BASTARD HILLS? (*SĀLĀ PAHĀḌMEṂ KYĀ HAI?*)

Springing quickly from its source,
it hurries here, and loiters there,
but never glances back;
instead, the river is kicking hard
against the sickly mountains
which stand like statues on its banks,
as it runs away, and leaves this land.

Young sons are walking out,
leaving the places they were born,
taking loved ones with them,
carrying bags, neatly tied
with red kerchiefs on their shoulders.
Khukurī knives hang from their waists,
dull and unpolished for years;
they tell their sick old parents
to look after homes, homes which are lifeless.

Soft petals of gentle flowers, tender leaves of green,
flying in every direction,
plucked up by unseasonal winds
blowing from unknown lands.
Trees stand bare and disfigured,
like soldiers on parade along mountain ranges.

Flocks of doves like destitutes
are driven from their homes
by incessant storms, the deluge
which ends the longest drought;
their bodies are soaked by rain:
no hope of food to eat,
no place for them to rest.

Thus there is nothing in the hills
on which to pen a poem,
you could even say there is nothing there
for anyone to write;
it's like the soldiers always say,
home for a few months' leave,
"What's in the bastard hills?"[11]

Surely there is something here:
dying mothers, newborn babies,
springs shedding sorrowful tears,
pools frozen like heaps of stone,
absolutely still,
where the rivers have left some dirty water
and a few frog shops
as they give up hope and leave,
a few old people tending their homes,
awaiting their time,
some mountains with finished faces,
some trees felled in their youth.

And there are the cooing destitutes,
piercing the heart, shedding tears of blood:
flocks of doves.

(no date; from *Samsāmayik Sājhā Kavitā* 1983)

11. *Sālā pahāḍ*: I have translated this as bastard (*sālā*) hills (*pahāḍ*). *Sālā*, with the basic meaning of "brother-in-law," is a common term of abuse. By addressing a man as *sālā*, one implies that one has had sexual relations with his sister. The term is also applied adjectivally to any object deserving of contempt, an application that is far beyond the original meaning. The soldiers' rhetorical question (*sālā pahāḍmeṃ kyā haiṃ?*) is asked in Hindi. (See Hutt 1989a.)

THUS A NATION PRETENDS TO LIVE
(*YASARĪ EUṬĀ RĀSHṬRA BĀNCHNE BAHĀNĀ GARCHA*)

Honored friend,
this is Māchapuchare, that is Annapūrṇa,
over there stands the Dhaulagiri range.[12]
You can see them with the naked eye,
you do not need binoculars.
Here I shall open a three-star hotel:
would you kindly make me a loan?

Dear guest,
this is the Koshī and that is the Gaṇḍak,
the blue over there is the Karṇālī.[13]
You may have read in some papers
about the selling of Nepal's rivers.
That was a lie, sir.
Those rivers have given our regions their names,
we plan to generate power from them:
could you give us some help?

Respected visitor,
this is Kathmandu Valley.
Here there are three cities:
Kathmandu, Lalitpur, Bhaktapur.
Please cover your nose with a handkerchief,
no sewage system is possible,
the building of toilets has not been feasible.
Our next five-year plan has a clean city campaign:
could you make a donation?

(no date; from *Samsāmayik Sājhā Kavitā* 1983)

AVINĀSH SHRESHṬHA (B. 1955)

Avināsh Shreshṭha was born in Gauhaṭī, the state capital of Assam in northeastern India. His voice is unique among the younger generation of Nepali poets, and his work has caused a stir in Kathmandu literary circles. Avināsh's poems are heavy with mystical symbolism; their beauty is indisputable, but their interpretation is the subject of vigorous debate.

Avināsh Shreshṭha's poems are collected in *Samvedanā o Samvedanā* (Feelings, Oh Feelings, 1981) and *Parevā: Setā-Kālā* (Doves: Black and White, 1984).

12. These mountains are seen prominently from Pokhara.
13. These are three of Nepal's most important rivers.

A SPELL (*MOHA*)

I do not know from which Mānasarovar there sprang
the Brahmāputra of my consciousness,[14]
I do not know how far it will be
to the final sea of its ending.

The fisherman fears poverty,
the fish is afraid of the fisherman,
sleep is startled by a dream,
eyes are made dizzy by sleep;
greetings from the restless sea,
palms of ebb and flow together,[15]
to the moon, to the sky.

Where does it hide, where?
pouring out boundless blue silence,
filling the eyes of the sky.
Has it collided somewhere
with the illusion of insoluble space,
or simply disappeared?

On a rain-soaked Indra-lotus night
in the month of Bhadau,[16]
I do not know who it was that walked,
joined to rumor, body fragrant,
across the mind's unpeopled forests,
unseen.

(1986; from *Kavitā* 1986)

HEADLAND (*ANTARĪP*)

A negro-black night
dozes in each eye
where cigarettes of disbelief are lit.

Where the solitude makes you forget your name,
the river your shape and the sea your limits,
there is a headland.

Oh Irāvatī,[17]
through what lonely place do you flow?

14. Mānasarovar, a sacred lake on the Tibetan plateau, is the source of the great Brahmāputra River.

15. This reference is to the gesture of greeting known as the *namaste*.

16. The month of Bhadau, or Bhadra, corresponds to the second half of August and the first half of September in the Western calendar. This is the season of the late monsoon rains.

17. Irāvatī is the sacred Rāvī River in northern India.

In what desolation have you hidden hate?
Where is the innocent headland
of your fleshless love?

One blue star still twinkles
on the sky's frightened breast
on nights sunken in chants of pain.

(1986; from *Kavitā* 1986)

BISHWABIMOHAN SHRESHṬHA (B. 1956)

Born in the Terhāṭhum district of eastern Nepal, Bishwabimohan Shreshṭha is recognized as one of the leading poets of the new generation and was awarded the Motī prize for poetry in 1987. The poem translated here describes the difficulty of pursuing a literary career in Nepal, where the struggle for basic needs is a more pressing concern.

Bishwabimohan Shreshṭha's poems are collected in *Bishwabimohankā Kehī Kavitāharū* (Some Poems by Bishwabimohan Shreshṭha, 1987).

SHOULD I EARN MY DAILY BREAD, OR SHOULD I WRITE A POEM? (*MA BHĀT JORŪṂ KI KAVITĀ LEKHŪṂ?*)

At home my aged mother
watches for her son
on every festive day,
wondering if he will come
to help her make ends meet;

Each night in her lodgings,
my wife watches the door,
hoping that her husband will bring
something sweet and fine;

My daughter wears torn pajamas
and runs round telling tales
to neighbors, strangers, friends:
this winter father will bring her
a fine new suit of clothes;

My son, sent home from school,
plays all day in the dust
with crowds of local children;
he hopes father will send him
back to school this term;

The little one's asleep now,
teasing milkless breasts,

his nakedness forevermore
mocks my very manhood;

Speak not of brothers and sisters:
for them no work could be found,
for them no spouse was chosen;

How much longer can I go on
in my tattered coat and patched-up jacket,
holding together heaven and hell?
Tell me, oh respected friend,
with such an evening in my arms,
should I earn my daily bread,
or should I write a poem?

Forget the radio, papers, speeches,
speak not of slogans, marches, placards,
and if some time remains
do not push me into darkness
with affectionate intent.
It is hunger I endure,
a greater Everest by far
than any ideal or doctrine.

The drying softness of life,
learning's gentle kindness:
only these can defeat hunger.
It is done: do not make me hesitate
by relating the Buddha's story,
if your dreams delay me,
if your temptations beguile me,
if I do not work these fingers to the bone,
if I neglect to sell my sweat,
my parents, my wife, my children,
will all grow hungry and die;
I am tired, a beaten warrior,
at war with the stomach's demands.

How much longer can I go on
in my tattered coat and patched-up jacket,
holding together heaven and hell?
Tell me, oh respected friend,
with such an evening in my arms,
should I earn my daily bread
or should I write a poem?

I always bear upon my head
an Annapūrṇa of need,
I always carry on my back
a Kanchenjungā of crisis,
how long can I fight this battle,

lifting a Māchāpuchare of costs
up onto my shoulders?

I believe that life should mean
flowing onward, a boon from God,
so do not mock my prayer.
Please try not to let me hear
of the horrors of the Falklands,
of massacres in Vietnam,
Afghanistan,
they are salt in my wounds.
Life is iron, I know you must
bite down hard upon it.
Life's a desolate shore, I know
you must water it with sweat,
but with what simile, what metaphor,
can I adorn and embellish this life?

How much longer can I go on
in my tattered coat and patched-up jacket,
holding together heaven and hell?
Tell me, oh respected friend,
with such an evening in my arms,
should I earn my daily bread
or should I write a poem?

(from B. Shreshṭha 1987; also included
in *Samsāmayik Sājhā Kavitā* 1983)

1. Bust of Bhānubhakta Āchārya, the *ādi kavi* (founder poet), at Darjeeling.

2. Bust of Lakshmīprasād Devkoṭā near his home in Dilli Bazar, Kathmandu.

3. A verse from Devkoṭā's "Like Nothing into Nothing," inscribed beneath the bust in Kathmandu.

4. Cover of the nineteenth edition of Lakshmīprasād Devkoṭā's classic *Munā-Madan*, published in 1988 in Kathmandu. Twenty-five thousand copies of this 43-page booklet were printed for this edition. A total of 140,000 copies have been produced since the fourteenth edition was published in 1976.

5. Siddhicharaṇ Shreshṭha at his home in Om Bahāl, Kathmandu.

7. Mohan Koirālā and his wife at their home in Dilli Bazar, Kathmandu.

6. Kedār Mān "Vyathit" at his home in Jyāthā Tol, Kathmandu.

9. Bānīrā Giri at her home in New Baneshwar, Kathmandu.

8. Pārijāt at her home at Mehpin, Kathmandu.

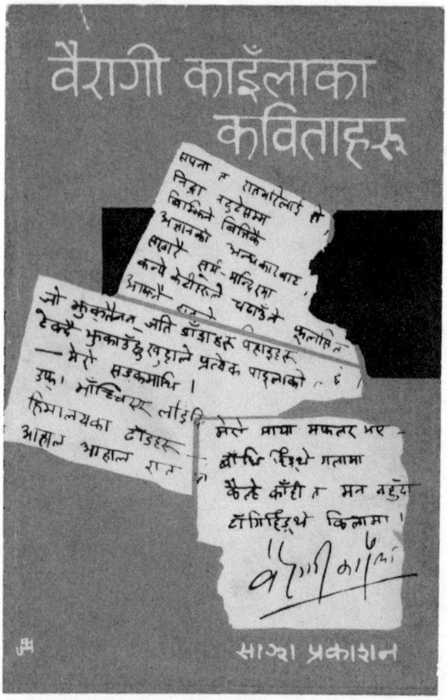

10. Cover of Bairāgī Kāinlā's collected poems, published in Kathmandu in 1974.

11. The eleventh edition of *Kathā Kusum*, published in 1981 in Darjeeling. *Kathā Kusum*, the first anthology of short stories in Nepali, was initially published in 1938.

PART TWO

Selected Short Stories

The Short Story in Nepali

Nepali literature is of enormous value to anyone who is interested in the culture and society of twentieth-century Nepal. Nor should it be forgotten that the world that Nepali literature describes is not confined to Nepal alone: at least 2 million Nepalis live in India. A recent volume of "Indian" Nepali stories contained works by authors from Darjeeling, Sikkim, Assam, Nagaland, and various other regions of Nepal's huge southern neighbor (Bhāratīya Nepālī Kathā 1982). The following selections are dominated by stories from Nepal, but Indian Nepali literature has not been wholly ignored and is represented by the Darjeeling writers Shivkumār Rāī and Indra Bahādur Rāī.

Verse genres are still the strongest area of Nepali literature. In the first section of this book, I have attempted to demonstrate the richness and variety of twentieth-century Nepali poetry. The Nepali short story, a genre that began to adopt its present form only during the early 1930s, has also developed a surprisingly high degree of sophistication within a relatively short space of time, as I hope my selection shows. Modern Nepali stories offer insights into the workings of Nepali society that have long been the stuff of sociological theses: caste, agrarian relations, social change, the status of women, and so on. Such insights are more immediate than those offered by scholarly works and are conveyed by implication and assumption rather than analysis and exposition. These translations illuminate the nature of life in twentieth-century Nepal in a way it has never been illuminated before.

In its present form, the Nepali short story is only a half century old. The only antecedents it has within the comparatively young literary tradition of the Nepali language are narratives translated from Sanskrit such as Shaktivallabha Arjyāl's rendering of the "Virāṭaparva" chapter of the Mahābhārata epic, which dates from 1770, or the less esoteric *Tale of Pinās* (*Pināsko Kathā*) from 1815. Although Nepali literary scholars try to prove otherwise (see, for instance, M. Sharmā 1978), it is clear that the short story genre has been adopted from Western literatures, probably via Hindi and Bengali, and that it is a product of the sweeping cultural and political changes that have occurred in Nepal since the turn of the century.

Several prototypes for the modern Nepali short story are to be found in the early issues of the state newspaper, the *Gorkhāpatra*, established in 1901. Although stylistically unremarkable and largely plagiaristic, many of these stories were nevertheless set in recognizably contemporary contexts and therefore marked a significant departure from the didactic, moralistic, and miraculous tales of earlier Nepali fiction. This trend toward social realism accelerated and bore its first full fruit during the 1930s in the important Kathmandu journal *Shāradā*. Several other periodical publications were also important in this process. The first truly original short story in Nepali is said to have appeared in *Gorkhālī* in 1915 (D. Shreshṭha 1982, 4), and by the time *Gorkhā Sansār* (*Gorkha World*) began publication in 1926, the crucial elements of originality, coherent plot structure, linguistic simplicity, and contemporary subject matter had begun to coalesce. Although published in Dehra Dun, an Indian military town in the Himalaya, *Gorkhā Sansār* was an important forum for progressive writers from Nepal who could not publish in their homeland because of the censorious attitudes of the Rāṇā rulers. "Annapūrṇa," a story by the Darjeeling lawyer Rūpnārāyaṇ Singh, which appeared in *Gorkhā Sansār* in 1927, is considered a landmark in the development of modern Nepali fiction (D. Shreshṭha 1982, 4; K. Pradhan 1984, 146).

With an exactitude rare in such matters, it can be asserted that the history of the modern Nepali short story began in 1935 when Guruprasād Mainālī's first story, "Nāso" (The Ward), was published in *Shāradā*. The first anthology of Nepali short stories appeared shortly afterward: this was the important *Kathā Kusum* (*Story Flower*), published by Darjeeling's Nepālī Sāhitya Sammelan in 1938 and now in its twelfth edition. *Kathā Kusum* contained stories by Bālkrishna Sama, Guruprasād Mainālī, Pushkar Shamsher, and Bishweshwar Prasād Koirālā.

Because the short story is a comparatively new phenomenon in Nepali, there is no scope or need for a detailed periodization of its history. There may be some merit, however, in attempting to assess the philosophical and literary influences at work in its development. Realism (*yathārthavād*) is the fundamental quality for which every Nepali story writer strives, although definitions of realism have varied from time to time. The basic tradition of social realism can be traced back to Mainālī: his stories owe much to the influence of the great Hindi/Urdu writer "Premchand" (real name Dhanpat Rāī, 1880–1936) and exhibit the same idealism and concern for the poor. Social realities were presented with an idealistic sheen, and few such stories lacked a moral or an improving message. This kind of story retains many exponents today: the redoubtable Bhīmnidhi Tiwārī, for instance, produced ten volumes of "Nepali social stories" (*Nepali sāmājik kahānī*). The typical features of stories in this genre are their sympathetic portrayals of poverty, opposition to superstition and ossified tradition, and the great attention they pay to the social status of women.

A logical extension of social realism are stories written to promulgate a particular political standpoint, usually Marxist, or to draw attention to a specific social issue. Such stories multiplied during the period of unprecedented freedom that followed the fall of the Rāṇās. Numerous stories by Ramesh Bikal are clear examples of this socialist realism.

As Nepal opened up during the 1950s, writers inevitably became familiar with the great figures of world literature and philosophy. Marx and Freud were obvious sources of political ideology and psychological insight, and many stories bore the stamp of Tolstoy, Sartre, Maupassant, and Tagore, among others. As a result, an element of psychological analysis became important in the Nepali story at a fairly early stage. Rather than presenting a simple narrative involving stereotypical characters whose motives and status remained unanalyzed, several Nepali writers began to investigate the mental processes of the unconscious and subconscious mind and to suggest that the old moral certainties could no longer remain unquestioned. The earliest examples of such innovative works are stories such as Bishweshwar Prasād Koirālā's "The Colonel's Horse" (*Karnelko Ghoḍā*), published in the late 1930s, in which a young woman who is married to an elderly colonel sublimates her sexual frustration in an infatuation with the colonel's stallion:

> A few days later, the colonel said that he wanted to ride the horse, and he went with his wife to the stable. But the horse threatened to bite him whenever he tried to approach it. If the colonel's wife began to walk away, however, the horse would whinny in distress, and she would come back to stroke it. Then it would snort and stamp its hooves in appreciation.
>
> With great difficulty, the colonel managed to mount, but the horse would not let him control it: it simply reared up and refused to budge. He was a skilled horseman, and so he did not fall off, but flew into a rage and began to beat it pitilessly with his whip. As soon as the first lash fell onto the horse's back, the colonel's wife cried out, "You cruel man!" But the horse still refused to move. The colonel had shut his eyes and was showering it with blows from his whip when it suddenly threw up its hind legs. Because he was busy whipping the beast, the colonel did not have

> hold of the reins, and he fell head first to the ground. The colonel's wife was already at the horse's side, stroking and caressing it and ignoring her husband who lay nearby, covered in dirt. The horse's nostrils were wide with anger, and wet breath came panting from them. The horse had won: its enemy lay defeated on the ground.
>
> The colonel's wife had no doubt about the horse's power: for her it was a matter of pride. She pressed her face fondly against its mane. She, too, had wanted to ride on its back, so she slipped her foot into a stirrup and climbed up. As she sat mounted on the horse with her husband lying on the ground below, she felt triumphant. Today she had a chance for revenge. Feeling an even greater love for the horse, she bent down with a look of supreme hatred to watch her husband licking the dust. Then she spurred the horse forward, and it skipped away as if it was bearing no more than a burden of flowers. (B. Koirālā [1949] 1968, 41–42)

Like social realism, psychological realism has since become a standard feature of much Nepali fiction, and these three philosophical strands of Nepali fiction—social realism, socialist realism, and psychological realism—dominated the short story until about 1960. It was then that a distinct reaction took place, as it did in poetry. Nepal's brief experiment with parliamentary democracy ended in 1960 when King Mahendra revoked the Constitution, and the literary atmosphere completely changed. The following decade saw the emergence of several literary movements, of which the most influential was the *Tesro Āyām,* which I have discussed in some detail in my introduction to the poetry of Bairāgī Kāinlā. The influence of this movement can be seen clearly in Indra Bahādur Rāī's story "Mainā's Mother Is Just Like Us" (*Hamī Jastai Mainākī Āmā,* 1964).

Several critics have argued that 1960 was the beginning of a "new age" in Nepali fiction.[1] It is certainly true that the character and tone of the Nepali short story have changed markedly since then. Several innovative writers began to publish their stories between 1960 and 1962: Kumār Gyavālī, Premā Shāh, and Parashu Pradhān are obvious examples, and the influence of Dhruba Chandra Gautam was formative. But the clearest signs of a radical change in Nepali fiction at this time are to be found in the works of Indra Bahādur Rāī, his *āyāmelī* colleague Ìshwar Ballabh, and Shankar Lāmichhāné. Lāmichhāné's "The Half-closed Eyes of the Buddha and the Slowly Setting Sun" (*Ardhamudit Nayan ra Ḍubna Lāgeko Ghām*) made an enormous impact on Nepali fiction when it was published in 1962. This was due in part to its unorthodox structure and partly to its theme, which turned away from the internal concerns of the writer's own society to consider a foreigner's perception of Nepal.

1. Shreshṭha (1982, 15), for instance, links the *navayug* (the new era) directly to the advent of the *Tesro Āyām* movement.

A number of other movements were instigated during the 1960s, but none was as significant as the *Tesro Āyām*. Pārijāt formed Rālphā, a group heavily influenced by existentialist and nihilistic thought with progressive social attitudes and a belief in the importance of the individual rather than the community. Pārijāt herself proved to be the only writer of note to emerge from this group. In later years, groups of young writers attempted to generate change with initiatives such as the Aswīkrit Jamāt (Unaccepted Generation), a heavily politicized movement, in 1968; the Amlekh (Free) movement in 1969; and the Boot Polish group in 1974. Each of these has had some effect, but none had such clear-cut aims as the *Tesro Āyām*. In practice, the writers of the new age have simply taken the old realism further and have stripped their literature of the last vestiges of sentimentalism and traditional belief. In their short stories, young writers have begun to make effective use of satire to oppose the limitation of individual freedom and to attack the traditional pillars of society, paying special attention to the conflict in values that rapid change is bringing to their lives.

THEMES OF NEPALI SHORT STORIES

It is of course impossible to classify a body of fictional literature under discrete and exclusive subject headings. It is possible, however, to define a number of themes that recur with regularity in the Nepali short story. The following discussion is not a thorough analysis of the whole of Nepali fiction; my aim is to identify a number of themes that occurred with striking regularity in the stories I read during this research. The sample is therefore inevitably limited, but it is far from random because I have concentrated on texts that are most frequently cited in works of Nepali criticism and analysis.

Village Life

More than 90 percent of Nepal's total population lives in rural areas, and there are few large urban centers in the hill regions that are the natural home of the Nepali language. Indeed, if a story is set in an urban environment, it is usually that of the Kathmandu Valley. It is not surprising that rural life is the backdrop to about one-third of these stories; although they may live in Kathmandu, many authors grew up in a village environment. A distinction can be drawn nevertheless between stories that are self-consciously "village stories," written either to paint an authentic picture of rural society or to point out some undesirable feature of it, and stories in which events simply happen to take place in a village context.

Village stories were rather more common during the early phase of the short story's development in Nepali. This can be accounted for, at least in part, by the popularity and influence of the Hindi/Urdu writer "Premchand." Almost all of Premchand's multitudinous stories are set in the villages of northern India. Despite his somewhat idealized, Gāndhīan view of rural life, he was often concerned about depicting the plight of the poor, oppressed by hypocritical priests and exploited by landowners and moneylenders. More than an echo of Premchand's fiction can be found in early village stories in Nepali.

"A Blaze in the Straw" (1935) is the most celebrated of Mainālī's ever-popular stories and is the archetypal village story. The original title, "Parālko Āgo," is rendered literally here, although there was a temptation to entitle it "A Storm in a Teacup." The concept behind the title is of a blazing row that flares up fiercely but burns out very quickly. The main purpose of the story is to paint a picture of a relationship between a man and his wife that is authentic and amusing and that ultimately imparts a kind of moral lesson. In this, Mainālī is undoubtedly influenced by Premchand, especially in the use of proverbs and rural colloquialisms (for a selection of Premchand's stories in translation, see Premchand 1988). "A Blaze in the Straw" has now entered the folklore of Nepali-speaking communities; it is acted out in school dramas throughout the region and was recently made into a feature film, complete with Bombay-style musical interludes.

Shivkumār Rāī is a noted writer from Darjeeling who developed this tradition further. Rāī's particular talent was to write simple but evocative tales based on his observation of characters in the everyday life of the Darjeeling area, and in this he closely resembled Mainālī. "The Price of Fish" (*Māchāko Mol*, 1945?) a melodramatic tale of the simple ambitions and untimely demise of a local fisherman, is one of the best-known stories of Indian Nepali literature:

> He cast his net into the same muddy pool. Again, the fish were mesmerized by the light from his torch. Twenty or thirty fell into his net. Rané found fish wherever he looked, in every basket he pulled out from around the dam. He felt neither hungry nor tired. His hopes grew wings, and he did not care how hard he worked.
>
> Black clouds rose up in the west; a flood of water thundered down from the peaks. Little did Rané know that Yamarāj[2] was coming, wading down with the torrent. He heard the waters dashing against the rocks, and he began to pick up his fish from the beach. But the river engulfed him and swept him away. Rané was dismayed by the loss of the fish he had labored so hard to catch; he did not realize that he was being borne away, too. As the flood washed him down river, he cried, "Is it so high then, the price of fish?" But before he could complete the sentence he was lost in the waters. (*Jhyālbāṭa* 1949, 236)

2. Yamarāj is the lord of death and the underworld.

Ramesh Bikal's "A Splendid Buffalo" (*Lāhurī Bhainsī*, c. 1962) is an example of a story in which the nature of rural life and society is the central topic. This is probably the most cynical depiction of village Nepal ever written and is justly famous. Its theme is reminiscent of that of Premchand's best-loved novel, *The Gift of a Cow* (*Godān*), first published in 1936. Lukhuré, a poor farmer or perhaps even a bonded laborer, has bought himself a buffalo—a symbol of wealth and prestige in the village. His is no ordinary buffalo, either, but a *lāhurī bhainsī*, an animal of high breeding. The *dwāré*, a powerful local official, cannot tolerate this; it is a blow to his own status. So he sets about depriving the gullible Lukhuré of his most cherished possession. Bikal conveys the atmosphere of village intrigue with consummate artistry: the dialogues are as authentic as Mainālī's, but the theme of an official's corruption and the sycophancy of his lackeys sets this story apart from earlier, more idealized descriptions of rural life.

"Will He Ever Return?" (*Tyo Pheri Pharkalā?* 1940) is set in a village on the main thoroughfare between Kathmandu and India before the modern highways were built and is Bhavānī Bhikshu's simplest and most popular story but possibly his most formulaic. It contains passages that are notable for their economy and effectiveness, but some parts of the narrative may strike a Western reader as overextended. It should be remembered that the readership for whom Bhikshu was writing fifty years ago liked nothing more than a tearful melodrama. A young woman, Sānī, falls in love with a traveler when he stays for one night at her mother's inn, and she spends the rest of her life waiting for him to return. If the story's plot has a weakness, it is the unlikeliness of Sānī falling in love with the traveler to the extent that she does: his attractions are not evident in Bhikshu's descriptions of him. Nevertheless, that a poor village girl should become infatuated with a high-caste sophisticate is to some extent credible. The most interesting aspects of the story, perhaps, are Bhikshu's ruminations on the nature of women and the unexpected psychological subtlety of his ending.

More recently, several writers have attempted to describe the stark contrast between life in the village and life in the town. Indra Bahādur Rāī's "The Storm Raged All Night Long" (*Rātbhari Hurī Chalyo*, 1960) is a straightforward narrative with little of the abstractedness of its author's later works. The story, which has not been included in this selection for reasons of space, tells of a man and his wife, known to us only as Kālé's mother and Kālé's father, a common form of reference in the Darjeeling district, who have moved out of the town to make a living as farmers. The wife goes into Darjeeling every morning to deliver the milk from their two cows to various households. After a violent summer storm, she decides that the hardship of life in the hills is not worth the slender reward it brings. After several encounters in the town next day, however, she changes her mind; she finds the townspeople arrogant and petty, particularly one woman who died during the night while trying to save her cat:

> She arrived on B. B. Gurung's verandah. The house had been full of people since early morning. A few stood outside, talking under umbrellas. Kālé's mother went around to the back to deliver the milk. She could not discover what was going on. Something must have happened—either to the husband or to the wife; there were no children. The fat wife used to come and go all day, her wooden sandals clacking. She went all over town carrying her white cat, Nini. The husband owned a dry-cleaning shop up on Laden-la Road.
>
> "What's happened? Why are all these people here?" she asked the woman who came from next door to collect the milk.
>
> "Nini's mother had a fall last night. She's unconscious."
>
> "Where did she fall?"
>
> She heard that the cat had been outside in the rain when the door was locked in the night. It must have mewed and mewed, but nobody heard it above the din of the storm. When the rain eased a little, there had been a search for the cat. They had looked outside and called and called, but the cat had not come. Nini's mother's sandal had slipped as she was going down the hill to look for the cat, and she had fallen down onto the road. A doctor had been called urgently, but he hadn't come at once. The woman was still unconscious.
>
> "It's all the fault of that stupid cat!" said Kālé's mother quietly. "That's it there, isn't it?"
>
> A white cat sat warming itself and licking its fur by the fireplace. Kālé's mother couldn't just walk away. She sat down on the doorstep, and soon the husband came out in tears. The woman had died.
>
> "How astonishing! What a shame!" Kālé's mother picked up her bag and the churn. (Rāī 1960, 8–9)

Several later stories view the village from the perspective of the town. Dhruba Chandra Gautam's satire in "The Fire" (*Āglāgi*, 1976) is aimed at the corruption of government officials and the ludicrous inappropriateness of projects devised at the "center" when they are translated into the realities of village society. In "A Small Fish Squats by the Dhobī Kholā" (*Sāno Māchhā Dhobī Kholāko Bagarmā*, 1983), Manu Brājākī mentions that his character Ganesh has been punished for accepting bribes by being transferred back to Kathmandu, where there are fewer opportunities for corruption.

Life in Kathmandu and Darjeeling

As I have mentioned, Kathmandu is the city to which Nepali writers most commonly refer, and the picture they paint of life there is generally a negative one. Ramesh Bikal's somewhat overextended "The Song of

New Road" (*Nayā Saḍakko Gīt*, 1960) describes a blind beggar with his pitch on a New Road pavement and is clearly meant to point out a contradiction between the grinding poverty of the majority of Nepalis and the veneer of prosperity apparent on New Road. New Road is the main thoroughfare of Kathmandu's busy commercial center, and with its supermarket, import shops, and tourists, it symbolizes for many writers the new age into which Nepal is passing. Bikal also paints a convincing picture of official attitudes to the urban poor, and his concluding passage contains a cynical view of democracy in Nepal:

> Sānī picked up the stick that lay nearby. The blind man stood up and moved forward, leaning on Sānī's shoulder. "How old are your skirt and blouse, Sānī?"
>
> "About two years old, I suppose. Why do you ask?" Sānī was puzzled by this unexpected question about her clothes.
>
> "Two years is a long time. Come on, let's find ourselves a corner to sit in."
>
> Sānī led the blind man down the edge of the main road. A jeep came up behind them, and a loudspeaker blared something about democracy . . . citizens . . . a friendly nation . . . a guest . . . welcoming with open hearts, and so on. The sound of the loudspeaker filled the air; then it gradually faded away into the distance.
>
> "What is it, Sānī?" asked the blind man. Then he turned to a shopkeeper and asked him, "What is it, shopkeeper?"
>
> "They're telling you to send your wife to the Women's Assembly to give a lecture. She should speak about democracy," said the shopkeeper. The air was suddenly filled with the sound of many people laughing.
>
> "Oh, demcarcy![3] How long is it now since demcarcy happened? We've had that for years, for years," muttered the blind man, and then his voice joined the modern culture of New Road. It mingled with the noise of all its new songs. (Bikal [1962] 1977, 44–45)

Parashu Pradhān's "A Relationship" (*Sambandha*, 1970) paints an equally grim picture of the wretched lot of the urban poor. For centuries, the people of the hill regions around Kathmandu have earned a living from portering goods and produce in and out of the capital. Many of them will sleep for a night on the covered platforms that stand in several street intersections. This is where Gyānchā, a Newār street cleaner, sees Gangā lying. Gangā is a woman with whom Gyānchā once had a fleeting relationship, the precise nature of which is not disclosed. But soon he discovers that she is dead and that no one will accept responsibility for her body.

Tāriṇī Prasād Koirālā's "It Depends upon Your Point of View" (*Drishṭikoṇ*, 1964) satirizes the moral hypocrisy of the professional upper strata

3. The beggar mispronounces the word *prajātantra*, "democracy," as *parjātantra*.

of Kathmandu society. With uncharacteristic indiscretion, Professor Niranjan has had a sexual encounter with a shopkeeper's daughter, a girl of low breeding and little education who is, above all, a Newār and therefore somewhat despised. The story describes his guilt and remorse the next morning.

Later stories adopt a more caustic tone. Stories describing the alienation of the urban young are a new phenomenon in Nepali fiction. Manu Brājākī's "A Small Fish Squats by the Dhobī Kholā" is a sardonically humorous account of the plight of a "small fish," a petty official in government service who cannot gain access to the lavatory at his lodgings and therefore has to squat beside the Dhobī Kholā, a river in Kathmandu, to open his bowels each morning. The small fish has been transferred to the capital from a post in a rural area after being caught accepting bribes. The point of the title is that the really "big fish," his senior colleagues, were equally corrupt but escaped all retribution because of their status. As the urban centers of the Kathmandu Valley continue to grow, it seems likely that the alienation that is typical of much modern Hindi fiction will begin to enter Nepali fiction, too.

Darjeeling, which in a sense has a Nepali literature all of its own, is the setting for most of its own writers' stories. Rāī's famous story "Mainā's Mother Is Just Like Us" (*Hāmī Jastai Maināki Āmā*, 1964) was strongly influenced by the tenets of the *Tesro Āyām* movement and is the most abstracted composition translated here. It expresses the historical and cultural consciousness of the poorer sections of Darjeeling's émigré Nepali community: farmers and workers driven out of eastern Nepal during the past few centuries by landlessness, poverty, and unemployment. The viewpoint is that of ever-present time, and Darjeeling's past, present, and future are seen through the eyes of a vegetable seller we know only as "Mainā's mother." "The woman selling vegetables in the market square is seen even before that market was constructed," writes Kumar Pradhan, "extending to the time of her mother's life and beyond to a remote nomadic past that is contained in the future" (1984, 159).

The Lives of Women

Five of these stories describe the plight of women in a male-dominated society and reflect a very widespread preoccupation with this particular issue within Nepali fiction as a whole. In many of his stories, Bishweshwar Prasād Koirālā attacked the tradition that permits elderly men of high caste and social status to take much younger wives or second wives. Koirālā and Premā Shāh both address the subject of widowhood in Hindu society. Koirālā's "To the Lowlands" (*Madhestira*, 1940?) is an early example of a Nepali short story that appears to have borrowed from Western literature. The story bears a striking resemblance to Maupassant's "Boule de Suif" (The Ball of Fat). Both Koirālā's and Maupassant's stories describe a group of people who have fallen on hard times and been thrown together and the way in which a woman from the fringes of society is taken advantage of during a time of common adversity, then shunned when things look brighter. In Maupassant's story, the refugees are escaping a Prussian invasion and the woman is a prostitute, whereas in Koirālā's they are simply landless, unemployed villagers and the woman is a widow. Widows, who may never remarry, occupy an unenviable position in traditional Hindu society. It cannot be proved that Koirālā consciously borrowed from Maupassant here, but his well-documented knowledge of world literatures makes it seem highly likely. "To the Lowlands," however, is a deceptively subtle and complex story and amounts to far more than a piece of literary imitation. In just a few pages, it comments on the sorry plight of the landless poor, the depopulation of the hills, the low social status of widows, and the exploitation of women by men.

Several noted women writers appeared in Nepali literary circles during the 1960s and gave the literature a more rounded perspective. Premā Shāh's "A Husband" (*Logné*, 1966) introduces us to another widow, Nirmalā, and describes her feelings and somewhat neurotic actions as she helps her younger sister prepare to meet her prospective husband. Pārijāt is perhaps better known as a novelist and poet, but she has also written several significant short stories. Like her poems, these often seem personal and subjective. It seems to me that many of her female characters seem to be based upon herself (although she denies this) or are drawn to challenge assumptions about, and stereotypes of, Nepali women:

> My house is on the main road; my room faces the street. Opening the window wide and watching the pleasant bustle going on outside has become a major part of my daily routine. I often watch from here, and I know all the passers-by. Office workers, students, sellers of bread and milk—I recognize them all. Let me tell you, this window is my pastime, and it leaves me with no free time at all. This is not to say that I have spent my whole life there. Once it was considered a sin even to peep outside, let alone to sit by an open window. Then came the revolution in 1950, my father died, I progressed in my education, and gradually times have changed. Now my relationship with the window is intimate. Since I completed my education and began work in a morning school, there has been no one to prevent me from sitting here and looking out. (in *Sājhā Kathā* [1968] 1979, 224)

Bhavānī Bhikshu's "Will He Ever Return?" and Daulat Bikram Bishṭha's "The Āndhī Kholā" (*Āndhī Kholā*) both describe the yearning of village girls whose loved ones have gone away; both are largely works of sentiment. Bijay Malla's "Sunglasses" (*Kālo Chashmā*, 1960) presents a strong contrast to such stories. By 1960, Nepali writers had produced a plethora of stories examining the nature of marriage and of relationships between men and women. Most of these were written from a reformist standpoint, with little moral ambiguity. In this story, however, Malla describes how a man is faced with a crisis in his marriage but reacts in an unexpected and unorthodox fashion.

Malla's brother, Govind Bahādur Goṭhālé, wrote a number of very long stories on similar themes for which room could not be found here. The most famous is "What Are You Doing, Shobhā?" (*Ke Garekī Shobhā?* 1959) in which Goṭhālé examines the mind of a widow who has become a prostitute. When first published, this story was innovatory for the unusual depth of its psychological analysis and its frank depiction of the hypocrisy inherent in Nepali society's attitude to prostitution. Shobhā is clearly a high-caste woman who has fallen into prostitution after being shunned by her family for a marriage of which they disapproved, a marriage that brought her unhappiness and, eventually, widowhood. The story focuses on the mental conflict Shobhā experiences when she learns that her mother is dying. A second innovation was the use of "flashbacks" to inform the reader of the events in Shobhā's life that had led to her fall from grace:

> Dhanmāyā had come downstairs. "Kānchī, where were you? What has happened to Shobhā's mother?"
>
> "I'm going," said Shobhā.
>
> "They've taken her to the river, at Pashupati," said Kānchī.
>
> Shobhā was on her way out of the door. "Where are you going?" asked Dhanmāyā.
>
> But she was already on her way down. Dhanmāyā leapt up and ran to the stairs. "Don't go," she said, trying to catch her hand. "Really, it's late. And it's a long way. . . . " She stopped. Shobhā was already at the foot of the stairs. Dhanmāyā shouted to her again, "Listen to what I say. Don't go. You'll be insulted. They won't let you near."
>
> She hurried across the ground floor but stopped abruptly at the door and peered out at the dark street. Something moved on its surface. A shaft of light spread down the street as a window opened at the top of the house, and Dhanmāyā shouted, "Shobhā, come back! Listen to me! Come back here!"
>
> Shobhā stood still, unable to go out onto the street. She saw her mother, already half-immersed in water. She saw herself approaching. Her mother looked away. Someone shook her—was it her sister-in-law?—and said, "Don't show your face here; don't send your mother to hell." Her father just hung his head. Shobhā slowly moved away. She did not even have the right to mourn. (Goṭhālé 1959, 91–92)

Poshaṇ Pāṇḍé's "A Sweater for Brother-in-law" (*Bhinājyuko Sveṭar*, 1964?) investigates a woman's feelings of insecurity in her marriage and is a further example of a male Nepali writer examining feminine psychology. The surprise ending of the story is one of Pāṇḍé's trademarks.

Finally, in "A Living Death" (*Mritajīvī*, 1982) Kishor Pahāḍī presents us with a story that is perhaps the most damning indictment of the status of women in Nepal's Hindu society. The prevalence of stories about downtrodden women in Nepali literature is one of its more interesting features, particularly as only one of these authors is a woman.

Caste, Class, and Ethnic Relations

The relations between castes in a Hindu society are somewhere in the background of most of these stories, but they form the principal theme of none. A Nepali reader will automatically understand that Mainālī's Juṭhé the tailor leads a happy life despite belonging to a lower caste than the hapless Chāmé. Similarly, the simple honest character of Pushkar Shamsher's Rané is communicated as much by the fact that he is a Gurung as it is by Shamsher's portrayal of him. Rané is the central character of "Circumstantial Evidence" (*Pariband*, 1938), the story of a wrongful conviction. This is one of the most famous Nepali stories and certainly Shamsher's best; because an English translation of the main part of this story is already in print, however, there seemed no need to include it here (Riccardi 1988, 4–7). The characterizations (particularly of Rané and the magistrate Lāmichhāné) are unusually strong and the dialogue unusually natural for a story of the period. Although not intended to make any comment on the society of its day, the story is interesting for its portrayal of Rané's naive honesty and for the hints it gives of the way in which justice was dispensed in the days of the Rāṇās. The following passage comes toward the end of the story, as the magistrate explains to Rané that he is sure to be found guilty:

> "Then you, an honest, er, Gurung; you got blood on your clothes while you were giving him water. Maybe you'd have washed it off if you'd noticed it. You went to report what had happened but as you thought it over, you thought, 'Oh no! Now they'll arrest me!' Then, er, you decided to slip away, without a thought for the consequences. Then when you were arrested, your heart beat like a drum, and you started to admit and deny all sorts of things, I don't really know why.
>
> "If you're really innocent, then perhaps this is how it happened. But what can you do? You're damned by the circumstantial evidence! And moreover, to get arrested beside the Rapti River just as you were getting away, to cover up what happened, and then when everything else was proved to deny only the murder itself—what are you left with now? Alright, if you hadn't run off, and if you'd told the truth from the start when the West number 2 court people came to sort it out, then perhaps there'd have been some hope. But now, er, now that the matter's been referred here there's not much chance at all." . . .

> Rané stared at the magistrate without reacting: the effect these words had had upon him was not clear from the expression on his face. His forehead was soaked in sweat. Perhaps it was because he was straining hard to understand, or perhaps it was because each and every syllable had sunk deep into his heart and his tears could not find a way out of his dry eyes. His lips moved once or twice. Perhaps he was mouthing the words "circumstantial evidence." (D. Shreshṭha 1987, 8–9)

The names of characters in every Nepali story implicitly reveal the caste or ethnic group to which they belong and thereby indicate their status relative to other characters. Rather more explicit reference is made to rank and class: the fact that Goṭhālé's prostitute, Shobhā, is the daughter of a *subbā*, a government official, is of great relevance to his story. Many stories by Ramesh Bikal revolve around the differences between their principal characters' status and those of their oppressors.

The Gurkha Soldier

The Gurkha soldier, or *lāhure*, as he is called in Nepali, makes several appearances here. Bishweshwar Prasād Koirālā's "The Soldier" (*Sipāhī*, 1938?) is the most carefully considered portrait of a Gurkha soldier ever written in Nepali. The main characteristic Koirālā attributes to the soldier is his complete freedom from responsibility and social convention. This, Koirālā implies, is something to be envied. But is it to be admired?

Rāī's "The Murderer" (*Jyānamārā?*) is another portrayal of an ex-soldier that questions the motives and mentality of its central character. The basic idea behind Rāī's story seems to owe much to Pushkar Shamsher's "Pariband," which I have discussed previously. On the basis of circumstantial evidence, an ex-Gurkha is convicted of the murder of his young wife's lover. Here, the coincidence is between the word for "bear" (*bhālu*) and the name of the murderer's victim. Despite this rather clumsy device, the story has many interesting qualities: the old Gurkha's character is well portrayed, and the way in which he turns out to be the only man in the village who knows nothing about his young wife's affair is a comment on such marriages. But the most telling passage comes at the end of the story, when Ujīrmān, the central character, admits to the murder he has not committed: is it that he has a sense of guilt for his past as a soldier in a foreign army, or is it that he simply wishes that he had indeed killed the policeman?

Bishṭha's "The Āndhī Kholā" addresses the subject of Nepalis leaving their homeland to serve in foreign armies as Gurkhas. The Āndhī Kholā is a river valley in the Gurung region of central Nepal from which many Gurkhas emanate. Bishṭha's main intention is clearly to paint a touching picture of a faithful wife waiting for her husband to return, but he also touches on the motives such men have for joining foreign armies.

Nepali poets have on many occasions attacked the men who leave Nepal to serve in foreign armies, criticizing them for a lack of patriotism (Hutt 1989a). In the short story, however, the approach has been milder; the very nature of the genre means that it lends itself better to measured descriptions than to polemic.

The Rāṇā Regime

The century of Rāṇā rule is etched on the minds of Nepalis as a period during which Nepal's progress and development was deliberately retarded. It is remembered as a time of exploitation, censorship, and oppression, but there is also a kind of nostalgia for the ostentatious grandeur of the age. Several of Bhavānī Bhikshu's stories are set in this time: one, *Maiyāsāheb* (The Lady Maiyā, 1956), an exceedingly long-winded account of an affair between a Rāṇā princess and a commoner, is nevertheless interesting for the wealth of social detail it contains. This book contains two stories that reflect two different aspects of this period of Nepal's history. Bhikshu's "Māujang Bābusāheb's Coat" (*Māujang Bābusāhebko Koṭ*, 1960) is a masterly analysis of the attitudes and beliefs of a senior Rāṇā in the years after the fall of his family's regime, in which an old coat comes to symbolize the glories of his past.

During the latter years of the autocratic Rāṇā government, many intellectuals and activists spent periods in jail, including most of Nepal's leading writers. Bijay Malla's "The Prisoner and the Dove" (*Parevā ra Kaidī*, 1977) recounts a disturbing incident from prison life based on Malla's own experiences.

Views on Tourism

Finally, this anthology includes two stories that refer to the mass tourism that has become a mainstay of Nepal's economy since the late 1960s. Lāmichhāné's story "The Half-closed Eyes of the Buddha and the Slowly Setting Sun" (*Ardhamudit Nayan ra Ḍubna Lāgeko Ghām*, 1962) is regarded as a classic of modern Nepali literature. Since foreign tourists began to visit Nepal during the 1950s, the popular Western view of Nepal has been of an idyllic Shangri-la. This famous story is composed of two monologues. The first comes from a tourist who has achieved a long-held ambition to visit Nepal. He brings with him his notions of the culture and history of Nepal, acquired from books published in the West. Before dinner in his hotel, he treats his guide to a rapturous description of all he hopes to see. Next day, the guide shows the tourist an aspect of contemporary Nepal of which he is unaware by taking him to visit a farmer whose son is completely paralyzed.

Parashu Pradhān's "The Telegram on the Table" (*Tebalmāthiko Tyas Ākāshvāṇī*, 1975) has the tourist industry as its background. From Pradhān's description of Krishna, a tourist guide in Kathmandu, it is clear that he is one of a new generation of Nepalis who has been so influenced by Western culture and his contact with tourists that his only desire is to escape from his native environment. A telegram brings bad news and forces him to face up to reality.

The Nepali poet Lakshmīprasād Devkoṭā once wrote that the short story was like a glimpse of life seen through a small window, thus inspiring the title of an early anthology, *Jhyālbāṭa* (From a Window). It is true that the genre reflects and portrays various aspects of life in Nepal and the adjoining regions of Himalayan India; hitherto, the Nepali short story has lacked the sophistication of fiction in other more developed South Asian literatures, but this genre is rapidly gaining ground. The changes and developments that have taken place during the brief history of the short story in Nepali are an important barometer of the cultural and intellectual climate of these societies, and it is my hope that this brief glimpse of Nepali fiction will inspire further, more detailed studies. In the field of Nepali literature there is ample scope for this, especially as my discussions in these pages have barely touched upon the existence of a surprisingly rich dramatic tradition and a growing number of novels.

The following selection is presented in approximate order of first publication, and brief biographical notes are given for each author. In general I feel that the stories demonstrate the authors' standpoints themselves and that the need for detailed analyses of individual literary philosophies is less pressing here than in Part One. The publication dates of several stories have not been easy to ascertain because many are drawn from anthologies that do not provide such information. In such cases, I admit to having made educated guesses on the basis of their language and style and the birth dates of their authors.

Guruprasād Mainālī (1900–1971)

Mainālī was one of the first generation of writers to develop the modern short story in Nepali. Little detailed biographical information on him is available, but it is known that he was born in Kānpur village, Kabre Palanchok district, and spent most of his life in government service. Some sources suggest that he was a high court judge. Mainālī left his birthplace for a village near Nuwākoṭ when young and spent his last years in Khairhanī, near Chitwan. In the interim, he occupied a large house in the Thāmel quarter of Kathmandu.

Mainālī's first stories appeared in *Shāradā* between 1935 and 1938. Only eleven have been published in all, but each is now considered a classic. His most famous stories are "The Ward" (*Nāso*), in which an elderly Brāhmaṇ who is without children is obliged to take a second wife in order to clear his way to paradise (translated in Riccardi 1988); "A Blaze in the Straw" (*Parālko Āgo*), translated here; and "The Martyr" (*Shahīd*), a story about a man who lays down his life in the struggle against the Rāṇās. All of Mainālī's stories were published in a collection entitled *Nāso* in 1969.

A BLAZE IN THE STRAW (*PARĀLKO ĀGO*)

Chāmé's wife Gaunthalī had a very sharp tongue. Even when he was civil to her, she'd invariably slant the issue and bring up something to fight about. Every few days man and wife would quarrel.

One evening, Chāmé came home from his ploughing to find that Gaunthalī had locked up the house and gone to the village to watch a wedding. After a whole day of ploughing, he was tired and hungry. Just as he was putting away the yoke and plough and tying up the ox, Gaunthalī came down the hill. When he saw her, Chāmé flared up in anger. The fire hadn't even been lit yet, let alone a meal prepared! Hurriedly, Gaunthalī unbolted the door and rushed off to fetch water. Chāmé kindled a fire in the hearth and filled his pipe with tobacco.

He sat smoking on the doorstep like a gathering storm cloud. Gaunthalī came back carrying the waterpot on her hip. She was just about to enter the house when Chāmé said, "This old widow's spent the whole day making eyes at the men, and still she's putting on airs!" and he gave her a kick. Gaunthalī staggered and fell in the doorway. The pot smashed, splashing water across the threshold. She was picking up the pieces and throwing them out into the yard when Chāmé yelled, "Don't stay another second in my house! Get out and go where you will!" and he dragged her out by her pigtail and threw her into the yard.

Gaunthalī had been a little to blame, and so she held her peace even when he kicked her. But when he grabbed her by her hair and threw her out, she let fly, "Take your leprous hands off me! My wretched parents in their stupidity have handed me over to a butcher! It would be better to drown than to be the wife of such a destitute corpse!"[1]

"This old widow must think her father's very rich! If he didn't do the ploughing for all the other villagers, he'd never get a bite to eat! And then she brags about her family!" and he kicked her again. Gaunthalī wailed at the top of her voice.

All the village children had come up onto the embankment to see the show. "Hey, you corpses, what show is going on here for you all to come and watch?" Chāmé picked up a stick and chased after them, but the children ran up the hill, laughing.

Gaunthalī was weeping, but Chāmé just spread out a rush mat and went to sleep on the verandah.

The next morning, Chāmé took the ploughing ox off to the paddy field with an empty stomach. When he came home in the evening, Gaunthalī had gone. The neighbors told him that she had packed up her clothes and gone off to her parents' home.

The buffalo was still in the yard and when it saw Chāmé it bellowed. He gave it fodder and untied the calf; then he fetched a pail and sat down to milk it. First, it gave a few measures of milk, but then it kicked Chāmé and skipped away. Chāmé fell backward into some dung and the pail fell three feet away. His trousers and waistcoat were covered with dung. On the wall there was a stout stick, which he snatched up in his hand, but after a couple of blows from that, the buffalo broke its tether and leapt off into Kokalé's maize field. Chāmé tried to tempt it away,

1. Nepali is rich in terms of personal abuse, as is evident from this story and several others in this selection. Maināli's favorites seem to have been "leper," "corpse," "butcher" (*kasāī*), *poḍé* (a low, ritually unclean caste of Newār), "widow," and "serf" (*bajiyā*).

but the buffalo jumped from one side to the other in terror. Soon the newly hoed maize field was flattened to straw. Kokalé's mother cursed Chāmé from the courtyard wall,

"Chāmé, may you become a barren corpse! A corpse that not even cholera can carry off! Yesterday you beat your wife, and today you beat your buffalo and destroy somebody else's income for the year! I've never seen such a temper! Look at this wretched serf's bravery! Last year, Dhanvīré laid you flat on your back with just one blow, and there you lay for a whole year, saying how brave you were! It may be alright to wallop a stranger, but why beat your wife or a dumb animal tied to a post? As soon as the evening comes around, you're causing some trouble or other, and the whole village is in an uproar!"

There was a wedding feast at Dhanvīré's house. All the village youths were blind drunk on the beer. Kokalé had dressed himself up in women's clothing, and he was beating a drum and dancing.[2] All the others had joined in with him, singing and clapping their hands. Just then, his sister arrived and told him about his maize field.

Kokalé ran off to the maize field in his petticoat. When the buffalo saw his attire, it stuck its tail in the air and leaped around even more. Kokalé was furious when he saw the flattened maize; the few remaining heads were just being crushed as he slapped Chāmé twice across the face. Poor Chāmé said nothing. Eventually it took four or five men half the night to chase the buffalo away.

Next morning, Chāmé was on his way back from the spring with the water pot on his shoulder when Juṭhé the tailor's[3] wife came down the hill. Juṭhé the tailor and Chāmé were the best of friends. He called Juṭhé's wife "sister-in-law." When she saw Chāmé carrying water, she said, "Oh, how bad it looks when a man fetches water!"

"Well, what choice do I have? I packed the wretch off to her mother's, so if I don't do it, who will?"

"If you beat her blindly, what choice did *she* have?"

"She's got a tongue like a razor. What can I do but beat her?"

"It's true, she is a bit cheeky, but just a mild beating would be enough."

"Oh, be quiet! I remember Juṭhé giving you a proper thrashing last Dasain! Well, did you answer him back?"

"Oh! Beat me once, you say! We're devoted now, but there was a time when never a day would go by without a thrashing! In the evenings he'd come back from the Tibetan village where he'd been drinking beer and beat me on some pretext or another . . . and then on festival days. . . .

2. For men to dress up and dance in women's clothing (to become a *mārunī*) is fairly common practice at village celebrations.

3. Juṭhé is a member of the lowly tailor caste (*damai*).

After a few rainy days my body still aches from it! But even after all these years I don't think I've ever answered him back."

"That's all very well. Do you mean that *I* made her cheeky by beating her? If she'd been as even-tempered as you, I'd have kept and cherished her as if she was a goddess!"

"That's as may be, but no woman need stick with a fool. How much longer are you going to keep on fetching your own water? Go tomorrow and bring her back."

"If she comes to her senses, well, the house is still here for her. But I'd sooner be a *poḍé* than go and get her!"

With his waistcoat over his half-sleeved shirt and lopsided Nepalese trousers, with his black cap gleaming with dirt and a vermilion *ṭīkā*[4] between his eyebrows, with his waterpot on his shoulder and his moustache set firm, Chāmé cut a dark and grimy figure.

One morning, Chāmé was sitting on his verandah smoking from the bamboo hookah when down the hill came Juṭhé the tailor. First came Juṭhé, carrying his son. Behind him came his wife with a small bundle of clothes tucked under her arm. When he saw Chāmé, Juṭhé laughed and called out.

"How are things, my lad?"

"Oh, not so bad, my brother!"

"You've sent your wife packing; now sit and enjoy yourself!"

Juṭhé and his wife had a very loving relationship. Whenever he went down to the village to do his sewing, Juṭhé would take his wife along. On their way, man and wife would discuss the joys and sorrows of the household, and then they'd chat on the way back, too. In the evening, Juṭhé would set the lamp up on its shelf and read some verses from the Virāṭaparva.[5] His wife would listen as she washed up the pots. If Juṭhé ever fell ill, his wife would seek out the shamans and healers in the village. Sometimes, on their way to do some tailoring for the Bishṭas,[6] Juṭhé would joke with his wife or stretch his neck and roll his eyes at other passers-by. His wife would giggle and turn aside, saying, "You may be getting old now, but you still know how to joke!"

Juṭhé was very religious, too. First thing in the morning, he'd bathe in the spring. Then he would anoint himself with ceremonial ashes by the place where the women dried their clothes and read out a verse such

4. A *ṭīkā* is a spot of paste applied to the forehead for religious or cosmetic purposes.
5. The Virāṭaparva is part of the great Hindu epic, the Mahābhārata.
6. Bishṭa is a Brāhmaṇ family name.

as, "Taking a form like that of the lightning, he flew in a flash to the sky."[7]

Chāmé was sad as he compared Juṭhé's home life to his own. At Juṭhé's house they would have finished their evening meal and would be reading from the Virāṭaparva, but at his house there would be shouting and yelling. Juṭhé and his wife had such affection for one another. They walked along, chatting about all sorts of things. But Chāmé's wife had quarrelled with him and run off home. It was a long time since their wedding, but he'd never known her to have had a pleasant word to say to him. And now his one and only buffalo wouldn't let him go near it. Off she'd gone to her mother's, leaving even the buffalo accustomed to only one person's hand! And then the buffalo had caused him to get his face slapped by Kokalé! He'd push the damned creature over a cliff if it wasn't for the moneylender, who'd come chasing him. If he didn't do the chores, he'd go hungry. It would have been better to have smothered himself in ashes and wandered off as a mendicant than to pass such a rotten life! But what would he do as a *jogī*? You have to go from house to house without making the dogs bark, or else you don't get fed! Anyway, people nowadays would just ridicule a sleek, fat, turbanned *jogī*, they'd say, "He's only become a *jogī* because it was too much trouble for him to hoe his fields!"[8]

Living in the wayside inns would be fine . . . unless he fell ill, in which case there would be no one to offer him even a drop of water! Whether people call out "Hail Nārāyaṇ!"[9] or not, the *jogī* calls it out himself and wanders from barnyard to barnyard in his ashes. This just seems a little cooler to a man who is being burned by the heat of worldly affairs when he views it from a distance!

During the first week after his wife's departure, Chāmé would snap at the very mention of her name. But as time went by, life began to seem empty. He thought to himself, "She may have been cheeky, but she was a lively girl. When she put her mind to it, she'd gather enough fodder to fill the buffalo to the brim. Every morning and evening she'd cook me something, but now that she's gone I've only cooked once or twice. Otherwise, I just get by on roasted barley. When she was here the buffalo gave milk regularly. She milked it herself. But now it's wary and timid. Everyone's telling me to go and fetch her. Juṭhé's wife says the same.

7. This verse is from the Nepali Rāmāyaṇa.

8. A *jogī* (or yogī) is a man who has renounced the world and all worldly possessions and travels from one pilgrimage site to another, living on alms.

9. Nārāyaṇ is a name for the god Vishnu.

She may or may not come of her own accord; but I'll have to go and get her some day."

The next day, after his morning meal, he prepared to go to his in-laws'. He took out his best clothes and put them on. Then he saw that Gaunthalī must have put some tobacco on top of his hat, for there was a stain there, and it was all split and torn, too! Chāmé was irate.

"Just look at the way that old widow carries on!" he fumed. "See how she treats the things she receives! It's high time she learned some manners! Perhaps if her father or grandfather had worn proper felt hats she'd have learnt, but her father walks about in a homespun hat and a nettle cloth cloak, so how could his daughter have been brought up properly? 'A Brāhmaṇ who has never eaten a mushroom can never know its flavor.' "[10]

He quickly brushed off his hat and set it on his head. He had no other waistcoat, so he put the same one on. He slung his cloak in a bundle across his back and set off with a ragged umbrella in his hand.

Pausing at a *chautārā*[11] near his in-laws' house, Chāmé wiped the sweat from his brow. The sound of Gaunthalī singing came to him from the edge of the forest above the village. She was resting there before carrying down a bundle of grass: "I would fly away, but I am no bird, I cannot bear to stay."

Chāmé gritted his teeth, "My buffalo can't get enough to eat, and its stomach rumbles and twangs like a village singer's violin! And here she is making the forest resound!"

After a short rest, Chāmé went slowly on up the hill. As he drew near an itching tree,[12] he began to drag his feet. He wondered what his in-laws were going to say. Slowly, he approached the gate. There he saw his mother-in-law beside the midden heap, scouring a pan. His father-in-law sat smoking on the verandah. Chāmé put his hands together and bowed in greeting to his mother-in-law, and she returned his salutation with her filthy hands. Then he went up to the verandah where his father-in-law handed him the hookah and bent down to touch his feet in respect. But Chāmé brought his knees together to prevent him.

Soon Gaunthalī arrived with her bundle of cut grass, wearing a fine bodice and a chintz skirt gathered up to her waist. On her arms there were bangles, and around her neck there was a necklace of coral; her bosom was full and a large vermilion ṭīkā enhanced her forehead. She wore a rhododendron flower in her hair, and she looked dusky and

10. This proverb refers to the fact that some highly orthodox Brāhmaṇs refrain from eating mushrooms.

11. A *chautārā* is a brick platform built around the base of a shady tree, where foot travelers may pause and rest by the wayside.

12. In Nepali, *chilāuné*.

beautiful. Chāmé was most gratified to see her; it seemed as if the goddess Lakshmī had entered the house in person![13]

After dusk had fallen, Gaunthalī came and touched Chāmé's feet in greeting. Chāmé was overjoyed. He felt like gathering her up and kissing her a thousand times, but she pushed his arms away and walked back into the house.

After the evening meal a quilt was spread out on the verandah for Chāmé. He lay down, but he wasn't in the least bit sleepy. He just lay there waiting for Gaunthalī to come. The meal was over; the pots had been washed. Then someone went upstairs carrying a lamp. Suddenly, the door was shut and bolted. Chāmé was stunned.

"Oh, why did I beat poor Gaunthalī that day? Women love to watch weddings. And she's a young woman, so if she goes off to watch a while, what of it? Should someone who can't put up with that punish his wife for it? To beat your wife for being late cooking the meal: what could be a more despicable act than that? Alright, beat her a little if she's cheeky. But if she comes home I certainly won't do it again. Just see if I don't respect her even more than brother Juṭhé respects his wife."

In his mind there was such turmoil. From beneath, the fleas were biting so hard!

In the morning he heard a door opening. Chāmé pricked up his ears: had Gaunthalī come? But then he saw his old father-in-law; he had come out to urinate in the drain. Chāmé hadn't had a wink of sleep all night.

It was time to let the animals out. Father-in-law sat on the wall and smoked, mother-in-law husked maize on the verandah, and Gaunthalī washed pots on the kitchen floor. A little bashfully, Chāmé said to his father-in-law,

"It's time to set to work in the fields, time to send your daughter home."

Father-in-law coughed and rested his cheek on the tube of the hookah. "I hear you called us poor and beggarly and all sorts of names," he said. "We may be poor, but we've never been beggars! We paid you our respect and gave her over to you. You persuade your wife yourself. Take her home; no one's stopping you!"

Chāmé was crestfallen. Soon Gaunthalī had finished her kitchen chores and was about to leave for the forest with her basket, but Chāmé caught her by the arm.

"Where are you off to with that basket? Come on, let's go home!"

"I'd rather die than go home with you!"

13. Lakshmī is the Hindu goddess of wealth and material good fortune.

"Where will you go if you don't come home?"
"Who cares? I'll go where I like. I'm a *joginī* now!"[14]
"Who'll feed the buffalo if you're a *joginī*?"
"Oh, cut your own grass and feed your own buffalo!"
"Now, don't be cross; just come quietly, won't you?"
"What? Just to quarrel and get thrashed?"
"I'm damned if I'll ever do that again!"
"Right, that's settled."

Soon Gaunthalī had dressed, gathered all of her belongings, prettied herself, and was ready to go. Her mother set a small parcel and a jar of curd before her. Gaunthalī picked up the parcel and went on ahead. Chāmé came along behind, swinging the jar from his hand. On the way they began to talk,

"How much milk does the buffalo give these days?"
"A *pāthī* a day."[15]
Gaunthalī pouted in derision.

The sun was setting behind the hills. Cowherds were driving their cows home in a cloud of dust, moving slowly up the slope. Chāmé and Gaunthalī came to the spring. There they saw Juṭhé's wife coming down the hill carrying a water pot in a blanket. When she saw Chāmé, she stuck out her tongue. Then she laughed and said, "Oh, it looks like a goose and gander with the bride out in front and the groom behind!"

"Don't laugh, my sister, there may be another quarrel some day—you never can tell!" said Gaunthalī with a smile.

"Oh, it won't be long before you quarrel again! But a squabble between a man and his wife is just a blaze in the straw!"

(from *Kathā Kusum* [1938] 1981; also included in *Nepālī Kathā Sangraha* [1973] 1988, vol. 2)

14. A *joginī* is a female *jogī*.
15. Please refer to the Glossary for details of Nepali currency, weights, and measures.

Bishweshwar Prasād Koirālā (1915–1982)

Better known in Nepal as "B. P.," the leader of the Nepali Congress Party that ousted the Rāṇās, Koirālā became Nepal's first elected prime minister in 1959. Before this, however, he had already become quite well known for his writing, which he began while studying law in Darjeeling during the 1930s.

Koirālā's first story, "Chandrabadan" (A Face Like the Moon), appeared in *Shāradā* in 1935, and three further stories were included in the seminal *Kathā-Kusum* anthology in 1938. The most common theme of his stories and novels (of which Koirālā published four) was the relationship between men and women, but a significant number of stories also dealt with social issues. The subject of politics, which dominated Koirālā's life, is conspicuous by its absence in his writings. Most of his stories are brief but exceptionally effective. Koirālā's stories are available in *Doshī Chashmā* (Faulty Glasses, 1949).

THE SOLDIER (*SIPĀHĪ*)

It is hard to travel alone in the hills. I had to walk for two or three days, but I met up with a soldier on the way who made the journey pass easily.

First he asked me, "Hey, young man, where are you headed?" shouting rudely at me from behind in a familiar tone. I turned to look back and saw a soldier in uniform coming up quickly with short, fast strides. I remembered the many things I had heard about the rough, cruel nature of military men and so I simply replied, "Ilām,"[1] in the hope that

1. Ilam is a district in the extreme east of Nepal, next to the Indian border.

this would shake him off. But by then he had already caught up with me.

"Aha!" he said casually, and as he grinned a gold tooth glittered, "I'm on my way there too. Now we shall keep each other company all day, shall we not, my brother?"

He wore a black coat, an army cap, and khaki trousers. In his coat pocket there glittered the clip of a cheap fountain pen. A Queen Anne watch was strapped to his wrist and was visible whenever he lifted his arm—he had a habit of raising his hands as he spoke. Around his throat he had tied a large red kerchief.

"I'm a soldier, but you, if the Lord does not deceive me, must be a student. Am I right?"

I smiled and confirmed that this was true.

"I can always tell who a person is, and what he does, from the clothes he wears and the way he speaks. I swear I've never been mistaken, at least in this. I can't really read or write. Well, I can sign my name each month and get through the Rāmāyaṇa:[2] that much I've learned in the barracks. But if I'd studied any harder I'd have turned out thin and pale, like you!"

I began to enjoy his talk. He spoke with familiarity to everyone we met on the path, saying, "Where are *you* off to then?"

People were nervous of his military appearance and gave him no reply. On encountering an older woman, he would address her as "mother-in-law" and enquire after the well-being of her daughters: "How is your little girl? Tell me won't you, oh mother-in-law of whom I'm so fond?"

He had no wish to know about me. He didn't have enough time to tell me everything about himself, so how could he even inquire?

"I'm stationed at Quetta.[3] I've been there a long time. I do have a wife, but she's back here in the hills, and she's sickly and good for nothing. But we've had two children, all the same. I haven't been home for ages, and I don't even want to go either. She'll have gone off with someone else by now, and my sons will have turned into rogues. Well, the little one seemed bright enough and I really hoped to educate him. But who could be bothered? My father didn't educate me, and I'm quite content. I found myself a wife in Quetta, too. Wherever you go you should have what you want."

I was really enjoying listening to the soldier because he spoke openly and concealed nothing from me. What was there for him to hide, any-

2. This reference is probably to the ever-popular Nepali Rāmāyaṇa, written in the nineteenth century by Bhānubhakta Āchārya; "get through the Rāmāyaṇa" is a translation of "*rāmāyaṇasamma bānchchu*—"I survive as far the Rāmāyaṇa." It is not clear whether the soldier is claiming to be able to read the text or just recite from it.

3. Quetta is a large town, now in the southwestern Pakistani province of Baluchistan.

way? Like the serious student I was, I asked, "But what is life in the army like for you people?"

"What's that you say? I swear to you, you know, we don't have the problems you have. Even our officer tells us to enjoy ourselves; he was the one who gave me leave to come here. Recently, there's been talk of war, and so I've come to train new recruits. I've already caught six, and that's the truth. If you become a soldier, you get to rinse out your mouth with milk. You get to keep the goat's horns as your trophy. I'm hardly trapping them; I'm doing them a favor. Our country's in need of soldiers." He puffed out cigarette smoke. "If you die in battle, you go straight to Heaven." His face was as grave as that of a man reciting from the scriptures.

The journey was passing by easily because of his interesting talk. Some girls were on their way home from cutting fodder, and they were coming toward us. The soldier winked and said, "Wait now, I'll tease them." He went ahead and greeted them and then said something to them that I couldn't hear. They all clucked their tongues in disgust and hurried away, but one threw her load of grass down onto the ground right there. With her hands on her hips and her whole body shaking, she cursed him roundly and showed him her teeth. My soldier friend laughed, clutching his stomach, and turned to me and declared, "What a fearsome woman! I'm sure she curses her husband like this. I'd swear to it, you know!"

So we walked on together. "It's very hard to understand these girls. Once, one of them got me in her clutches. Yes. . . ," he sighed. Then he looked as stern as a stone statue, and his legs moved like automatic machines. Straight up ahead, the yellow sun was sinking behind a hill. With great curiosity, I asked, "Well, what happened?"

"Yes, as I was saying. I, too, loved a girl once; I don't know how it happened. I had spent a lot of time laughing and playing with her and then one day, a Sunday, I found myself beginning to love her. That day was my day off, and as soon as it got dark I hurried to her house." He began to pant. "That day, she was wearing a blue gown, the wretch. She looked very pretty that day."

Just then we began to climb steeply. "Wait, I'll go and buy a couple of sugarcanes. Going uphill is easier if you've a stick to lean on, and when you get to the top you can suck it and it refreshes you. Isn't that a good idea?" He went off and returned with two sugarcanes. Giving one to me, he went on talking, "But that girl really deceived me. She went off with a captain. Her pretty clothes attracted him, but I assure you she won't stick with that old captain. She enjoys flitting around, that pretty girl." A light breeze swept his last sentence away.

I was pondering over this and I made no comment. Seeing me quiet, he laughed, "I bet you a bottle of *raksī* you're thinking about your wife.[4] Aren't you now? Tell me the truth! . . ."

I didn't answer him. Then after a while, I said, "Tell me, brother soldier, how do you go into battle? All the bombs, bullets, death—I can't even imagine such a dreadful thing."

He laughed scornfully and slapped me on the shoulder, "It's no place for a soft man like you. But I swear to you, I enjoy myself in battle."

Talking like this, we came to a place where we could spend the night. There were still two hours of daylight left, but the hills to the west had already covered the sun, and darkness was falling quickly to the sound of cascading waters.

"Now I can't go on," I said. "It's time to look for somewhere to stay."

"Don't worry about that. I know every stone here; it's where my forefathers came from. Come, I'll take you to a shop; I know the old woman who owns it. There was a time when men sat all around her, my father among them. Her shop did very well then. But nowadays no one even casts her a glance from a blind eye. I swear to you, if it wasn't for her daughter, I wouldn't go there now either."

As he spoke we came to the shop. It was old and built of timber that had rotted in the rains. The front of the building had subsided, and so people had to stoop down before they could enter.

We went inside. The smoke that filled the room made the pale light of a solitary oil lamp even dimmer. And because my eyes were heavy with fatigue, the scene inside seemed almost unreal. Two hillsmen were drinking tea and eating pieces of stale old bread. They talked loudly and slapped the table from time to time. I saw a fire burning in one corner, with a teakettle placed above it: this was the cause of the smoke. To one side, there was an odd, shelved cupboard with a broken glass front. Inside it I could see an old Lily biscuit tin, an empty box that had contained orange pekoe tea, and a few glasses. A fat old woman sat with her elbows on the table, listening intently to the men's conversation. Occasionally, she would say a few words, and from time to time she laughed out loud.

The soldier entered the room ahead of me, and as soon as she saw him the woman stood up. Looking him up and down, she said, "Hey, what are *you* doing here? Have you lost your way?"

"No, I'm not lost! Where's that daughter of yours?" Waving his hands, he began to pace up and down as if he owned the place.

"She's out, but she's due home soon. I thought you had forgotten us."

At that moment, a plumpish young woman came into the room and

4. *Raksī* is the ubiquitous liquor of the Nepalese hills. It is distilled from barley, millet, rice, and almost anything else.

said carelessly, "Let him forget! Why should anyone spare a thought for us?" She wore a dirty print skirt and the black smudge of her cheeks was visible, even through the gloom. Above her skirt, a piece of dirty cloth was tied around her waist. She was not especially pretty, but no doubt she had the natural attractiveness of youth.

When he saw her, the soldier skipped over to her. "Oh, you won't believe me, but it's you that draws me back here again. Who could possibly forget you? As soon as I arrived, I asked your mother about you. And then you turned up in person. Tell me, what oath should I swear?"

"Enough, enough! Don't say anything more. You say a lot of things when you're in my sight, but afterward . . ." She went into another small room and the soldier hurried after her. Inside that room, she lit a lamp and lay down on a mat. The soldier sat down in the doorway and began to talk.

"Tell me then," she said, "what have you brought for me?"

I was feeling drowsy, so I paid little attention to their conversation. But they were still talking much later on, even when everyone else had eaten and gone to bed. The woman told him to bring her a framed Indian mirror when he returned next time. The soldier replied that he wouldn't just bring her a mirror but a dress as well, made from twenty hands of printed cotton. I was tired and I quickly fell fast asleep.

Early the next morning, the soldier shook me awake. There were still two hours to go before sunrise, and it was very cold outside. A chilly wind blew down between the ranges, and the sound of the river nearby was loud. No one else was up, and the cocks had just begun to crow. The hills all around were dark and silent and treeless because it became very cold in that place. I got up, rubbing my eyes.

"Little master," said the soldier, "I bid you farewell. We go different ways from here." He shook me by the shoulders until they hurt. I felt quite sorry; I had begun to grow fond of him, but he cared for no one. He strode off down his path, I stood there watching him go.

Many times I have seen stone memorials to soldiers killed in battle. But this was the only chance I ever had to meet a soldier in the flesh.

(from B. Koirālā [1949] 1968; also included in *Kathā Kusum* [1938] 1981)

TO THE LOWLANDS (*MADHESTIRA*)

Morning came to the confluence of the Sunkosī and Tāmākosī rivers.[5] The Sunkosī came down from the north in a rushing torrent and mixed

5. These two rivers in eastern Nepal meet in the Janakpur zone near the southern margin of the hill country.

into the Tāmākosī, which flowed from the east. There could be few men capable of fording the Sunkosī, but anyone with a strong pair of legs could cross the Tāmākosī. No greenery grew on either bank of these two rivers; the trees and shrubs seemed to stand back in awe.

The earth's crust seemed to burst open at the touch of the sun's first rays. Four or five people rose from where they had been sleeping, curled up on the ground. Each asked the same question as he awoke: what were they going to eat? They turned to one another as if reading each other's minds. The widow was looking at Goré, but she addressed them all, "Well, what food did you bring when you set out? Did you think about what you would eat?"

Her words surprised them all. "*I* don't even have a *house* to live in!" said Bhoṭé.[6]

"I did once," said Buḍho. "Now I have nothing. But child, if you do have somewhere to live, what are you doing here?"

I might call these four homeless people beggars or coolies. When they found work, they were coolies; when they did not, they were beggars. But the widow in their midst, a woman who had her own home, was a swan among a flock of crows. Like the goddess Annapūrṇa, she pulled out some *chiurā* from her bundle.[7] She shared it out between them and gave them each a lump of sugar, too. Their eyes all brightened and they felt great respect for her. She added to Goré's share from her own.

"You're young; you must be hungrier than the others," she said. "I'm on my way to the lowlands. I have no husband. My in-laws are not blind. My brother-in-law was disrespectful. I couldn't stay in that house with no husband."

This statement had a profound effect on the others. It was no mean thing for a woman to abandon a place where food was freely available just because she had lost her husband. Their respect for the widow increased.

"Where are you all going?" she inquired. "I didn't see you eat anything last night. You all went to sleep just like that. I had no companion, so I slept nearby. All night long I felt fond of you."

Bhoṭé was greatly surprised. "Why should you feel fond of us? We're not your husband, your sons, your father."

"But you are people, nonetheless," said the widow.

The rice had gone into stomachs that had been empty all the previous day. Enlivened, they began to talk loudly and excitedly.

6. The characters of this story are named Goré, "the fair one"; Bhoṭé, "the Tibetan"; Buḍho, "the old man"; and Dhané, "the rich one."

7. Annapūrṇa is a goddess of plenty who brings good harvests. *Chiurā* is parched rice, a common staple among the poorer people of Nepal.

"Young lady, we four are not related to each other," said Buḍho. "But we are all homeless. There's no work here anymore. We're off to look for work somewhere. From what you say, it seems we should head for the lowlands. What do you say, my friends? Shall we go there? In the lowlands you can eat your fill. I once carried a load down there."

They all decided to go to the plains. Four men and a woman took the road for the south. Buḍho told them about his past. Once, he earned a lot of money, farming 17 *ropanī*.[8] Then everything had just gone wrong. He had been young then, and so he had been able to take the browband onto his head and make a living as a porter. But now there wasn't even that to resort to. Or else why would an old man like him be wandering around feeling hungry? It was time for him to die now. But the pangs of hunger forced him to move from place to place.

"I want to set up a lovely home in the lowlands," said the widow. "I'll take up farming. They say it's easy there. They say you can get land just like that. I couldn't stand any more of my in-laws' complaints. And the place where my husband died filled me with dread."

Bhoṭé and Dhané listened with interest but said nothing themselves. Goré seemed weary; he trailed behind, dragging his feet. The widow stopped to wait for him. When she stopped, everyone else stopped, too.

"Are you feeling tired, Goré?" she asked as he approached. "The sun is hot. Here, put this on your head." She took off the white cloth she wore on her head and put it onto Goré's. Then they all went on. Buḍho was old in name only; he strode out ahead of everyone else. Bhoṭé and Dhané walked beside him, listening to his tales. Noting their interest, Buḍho became bolder and began to mix fact with fiction. Bhoṭé and Dhané listened in awe.

Goré and the widow came slowly up behind. Goré was about twenty-five, the widow about thirty. Goré was shy and taciturn. His eyes were dull and his cheeks sunken from many long days of arduous labor.

"What will you do in the lowlands?" the widow asked him.

"Who knows?" replied Goré.

"Won't you settle down? Don't you fancy farming?"

"What about money?" said Goré.

"It's easy to farm in the lowlands. You get the fields for nothing there. How old are you, after all? Settle down in a home of your own! Look after a wife; bring up children! How much longer can you go on like this?"

Abruptly, she suddenly asked him, "Don't you like women, then?"

He looked up sharply, "Why shouldn't I like women?"

8. A *ropanī* is an extremely small area of land: about 5,000 square feet.

"In the lowlands, I shall set up home and grow some crops," she began. "But a home's not a home without a man. So I just thought—why don't you and I set up house together?"

Goré looked at the widow in astonishment, and she was rather taken aback.

"Am I not good enough for you? So what if I'm old? My longing is like a flame in my heart. Won't I ever have children? Won't I ever have sons and daughters, a home of my own, a man of my own?"

The widow was on the verge of tears. She blushed, hung her head, and walked on in silence. For a long time they walked without saying anything. But as the evening drew in she broke the silence.

"Goré, I have a little jewelry. Some money, too. We could buy some land. I could make a home. If you were mine, it would all be yours."

A little further on, the three others were sitting on a large boulder, waiting for them. Buḍho saw them in the distance and he called out, "Shall we stop here? What is there to eat?"

All eyes were on the widow. "There's a little *chiurā* left," she said. "Not enough to fill us up, but it will keep us going."

They sat down to eat; then they slept right there, curled up by the wayside with the sky as their roof. After walking all day, they were asleep as soon as they lay down.

Buḍho got up with the first morning sunbeams and began to hack and cough. They all got up, but there was no sign of Goré. The widow was anxious. "Where's Goré?" she asked.

"Oh, he must have wandered off somewhere," said Buḍho calmly. "Now we must get going. There's nothing to eat. We must get there by dusk. There may be some way of getting food there."

The widow's heart was heavy. She was surprised by her companions' lack of concern. Were they not even the slightest bit saddened by the disappearance of someone who had been their comrade through such hard times? She began to collect her belongings, and then her heart came into her mouth—the bag of jewels was gone!

They were all ready to set off, but the widow just sat there going through her bags and bundles.

"What are you doing?" asked Buḍho. "Let's be off! We must be there before nightfall, or we'll have to sleep hungry again."

"My jewels have gone!" sobbed the widow.

They stared at her in amazement. "Where were you off to, carrying jewels?" Buḍho exclaimed. "Goré must have taken them. So they're stolen now, and I'm not surprised. No point crying about it!"

The widow was angry. "Shut up, Buḍho," she shouted. "I'd thought it all out, what I'd do with those jewels. I was going to buy some land, get married again, set up home, have a son. . . . Now my hopes are all destroyed." She wept and wailed loudly.

Buḍho patted her on the shoulder. "Why are you weeping, child? What's stolen is stolen. Something will turn up in the lowlands. You'll find a husband. A home as well—don't fret. Come on, let's be on our way."

The widow stood up, staring blankly, and fell in behind Buḍho.

Up on the top of a distant hill, Buḍho was full of excitement. He pointed down to the wide green plain in the south that stretched as far as the eye could see. "There it is," he said. "The lowlands! There's our salvation! There we will eat our fill!"

Dhané's and Bhoṭé's eyes flickered with joy. Even into their cheeks, withered by hunger, there came a flush of happiness. They grinned and grinned all over their faces. But the widow was indifferent. She was in the twilight of her youth now. She had hoped that her jewels and her money would attract a young man to her, a man she could make her own. She had longed to fulfill the dream of her youth: her own little home, sons and daughters. It had all collapsed like a house of cards. She imitated her companions and gazed with joyless eyes down to the plains in the south.

(first published in *Khojī*, a Darjeeling magazine, sometime after 1938; from B. Koirālā [1949] 1968; also included in *Sājhā Kathā* [1968] 1979)

Bhavānī Bhikshu (1914–1981)

Bhikshu was born at Taulīhavā village in the Kapilvastu district of the Tarāī, but he spent much of his life in Kathmandu. He made his first appearance in Nepali literature with an essay on criticism, originally written in Hindi, that was translated into Nepali and published in *Shāradā* in 1936. His first story, "Mankind" (*Mānav*), was published two years later, and he soon established a reputation as a poet. Bhikshu edited *Shāradā* for several years after 1940, when the former editor, the poet Siddhicharaṇ Shreshṭha, was jailed for his political opinions, and Bhikshu worked for the Royal Nepal Academy after its foundation in 1957. Bhikshu's life was not without its sadnesses: he had lost two wives, one of whom deserted him, by 1952. This might account for the innate pathos of many of his stories and for his long ruminations on the nature of love.

Bhikshu's mother tongue was not Nepali but Awadhi, a dialect of Hindi, and he received his basic education in Hindi at Indore. His writings in Nepali are often criticized because his prose lacks the spontaneity of a mother-tongue writer, his sentences are sometimes awkwardly constructed, and his vocabulary tends to be somewhat grandiose. Nevertheless, his stories are regarded highly for their thoughtfulness and subtlety. Most have women as their central characters, and Nepali critics heap praise on Bhikshu for his analyses of female psychology. I suggest that Bhikshu's most interesting stories are those such as "Winning and Losing" (*Hārjīt*) that describe village life in the Tarāī and those that deal with topics from the Rāṇā period. Bhikshu also authored two novels. Bhikshu's stories are available in four collections: *Gunakesharī* (1953), *Maiyāsāheb* (1960) (both named after the principal female characters of particular stories), *Āvarta* (Whirlpool, 1967), and *Avāntara* (In the Middle, 1977).

WILL HE EVER RETURN? (*TYO PHERI PHARKALĀ?*)

The narrow hill path was a difficult, strenuous, arduous trail that climbed higher and higher by degrees. Looking along it into the far distance, you could see nothing to make you think that you had seen a man.

The sun god[1] had hidden his face behind the mountains in the west, but his blush spread up to the dark hills' summits. The streams still sang their continual song, uninterested in and indifferent to the anxieties of the world. The dim half-light was meandering into darkness.

A traveler was on his way up from the plains. As Sānī[2] stood in the doorway of her house, one foot upon the staircase of maturity, he asked her, "Can I get lodgings here tonight?"

"I don't know; you'll have to ask Mother."

"Mother? I don't know who your mother is or where to find her. Show me whom to ask."

"Mother! Mother!" a sharp sweet voice from a shapely throat echoed around the hills, but nobody came in response. She waited for a moment; then she said, "Wait, I'll fetch her," and she went off. After a while she returned with an elderly woman.

"Here, this is my mother. Where are your porters?"

"I've only one porter, and he's old and slow. That's why I have to stop here, though I'd hoped to reach Chitlāng today. I know some of the shopkeepers there; I'd have found good lodgings. This is a liquor shop, isn't it?"

"It is. . . ," the old woman replied with a mixture of surprise and disdain.

"So what if it is?" Sānī said quickly. "It would be the same at Chitlāng, you know. And our side room is clean."

"Well," asked the old woman, "will you have a drink and something to eat?"

"I'll have a meal, but I won't take any drink. I have my own pots and utensils with me."[3]

Sānī leaned over and put her face close to her mother's. "Why mother, he'll buy rice, lentils, oil and firewood, salt, spice, vegetables. . . . If he cooks in the next room and sleeps in the side room, that will be fine."

1. The sun is identified with the Hindu deity Sūrya, or Sūrje.

2. Sānī is a pet name meaning "little girl."

3. The traveler's caste status is apparently too high for him to accept food from anyone but a Brāhmaṇ.

"May I see the room? Just to see that it's clean. If it's not . . ."

"Why shouldn't it be? Take a look—there's nothing in there; it's newly painted. If you want I'll put a mat down there for you. See now, your porter's arrived. Will you stay?"

"Come, Sānī." The old woman climbed the stairs.

Sānī stood by the door as the porter set down his load. "Such a heavy load, such a steep path," he groaned. "That'll be 9 sukā, including the head porter's cut and expenses, too. My God!"

The curiosity that filled Sānī's face contained a trace of hopefulness, of trust and satisfaction as she stood there in silence. When he had inspected the rooms, the traveler decided to stay the night and Sānī felt relieved. With the porter's help, she put a mat in one of the rooms. As soon as the traveler had spread out his bed on the ground and heaved a contented sigh, the porter said, "Right, I'll be off now sir, I'm exhausted. I must eat, too. You should give me a few annas for a snack."

"Here . . . ," the traveler tossed him 4 paisā. The porter picked up the coins, looking pleased, and was about to leave when Sānī said, "Tell me, what should we bring for your meal? It will be dark soon. I see you have a lantern—do you need paraffin for it?"

The traveler did not reply but addressed the porter instead. "Old man, get the pots from the basket, and go and wash them in the river." Then he turned to Sānī. "I'll need a pitcher, too, so that he can bring some water before he goes for his meal."

"Yes, I'll bring one down right now."

"But is it a clean one?"

"What dirt gets into a water pot? If you're not happy with it, he can easily clean it in the river before he fills it up." The young girl's hesitancy showed clearly on her face.

The porter had pulled the pots from the basket, and as soon as Sānī brought a little brass pitcher down from upstairs he went off to the river. The traveler looked at Sānī in the evening half-light. Although her clothes were dirty, advertising her poverty, her face was not at all ugly. In her cheeks he saw the lovely gifts that hard work and the mountain air had bestowed on her. She had a natural rosiness and was just becoming mature. Her eyes were round and bright, and their pupils were dark and quick. Boundless curiosity and excitement were playing in those eyes.

"So . . . what shall I bring for your meal?" she asked, with a caution born of their being alone.

"One *mānā* of fine old rice," said the traveler, "a quarter of lentils, 2 paisā worth of whatever vegetables you can get here, 2 annas worth of ghee. . . . That should be enough."

Sānī went upstairs, and after a while she returned with everything he had asked for. The porter had already departed, having put the pots and the water in the next room. The cooking hearth and the eating place were both newly painted and clean.

"This isn't very good rice," said the traveler, inspecting it.

"No. But you can't get better rice than that here. If you could, I'd have brought you some. And as for vegetables—there's nothing but potatoes."

"Oh well, if that's so, never mind," said the traveler, smiling slightly. "I'll have to be content with whatever I can get."

"May I go now?" asked Sānī.

"Yes." But for some reason he felt like looking at her again. Their eyes met; then the girl went upstairs, hanging her head in embarrassment. But she suddenly turned around and said, with some confidence and in a natural tone, "To cook the vegetables you'll need some oil and some firewood. Should I bring salt, spices, and paraffin for your lantern?"

"Oh, I'm forgetting! I'll cook the vegetables in ghee, perhaps. I don't want any spices. But bring me 1 paisā worth of salt and turmeric and, you know, 4 paisā of firewood, and for the lantern 6 paisā of oil will do. Got that?"

Sānī brought him these things quickly, and then she went upstairs. She ate with her mother, and after fifteen or twenty minutes she went into her bedroom and shut the door from inside.

It was only half-past seven in the evening, but it was already very dark outside. Those few houses were like butterflies in the laps of the great hard mountains, and they stood in such silence it seemed all the life had left their bodies. The regular, monotonous roar of the streams could still be heard, but still the fearsome emptiness deepened.[4]

As she lay on her bed, thinking who knows what, Sānī suddenly heard a knocking sound coming from the traveler's room. "He can't have had his meal yet." She remained engrossed in her thoughts, "He might know how to cook; he might not. Perhaps he dropped the vegetables as he was lifting them off the fire. What man knows how to cook! He has always lived in the plains; who would have cooked for him there? Maybe he took on a Brāhmaṇ. But how could he have? It's expensive down in the plains, and he doesn't look like a rich merchant. If he was, he'd be like those others who come by here time after time. There'd have been great heavy tin trunks, filled to the brim, three or four leather bags of various sizes, a folding bed, a servant, and lots of porters. And he himself would have arrived in a sedan chair and sat upon a carpet. There's

4. Nepalis tend not to romanticize the natural grandeur of the mountain regions. On the contrary, the absence of towns and people is something to be feared.

nothing of this. I reckon he must have had a job somewhere in the plains. A man who works for somebody else could hardly take on a Brāhmaṇ cook!"

Then her thoughts ran off in another direction. "If that's so, he's probably got a wife!" She felt a blow to her heart and her inner thoughts fell still. Outside, the river's unceasing voice roared on. The thoughts she had assembled became a little disordered, and so she heaved a sigh. But her mood could not be averted for long, and the sweet imaginings she craved covered her once more. Breathing more lightly, she tried to sleep. Had the traveler finished his meal and gone to bed? She heard no sounds downstairs, so he must have. But then that noise again—"It must be the mice. . . . No it's not; it's that poor man again. . . . " She did not dare to indulge herself in silent thoughts of sympathy anymore. After a moment, she jumped up, struck a match, and lit the lamp in the niche at the head of her bed. A feeble, smoky light fingered the darkness as she picked up the lamp and went carefully downstairs. Her heart was thumping; was the old woman asleep yet? She felt a twinge of fear.

Once she had arrived downstairs, she thought, "But . . . why am I down here? I have no jobs to do downstairs." In the traveler's room there was the soft, calm light of his lantern. She looked at him just once, then turned away. He was asleep in his white quilt—calm, still, and unchanged. A frightening desire tugged hard at her very soul and began to thump along with her heart. A strange mixture of inexpressible happiness and courage, of fear and sorrow, began to flow through her veins. She returned upstairs in that same agitation, with those feelings still flowing through her, and fell onto her own dirty bed.

Next morning, the traveler rose and left early. The unexpressed infatuation and strange unspoken hopes that now glittered in Sānī's eyes followed him until he was far away on the top of the hill, and then they came back. She could not say why, but her heart became heavy and filled with tearful emotion. A question arose again and again in her mind—would he ever return?

Her question remained unanswered: the traveler did not return. After a while, she was married and moved to her own home. As if by a commonplace rule, she became caught up in household duties and the love and affection of her husband. She brought no awkwardness to their behavior. But the question that Sānī, a woman from a village culture, clutched in her innermost heart as if it was a gift from God troubled her several times each day.

When she was in her husband's house, she sometimes became apprehensive, and her apprehension caused terrible inner conflict. "Here I am; what if that traveler returns?" She was not brave enough to ponder the question further. What a terrible worry it was for her! Better if he never came back; better that her life should come to its end even as she was watching for him. But Sānī was not strong enough to hope that fate would ordain them never to meet again. Her longing, her eternal wait, the daily hopelessness to which she had become accustomed—all were mixed into her very breath. That was what her life consisted of. Holding onto this, she was the woman of the home, her mother-in-law's daughter-in-law, her husband's wife. Could poor Sānī continue to be all of these things in this state, shattered perhaps by some powerful curse? How could she wish this from her heart?

But Sānī could still be a proper wife; this was no impediment. She would certainly have cursed anyone who suggested that her marriage contained any kind of deceit or shortcoming. A woman's heart is big enough for an affection for children, for mother and father, for friends and relations of the natal home, and for the in-laws of the husband's home, and so Sānī's heart held some echo for that traveler, too. A woman is her husband's wife: this is as true as the shining sun, but only so far as being a wife is concerned. A woman is not merely a wife! She is other things too—a sister, a daughter-in-law, a mother. Besides all of these, she is love personified. If the love of women had not been sown throughout this world, would the world not be like the dead wood of a dried-out tree?

As he left, the traveler said that he might have to come back after two weeks. Sānī still remembered that two-week wait. The first week ended in depression and a feeling of emptiness, but from the eighth day on she began to hope that each day would be the day of his return. She remembered the strange feeling, the mysterious hope and excitement with which she reached the hilltop on that eighth day, when she went out to cut grass for the cow. Setting down her load, she sat on a rock and lost herself in happy dreaming. She stared intently at the road from Nepal,[5] and when she saw some people coming her fantasy became more joyful and exciting.

"This is how he will come today, bearing all the happiness of the world. He will spread the happiness of our previous meeting by smiling just a little; again he'll lodge with us for a day. But what if he doesn't stay with us? . . . Chi! Such bad thoughts! He was perfectly comfortable at our house; he suffered no inconvenience. I did all the work myself. He cooked and ate well before he slept. Why would he not stay with us again?" She kept her hope burning with new dreams every day, and the days went by. At last the day she had longed for arrived. Sānī recalled how she woke up in the night, three hours before the dawn. She opened the door and looked outside and saw that much of the night had still to

5. This reference is to the Kathmandu Valley.

pass. The moon shone brightly, and the sky was clear. The rushing sound of the river was like a song of delighted welcome. The sky, the abode of God, smiled down in the moonlight. In a few hours' time, the burning sun would come out. Its golden rays would spread over the hilltops. That day would be the festival of his returning. Tomorrow he would come. At first light he would set out to meet her and bring her great joy. She sat engrossed in these dreams for ages, overwhelmed by the happiness she imagined. Then she heaved a long sigh, as if anxious, and returned to lie uneasily on her bed. Later, the dawn came, the sun rose, and Sānī waited restlessly. Then it was dusk, the night fell, and after her fortnight of waiting Sānī was left with the fact that he had not come. With tears in her eyes, sorrow in her heart, darkness in her soul, a lump in her throat, and her body filled with regret, this knowledge was all she had for consolation.

Alas, the feeble heart of a woman! How much do you have to sacrifice? How much pleasure, attachment, and love, and who knows what else, have you stored away for your offering?

Two more weeks went by. The course of her life began to change—from beginning to end, it seemed. The change went deep inside her, and her question, "Will he come back?" was joined by the knowledge that he had not come. Where would her journeying cease? Where was its end and destination? Was it within the rest of her life or beyond its end?

The narrow hill path was a difficult, strenuous, arduous trail that climbed higher and higher by degrees. Looking along it into the far distance, you could see nothing to make you think that you had seen a man. . . .

The times were changing. Sānī's mother went to meet with eternity, from which no one ever returns. Sānī went back to her home to run the old business. While living in her husband's house, she had always worried that the traveler had already gone by. Thousands of people went down to the plains from Nepal by that Mārkhu road, but the traveller. . . .

"He'll surely come back one day." Catching hold of a thin, weak thread to lead her despairing hopes on, she made them stretch even further. How delicate, how lovely, how long it was, this thin thread of desperate wishing. Someone else was tugging hard on the thread of life and her youthfulness, but did Sānī know? She was aware of little more than that charming memory from her past, that momentary dream that lasted for only a day. The person for whom she had made her sacrifice, in gratitude for the first gift of youth, would surely return one day. Every day she busied herself in renewing her treasure. How could she know that the thread of her life was being pulled along? Love is the path of life. Sacrifice is its ultimate aim. Once you reach your destination, you are given the end of existence.

After she had opened the shop one evening, Sānī stood in the doorway with her thoughts elsewhere. She had been standing like this in the peaceful half-light on just such an evening when the traveler had come, her symbol of love. She had stood there like this so many times since, waiting without hope, her heart filled with demolished dreams and sorrow. But he had not come back. In response to all these false welcomes, she had acquired a quiet sadness and eyes filled with tears. Again today she stood there waiting. Either for the traveler or for the silent sorrow she knew so well.

A man well past his prime came up to her and asked, "Can I get lodgings here tonight?"

She thought her heart would stop. She was struck by a thunderbolt from the past! Sānī could do nothing but stare and stare at his face.

"Are there lodgings here or not?" the question came again. Sānī's face shone brightly at first, but then it darkened and dulled. She stared into space and said sadly, "Where are your porters?"

"They're on their way," said the traveler, and sat down on a rock. "It's ages since I went to Nepal from the plains. I never managed to go back at all. Now at last I'm going back, but everything seems to have changed—the path, the hills. . . . I stayed in this house on my way to Nepal, so I thought I might stay here again, if the house was still here. I set out with that in mind, and now at last I've arrived. Where's the old woman? You, you must be Sānī? . . . "

For Sānī, his words were harder than a thunderbolt, more tumultuous than the roar at the end of the world. She felt frightened. She was not ready to welcome the end of all those days of waiting, of the misery that had filled her, with such ease and informality. Man! You are all the hope, pain, longing, despair, dreams, and joy that have filled Sānī's life, and yet you do not know! With your simple question, your unexpected arrival, you have brought to its climax the story that has pervaded this life. How could you know, why should you know, how shattered this woman's heart has been?

Sānī's voice was like a sound from a distant skyline. "Yes, I'm Sānī," she said.

"I know, I recognized you. But you . . . you've become old." He smiled.

Sānī's eyes were opened at last. She saw her wrinkled skin and realized how much time had passed. Clearly she saw that her journey was almost over. The evening of her life had arrived with the end of all her hopes. The world was changing; she was out of place in the present. She felt tired; her body was weary from standing. She sat down right there in the doorway.

As soon as it was morning, the traveler went on his way, just as he had before. From that day on the purpose of her life disappeared. "You've become old"—a single comment from the traveler had consumed all the zeal with which she had clung on to her hope, all the youth and enthusiasm she had maintained. Then that woman was finished, along with the dumb hopes she had had for her life and her silent, unbroken sorrow. But that was not all—the question she had loved more than her soul, that she had fostered until it filled her life and was dear and familiar to her, her question vanished, too, in the darkness of deep regret: "Will he ever return?"

(originally published in 1940; from Bhikshu 1960a)

MĀUJANG BĀBUSĀHEB'S COAT (*MĀUJANG BĀBUSĀHEBKO KOṬ*)

To tell the truth, Māujang Bābusāheb and his coat were one and the same thing.[6] If you ever saw that long, pink Benson[7] overcoat, walking, moving, sitting, or gesticulating at a show, a feast, or an argument, or at the scene of a quarrel or a tragedy, it always turned out to be Māujang Bābusāheb, along with his whole indomitable existence. Precisely when the coat had begun to represent Māujang Bābusāheb was a matter for research; only one or two people could hazard a guess, even among the few surviving ancients. But nowadays there are few who are reluctant to relate all sorts of historical tales.

Māujang Bābusāheb was a Rāṇā aristocrat, a bad-tempered, rude, and irrepressible character who held *birtā* land in Nepalganj district.[8] Somehow everyone still remembered what used to happen fifteen years before democracy. An army of dogs lived at Bābusāheb's village house—three or four of them were big and ferocious; the others were small and fine-haired. They used to terrify every visitor by being the first to offer a welcome and were a prominent and fearful memory in that Tarāī province. The coat had come to represent a multitude of terrors for the men of this world of agricultural laborers. It reminded them of forcible seizures of houses and fields, of thrashings and beatings, of insults and wild abuse when Bābusāheb's thick lips, set in a wide, red face that was sweaty and insistent, spat out a stream of foam. . . . And when the high Rāṇā officials of the area, ranked in a certain order with members of the Thāpās or some other clan first,[9] bowed down before him for everyone to see, that long pink coat was being honored, too. Through this combination of pomp, grandeur, and terror, he became known by the

6. Bābusāheb is an honorific title.

7. Benson is a particularly expensive variety of cloth.

8. *Birtā* land was granted to a person employed by, or simply in the favor of, the Nepal government. This person could then work the land and derive income from it. Nepalganj is a large market town near the southern border with India.

9. The Rāṇā period was characterized by continual infighting among the various ruling families, including the Thāpās.

name of Māujang Bābusāheb, instead of by his real name, which was perhaps Humāyun Jang Bahādur Rāṇā. The name was on everyone's lips, and people uttered it with fear.

Just as the Gāndharvas' bow symbolized Arjuṇ during the Mahābhārata era, so that coat represented Māujang Bābusāheb's tyranny during those Rāṇā times.[10] No one even dared to mention that invincible, glorious coat. The insolence of time had made it fade until it was gray and pale, but it still seemed bright to everyone. But after democracy came,[11] people became impudent and looked scornfully at both Bābusāheb and his coat. Everyone laughed at it now. Some even picked up a rumor somewhere and began to say that the coat had been a reward from P.K.J.[12] Then it went still further, and some who had inquired into the coat's ancient history discovered that it had been given to Bābusāheb in Nepal[13] when he attended the wedding of that P.K.J.'s parasol bearer. He had been picked out to receive the gift because of the clothes he was wearing.

By some misfortune, Māujang Bābusāheb got wind of these rumors one day. He stared at his coat, which hung from a nail in the wall. Even in these days of democracy he recalled the events of the past. He remembered how a sweet smell had arisen from the coat and scented the air on the day it was given to him. Everyone else who was there had looked at it with envy. He remembered how smoothly his hands had slid into the linen lining in its arms when he had first put it on. That coat on its nail had fitted him perfectly—it symbolized nobility, prosperity, and honor and made him feel gratified and self-confident. When he came home with it, how astonished the Rānī Sāheb who accompanied him had been![14] She took the coat from him, but before she hung it up she turned it over and over in her hands. She saw the lining glistening and caressed it gently. Yes, and then Bābusāheb had been annoyed. He had scolded her: "What are you doing, you hill farmer's daughter? Don't you realize it will get dirty if you stroke it like that?"

The Rānī Sāheb had hung it up, still smiling though she was frightened. And then when he was alone in the room Bābusāheb had got up quietly and stroked the coat himself. He was filled with awe and amaze-

10. Arjuṇ was the warrior on the battlefield to whom Krishna delivered his famous sermon on duty (dharma) during the great war between the Kauravas and the Pāṇḍavas recounted in the Mahābhārata. Arjuṇ's prowess as an archer was largely due to his possession of the bow belonging to the Gāndharvas, the celestial musicians.

11. Democracy came after the downfall of the Rāṇās in 1950–1951.

12. P.K.J. are probably the initials of a fairly obscure Rāṇā, whom I have been unable to identify.

13. "Nepal" refers to Kathmandu.

14. Rānī Sāheb is an honorific title for the senior wife of a high Rāṇā. As a high-ranking Rāṇā, Māujang may have had several wives.

ment as he read the label, sewn inside one of the pockets, as if it were a holy text. He read it, piecing it together from the knowledge of English letters that enabled him to write his name. "Whiteway Ladler and Company, Tailoring and Outfit Department," it said. This was really evidence of the coat's royal magnificence, its incredible nobility and sophistication. Then Bābusāheb recalled the many times after that, the many opportunities and occasions, the many people to whom he had shown that label, and the limitless pride he had felt. Lord! In this strange alien time, how disgraceful that a coat like this should be treated with such contempt!

Bābusāheb jumped up and took the coat out into the light to inspect it properly.

"What a *grand* thing it is, what excellent *art* this is. Carefully sewn without a piece out of place! Even Brahmā[15] himself cannot have taken such care when he sculpted the human body!"

He looked at the coat's collar as he thought this. It was grubby and split; some threads were hanging loose.

"This makes it look less grand, does it not? But everything gets old, even people. Does aging have any effect on someone's caste, reputation, pride, or nobility? Such a coat! Now that the Whiteway Ladler Company is under the rule of the Hindustanis, even it could not produce another coat like this! Those craftsmen will already have left, unable to make a living. Who wears such expensive coats now? Where could you get cloth like this now, let alone a coat? It won't even be made in England any more. You just don't see such things nowadays. Even the English are going downhill, poor wretches! When they held Hindustan, they were so glorious. The most advanced society in the whole world! London was our capital then, I suppose. But where's that old spendor nowadays, even in Kathmandu?"

Bābusāheb went on remembering. He recalled the generals'[16] palace: such ornamentation! Iron bedsteads with brass decorations—fairies, creepers, flowers, and so on, all made by real artists—*double spring*, how soft they were! Huge, huge rooms, their walls covered with enormous portraits in golden frames, of kings and generals, and the kings and queens of England, Germany, Russia, Rome. . . . Each one worth more than 10,000! Huge cupboards, racks, and bookshelves, chairs and tables of every design. The polish seemed to be made from gold! Then there were *sofa sets* covered with silk and velvet, and tasseled curtains—there was no end to it! The walls, the ceilings, even the staircases, were an exhibition of marvels and magnificent things. Silver was an everyday thing;

15. Brahmā is the Hindu deity who created the universe.

16. Every high Rāṇā official assumed a military rank, which sometimes became hereditary.

gold was no concern. So many great vessels and pots of silver and gold, beautiful vases. So many servant girls and attendants, dressed in lovely clothes. An army of children, servants, *subbās*, parasol bearers, *mukhiyās*.[17] Motors and horses and buggies . . . could all those wonders be remembered now? Bābusāheb remembered the crowds that used to fill the palace and the servants' quarters, the press of people, the running about that went on. That was real grandeur then! What had become of it now?

He inspected his coat once again: a symbol of a proud noble past, a coat of Benson cloth, made in Whiteway's Tailoring Department. He rose and hung it up on the nail again. Then, in a haughty state of mind, he sat down in his seat with particular gravity. Intuitively he knew that the rumors were not important. Those Congress wretches only made fun of it to hide the jealousy they felt.[18] They couldn't stand its nobility. The bastards simply envied him. Liars and petty, mean men all, yes, oh yes, they were truly great! When the principal officer came and they had welcomed him (Bābusāheb reassumed the attitude of his past), how respectfully he had stared at Bābusāheb in his coat. Not to mention the *subbās* and the lieutenants: jobs given to little men for their services to the *hakīm*. An English district collector had come from Mugalān once;[19] even that Mr. Cornish could not rest content without a long look at the coat when they invited him to go hunting.

Bābusāheb recalled the many moments of glory when his coat had brought its high class and its brilliant, silently stated nobility to festivals, meetings, receptions, rituals, and wedding feasts. He brought its splendid history back to mind and felt his old completeness in the personal pride this generated. Wherever he went, and for whatever reason, this pink coat became the center of attention. With immense gravity, Bābusāheb said to himself, "They're all rogues, the lot of them! Is this some ordinary coat? No! It is something very special, very, very special indeed!"

The central government's home minister was coming out on a tour, and the committee that was organizing a reception for him had called Māujang Bābusāheb to a meeting. The day before he went to Nepalganj, Bābusāheb carefully began to brush down the coat that Whiteway Ladler's had made. Clouds of dust rose into the air. Chi! They never brushed it, ever! He scolded the whole household, from the servants right up to the Rānī Sāheb herself.

17. A *mukhiyā* is a government official of the third rank; a *subbā* is a government official one rank higher than a *mukhiyā*.

18. The Nepali Congress was the main political party among the forces that eventually ousted the Rāṇās in 1950–1951.

19. Mugalān, "the land of the Mughals," is an old name for India.

"What's this now? If I don't tell you what to do, you just don't see the jobs! All this dust on such a fine coat! This is what's made the color fade! Would a coat like this fade otherwise? It's Benson cloth, but now you've let it fill with dust and the original color's finished! Oxen! The more you brush, the more dust you find!"

Eventually he finished brushing it and hung it up again. He covered it with a piece of cloth. But one thing kept on pricking him—how creased the coat had become. It would have to be ironed. But who could he give it to in the village? It was a complex problem. He was due at the *baṛā hakīm*'s house at eight the next morning. . . . [20]

Next day, Bābusāheb wrapped up the coat and set off for Nepalganj, with a servant carrying the bundle. In a corner of the bazaar he came to Gurdin the *dhobī*'s house[21] and called, "Hey Gurdin! Just iron my coat, and take care!"

Gurdin looked at it with an expert eye. "Alright sir. I'll have to heat the iron. Send your man in a little while, and I'll have it ready."

What Gurdin said was fair enough, but he knew what *dhobī*s were like. If he didn't do it in time, or if he scorched it because he didn't know what sort of cloth it was . . . Bābusāheb was not content.

"No, I'll go to that shop over there and smoke a cigarette. Heat the iron quickly, and I'll show you how to iron it. It's no ordinary coat, you know. You'll have to do as I tell you."

Gurdin's pride was injured. "How many expensive coats and trousers and clothes of all kinds have I ironed with these hands! Teaching me how to iron this pathetic, ragged old coat, indeed!" But he did not say this to Bābusāheb. He just said, "Fine." Then when Bābusāheb had left for the shop, Gurdin was gripped by anger and took his private revenge by throwing the coat down hard onto a pile of clothes in the corner. Soon the iron had warmed up. When he had spread out the clothes on his table and put the coat down, Bābusāheb, who had been watching from a distance, came and seated himself close by on a three-legged stool.

Gurdin had barely touched the iron to the arm of the coat when Bābusāheb shouted, "Hey, you ox! Damp it first, damp it first! It's scorched, it's scorched!"

Gurdin was mystified and stared blankly at him. "Sir, the iron hasn't warmed up properly yet. It's hardly warm; it's a cold iron. Do you think I know so little?" Then he bent low over his ironing. Gradually the iron became warmer. At every opportunity, Bābusāheb still told him to

20. *Baṛā hakīm*, "great *hakīm*," is the most senior local government official.

21. A *dhobī* is a professional washerman. Gurdin is a Muslin name.

dampen the coat, and Gurdin went on muttering angrily at the insult. Several technical things happened, but at last the ironing was done.

Bābusāheb put the coat on while it was still warm, and he was about to leave when the *dhobī* said, "Sir, I haven't even begun the day's business. I did this job first thing in the morning."

Māujang Bābusāheb tossed him 2 paisā. "There, you've had a month's income now. You'll take money before you've opened, won't you?" Then he walked out, saying firmly, "Now everyone will realize what this coat really is! As soon as it's been brushed down and ironed, it's back to its old glory. Something of quality demands greater care and attention. I'm a fool—should such a coat be hung on a nail? But what can I do in such circumstances? I have to support an army of people; my income is just this pathetic *birtā*." But then Bābusāheb was alarmed at his own thoughts: "But a *birtā*'s a *birtā*, after all—something given by the king, to be proud of. It supported me, and I did as much as I could, without any other means. What would my income have been without it?"

He glanced at his coat. His old pride flared up again, and his habitual vigor, power, and arrogance replaced the sense of deficiency he had been feeling just a moment before. Silently, he contemplated the unchallenged might, the undefeated power that had been his until so recently, and before he knew it he had entered the *baṛā hakīm*'s gate and was standing on his verandah. Twenty-five men were sitting there, talking. As soon as he saw him the *baṛā hakīm* said, "Come in, Bābusāheb; you're late. You'll have to make a door yourself!" He laughed and ushered Bābusāheb to a seat.

Bābusāheb quietly checked his coat in the place where the *baṛā hakīm* had touched his arm to make sure it hadn't been creased. The discussion about the reception continued, and although Bābusāheb chipped in now and then with a "yes" or a "no," his thoughts were elsewhere: "As soon as he touched my coat, the *baṛā hakīm* will have realized what sort of a garment this is! No joking: quality is quality, after all."

But then a Tarāī congressman butted in, "Why, Bābusāheb, are you going to wear that coat even when the minister comes? The weather's getting hot, you know!"

Bābusāheb stared at his face for a moment. "How uppity the lower castes are becoming," he thought. "Should I come dressed in a 4-paisā vest and loincloth just because it's warm? The minister's coming from Nepal, so he'll be wearing a woolen coat. However hot it is, the generals always wear uniforms made of soft cashmere. You haven't a clue about these things—is this how affairs of state are conducted?" He showed his contempt by remaining silent as the discussion went on. Whenever he saw a smile on the face of that congressman in his khaki jacket, Bābusāheb muttered to himself, "What to do? It's a different age now. This wretch would never have dared to make fun of this coat before."

Then he realized that the *baṛā hakīm* kept glancing at his collar, and he thought he would die of shame because the collar was filthy and torn. Bābusāheb was unbearably embarrassed, and his big face turned red. He could not sit there any longer. Somehow, he managed to stick it out for ten minutes more; then he took his leave and went out of the room. Even as he stepped down from the verandah, the sound of laughter reached his ears. What could have caused such laughter? It could have been nothing else—they were laughing at his torn collar, for sure. Bābusāheb's eyes dampened with a mixture of sorrow and helpless anger, and he walked quickly to the main street. By the time he reached it, he was in control of his tears. The whole world was jealous of this coat's noble appearance, of its unending glory, he thought. Everyone was conspiring to bring down his reputation.

"Lord, such small-minded envy! To rob a poor coat of its honor! A lifeless, senseless coat! Now quality is considered a flaw—that's what's happened, you know! This is a mean-minded age. Greatness and honesty are sins now. And this is called democracy! . . ."

Back home again, Bābusāheb spent the whole night in thoughts like these. He resolved that the respectability and honor of the coat made by Whiteway Ladler Company would not be allowed to disappear, for as long as he lived. . . .

There were only eight days to go before the minister's visit. The coat would have to be restored by then. It deserved to have its true nobility back; this wasn't something that could be humbled or diminished. He decided to go to Lucknow to have it dry-cleaned and repaired.[22] But even at a rough estimate this would cost 40 or 50 rupees. Several members of the household suggested, "Just add another 40 or 50 and buy another coat. That would be better."

But Bābusāheb smiled, as if he pitied their ignorance. "What are you thinking of? Do you think I could find a coat as good as this one, even for 100? Know-it-alls! Even if I had ten new coats, they could not compare with this one! It's only because I've neglected it, you know. I'm going to Lucknow, for certain. Just wait and see how it looks when I get back!"

Bābusāheb was determined to go, but money was a problem. Even if he bought a second-class ticket, the return journey would cost at least 20 rupees. Even if he stayed at the cheapest hotel in Lucknow and ate

22. Lucknow is a large city in the north Indian state of Uttar Pradesh, about one day's journey from Nepalganj.

only the simplest food, it would cost 9 or 10 a day. He would have to stay for four days: that meant 40 rupees. Then there was the dry-cleaning and repair—10 rupees, at most. Then perhaps 4 rupees a day for traveling around—not in a taxi, in a *tongā*[23]—and add cigarettes, *pān*,[24] and so on—it wouldn't be less than 100 in all. And even if he kept to this, he would have to bring something small back from Lucknow for the children, the servants, and Rānī Sāheb, too. At least 200 in all! Two hundred rupees to clean an old coat! Two hundred! Two hundred! Those two words filled his brain. Then the sound of laughter from the *baṛā hakīm's* house echoed in his ears again, and he pulled himself together.

"Why must it cost me 200? I'll go second class from Nepalganj to Gonda; then I'll go on from there in third class. Who will recognize me, after all? Then in Lucknow, Chedī Lāl's *dharamshālā* has good rooms; he'll let me stay four days.[25] If I eat somewhere really cheap, 1 rupee per meal will be enough. It is four days after all! Even if it costs 50 rupees, the coat will come back ready." Bābusāheb felt much better, and he called a servant to fill his pipe.

In the end, Bābusāheb brought the coat back restored. There had been one problem in Lucknow: if the coat was darned after it had been washed, would the cleaning not have made it even more ragged than before? If so, the darning would turn out to be very costly. On the other hand, if he had it darned first, there was a danger that it might come apart again while it was being washed. Bābusāheb solved this problem cleverly. He took it first to be darned.

"Every thread in this coat is rotten," the darner said. "It'll be very difficult to mend it."

But with great skill Bābusāheb persuaded him. In later days, Bābusāheb would describe in detail the care the darner had taken to mend it once he had begun. Then when he took it to the dry-cleaners', the manager had expressed concern when he saw how decrepit it was. But Bābusāheb got him to write "not torn anywhere" on the receipt and made plain his intention to offer a tip. Bābusāheb amazed everyone with his account of how lovingly it had been cleaned after that.

"If I hadn't gone there in person, the coat would have been ruined," he said, immensely satisfied with his cunning.

When the coat came back from the shop, in plastic packing with the company's name stamped on it, Bābusāheb did not unwrap it. He could

23. A *tongā* is a pony and trap.

24. *Pān* refers to certain nuts, particularly betel, and pastes wrapped in a betel leaf and eaten as the Indian equivalent of chewing gum.

25. A *dharamshālā* is a simple, cheap hostel for the accommodation of pilgrims.

see the mended collar and the color of the coat through the plastic cover. He showed it to anyone who showed an interest. Why let the dust in by unwrapping it? And yes, Bābusāheb brought them all a gift from Lucknow: lemon sweets for the children, plastic slides for the servant girls' hair, an amazing machine that threaded needles for the old cook. The thread went in even if you shut your eyes! And a bottle of Spring Flowers oil for the Rānī Sāheb. The whole lot cost him only 3 rupees, and everyone was happy.

Now Bābusāheb waited impatiently for the minister's visit. Time passed by impossibly slowly, but at last the day arrived. The minister came at eleven in the morning; Bābusāheb was to attend a party in his honor at four. Early that morning, he shaved, trimmed his moustache, bathed, and sat down all prepared. At exactly three he was dressed in the clothes he was going to wear; then he sat and smoked. At half-past three, when it was time to leave, the coat was taken from its plastic packing. Well! No one would have thought that it was really the same coat! It had a completely new splendor, as if it had regained the youthfulness of a quarter century before. A servant woman dressed Bābusāheb in it, taking great care not to crush or crease it. Bābusāheb could not help feeling grateful, and he remembered that she was their oldest servant. How long had she served them? He felt a strong impulse to reward her, but his pockets were empty. So he suppressed that brief, generous thought regretfully; if he asked the Rānī Sāheb for money, he knew she would deny that she had any. Despite the return of his old grandeur, his helplessness in such a petty matter wrung his heart, and he held back tears of self-pity. Moreover, he felt remorse for not having been able to defend the honor of the coat he was wearing: a coat that had earned him his former glory but that had been so grossly insulted. Actually, in his feeling of greatness today, all his tyranny, barbarity, and ill-temper seemed to have disappeared. It was as if the noble nature of a loftily humanitarian, forgiving benefactor had welled up inside him. He regarded them all with great affection and silently wished them well.

Bābusāheb arrived at the reception in an exceedingly straightforward and positive frame of mind. As soon as he entered, everyone looked at his coat. For an instant they all stared at it, wide-eyed, and although smiles came to their mouths none of them actually laughed. Bābusāheb took note of this, but today he felt no anger, no irritation, nothing at all of that sort. He was on a lofty mental plane where such impulses were pacified and stilled of themselves.

The convenor introduced Bābusāheb to the minister and seated him on the dais. Bābusāheb chatted to everyone with a civility and politeness appropriate to the occasion. At last the tea party was over and everyone left one by one, bidding the minister farewell as they departed. As Bābusāheb left, he thrust his hands into his coat's lower pockets, as was his habit. At the same time, a local congressman came out, too. He took Bābusāheb by the arm and walked beside him, talking. On any other occasion, Bābusāheb would not have tolerated the insolent intimacy of the lowlander, but today he was a different man and so he walked on, talking happily with him. But unfortunately, someone called to that congressman from behind, and he turned around without letting go of Bābusāheb's arm. Bābusāheb's arm was jolted, and because his hand was in his pocket, the old coat ripped from the top corner of the pocket to the bottom of the garment.

Jhaarrrrrrrrr! . . . A thousand earthquakes happened all at once, Bābusāheb's heart was rocked by a blow that felt like the end of the world. The whole world seemed to collapse; the seven oceans came welling up into Bābusāheb's eyes.

But could the mighty Māujang Bābusāheb weep and wail in front of that worthless man? In the old days, he would have set the Alsatian on him and had him torn to pieces. But he did not have that option today; Bābusāheb's attitude was no longer one of high and mighty greatness. With an immense effort, he suppressed a feeling of total anguish. Bābusāheb was neither dumb with grief, nor did he even permit himself a cry of rage. All he said was, "Oh, what's happened?" and managed to calm himself with a careless gesture.

Slowly he walked outside, took off his coat, and handed it to his man, who stood there waiting for him. Once the congressman had taken his leave, Bābusāheb went on his way, walking gravely and in silence. Although dressed now only in shirt and trousers, he did not lower his gaze in shame; and when he had peacefully, firmly, finished his walk and entered his house, he sat down in his usual chair. The man followed him in, hung the coat up on the same old nail, and then went out again. Bābusāheb stared at the coat on its nail. The linen that was hanging from the torn pocket was like its tongue sticking out at him. "What's this now, eh?" it seemed to say. "Now what will you do?" He sat staring at it, dry-eyed, for ages. After a while—perhaps because she had heard about the coat being torn—the Rānī Sāheb came running in and looked closely at it.

"What has happened, eh? How did this happen? Oh Lord, now what will you do?"

"Nothing has happened." Despite the terrible accident, Bābusāheb spoke peaceably, even in his own home. "Nothing has happened. I just went to meet the minister, and then I came home. The Rāṇās' rule is ended."

(written in 1960; from Bhikshu 1960b)

Shivkumār Rāī (b. 1916)

Rāī was born at Rinãk in Sikkim but made his home at Kurseong in the Darjeeling district of West Bengal. He studied for a while at Gyantse in Tibet before gaining his B.A. from Calcutta University in 1941. Rāī's career was primarily political: he was one of the founding members of the Gorkhā League, an organization that represented Nepalis resident in India, and the first Nepali to hold a ministerial position in the government of West Bengal. Later, he became a producer of Nepali programs for All India Radio.

Rāī's first story appeared in *Shāradā* in 1944. His writings are varied; most of the stories in *Frontier* (*Phranṭiyar*), his first collection, are set among the tribal communities of the northeast frontier states, and others deal with topics ranging from a mountaineering accident to the life of a dancing girl in a Mughal court. Rāī's finest stories are those that describe the lives of the lower classes of the Darjeeling district. He is no experimentalist; he tells his stories in a straightforward and unpretentious manner, but his characterizations and descriptions of scenery are among the finest in Nepali fiction. Rāī's stories are published in three collections: *Frontier* (1951), *Yātrī* (The Traveler, 1956), and *Khahare* (Monsoon Stream, 1976). (The latter received a Sāhitya Akademi Award in 1978.)

THE MURDERER (*JYĀNAMĀRĀ?*)

The long summer downpour came to an end, and the setting sun glinted through dwindling evening clouds. The shadows of banyan and *pīpal* trees grew long above the spring, reaching out and touching a grinding stone that leaned against the courtyard wall. It was busy at the spring:

the farmers had planted the last crop of the year, and now they were washing the mud from their arms and legs and cleaning their tools. Soon they all went home. But Ujīrmān, who had gone to water the cardamom field, still did not return.

During the Second World War, Ujīrmān had fought the Japanese in Burma and at Kohima. His left hand lacked its little finger: he claimed that the Japanese had cut it off in hand-to-hand combat. Whenever someone asked him how he had lost it, he became very animated.

"It got cut off, what!" he would exclaim. "It was when we were facing the Japanese in the assault on Burma. But I chopped the radishes off three of them, what! Their weapons were as much use as monkeys' tails. Our knives may not have been sharp, but they were light and quick. We were advancing when they attacked with machine-gun fire, so we halted and quickly took cover. I had jumped into a ditch, and I was firing away when three of them came up on me from behind. And that was that: I killed the lot of them. I didn't notice my finger was gone until I got back to camp. What! I had to spend a month in the hospital!"

Ujīrmān was a short stocky man in his late thirties, with bulging calves and knotted biceps. He still seemed quick and agile. Everyone knew he never missed his mark when he went out hunting. Young boys often ran along behind him, shouting, "If you want meat, just follow brother Ujīrmān!"

Most of the village called him "brother," and sometimes, when the village council developed a craving for meat, they would give him a gun and a couple of cartridges and tell him, "Off you go then, brother. Have a look down at Dussenī forest, and see what you can find."

Once he had entered the forest, Ujīrmān never came back empty-handed. He would always return with at least a few pigeons, or some other kind of bird, if not with a deer or a jungle fowl.

No one knew who his first wife had been, and there were no children from that marriage, either. Now that the last ripples of his youth were beginning to lap against the shore, Ujīrmān felt the need of a young woman. Perhaps he feared that there would be nobody to light his pyre or perform the last rites for him when he died, or perhaps he simply wanted someone to keep him company in his old age. Maybe it was just because Putalī was pretty that he was attracted to her. Only he knew his motives. But whatever the reason might be, he felt he had to take a young woman for his wife, and so he did. His domestic affairs were no business of the outside world.

Truly, if any man caught a glimpse of Putalī he always had to look again. Sixteen or seventeen, and in the first flush of maturity, she was tall, lovely, and straightforward in manner, with a complexion as fair as wheat, and she always wore the hint of a smile. The village lads called her "sister-in-law," perhaps because this established a relationship between them that made them all feel at ease. There were plenty of youths who would tease and joke, but she answered them cheekily, too. Ujīrmān knew all about this, but he was a big-hearted soldier, and it caused him no concern. He saw no harm in simple fun.

One evening, when it had grown quite dark, Ujīrmān burst into the local police post with a gun in his hands. Sergeant Bīr Bahādur was the officer in charge, with four men under his command. He sat writing in the dim lamplight with his spectacles halfway down his nose. The broken lampshade had been patched with scraps of paper, and the oil it burned gave off a grimy smoke, and so it only lit a small area around the table. For a moment, the sergeant was startled when he saw Ujīrmān sweating and panting before him. He pushed the lamp higher to see him properly.

"What are you doing here at this time of night?" he asked.

Ujīrmān hesitated. "Sergeant, what!" he said at last. "I did something awful today. I killed Officer Bhālu by mistake."

The sergeant stared at him, perplexed, "What? Are you saying you've killed a *bhālu,*[1] or do you mean policeman number 88?"

"I thought I was firing at a *bhālu,* but it was Officer Bhālu. Just look outside, won't you? I'm here to report what happened."

Ujīrmān's shoulder was covered with blood, and Officer Bhālu lay dead outside.

The sergeant's heart pounded so fiercely, he could hardly move his pen. From time to time, he tore the paper or spilled drops of ink. At last he managed to steady his hand and complete his report. . . .

Yesterday, Ujīrmān had gone to irrigate the cardamom field with Sundanté and Harké's father, and they'd seen a bear near the Mangar cliff. Today, he went up there alone because everyone else was down in the valleys planting the fields. Before he set out that morning, he had borrowed a gun from the council, partly for his own protection and partly because he hoped to meet with some game on the way home. Dusk fell very suddenly in the forest below the cliff, and soon it became impossible for him to pick things out in the darkness. Then he heard the sound of cracking branches and stones slithering down the hillside just below the path. So he stopped and stood dead still, looking toward where the sounds were coming from, but he saw nothing in the darkness.

"Who's there?" he cried, and the noises stopped for a moment. But then he heard them again and saw something black slip behind a leafy fig tree. Suddenly he remembered the bear he had seen the day before, and now he clearly saw a bear hiding there, eating seeds from the tree. As he watched, it got up and began to lollop toward him. He hurriedly

1. A *bhālu* is a bear.

took aim and fired: BANG! The bear gave a yelp and fell flat on its back. His heart missed a beat, and he walked over to look at it, but near the fig tree he found the body of Officer Bhālu, covered in blood. On his way back from a patrol, he had probably squatted down there to defecate.

So Ujīrmān had picked up the body and presented himself at the police post. When he had finished his account of these events, he was close to tears.

"Please save me, sergeant," he said. "I made a mistake, what! If anything should happen to me, my Putalī will be so sad!"

Sergeant Bīr Bahādur was in the government's favor. He felt very sorry for Ujīrmān, but he couldn't shirk his responsibilities. That night he locked Ujīrmān in the guardroom and next morning had him transferred to the police station in the town. The news went round like a forest fire, and people said all sorts of things.

"The poor man's ruined, and all for nothing. That's what happens once your luck is out."

"No, no, it's always the same when a man has a pretty wife. Everyone looks at her. On days when Ujīrmān wasn't at home, Officer Bhālu was always calling by. Do you think he was just bringing her sugarcane?"

The old council headman knew Ujīrmān well. "I saw him only yesterday evening. 'There!' he said to me, 'That Bhālu has gone too far today!' The poor man was deluded. Once the stars are against you, there's nothing you can do."

The police went about their investigation quickly. Ujīrmān stood in court as a man accused of murder, and there were witnesses and evidence, too, of things that did or did not happen. On the opening day of the trial, he felt heartened to see people from his village in the courtroom. Little did he know that they were there as witnesses for the prosecution and had come to do him down. The village council had tried hard to get him released on bail, but their efforts met with no success. They had employed an advocate to plead his case for him.

"When the judge asks you whether or not you're guilty, say 'not guilty' and leave everything else to me," the advocate had instructed him. And that was how it happened.

"Are you guilty or not guilty?" asked the judge.

"Not guilty, my lord, what!"

The police presented their case and added plenty of spice to it. The officer laid the file before the judge and said, "My lord, marrying a pretty girl was disastrous for Ujīrmān. Lots of the village lads came and went regularly at his house, and it was only natural for him to worry about the rumors that were going around concerning his wife. They caused constant squabbles between Ujīrmān and Putalī. While Ujīrmān was down in the fields, Officer Bhālu would visit his house and chat to

Putalī for hours. So it was only natural that Ujīrmān became suspicious. And it is clear from the evidence before me that Putalī welcomed Bhālu's advances. Last year, on Māghé Sankrānti Day, many of the villagers saw Putalī and Bhālu together at the fair.[2] Ujīrmān was away at the time."

The policeman opened a parcel. "My lord, this is a sweater that Putalī knitted for Officer Bhālu. She knitted socks and scarves for him, too. Ujīrmān must have known that they were planning to run away together the following Wednesday. Officer Bhālu had been granted one month's leave, and they intended to elope to the hills. It was because Ujīrmān had found out about this that he devised a plan to kill Officer Bhālu. Once, as he was setting off on a hunting trip, he made a strange remark to Māité's father. 'The police are very devious,' he said, but when he was asked what he meant by this he did not answer. Surely he must have been thinking about the affair that was going on between his wife and Officer Bhālu. He and Putalī quarreled on the morning before the murder. Ujīrmān said, 'No, no, you can't change my mind. You can't stop me. Today it's either Officer Bhālu or me. I shan't rest till I've killed him.' And two of the villagers saw him going down the hill with a gun. So this is proof of the fact that Ujīrmān was full of anger and jealousy. He knew that Bhālu would come along that path on his way back from Daudāhā, so he caught Bhālu on his own there and put an end to him."

Ujīrmān sat and listened in astonishment, burning with rage as he heard his wife slandered. He loved his Putalī, and he trusted her, too. "My wife is young," he thought to himself. "She likes to have fun. But she would never behave like that. If she had disgraced herself as he says she did, I'd have strangled her myself."

One after another, the witnesses gave their accounts. Shikārī Damai and Musé's father stood up in court and said, "It's true; we did see them together on Māghé Sankrānti Day, my lord."

Māité's father talked about the day when he saw Ujīrmān going out hunting: "It's true, my lord; Ujīrmān did say that the police were devious and not to be trusted. He'd quarreled with Putalī that morning as well."

Next came Kānchā Bijuvā. "My lord, I'd spent the night at Lālmān's house in the Magar village,[3] and that morning I was on my way home with Māité. As we passed Ujīrmān's house I heard them arguing inside. 'Why don't you leave it alone, what's the point of killing?' Putalī was saying. Ujīrmān was shouting angrily, 'Let me be, you whore! I will not rest till I've killed that *bhālu*. Today it's either him or me!' I don't know,

2. Māghé Sankrānti is an important festival on the first of Māgh (January–February). A feature of this festival is that fairs are held throughout the region. These are often occasions for courtship between young men and women.

3. The Magar are an ethnic group from west-central Nepal who speak a Tibeto-Burman language.

my lord; at the time we thought he was talking about a bear. Little did we know that it was Officer Bhālu he was jealous of!"

The judge became rather stern. "Just tell the court what happened. It's not for you to add your own interpretations."

"That's all I know, my lord," said Kānchā, startled. "But I did see him going out with a gun."

Ujīrmān stood there deep in his thoughts; inside, he was furious. Suddenly he heard someone call Putalī's name, and he looked up as she was led into the courtroom. She looked all around, but when her eyes met Ujīrmān's she turned away and hung her head. He wondered why she had lowered her gaze, but then he thought, "Well, she's never been in a court before; she must be nervous in front of all these people. Now my Putalī will defend her husband's honor and give sharp replies to all their questions."

A man and his wife stood on either side of the judge. One was there as a criminal, the other to prove that he was a killer. One was there as the accused, the other as a witness to confirm the accusation. The questioning began. A police officer showed her a blue sweater and asked, "Did you knit this?"

"Yes."

"When it was finished, to whom did you give it?"

"Officer Bhālu."

"Why did you give it to him?"

"Last year, did you go to the Māghé Sankrānti fair with Officer Bhālu?"

"Yes I did. So what?"

"What was your relationship with Officer Bhālu?"

"Had your husband discovered that you were planning to run away to the hills with Officer Bhālu?"

Ujīrmān's lawyer interrupted. "My lord, I object. The question is not relevant. It has nothing to do with the incident."

"My lord, it is of course wholly relevant. It is necessary for us to know what effect the elopement plan had upon Ujīrmān."

"Objection overruled," said the judge. "Proceed."

The policeman repeated his question. "Had your husband discovered that you were planning to run away to the hills with Officer Bhālu?"

"He had not."

"Did you tell Officer Bhālu not to come that evening because your husband had found out and was going to kill him?"

"In the end, he came every day, didn't he!"

"Just give me a simple answer. Did you or didn't you?"

"I did."

"The morning before Officer Bhālu was killed, did you and Ujīrmān quarrel, and did Ujīrmān say, 'Leave it, don't try to change my mind. Today it's either Officer Bhālu or me?' "

"Yes, we did have a row. But it was the bear he said he would kill."

The policeman turned to the judge.

"My lord, if a man is setting out to kill a bear, he never goes into the forest alone. She's trying to save her husband. She has already admitted that she told Officer Bhālu not to go out that evening because her husband was going to kill him. We know already that Ujīrmān was furiously jealous of Bhālu. Without telling anybody, he went down into the forest on his own simply in order to kill him. When Ujīrmān fired the gun, he knew exactly what he was doing."

Ujīrmān was holding his breath. He felt the ground crumbling beneath his feet, and he was lost for words. He stared dumbly at his feet. The judge turned to him.

"Have you anything to say?"

Ujīrmān's eyes blazed like a lion's, and he clenched his fists. All at once he stood up and bellowed, "I am guilty, my lord. I did put an end to that adulterer. I did fire the gun simply to kill that wretch. What! I am prepared to go to prison."

For a moment, the whole court was stunned. His lawyer turned to the judge and said, "My lord, I request a few days' adjournment. Because of what his wife has been through, the prisoner is not in his right mind."

But Ujīrmān interrupted, "I have not gone mad, my lord. I certainly did kill him, what, and I've no regrets! Ha ha ha." He began to laugh out loud.

The judge was banging the desk with his gavel, but Ujīrmān went on laughing. He laughed and laughed until the whole court shook with his laughter.

(from *Sājhā Kathā* [1968] 1979)

Daulat Bikram Bishṭha (b. 1926)

Bishṭha was born in the eastern district of Bhojpur and is one of Nepal's few truly accomplished novelists. Six novels by Bishṭha have been published, and several have earned him literary prizes. His stories are extremely varied and include psychological portraits, portrayals of oppression, and simple romances. Bishṭha's stories are collected in *Pradarshinī* (Exhibition, 1966), *Gālāko Lālī* (The Blush of a Face, 1968), *Chāyā* (Shadow, 1974), *Ghāukā Satra Chakkā* (The Seventeen Wheels of a Wound, 1978).

THE ĀNDHĪ KHOLĀ (*ĀNDHĪ KHOLĀ*)

Gangī goes on watching. It is midday, and some young lads from the Āndhī Kholā are on their way down to Gorakhpur to enlist at the cantonment there.[1] They follow a recruiting sergeant along the level path, singing as they come. She is affected by the melody of their song; its refrain touches her heart:

> Mother, mother, do not weep so,
> My letters will come to you time after time,
> Just like the sentries patrolling.

It holds a peculiar magic for her. The young men are taking this chance to sell their lives and pay off their debts: the chance is born of the tension between India and China. They sing to the beat of a drum,

1. Gorakhpur is a town in northern Uttar Pradesh to which aspiring young recruits used to travel during the period of British rule.

and Gangī's whole body repeats their refrain. As they pass by in front of her, she suddenly remembers him. His image reappears, like the dawn mists that weave their way up the western ridge from the valley of Āndhī Kholā. For Gangī has not forgotten; it seems like only yesterday. She feels that even now he is climbing the steep hill path out of the valley, following the recruiter, to join the war with the Germans. Twenty-five years seem to have flown by, and still she watches that hillside.

The young men are off to earn their rice abroad and maybe to throw their lives away. They begin to disappear as they go down the slope. But Gangī goes on watching. Even when they are all out of sight, she still thinks she hears their song on the wind. . . .

He was singing the same song when he crossed the pass and disappeared for ever. She was nineteen at the time. All the other young folk of the village used to tell her how pretty she was. Then she had been fleet of foot, able to run through the forests and over the hills, as light as a flower blossom. She used to go out with him, like a lively young doe, to cut grass for the livestock. As she drowsed in the shade of a *pīpal* tree, she often heard him singing that song.

There is a particular incident she wants to remember, but at the moment she can't recall it. She gazes up at the mountain peak, which seems to be fixed to the clouds, but a strange uneasy feeling persists.

Once, Gangī was on her way down to the valley, ostensibly to cut grass. But she was looking out for him, and suddenly she saw his figure at a bend in the path. She was struck by a mixture of joy and fear, and with her hand on her pounding breast, she hid like a bird in the roots of a tree by the Āndhī Kholā. Slowly, she inched her way toward the riverbank, waiting for a chance to escape without him spotting her. She jumped over one boulder and down onto another, chuckling quietly in delight. But then she thought she heard him breathing on the far side of the rocks.

Her heart still pounded, but she tried to hold her breath and jump the other way. He sounded very near, but he didn't seem to have discovered her. Perhaps he wanted to let her run for a little longer. Leaving the shelter of her rock, she jumped behind another. Then all at once she was in his arms. There she was, enfolded in his embrace, entangled with him like a bashful flower. So she put her foot into the river and splashed him with water.

Gangī smiles to herself: this was what she had tried to remember. The memory brings her comfort and relief; it is as if she has laid down a heavy load. Feeling a little lighter in spirit, she looks up the sheer hillside again. She sees the young men's dark shadows filing up the steep, twisting path. Their song and the beating of the drum come to her once more. As she watches those figures, it is as if she is searching for something she has lost. They are becoming smaller and smaller, just as he did as she watched him go. Gangī feels herself becoming smaller; she becomes as small as a seven-year-old girl.

When she was seven, she once went out at sunset to look for a goat that she feared might have been lost at the edge of the fields. She didn't know that his ten-year-old body was hidden up in a mulberry tree. He leapt down in front of her and gave her a terrific fright. She quarreled with him and compared his family to hers. There was a telephone in her uncle's house, she bragged, but at his uncle's house the mice were singing about all the rice they'd stolen. In her uncle's house, they played harmoniums, but at his there was a leaky roof. The rains came through in the summer, she mocked.[2] He became so cross with her that he slapped her in the face. Then she told his father about it, and he got a hiding. After he had taken his thrashing, she went and consoled him. From then on, she always consoled him.

How blue the memory makes her feel. It is as if she still feels his hand on her face. Lovingly, she strokes her cheek. . . . As if trying to hold back the tears, she looks up at the hillside once again, where it descends indifferently to the valley floor. The young men are nearly at the top, but because they are far away, she cannot hear their song anymore. Her eyes fall upon the distant, forested hill that overtops the ridge. What is the world like beyond the hills? Gangī cannot imagine; she just looks out from unblinking eyes.

Oh, her heart still pains her. It was at exactly this time of day, when evening was drawing in, that he sat outside, looking desolate. He just sat there in silence, deep in his thoughts. Gangī looked at him.

"What's the matter? Aren't you well?" she asked.

But he did not reply. Trying to start some conversation, she talked about various things, but her man remained as aloof as a rock, buffeted and broken by the Āndhī Kholā. Gangī was still trying to think of some way to cheer him up when he announced, "Tomorrow I am going to sign up in the war against the Germans."

Gangī felt as if she had tumbled down a waterfall. Without giving her any chance to question him, he set off for the village. Then Gangī was gripped by fear—that day his voice lacked its usual jocularity. She cast around for hope, but the more she did so, the more she became convinced—he was going to the war, for sure. His land was in a rich man's

2. Young Gurungs, as well as members of other ethnic groups in the Himalaya, often bring a semiritualized form of mockery into their flirtations. The accusations and counteraccusations may be sung.

hands; his livestock were all mortgaged. He was not prepared to wrestle with poverty every day of his life.

After the evening meal, Gangī went and sought him out. At first, he was impatient with her, but then he murmured sweetly, "The river is for bathing in, Gangī. Or else, why would people jump in? I'm not running away from hardship. The war will pay off our debts and fill our stomachs. And I'm not going alone, after all."

Gangī did not understand at all. She simply laid her head on his chest and sobbed, choked with grief. She hugged him tightly, as if she hoped that he would not go and desert his wife like Gautam Buddha, and listened to the awesome roar of the river in the night. As she listened she fell asleep. In her sleep, she dreamed that the clear water tumbling down from the mountains was turning cloudy as it descended. First, it submerged the boulders where they had played hide-and-seek, then the woods where they had wandered since childhood, teasing each other and joking. The waters rose higher, until she was afraid that the very hills would collapse and engulf her.

She woke from her dream in terror and listened for a moment to the thundering Āndhī Kholā, which shattered the empty silence of the night. He was still sleeping right there beside her. Sighing mournfully, she held him tight and pressed her face against his. As she went back to sleep she felt his warm breath on her cheek. She clung so tightly it was as if she was trying to imprison him, as if her hold on him would not be broken even if the river flooded and engulfed them both. She fell asleep to the warm sound of his breathing and his sweet heartbeat.

Next morning, she found that he was gone from her arms. Chilled, she rushed to open a window and look outside. The sun had already risen over the peaks beyond the river. She went out, still fastening her clothes, but she could not see him anywhere: not on the steps or in the yard. She ran to the village, but he was not there. Nor did she find him beside the Āndhī Kholā. Standing by the resting place, she looked up at the mountainside.

He was becoming smaller and smaller as he went up the hill. She felt that he had torn himself from her arms and forsaken that place forever. His song came down to her on the wind, spreading sadness all around:

> Mother, mother, do not weep so,
> My letters will come to you time after time,
> Just like the sentries patrolling.

Gangī watched him go, and as she watched, the leaves fell from the trees. As she watched, the leaves grew on the trees once more. Twenty-five years had passed, watching day and night. But still she watches. One day, he might eventually come back down that path.

Gradually, the young men vanish. There is only the empty path twisting up that fearsome slope. Gangī is still watching as the dusk, then the night, comes down on the Āndhī Kholā. She is hidden by the empty, silent night in which nothing can be seen. But Gangī goes on watching.

(from *Sājhā Kathā* [1968] 1979)

Bijay Malla (b. 1925)

Bijay Malla is the son of Riddhibahādur Malla, the first editor of *Shāradā*, and the younger brother of Govind Bahādur Goṭhālé. Bijay Malla was educated at Banāras Hindu University and at Trichandra College in Kathmandu. Both Goṭhālé and Bijay Malla were strongly influenced by their childhood in the literary household where *Shāradā* was produced, as well as by Bhavānī Bhikshu, who was the journal's third editor. Malla spent two years in jail for his anti-Rāṇā political activities during the late 1940s (hence the second story translated here) and was until 1990 the secretary of the Royal Nepal Academy.

Malla began by writing prose poetry and drama and quickly developed a self-consciously modern style of prose that strongly resembles his speech: rapid and confiding. His stories, which are almost always set in Kathmandu, observe life from a variety of unusual angles. "The Engineer's Head" (*Injinīrko Ṭāuko*), a story for which there has not been space in this book, is another interesting parable of humankind in the age of technology. Malla is also noted for his poetry, several dramas, and two novels. Malla's stories are published in two collections: *Ek Bāṭo Anek Moḍ* (One Road, Many Turnings, 1969) and *Parevā ra Kaidī* (The Prisoner and the Dove, 1977). Malla was awarded the Sājhā Puraskār for *Ek Bāṭo Anek Moḍ* in 1970.

SUNGLASSES (*KĀLO CHASHMĀ*)

It was raining a little. As I left the house in the dusk, I told my wife that I wouldn't be back that night. But my work finished earlier than I had expected and I came home at about two in the morning. I knew the front door would be locked, so I went to the back door, which was sometimes forgetfully left open. Even if it was shut, it could be opened by shaking the door frame hard; the lock was not especially strong. I was reluctant to call out and wake someone up when they were fast asleep. I felt this would cause an unnecessary fuss.

I was soaked through by the rain, but the back door was open. I went inside and crept up the stairs to the first floor, the second floor. The door to the room was shut. I pushed it gently: it was locked. So I thought I would go across the balcony into the back room to lie down. The room was dark; I pressed the switch and the electric bulb glared brightly.

I mopped my brow and dabbed my face with my handkerchief. Then I noticed the sound of someone breathing. I turned and looked: someone was asleep on the bed. I shook the water from my coat, shirt, and trousers. Sometimes my wife tires of her room and sleeps somewhere else. For that reason, every room is prettified! I laughed to myself.

Then suddenly I began to doubt that it really was my wife sleeping there because the door to my room was locked. So I wiped my eyes and peered over. Yes, it was her, alright. And there was someone else there, too, with fat thighs. I quietly moved closer.

They were both fast asleep. My wife was sleeping with her head resting on our neighbor's brawny shoulder and her forehead pressed against his cheek. Her breast was partially bared. The man was sleeping with his arms around her, squeezing her tightly with his thighs. They had obviously fallen asleep in great contentment. As I looked at them, I suddenly thought of two white roses entwined and blossoming together.

For a while I watched their contented faces and felt that there should be places in every life where the earth's creatures can play and enjoy themselves, and so sustain their lives. If they could live out their time in games, they would consider it an accomplishment.

I moved back a little, in case they woke up, but they were fast asleep. They did not lie still, however: they both moved their arms, as if searching for something on each other's breast. The white skin shone on their plump legs. I just stood and stared. I felt as if this man and this woman were the first people of creation. I felt like a spectator. Watching this charming scene was like watching some great event. So I watched.

Suddenly it occurred to me that I was watching my own wife sleeping shamelessly before me, in an immoral liaison with another man. I should be embarrassed. I should think this improper. I should feel violently angry, outraged, repugnant, and vengeful as a witness to such a reprehensible deed.

But still I watched the two of them, these two flower blossoms, with wide eyes. Really, they were beautiful.

All at once I remembered a story I had heard someplace, sometime, from a political friend who had been to jail. I do not remember it well, but he told me about a madman there who had stabbed his wife with a *khukurī* when he discovered her sleeping with an unmarried man. If his dog had only barked when it heard him coming home, his wife would have woken up and the man would have escaped. He would have gone on thinking that his wife was pure. But the dog had not barked, and he had caught his wife with the man. So he took the dog outside and killed it. And then there was his horse: if it hadn't brought him home so quickly from so far away, he wouldn't have seen her sleeping with that man. So he killed the horse for its crime, too; then he turned himself in and was sent to jail.

The story might have been invented, or it might have been true, but it was certainly instructive.

I smiled as this memory came back to me. The young couple who slept before me now were playing. The earth itself was their right. All they wanted to do was to enjoy a game of hide-and-seek. One day they would get caught up in the complex problems of morality and social convention. They would be frightened and even curse themselves. Questions of sacredness and defilement would pursue them. If they were unable to bear this, they might even go mad. But why should I hope for that? What difference did it make to me?

Why would I wish to be ungenerous to those who enjoy the pleasures of the flesh? I was watching them in their nakedness.

Even as they slept, there were traces of loving smiles on their faces. Their limbs were tangled up together. They murmured their satisfaction quietly in their sleep, as if swept along by joyous music. Their rounded arms, breasts, thighs, and calves were like those of stone images. Was their fulfillment limited to only this level?

So why should morality trouble them? The problem would begin as soon as they woke up and saw me. Could they put up with this question of morals? Would the sensual contentment they so recently found not disappear completely when they realized their corruption? Poor things! I didn't want any kind of question to overturn or disrupt the fulfillment they enjoyed or to pursue and worry them for the rest of their lives. I watched their peaceful attitude for a little longer before I switched off the light. Let them sleep in comfort, I thought, and I tiptoed out onto the balcony.

Next morning, I was up first. My wife was in a carefree, contented mood; she was cheerfully doing the housework.

"When did you come home?" she asked.

"A little while ago," I answered, smiling.

She was as light as a blossom; there was no awkwardness in her. She flitted to and fro, up and down, like a butterfly, busy in her work. Even I was surprised to see how happy she was. But anyone would behave like this if they had found fulfillment on their own mental plane. Did her happiness make any difference to me? How pleasant, how joyous their private world was!

She brought me fried eggs and tea in my room. Her slender, pretty body was certainly rather attractive. She picked up my clothes and my coat and brushed them down. They were dirty and soiled from the rain and from being left on the floor.

"So," she said, "you got soaked in the rain last night, and you stayed behind somewhere?" There was a sweetness in her voice. Today she seemed utterly charming.

Then my neighbor came in. He was ill at ease as soon as he saw me. His sense of moral weakness had gone, and his awkwardness made my wife's expression tense. For a moment, she was bewildered and doubtful. I smiled and offered him some tea, and they both relaxed a little.

As if paying no particular attention to them, I leafed through a magazine. Their uneasiness gradually diminished. When I looked surreptitiously at them I saw that smiles and a new world of dreams were dancing again in their eyes. Soft, tender emotions made their faces transparent, and they looked like an innocent boy and girl. Why should I thrust such delicate people into pain or sorrow? If the poor things ever discovered that I knew even a little about their innermost secret, the cruel restraints of guilt and convention would begin to trouble them. In reality, they were not contemptuous of the need for social approval, nor were they rebelling against it. Those eyes contained dreams and desires, beautiful, sweet! The first flowers of creation!

I did not realize that I was looking at them curiously. They became uncomfortable, and their conversation stopped in midflow. They surely feared that I knew something then. They were unsure of themselves and uneasy. My wife felt like getting up and going outside. They seemed suspicious of me and unable to understand my indifferent gaze. I smiled to myself.

I didn't want to cause them any pain. They should not have to worry about whether I knew or whether I was going to find out. It would be no great achievement to shatter the world they were playing in. But what good would it do me? Let them enjoy themselves in their own world! Moral questions could easily destroy their world of sensuality. So let me not find out—that would be best.

Most emotions can be seen in the eyes. So I decided that I would wear sunglasses from then on to hide them. Then their world would be safe.

Seeing me thinking to myself, they were suddenly agitated; a change came over them, as if they had the mentality of guilty criminals. Their contentment vanished; the soft dreams disappeared from their eyes; they wanted to get away from me to hide the signs of their fear. How conscious they were of the prohibitive rules of society! How easy it was to know which level their touchstone of judgment was on!

But I didn't want to cause them sorrow or fear. I stood up and decided to buy some goggles. I would wear them over my eyes. They should not feel any fear in my presence. Let them go on playing happily. Why should I deny that their world exists?

I turned around carefully, so that they would not see. Gentle emotions were in their eyes; a sweetness was on their lips. I had to buy some sunglasses then. If I wore sunglasses, I would become obviously aloof from the forms of social, moral man.

Goggles, sunglasses.

(first published c. 1960; from Malla 1977)

THE PRISONER AND THE DOVE (*PAREVĀ RA KAIDĪ*)

Sometimes something occurs in your life that is highly unlikely and totally unexpected, but the insight you gain from such an event can contribute to a change in the whole course of your life. The event I shall describe to you here was really quite an ordinary one.

We political prisoners were locked up in jail number —, also known as the round house. It was the time when the autocratic Rāṇās were ruling. We were among those who had joined a movement to bring democracy to our land. In the course of our struggle, most of us had ended up in various jails to endure punishment and privation. We all agreed that the Rāṇās' regime should be brought to an end, although each of us belonged to a different political persuasion. But we were forced to put on a show of unity in front of the warders and the regime and to behave as if we were unanimous in our values, without letting our differences become evident.

Thus, our daily relations inside the round house were like those of a family. We collected together the "offerings" they gave us in jail—one and a half *mānā* of paddy, a handful of firewood, a little salt and chili pepper, 1 paisā of dal, and a quarter of oil each week—and added it to the rice, lentils, ghee, and so on that came from various prisoners' homes. Thus we maintained a kind of diet. We also divided the various jobs up among us: some of us were cooks; others were washers-up; others sifted the poor-quality rice they gave us. We twelve young men ran our kitchen like this, and our tasks kept us busy in one way or another all day long. We lacked facilities for reading or writing, but domestic chores helped the time to pass without us being aware of it.

We had several other means of entertainment. There were cards and a *carram* board, and by good fortune we also had four pairs of doves. These had been cared for by a prisoner who was transferred shortly after our arrival. We felt obliged to take over his responsibility for them. At first, we feared that the doves might be a burden on us, but as we fed, tended, and played with the simple domestic creatures, they became quite attached to us. We all became very fond of them, too, when they hatched their eggs and produced little chicks. I hadn't realized that doves could become so tame and so friendly toward humans.

We gave each of them a name, according to its character, color, or shape: there were Victoria, Menkā, Dushyant, Shakuntalā, Lālpāté, Sāvitrī, Jurelī, and so on. The young doves we had reared would fly onto our shoulders or come and sit on the tips of our fingers. Sometimes they came cooing to light upon our heads or our bodies. At mealtimes, and when we scattered grain for them, the doves would congregate, each round its own master, and we gave special attention to our own particular birds. We would toss the adult birds into the air, and as they flew across the sky above the compound, mounting higher and higher, we thought of the world outside and longed to leave the jail. But they always flew back inside to come and settle on our shoulders and then to an open space where we had set up some cages for them like a dovecote. The jail was truly their home.

In the evenings, we were separated from them and shut away in our iron traps. Soldiers and jailers came and locked each cell, then locked the front gate and the two rear gates. Now and then we could hear the sound of the doves, and the soldiers' voices rang out from the watch-towers all through the night: "Be alert!" "Be alert!"

Early in the morning they would come to open up, unlocking the iron doors. Then the doves would fly to us, cooing. We would go out to sit on a dais in the yard, where we scattered food for them, and they would come to peck it up. One of the cockbirds would act out his love for his mate by cooing and dancing and fluttering along behind her. Then he would fly up onto the roof and join with her there. The hens would sit feeding their chicks. We would tarry a while to watch and enjoy these scenes, and then our daily work would begin.

We had come to identify so closely with these doves that we would search for any bird that did not come out into the compound in the morning. Sometimes, one would be found laying an egg or incubating. We so forgot ourselves in our care for the doves that we became almost oblivious to the passing of the days. We felt that the hardships of life in prison weighed less heavily on us because of them.

Even the prison workers were affected as they watched us passing our time in this pleasurable relationship. We even cut down on our own food and fed the doves mustard seeds that we had brought in from outside. So they became sturdy and strong; they could fly high up into the sky, and we watched them happily. Once or twice they were attacked by hawks, but the doves always returned home safely. We were overjoyed on such occasions and fed them especially large portions of grain.

After some time, we realized that the prison workers were not looking so kindly upon the source of our enjoyment and pleasure. One day, they were reluctant to bring us the mustard seeds we had had bought for us outside. Subsequently, we discovered one of the doves decapitated and flung to the ground, and we all became very sad and angry. We felt that we had been provoked, and we were as miserable and worried all through that day as we would have been if a member of our family had died. We were furious with the prison orderlies, and one or two of us even shouted angrily at them. They completely denied having killed the dove, but we were well acquainted with their mentality and put little faith in their protestations of innocence. We thought they might have killed the dove in order to eat it but had thrown it away so that the soldiers who had come to lock up would not see. From that day on, we were all vigilant: we counted the doves at lockup time and remained wakeful after dark.

Because of all this, relations between us and the orderlies gradually worsened. They would not come to our compound when we called them or buy us the things we needed. They would not call a doctor if one of us fell sick or even a barber to cut our hair. If ever our families sent something in for us, they would delay and procrastinate before handing it over. With a display of blatant hostility, they caused us the maximum possible hardship. We, too, decided to take only those things we needed and that were due to us and not to ask for any favors. This internal and external war between us went on and on.

One afternoon, the sun was blazing down and everyone lay in their cells, sleeping or talking quietly. I was suffering from an upset stomach, and I was on my way to the latrine when I caught a glimpse of someone going into the dovecote. When I saw that it was one of our group, my fear for the birds' safety was dispelled. The open area where the dovecote stood was in front of the latrine, from which one could see everything outside through a sackcloth partition. Most of us were of the firm opinion that this friend of ours was rather dull and uneducated, and so we had kept him off the more delicate tasks. During our discussions, and when a decision had to be taken, we attached little importance to what he said. He was not in the least interested in looking after the doves, and because he showed scant enthusiasm for games and his manners were coarse, he was obliged to live a life apart from us. He often wrangled with us and became irritated, so he lived hungrily on his own.

So on that day I was surprised to see him picking up the doves and caressing them. He held them to his face and kissed them. However he might have seemed on other occasions, I now became aware of another aspect of his character as I watched him consoling himself all alone in this display of affection. Suddenly, however, I was startled to see that he had grasped hold of one of the henbirds forcibly and had thrust its beak into his mouth. A strange change of mood showed on his face as it flapped its wings and struggled to be free. The dove was fluttering frantically, and he was holding on hard and sucking with excited desire. Suddenly, the dove fell to the ground. He calmed himself for a moment, stared blankly at the fallen dove, and then walked out.

I left the latrine and walked toward the dovecote, pretending to be unaware of what had taken place. There I saw the body and the head of the dove lying on the ground. I felt no shock or surprise. What I had witnessed was a clear glimpse into the mind of a man who had been kept away from his home for many years. Could I claim that such a thing was not latent inside me, too?

(from Malla 1977)

Ramesh Bikal (b. 1932)

Bikal, whose real name is Rameshvar Prasād Chālisé, was born near Gokarṇa in the Kathmandu Valley, passed a B.Ed. in 1960, and has worked in education for much of his life. His earlier stories express his socialist beliefs and antiestablishment instincts, for which he was imprisoned on three occasions between 1949 and 1952. His analyses of rural life are especially progressive, and Bikal's success in describing and empathizing with the lives of the common people of his country is without parallel in Nepali. Stories such as "A Splendid Buffalo," "The Song of New Road" (*Nayā Saḍakko Gīt*), "Footpath Ministers," and "The Chautārā at the Pass" (*Bhanjyāngko Chautāro*) are among the finest in Nepali literature. Bikal has more recently turned to stories about sexual relations—following a trend, perhaps—for which he is sometimes criticized.

Bikal's stories are published in eight volumes: *Birāno Deshmā* (In an Empty Land, 1959), *Nayā Saḍakko Gīt* (The Song of New Road, 1962), *13 Ramāilā Kathāharū* (13 Enjoyable Stories, 1967), *Āja Pheri Arko Tannā Pherincha* (Today Yet Another Bedspread Is Changed, 1967), *Euṭā Buḍho Violin Āshāvariko Dhunmā* (An Old Violin in the Āshāvari Tune, 1968), *Agenāko Ḍilmā* (On the Edge of the Hearth, 1968), *Urmilā Bhāujyū* (Sister-in-Law Urmilā, 1968), and *21 Ramāilā Kathāharū* (21 Enjoyable Stories, 1968). Bikal was awarded the Madan Puraskār for *Nayā Saḍakko Gīt* and was the first story writer to receive such a prize.

A SPLENDID BUFFALO (*LĀHURĪ BHAINSĪ*)

"What's going on at Lukhuré's place, eh? His house is full of people!" The *dwāré* looked out over his wall and saw a jet-black creature there. "What's that in Lukhuré's yard?" he asked impatiently, as if there should always be someone at hand to answer his questions or to tell him that what he said was true. He looked around, but there was no one near. Abashed, he called down to Rāmbīré Ghartī in the field, "Rāmé, hey, Rāmé! What's all the fuss at Lukhuré's place? Look! Is that a black cow there? What is it?"

"Eh? Oh, I think Lukhuré said something the other day about going to buy a buffalo. He must have brought it home today," muttered Rāmbīré as he came up the steps to the *dwāré*'s house. He touched his head to the *dwāré*'s feet, then shaded his eyes and looked over towards Lukhuré's house.

"Hey, it is you know! It certainly is a buffalo! The serf has brought a buffalo home!"[1]

"Lukhuré's bought a buffalo?" said the *dwāré* in amazement. He'd never have believed such a thing, even in a dream. If this were true, it was the most astonishing thing and something of a misdemeanor. He had always intended to get a good buffalo himself, but he'd been putting it off for years. Now that wretch Lukhuré had got one! How could this be? It felt like a blow to his status, indeed, and made him feel uneasy. It was as if someone had pricked him with a gramophone needle.

"What kind of buffalo has he got, then, Lukhuré the serf?"

"I don't know, I'm sure. He said he was going to look out for something that cost up to a hundred a hoof." Rāmbīré spoke absentmindedly, staring hard at Lukhuré's yard. Perhaps Rāmbīré was wandering pleasurably through a dream in which a buffalo was tethered outside his door, too, with a great deal of excitement going on around it.

The *dwāré* could not contain his curiosity, and a terrible compulsion led him toward Lukhuré's house. "Come on," he said. "Let's have a look. Let's see what kind of buffalo that serf has got for himself."

Lukhuré's yard was full of people, and Poḍé, his four-year-old son, ran round and round the buffalo, clapping his hands. His feet had hardly touched the ground since father brought it home to Ānkurī Bhanjyāng.[2] Long before the buffalo arrived, Poḍé had told all his friends about it and assembled them in the yard. As soon as his father stepped inside, he rushed up to him happily and swung from his coat.

"Father, have you brought our buffalo? Have you? Hey Gopé, look! Look at the buffalo my father's brought home! It's our buffalo, you know! Every evening we'll have buckets and buckets of milk! It looks beautiful, too! And we'll take ghee to the town and sell it there.[3] Then we'll buy ourselves some good coats with the money! Won't we, father? Don't you think so?"

1. The reference to Lukhuré as a "serf" may be literal or simply contemptuous.
2. The story is set in a hill village, as its name suggests: a *bhanjyāng* is a pass or col.
3. Ghee (Nepali *ghiu*) is a kind of cooking oil made from butter.

"Yes, oh yes. When I next go to town I'll buy you a lovely coat." Lukhuré wore a gentle smile; today he was delighted. For a change, his son's insistent demands did not make him snap. His old remorse was gone. The hopelessness that caused bitterness and envy had come to an end for him. Today a splendid buffalo, all fit and healthy, was tethered in his yard. Standing there on his doorstep, it was like the wishing tree, granting his small son's demands and fulfilling his age-old dream. He gazed at it with love and affection. Even the cold evening wind felt like the gentle hand of fortune or a mother's loving caress. He approached the buffalo slowly. It was a marvelous creature, for sure. It had big heavy udders, a black body so sleek that the flies simply slipped down from its hide, and short, stubby horns. A thrill ran through his body, and he patted it fondly.

Lukhuré was not alone in his feelings; Ghainṭī, his wife, was delighted, too. She obeyed her husband's every command without her usual wranglings. Usually, she would answer him back with all sorts of rude words if he asked for even a cup of water, but today he found that it was offered without even having to ask. She cooked some soup voluntarily, too, from some old leftover corn flour and filled up two baskets with grass. Then she heaped it up on the doorstep, saying, "This will do for this evening." Now she was hurrying in and out with great enthusiasm. Lukhuré was pleased as he watched her bustling about; it was all thanks to his splendid buffalo. Usually, a whole day could go by without her even looking happy or uttering a pleasant word. Where had the old Ghainṭī gone now, that embodiment of strife and malevolence who always answered back at length and misinterpreted even compliments in the most unpleasant ways? Where had this new Ghainṭī come from, cheery and smiling, an image of love and helpfulness? Lukhuré watched her and grinned. All around, he saw nature smiling. A vermilion pinkness spread up to the top of the mountains in the west. The forests, the hills, the very leaves of the trees beside his house, all seemed to share his pleasure. He forgot how tired he felt after the long walk home and began to attend to his buffalo, as excited as a twenty-year-old. He warmed the broth and fed some to it, then washed off the dried dung that caked its flanks. From his own hands he fed it some oil; then he stroked it with such dedication that it seemed the two of them would merge into one.

Then the *dwāré* entered Lukhuré's yard. With the *dwāré* came Rāmbīré, and Ghamāné and Khulāl, too. The *dwāré* fixed his gaze on the splendid, attractive buffalo. His eyes were like those of a kite when it spots a carcass far below. The others launched an assault of thoughts at it, too, and looked at it with covetous eyes.

"What did you pay for that, eh, Lukhuré?" Lukhuré was engrossed in his animal, and he jumped when he heard these sugary tones. Startled, he looked up and saw the *dwāré*, so Lukhuré rose hurriedly, walked over to the *dwāré*, and bowed down at his feet. Cautiously, Lukhuré said, "Well, sir, it actually cost me 120 a hoof. What do you think?" Then he looked curiously at the *dwāré*.

The *dwāré* was not overpleased by the unusual tone of satisfaction he detected in Lukhuré's voice or by the happy glint in his eye. The *dwāré* felt a prickling sensation, and his tongue tasted sour. He grimaced in distaste and his eyes flashed angrily, but he managed to conceal these unsuitable reactions with his usual smarmy attitude.

"Why, who can say? Who knows with these buffaloes?" he said, inspecting the animal thoroughly. He stooped to look at its udders; then walked right round it, assessing its body, its eyes, its horns. . . . Really, it was in excellent condition. It made him yearn for it. The *dwāré*'s mind darkened, like a cloth that is stained by smoke.

"You gave rather a lot for it. How much milk will it give? Just because it has good udders doesn't mean that it's of any use. You won't afford to eat meat just because it's fat."[4] He turned up his nose and narrowed his eyes. Lukhuré was afraid.

"What's wrong?" He looked apprehensively into the *dwāré*'s eyes but could see no change of mood there: all his crookedness was hidden under his moustache. Then the *dwāré* returned his gaze and Lukhuré's eyes turned gray with fear. The *dwāré* examined the buffalo a second time, walking all around it. At last he said with great gravity and with as much sympathy as he could muster, "This buffalo is short of breath. Look, Rāmbīré, am I wrong?"

Rāmbīré glanced at the *dwāré*; then he, too, walked round the buffalo to inspect it. Khulāl and Ghamāné repeated the performance. Eventually, Rāmbīré declared, "Would the *dwāré*'s eyes deceive him?" He spoke as if there was nothing else he could say. "You've seen lots of buffaloes like this, haven't you, brother Ghamāné? It is short of breath, is it not?"

Ghamāné and Khulāl affirmed in unison that it was indeed, and although it was not clear what Rāmbīré really thought, the *dwāré* quickly turned this to his advantage.

"It's not easy to deceive me, you know. How many buffaloes have I dealt with in my time? If its eyes were not in good condition, the whole animal would be worthless."

Lukhuré began to see stars; it was as if Rāhu in the darkness was going to gulp down the moon of his long-cherished dream.[5] It was as if he had fallen into a ditch of total darkness through no fault of his own. There was not even a blade of grass to clutch at: oh Lord!

4. The *dwāré* means that its milk will not earn him enough for him to supplement his family's meagre diet with meat, an expensive luxury item.

5. Rāhu is the name of a demon who seizes the sun and moon and thus causes eclipses.

"But Dhakāl at Jyāmdī village swore to me! If there was anything wrong with it, he said, he'd give me all my money back." He groped for a way out.

"Who, that dirty bastard Dhakāl?" The *dwāré* frowned. "If you start believing what he says, you're lost! How many people has he tossed into the mire? What do you say, Rāmé? Do I lie?"

"No, sir! If this buffalo isn't sick, you can pour beer down my throat!" said Rāmbīré firmly. Then he searched the *dwāré*'s eyes to assess the impact of his words.

Lukhuré sat down in the yard and held his head in his hands. His garden of dreams was suddenly blighted by frost. His joyous skies grew dark with remorse. His vision blurred, and the smiling sky, singing birds, and dancing leaves all disappeared. He panicked and broke into a sweat. Were his hopes completely shattered? Had he wasted so much money, money he'd splashed out like water, on something that had no value? Had fate cheated him like that? Even as he watched, everything vanished into a dark cloud: Ghainṭī, little Poḍé, his house, and everything else that was his. A groan of anguish burst from his lips, "Oh Lord! That damned scoundrel! I'll go tomorrow and put this old cow back on his doorstep!"

The little boy had been gamboling about as if he was the emperor of the world. But now he noticed the sudden change in his father's mood and looked fearfully up at him. Ghainṭī had been raining down favors for all she was worth, but now she leaned on the door frame, blowing out with rage, like a cake of dried dung when it falls into water.

The *dwāré* went home, biting back a cunning grin. Ghamāné and Khulāl followed behind him. "No point grieving over it," said Rāmbīré, putting his hand on Lukhuré's shoulder. "What had to be has happened. You should have asked a few people for some advice." Then he went home, too. The unfortunate house and the little family that lived there were left alone to bewail their fate.

That evening, the buffalo did indeed give very little milk. Actually, this was quite inevitable because it had just been driven along for ten miles, but the natural shortage just made Lukhuré feel even more suspicious.

"Did it really give little milk?" he thought. "Why would that happen if there were not something wrong with it?"

All night long, he tossed and turned in his bed, feeling as if he was being stung all over by hornets. On one side were his son's ambitions—he had begged for a buffalo day and night—all pulverized to dust now. On the other side was all that money wasted. He was hardly going to be able to pull such a sum from his pocket. Money was like the dirt on his son's hands—here today, gone tomorrow. Today he earned it; the next day it was spent. How many lifetimes would it take to pay off his debt to Nepal Bāhun?[6]

"Oh Lord, that bastard Dhakāl has really ruined the poor!" Lukhuré turned from side to side. In the darkness, his 250 rupees became an image of Nepal Bāhun, as black as iron, and danced before his eyes. Long claws came out of its fingers and started to come toward him.

Lukhuré groaned, then screamed out in the dark. Instead of making Ghaințī feel sorry for her husband, his cries just fueled her violent anger: "You were a cursed idiot! You should have taken some people along who knew better, instead of taking all that money and throwing it down a hole! You've gone completely mad!"

Until this evening, she had been the epitome of love and kindness. Now she had become an emanation of the fearsome goddess. She had been so keen to have a buffalo she had given him the very jewels from her nose and ears. And now the debt was huge. It was hardly surprising that she was furious.

"You've given over our whole house and everything we possess to the moneylender. You've even stripped me bare of my jewels. And then you looked like a blind man at the thing you were buying. Take it back where it came from first thing in the morning. Throw the rotten carcass down on his threshold; then come straight back, you blind fool!"

Lukhuré's wife's long tirades were the most unbearable aspect of the whole affair. They made him reel. "Oh Lord, if such a lovely looking buffalo hadn't been sick, I wouldn't have had to suffer all this."

But what if it suddenly dropped down dead? Lukhuré was gripped by terror at the thought. He kindled a fire in the hearth and lit the lamp. What if it dropped right there, tethered to its peg? He rushed out to the stall and set the lamp in a niche. The buffalo was still tied up there, just as before. Sleek, black, and heavy uddered—a thoroughly splendid buffalo. He stroked it; it was so beautiful. There was no sign of any change in its condition. He sighed, but his sigh was disconsolate. If only there'd been nothing wrong with it. . . .

"You don't keep a buffalo just because it's nice to look at. . . . And if you want to fool me . . . how many buffaloes like this have I dealt with?" The *dwāré*'s words still rang in his ears. To deceive him would be no joke. Lukhuré felt utterly miserable. He went back and laid down on his bed, but the sounds of the night could not lull him to sleep. And his wife's sharp words broke his heart to pieces. "Cursed idiot! You're wondering what you would do if it dropped down dead, aren't you! Wasting money on such a worthless creature!" But really—what if it *did* drop down dead out there? Lukhuré shook with worry; then he stood up

6. Nepal Bāhun, whose name simply means "Nepal Brāhmaṇ," is the local moneylender.

angrily again and went to take another good look. Once he had felt every part of its body, he went back to bed. But Ghainṭī's words were as sharp as needles, and she went on goading him all night. In the dark he looked over at her regretfully, silently begging her for forgiveness.

Actually, even Ghainṭī was going too far. What could poor Lukhuré do? He hadn't meant to throw his money away. It was fate that had really robbed them; it had been kind to that bloody Dhakāl. Why couldn't the woman understand this?

"Oh Lord, may that bloody, scrounging Brāhmaṇ be turned to ashes! He brings only misery to the poor. Surely he'll get burned one day by the money he's taken from them!"

"It's you that got burned! Why are you dreaming about someone else getting burned? What are you planning now, you fool, slaughtering it and selling the meat?" Ghainṭī's voice shook with anger and hurt.

What could Lukhuré do? He'd have to drive it all those miles again if he was going to take it back. Then Dhakāl would only insult him and send him away again. If the bastard was so gracious that he was always giving people refunds, he'd hardly have deceived him and robbed him in the first place! Lukhuré threw himself down like a dead man.

The next day, the village elders were assembled outside the *dwāré*'s house. It's a custom in the villages for them to gather each morning and evening at some respected person's house to smoke, talk, and share one another's sorrows. All the affairs of the village are discussed on such occasions; this was going on now. Lukhuré came along, looking gloomy. He bowed to the *dwāré* and sat very nervously to one side of him.

"What is it, Lukhé?[7] What do you have to say?" asked the *dwāré* in an insincere tone. "Did the buffalo give plenty of milk yesterday?"

"No, sir. It hardly gave any at all," replied Lukhuré miserably. He was truly in the depths of despair.

"Just as I said. . . . " The *dwāré* turned to the others. "This Lukhé is a simple, honest man. That bloody Brāhmaṇ tilled land down in the plains before he came here. What does he care? He has completely defrauded him. He's always the same. Was it right for him to take so much money from an ignorant, innocent man like this? I've been there too, you know." He puffed at the tobacco that Kānchī Ghartinī had passed him, blowing ashes into the air.

"There now, you see? That's what it means when people say that you never realize when something is going to go wrong. Now he's emptied his purse for a sickly buffalo. . . . And who will buy it from him?" Buḍhāthokī looked at Lukhuré's miserable face.

7. The *dwāre* is patronizing Lukhuré when addressing him with the diminutive form of his name.

"Who else would be blind enough to put all his money on a sickly buffalo? Tell me that!" said the *dwāré*, shaking his head in contempt.

"You'll have got yourself into debt over this, I suppose?" said Ghamāné.

"If this man's buffalo isn't sick, make me eat forbidden food!" gravely declared Sītārām Paṇḍit, the *dwāré*'s priest, and wiped his nose on the back of his hand. Then he looked at the *dwāré*. In fact, he had never even seen Lukhuré's buffalo, but he would not hesitate to find fault with a motorcar bought by some stranger in Bombay, not to mention a local buffalo, if he thought it would please his master. With this combined assault of truth and falsehood, no glimmer of hope was left in Lukhuré's mind. Desperately, he began to wail, "Oh *dwāré*, I am ruined! The bloody scoundrel's destroyed me! I'm so desperate I feel like giving everything up and leaving the world behind!"

"But what does this have to do with us? It was your own decision, not ours. You trusted your own judgment. Nor did we advise you. What do you say to that?" The *dwāré* seemed very severe, and Lukhuré was overcome.

"Sir, I admit it. I was so stupid. I chopped myself in the knee with an ax! But what can I do now? My wife's jewelry didn't fetch much. How will I pay off the 250 I borrowed from Nepal Bāhun? Oh Lord, what can I do?" Lukhuré's voice trembled; he seemed to stagger under an immense burden of remorse.

"There's no other way out," Rāmbīré spoke up from the corner. "You'll just have to take the rotten thing back."

"This unworthy Rāmé's words are not worth our attention." The *dwāré* dismissed this suggestion peremptorily. "You don't know that avaricious scoundrel. He will tell you anything you want to hear. But once your money's in his hands, all you'll get from him is abuse."

"Sir, I've had it. What should I do? I'm ruined." Lukhuré floundered like a fish out of water.

"You're in big trouble; it's true," Rāmbīré spoke more kindly than the others. His voice was tinged with sympathy. "Come, *dwāré*. Lukhé is a poor man of our village, and he's in a fix. If you don't consider the problem, who else can he turn to?"

"What do you mean, Rāmé? Are you suggesting that I should jump into the pit just so he can get out?" The *dwāré*'s tone was sarcastic.

"No, sir. Fifty rupees, or 100, is nothing to a man like you. But for a poor man it can mean the end. If you don't do it, who will?" Rāmbīré pressed his case, and Buḍhāthokī backed him up.

"Yes, sir, you should help the poor man out. He has no one to turn to. He serves as well as he is able."

The *dwāré* pretended to think the matter over for a long time. At last, he announced very gravely, "Are you all of one mind, then? If so, what can I say? It's an act of charity for one poor man. Although . . . no, not even Lukhuré need consider as low a price as 150. But, of course, I'm taking a risk, too. Either I'm getting a buffalo for 150, or I'm ruining myself. But of course, if it's an act of charity . . . 150, Lukhuré, what do you say?" It was as if he was setting down a great load of beneficence, borne through many lifetimes.

"The *dwāré*'s words are fitting. To spend money on such a buffalo is like investing in a carcass. There's no wrong being done to Lukhuré if 150 is written off." This grave statement came from Sītārām Paṇḍit. He was the religious leader of the village, and so his words were like scripture itself. He was like the unopposed chairman, and his decision was final.

"There, that's the opinion of our respected priest. What do you say to that?" The *dwāré* turned to Lukhuré. "Well, what do you say?"

His eyes were piercing. What could Lukhuré say, poor man? He looked around at them all. Except for the *dwāré*, Buḍhāthokī, Rāmé, and the Paṇḍit, they were all silent. There was helplessness in their faces. They hung their heads, unable to look Lukhuré straight in the eye.

That same evening, there were great goings-on at the *dwāré*'s house. A splendid buffalo was tethered in his yard: sleek, black, and heavy uddered. A half dozen of the headman's children crowded all around it. The *dwāré* was attending to it with the keenness of a twenty-year-old.

As he fed it some hay, he looked over to Lukhuré's yard. There wasn't much to see there now. Father and son were both standing up on their wall. Then Rāmbīré came in and bowed down at the *dwāré*'s feet.

"What do you say then, Rāmé? Isn't she a gem?"

"Certainly, sir, she's one in a million!"

They both looked over at Lukhuré's house. The outline of Lukhuré and his son, standing there staring at the buffalo, gradually faded into the soil as dusk's earthy shadow descended from the hilltops.

(from Bikal [1962] 1977; also included in *Sājhā Kathā* [1968] 1979)

Shankar Lāmichhāné (1928–1975)

Lāmichhāné was born in Kathmandu but lived with an uncle in Banāras until he was eleven. After receiving some basic education at Trichandra College in the capital, he took his first job at the age of twenty-two and worked for a number of governmental and cultural institutions in Kathmandu. In his later years he became the manager of a handicrafts store. Lāmichhāné was an admirer of modern American fiction and frequently mixed with foreign visitors to Nepal. His stories are heavy with symbolism, often lacking a conventional plot and more closely resembling essays, but his prose is rich, fluent, and mature. Most of Lāmichhāné's stories are collected in *Gaunthalīko Guṇḍ* (Swallow's Nest, 1968).

THE HALF-CLOSED EYES OF THE BUDDHA AND THE SLOWLY SETTING SUN (*ARDHAMUDIT NAYAN RA ḌUBNA LĀGEKO GHĀM*)

Oh guide, you do not, you cannot understand the joy we Westerners feel when we first set foot upon the soil of your country![1]

As the Dakota crosses the Four Passes,[2] we see this green valley with its geometric fields, its earthen houses of red, yellow, and white. The scent of soil and mountains is in the air, and there's an age-old peacefulness in the atmosphere. You were born amongst all of this, and so perhaps you feel that the embrace of these blue hills' outspread arms confines you. But we live in the plains or beside the sea. Our vision founders on an horizon of land or sea, and so we know the affection

1. An abridged version of this translation was published in *Bazaar South Asian Arts Magazine* (London), Spring 1988.
2. The Four Passes (Chār Bhanjyāng) is a name for the Kathmandu Valley.

with which the breast of these hills forever clings to your sight. You have never had to suffer the feeling of insignificance that is caused by a vast distance. Perhaps we are always adrift in vastness, my friend; perhaps that is why this, your enclosure, appeals to us! Has it ever occurred to you that the half-closed eyes of the Buddha seem to welcome you, even at the airport?[3] It is as if one acquires a calmness, as if one is returning once more to a resting place.

You have always known only how to give to the West. You've given us religion and the Purāṇas, images of brass and ornaments of ivory, manuscripts of palm leaves and inscriptions on copperplate. You gave us a civilization and its wisdom and garlands of jasmine flowers around our necks. You have continued in your giving, ignorant of what others call "taking," innocent of the notion of ownership. The very word *indulgence* is unknown to you. My friend, I know your history. Before I came here I spent several years in our libraries, leafing through the pages of your priceless volumes. You are a guide who will lead me down the streets and alleyways of the present, but I could take you along your ancient ways. Even now I can see it clearly: the valley is filled with water, and a lotus flower blooms where Swyambhūnāth now stands. Manjushrī strikes with his sword at Chobhār.[4] I see monks and nuns receiving alms and spreading the law in the nooks and crannies of the Kāsṭhamaṇḍapa.[5] Behold the eyes of these shaven-headed monks. You cannot meet their gaze! It is called the *samyak* gaze. Do you know what that means? It is perception, pure and without contamination; sight that perceives everything in its true form. I'll have just one more drink before dinner. . . .

You live in a house like a temple, but you are unaware of its beauty, its enchantment. In these wooden images, these multifarious ornamentations, these many styles, there is the flowing music of a chisel in the hands of an artist. Do you not feel it? Tell me about those happy, prosperous young artists working in the fields all day and creating beautiful images of their personal deities in their spare time, who are now covered by the dusts of the past.

3. The great dome-shaped Buddhist reliquaries known as *stūpas* are a striking feature of the Kathmandu Valley landscape. Onto many of these monuments there are painted a pair of enigmatic eyes.

4. In the remote geological past, the Kathmandu Valley was filled by a lake. A famous Buddhist legend says that a miraculous flame became manifest upon the surface of this lake, above the present site of Swyambhū hill. The Bodhisattva Manjushrī came down from the north to see this miracle and declared that it was a sign that the lake should be drained so that human beings could inhabit the valley. He struck with his sword at Chobhār, cleaving the hills to the south of the valley to let the waters escape.

5. The Kāsṭhamaṇḍapa is reputed to be the oldest building in Kathmandu; the city itself was probably named after this temple, which is said to have been built from the wood of a single tree.

Once, an artist was adding the finishing touches to a wooden image when his fair, tiny wife came by, carrying her baby on her back, and poured him *rakṣī* from a jug. The foam bubbled over and congealed. Is it true that it was that foam that inspired the artist to construct a roof of tiles? Oh, your land is truly great, this country where so many different cultures found their home. Aryans, non-Aryans, Hindus, and Buddhists all came and obtained a rebirth here. It must be the effect of your country's soil, my friend; it was the soil that enabled all these races to flourish together here. Come, I'll drink one more small one, it's not dinnertime yet. . . .

I am greatly indebted to you for you have served me both Nepali and Newārī food. Ah, *mo-mos*![6] . . . Just picture the scene: it is winter and an old man sits in the upper storey of his house, lit only by the fire. Perhaps the smoke is filling the room like fog from floor to ceiling. Perhaps he is telling his grandson about each and every Nepali item that Princess Bhrikuṭī took with her when King Amshuvarmān sent her off to Tibet.[7] The old lady smokes tobacco from a bamboo hookah, and, mindful of the old man, she carries on making fresh *mo-mos*. The son's wife puts some of them onto a brass plate, and the old man's words are garbled and obscured by his mouthful. The grandson laughs, and the old man tries to swallow quickly, so he burns his tongue and, unabashed, pours out a stream of ribald curses. . . . These are scenes that cannot be read in an old book in a library, and that is why I've had to come to Kathmandu and soak myself in its atmosphere, for which I'm greatly obliged to you. . . . Now, cheers once again, to your great country, and to mine!

Oh, and another thing that is not to be found in any book is the smile on the faces of these people. It is a smile of welcome, as if our meeting were neither accidental nor our first. It's as if I was the farmer's eldest son, coming home after a long day's work in the fields, as if my labors had been fruitful and I was content and at ease with my father. It's as if I have taken the world's most beautiful woman for my wife and have brought her along behind me, and my mother is smiling a welcome from the door. It's as if my sister's husband and I were the closest of friends and we, her brother and her husband, were coming along with our arms around one another, singing songs of drunkenness. It's as if—I cannot explain; however much I try, I cannot describe it fully. That smile is full of wisdom; it is a smile from the soul, a smile peculiar to this place. . . . One more drink, to your Nepalese smile, that sweet smile!

6. *Mo-mos* are steamed meat dumplings, a Tibetan delicacy.

7. The Tibetan king Songsten Gampo (r. 627–650), who established Buddhism in Tibet, took two wives. One was a Chinese princess; the other was Bhrikuṭī, daughter of the Nepalese king Amshuvarmān. Both of these princesses have been credited by various scholars with the king's conversion to Buddhism.

And then there are the eyes. The eyes of the carved lattice windows, the eyes painted on the door panels. The eyes on the *stūpas*, the eyes of the people. And the eyes of the Himalaya, which peep out from the gaps between the hills like those of a neighbor's boy when he jumps up to see the peach tree in your garden. This is a land of eyes, a land guarded by the half-closed eyes of the Lord Buddha.

Even if all of the world's history books were destroyed today, your eyes would build a new culture; they would reassemble a civilization. My appetite for eyes is still not satiated. Tomorrow I shall go to a lonely place where there is a *stūpa* with eyes that are clear. There I want to see the pleasant light of sunset reflected in the eyes of the Buddha. Show me beautiful, full eyes, eyes without equal, eyes whose memory will make this journey of mine unforgettable. . . . Come, let's go to eat dinner.

Come, my guest; today I am to show you some eyes.

This is Chobhār hill, where you people come to see the cleft that was made by Manjushrī's sword and the outflow of the Bāgmatī River. Today I'll take you up the hill where few of our guests ever go and no tourist's car can proceed. There (in your words) the dust of time has not yet covered the culture of the past. Do you see this worn old rock? A young village artist has drawn some birds on it. Nearby, he has sketched a temple, leaving out any mention of the religion to which it belongs. Further up the hill, in the middle of the village, stands the temple of Ādināth.[8] In the temple courtyard there is a shrine of Shiva, several Buddha images, and many prayer wheels, inscribed *Om mani padme hum*.[9] You say it is a living example of Nepalese tolerance and coexistence. Children play happily there, unconcerned by the variety of their gods, religions, and philosophies. But my guest, I will not take you there.

You have already seen much of such things, and you have understood them and even preached them. Today I'll take you to a house where I feel sure you will find the pulse of our reality. They are a farmer's family, probably owning a few fields here and there, where they work and sweat to pay off half the proceeds to someone in the city. There is no smoke to fill their upstairs room, they cook no *mo-mos* in their hearth, nor do they discuss Bhrikuṭī's dowry in their winters. There is a child in the home, who is certainly no divine incarnation, either. Attacked by polio and born into a poor farmer's household, the child is surely incapable of spreading the law or of making any contribution to this earth. He has taken birth here in one of his maker's strangest forms of creation.

8. This is an epithet meaning "primordial lord," under which the Buddha is worshipped at a temple near Chobhār; also a name for Shiva.

9. "Hail to the jewel in the lotus" (a famous Tibetan Buddhist mantra).

And moreover, my friend—oh, the climb has tired you; would you like some filtered water from the thermos flask?—my intention is not to show him to you as any kind of symbol. Yesterday you were swept along by waves of emotion, inspired by your "Black and White" whisky, and you urged me to show you eyes that would forever remind you of your visit to Nepal. So I have brought you here to show you eyes like that.

The child's whole body is useless; he cannot speak, move his hands, chew his food, or even spit. His eyes are the only living parts of his body and it is only his eyes that indicate that he is actually alive. I don't know whether his eyes have the *samyak* gaze or not. I don't even understand the term, but his face is certainly devoid of all emotion. His gaze is uninterested, without resolution or expression; it is inactive and listless, unexercised and lacking any measure of contemplation. (Perhaps I have begun to speak unwittingly in the terms of the Aryan eightfold path, which will either be your influence or a virtue bestowed upon me by the child.)

My guest, these are the eyes you wanted. A living being accumulates many capabilities in one lifetime. It feels happy and it smiles; it feels sad and it weeps. If it feels cold, it seeks warmth, and if it is hungry, it prepares food to eat. It seeks to learn what it doesn't already know, and it succeeds or it fails. It has many experiences, some bitter, some sweet, and these it relates when company, occasion, and mood seem suited. How commonplace all of these actions are! My guest, yesterday you said that we Eastern peoples were always making contributions to the West, did you not? (Shall I give you some water? Are you out of breath?) Here is a child who can neither give nor take anything at all. Just put yourself in his position for a moment. You want your finger to do something, but your finger refuses. You want to speak, but speech will not come to you. Every vein, nerve, and bone is powerless to heed the commands of your brain, and yet . . . you are alive. I know that this disease occurs in your country, too. But the ability to endure it and to maintain a total indifference in the eyes, even, perhaps, to foster the *samyak* gaze, this capacity for remaining speechless, inactive, powerless, and immobile, and yet to survive without complaint . . . this can surely only be found in an Easterner!

Come, come closer. I have lied to his parents; I have told them that you are a doctor. Look . . . their faith in you shows in their eyes. There is intimacy, kindliness, and gratitude in their eyes, as if your coming here were preordained. That smile you described is on their faces, as if you were their eldest son who has brought a life-restoring remedy across the seven seas for your brother. The old peasant woman is smiling, isn't she? It's as if she's rejoicing at the birth of her first grandchild from your wife, the beauty of the world. I know that this same smile will remain on their faces as long as you are here. I know that it will be extinguished when you turn to go. Once you've gone they'll sink back into the same old darkness.

The child has a sister whose body functions properly. He watches her as she crawls around, picking up everything she comes across and putting it into her mouth, knocking over the beer, overturning the cooking stone. Just for an instant, the ambition to emulate her is reflected in his eyes, but then it is reabsorbed into the same old indifference. Once his mother was scolding his sister, and a light gleamed in his eyes. I couldn't tell you to which era its vision belonged, but I realized that he wanted to speak. With a gaze devoid of language, gesture, or voice, he wanted to say, "Mother, how can you appreciate what fun it is to fall over? To crawl through the green dub grass and rub the skin off your knees, to shed a couple of drops of blood like smeared tears, and graze your flesh a little. To feel pain and to cry, to call out for help. That pain would be such a sweet experience. She can rub her snot or spittle into her own grazes, or pull out the thorn that has pricked her, and throw it away. Or she could pull off a scab that has healed over a buried splinter of glass or spend a few days resting under her quilt. She can climb up onto the storage jar to try to pull a picture down from the wall, and when the peg slips out and the picture falls and the glass smashes with a wonderful noise, she feels a wave of fear as she realizes her guilt. She has grown up, learning from experience the facts that fire can burn her and water makes her wet, that nettles cause blisters and beer makes her dizzy. That if she falls she might be hurt or break a bone, that if something else falls it will probably break. That if someone dies, she is able to weep, and if someone laughs, she can laugh right back; if someone makes fun of her, she can strike them, and if someone steals from her, she can steal from them. My sister, who learns and remembers each and every new word she hears, is the result of the self-sacrificing practice of thousands of years of human language. She embodies a history, a tradition, and a culture, and it is in her very ability to speak that the future is born. But not in one like me, who cannot even move his lips. In my body, in its strength and gestures, an unbroken cycle of historical and human development has come to its conclusion. A long labor, a chain of events, a lengthy endeavor, and an endlessness are all at an end. The future ends and is broken abruptly."

And these are the eyes, my guest, that look at you but see nothing; this is the gaze that is incapable of self-manifestation. This is beauty that is complete and has no other expression.

These are eyes surrounded by mountains; their lashes are rows of fields where rice ripens in the rains and wheat ripens in the winter.

These are the eyes that welcome you, and these are eyes that build. And in these eyes hides the end of life. Look! They are just as beautiful as the setting sun's reflection in the eyes of the Buddha!

(first published 1962; from *Sājhā Kathā* [1968] 1979; also included in *Nepālī Kathā Sangraha* [1973] 1988, vol. 2)

Indra Bahādur Rāī (b. 1928)

Rāī is one of the most original and influential Nepali writers to have appeared in recent years. His earliest stories, collected in *Bipanā Katipaya* (So Many Waking Moments, 1960), were written in a naturalistic style. The second collection—*Kathāsthā* (The Faith of Stories)—showed a dramatic change of approach and philosophy, as Rāī formulated the views on literature that became the basis of the *Tesro Āyām* movement. *Kathāsthā* is divided into two sections: "Kathā" (Stories) and "Āsthā" (Faith), in which Rāī propounded his dimensionalist philosophy, beginning: "Let us write totality; let us live totality."

These stories were written in a style that was new in Nepali literature, and they displayed a completely novel attitude to plot, verb tense, and time. Much use was made of the language of modern and abstract art. "The Journey of a Thought" (*Euṭā Vichārko Yātrāpath*); "Black-out, Cashew Nuts, My Son" (*Black-out, Kājubadam, Chorā*); and "The Ordinariness of a Day" (*Euṭā Dinko Sāmānyatā*) are story titles from *Kathāsthā* that suggest the unorthodox nature of Rāī's work. Rāī is also a respected critic in a literature that is short of authoritative and objective commentators, and in 1964 he published an important novel, *Today There's A Show* (*Āja Ramitā Cha*). Rāī's stories are published in two collections: *Bipanā Katipaya* (1960) and *Kathāsthā* (1971).

MAINĀ'S MOTHER IS JUST LIKE US
(*HĀMĪ JASTAI MAINĀKĪ ĀMĀ*)

Waking a bundle of greens and lifting it from where it lies sleeping on the asphalt, then hugging it as if it is his wife, a customer asks, "How much for these greens?"

"Those are 6 paisā."

Injustice cries out, surrounding the man's self-interest with rage: he still remembers living in the forests, where it was possible to get them for nothing.

"They've turned yellow," he suggested (if they had, he would have rejected them immediately), and then he walked away.

Mainā's mother sat and waited for another customer.

"No point living in Darjeeling now," a man is saying. "Everyone here is looking for work. If you've studied, it gets you nowhere. We can't get enough to eat living here. When we came there were very few people, but now many more have come and our numbers have increased. There's not even enough grass for our animals. We should move somewhere else. The rains don't fall here anymore; the trees are bare. We should look for a new place. By sunset tomorrow we should be gone, with our women, our children, and all our belongings loaded into ox carts. Put strong young men at the front and the rear. Drive the livestock gently. We should walk until evening, then lodge for the night. When we are a hundred miles away we'll decide where we are headed."

"Over the hills to Assam. We should move to the northeast."

"Meet some of the people who came here later. Tell them the Nepalis came and set up a branch here many ages ago, a small town called Darjeeling. They've already found signs of very ancient settlements. For a hundred years or more they forgot themselves in this little toy town. Its little roads, little machines, little houses are the proof. There was very little to support them, so they became wanderers, scattered through the great land of India. Bunched together, they would all have died. The time had passed when they could have moved and advanced their civilization: their immediate needs were what forced them to abandon their homes."

"Yes, we should move somewhere new."

Mainā's mother was sprinkling water over her greens. If thoroughly drenched, their leaves would stay fresh; the cold spring water would make them last longer. Everything might be saved. But there is no water.

She covered the body of the bundles with a small grimy cloth. "You're back?" she asked the woman who stood there now.

"Are they sold?" she looked at the sleeping greens. "How much has been sold?"

"I haven't sold any."

"Oh! I shouldn't have tried to sell them here! I could have sold them easily somewhere else." The woman came tired from an age-long distance. She sat right down on the ground.

"Give me the few pennies you have. My baby's father is sick at home. I don't know if he's dead or alive." She stood up abruptly, suddenly fearful.

From here, you can see water falling into an ancient pond: circles spread out where each drop sets its feet. The rain makes the forest cry out; there is news that the rains are heavy this year. On the path that rounds the pool to the right, two or three bodies run hurriedly. One comes up to the tent and stands outside. He is a man she knows, and he smiles. He smiles in the pouring rain and says, "It's pelting down, isn't it!" He had pulled his trousers up above his knees.

"Where have you been to up there?" asks Mainā's mother, looking at legs like roof pillars, just as her mother's mother had done.

"I'm looking at a place up there. People have covered the hillside with cow pastures, I'm looking for some place higher up. They say Darjeeling will be a big town when people have covered it all."

"Everyone says the same," he heard in reply.

Suddenly the din of the rain outside says, "Be silent!" Inside the tent a fire burns between three stones and the rain keeps all the woodsmoke inside. The man with roof pillar legs found a plank and sat down.

"Hey, the water is coming in!" He stood up again, and the woman selling tea got up, too. Water ran in under the tent walls.

"Have you nothing to dig with?"

"No, I have nothing."

He picked up a piece of wood and went outside. Lashed by the rain, he began to dig a channel. The woman saw the fresh soil piling up. She saw that the water had stopped coming in and that she was encircled.

"That's it! The water's stopped!" she said, but the man continued to make good somewhere outside.

The rain clouds moved away. When the sun comes out, the forest's greens all turn to yellow. The strong man was still outside breaking the soil.

"Do I hear that they plan to fill in this pond and build a bazaar?" the shopkeeper asked, approaching him.

"Yes, that's right."

"Will they drain the pond?"

"They're going to demolish that bank over there."

"The pastures and the villages will all be washed away; they say there will be landslides."

"Who said so?" The man stood up.

"We're moving further up, too."

"Do you think I'm running away?" asked the man defensively.

"I've heard that all the plants and grasses here are medicines. If you knew which ones, you could cut them and sell them," said someone without a single penny in his pocket, clutching a small bag of rice.

"I've heard that there are mines underground near our house. There might be a copper mine right there in my garden. We should make the lowlands pay for water from our rivers," said another person, just coming home.

A rock swished down from overhead (man goes to the moon). Mainā's mother dodged it; it just missed her. Then came a stave (live as men). It caught her in the chest; she doubled up and fell.[1] All her sorrows stand before her; they come continually to her home. Joys for her are unknown and haughty. She wanted to sink underground in case great news came rolling down and crushed her. Her load of weighty hopes buried her deep, but she struggled to rise up and become a mountain.

Suddenly, she felt inspired to say—we came here looking for a place where we could see the Himalaya clearly. Now we don't want to go anywhere else. All of us should have a house where we can open the window each morning and look at the Himalaya. Here man is unhealthy; he quickly tires of most things; his thirst is quickly quenched. But with one thing we are never fed up, and that is the Himalaya. Wherever we go we will take this land with us, wrapped up in little bundles. We will make a five-year-old carry our possessions. . . .

The bundles of greens threw off the cloth that covered them and stood upright. Each bundle opened; each stalk came away. They yawned and cast their sleep aside. A light evening breeze was blowing; the small yellow mustard flowers jostled and swayed.

There is a small tree that has lifted its branches way up high. Her mind crawled still higher on a level branch, and she felt dizzy looking down. Her hands touched the grass at its base to uproot and weed it out. A well of smooth water had collected beside a tomato plant; she thought she might pick up a rotten old tin and water the plant. She sighs with pleasure as she sees something planted on the bank of the field. Bamboo bushes stand there, filling her eyes. Her eyes watch a leaf wafting down, making her wait for her own existence. She goes far across the brown ridges of the fields. On a piece of rising ground, luxuriant grass is growing. From the end of a garden she walks steeply uphill, moving from terrace to terrace. . . .

Why then did you come here?
Why then did you come here?

1. This bizarre and apparently meaningless juxtaposition of obscure images is typical of dimensionalist writings.

Why then did you come here?
Why then did you come here?[2]

A grinding stone, some dishes, in the bazaar. The marketplace is selling off the honor, the profits, and the losses of a thousand homes. A grinding stone should guard the porch of a home; it should become a part of the body of a house and hold firm to its floor. It should not wander around like this; the only things it should encounter are the sun each morning and the sun each evening. Young women sit around it, discussing things deep in their hearts. It is always bad when it comes into the market. Those black medicinal stems and roots should be stored away in tins and sacks inside every home. Those dishes should be kept on shelves. The place where the family sits down to eat at home is the only place to scatter such things around. To Mainā's mother, this bazaar looks like someone's home. It's as if a thousand households have been broken open. Why do a thousand homes stand neglected here? She felt like joining them all together, with children sucking and chewing on sugarcanes and daughters pounding grain. Our household things have all been put outside with us in the bazaar. First, man left home, then his belongings came after him, and now they are here in the bazaar, waiting to take him back. Mainā's mother tries to go home: suddenly, she is afraid of this bright, open afternoon. . . .

Hearing a noise, Hanumān hid in the leaves,
Quickly came Rāvaṇ along with his wives,
"When will Rāma come to kill me?
He has not saved Sītā, whom I've abducted,
Though I have seen him in my dreams."
Seeing the wicked one come near, Sītā bowed her head,
Holding fast to the vision of Rāma's lotus feet.[3]

She looked all around to bring herself back to reality. Like black dots, men climb the stairs and talk to each other. Their talking never ceases. Wherever she looked she saw more people. The whole scene becomes noise; everyone she sees is talking. They split up and come toward her, blocking her view. Their bags sway and collide with the tents.

The color of the flag has gone into the shadows; a loudspeaker blares in her ear.[4] A small boy runs by. Three people came and went; another

2. This is from a folk song about the Nepalis of Darjeeling by the late Agam Singh Giri.

3. From the Nepali Rāmāyaṇa—Rāvaṇ, the demon-king of Lankā, abducts Sītā, wife of Rāma, the princely incarnation of Vishnu. Rāma sends his most faithful disciple, the monkey-god Hanumān, to Lankā to recover her.

4. This reference is to the political unrest that has occurred sporadically in Darjeeling during the past few decades.

passed by engrossed in thought. One is walking past in a hurry. (I was born here, here I live, this I have, this I sell. I must find happiness with this simple wealth: this is my stand.) A dog is chased away; dirty papers have blown off into the distance; many voices are shouting. The bazaar is stirring, itching, lazily scratching. The sun is up on an electric pylon.

"Why did you come here?" asked an invisible person. A man walked by in front of her; he turned and asked her the same question. All the people standing in the street queued up to ask her; all the people inside the buildings opened their windows and asked her the question in high shrieking voices, staring at her from sharp eyes, taking aim with gaping mouths. She hid her face with her dirty shawl and peered out through the chinks of her window: an old fear. The whole bazaar left its work and came toward her. A thousand faces surrounded her, asking, "Why did you come here?"

The greens would be trampled—she turned cold with fear and leapt to her feet to gather them up.

In the evening she was keenly selling her greens. When night had fallen she covered the spot with a basket and a wooden box, reserving it for tomorrow.

(first published 1964; from *Bhāratīya Nepālī Kathā* 1982; also included in *Nepālī Kathā Sangraha* [1973] 1988, vol. 2)

Poshaṇ Pāṇḍé (b. 1932)

A surprise ending and a carefully constructed plot are the characteristic features of Pāṇḍé's stories. Many relate minor incidents from daily life or adopt everyday items as symbols of conflict, jealousy, or anger. Although "A Sweater for Brother-in-law" (*Bhinājyūko Svetar*) is generally recognized as his greatest story, it has a great deal in common with other, equally subtle tales such as "Krishna Dās's Wall Clock" (*Krishnadāsko Bhittā-Ghaḍī*), "Fingers" (*Auṃlā*), and "Rādheshyām's Bicycle" (*Rādheshyāmko Sāikal*). The popularity of Pāṇḍé's stories is evident from the recent publication of a fourth edition of his first collection. Pāṇḍé's stories are published in three volumes: *Ānkhījhyāl* (Lattice Window, 1964), *Mānas* (The Mind, 1968), and *Hiuṃmā Paḍekā Ḍobaharū* (Marks in the Snow, 1975).

A SWEATER FOR BROTHER-IN-LAW (*BHINĀJYŪKO SVEṬAR*)

Sabitā came gamboling over to Shāntī and said, "Sister! Brother-in-law says we're going to the cinema!"

"Tell him I'm not going," Shāntī spoke quietly, but her tone was severe.

Sabitā stood there for a moment, nonplussed. Her sister was so dull, she thought, she was indifferent to fun. How much older was she, after all? There was only five years between them. Sabitā left, silently scorning her sister's foolishness, but before she had gone very far Shāntī called her back.

"Did you offer to come and tell me?" she asked. "Or did he send you to me himself?" She put on a more cheerful expression.

Sabitā was puzzled. She knelt down and toyed with her sister's plait. "I was sitting out in the garden enjoying the sunshine," she began, in a voice as timid as her nature, "and brother-in-law came and asked me if I'd like to go to the cinema. So I said I'd come and ask you."

The cheerfulness fell from Shāntī's face, like a drop of shining dew falling from a blade of grass in a light morning breeze. But this time she had nothing cross to say. "Alright," she said, "I'll come."

"Good, sister!" Sabitā's gladness burst from her like a cascading stream. Her feelings were easily read in her face. Still, a doubt lingered on deep inside Shāntī. Time and again she tried to dispel it, but it went on confronting and nagging her.

Sabitā had come to stay with her elder sister some months before. They had been great friends since childhood. Shāntī still felt like kissing her sometimes for her childish ways and liveliness: Sabitā still played hide-and-seek and blindman's buff. Her behavior and manner remained unchanged, but although she did not realize it, she was gradually maturing. Shāntī no longer enjoyed such games; sometimes her nostalgia prompted her to play, but she was too hesitant, too self-conscious. Indeed, she was very different from her sister.

Shāntī was plagued by worry because she had never made her husband happy. Whenever Sabitā praised him, or told her how wonderful he was, she would feel strangely wounded, strangely envious. But she never said anything to Sabitā about how she was becoming tangled up inside, as if some spider was weaving its web in the darkness of her mind.

One day, Shāntī was sitting on the verandah combing her hair, with a small mirror before her. As she looked into it she suddenly thought she looked old. Strands of her hair fell out as she combed, and her face was flecked with dandruff. Hurriedly, she powdered her cheeks, and her face turned as white as snow. Then Sabitā arrived, wearing mascara around her big eyes, in soft white cotton trousers and a pajama top of embroidered silk. Roses were blooming in her cheeks, and her body was young and healthy.

"Why sister, these hairs are gray!" Sabitā picked one up and placed it in Shāntī's hand.

Shāntī looked at her sister's hair. She inspected her from head to toe, but she couldn't find anything to put into Sabitā's hand in return. So she just sat there, fingering the gray hair. "Oh," she said.

"Brother-in-law is here!" said Sabitā, overjoyed. As Gopīnāth approached them, she said flirtatiously, "Brother-in-law, sister's hair's going gray. Get her some oil to turn it black, won't you?"

Shāntī did not like her sister's sympathy one little bit. She was furious. She saw her husband looking oddly at Sabitā.

"I'll buy her some at the show tomorrow," he said.

It was suffocating at the show that day. Crowds of people were crammed together everywhere; there was hardly room to blink. They found a ferris wheel—Sabitā wanted a ride, so Gopīnāth bought a ticket. Shāntī refused, although Sabitā tried to persuade her.

"Come on, sister, why not? It's a special day today, you know! Oh, what's wrong with my sister? She won't do anything!"

"You go. Brother-in-law will go with you, won't he? I'm feeling faint, I'll just sit down here for a while."

"Right, right, why force someone when they're feeling faint?" Gopīnāth found them a seat.

Shāntī wept a little, making sure nobody saw her. She leaned against a bamboo post and dried her eyes. The wheel turned round, and Sabitā and Gopīnāth went round with it. Shāntī was unable to watch; she really did feel giddy now. She turned and walked away with a weary expression on her face.

In a part of the show that was especially full, Shāntī became lost in the crowds. She didn't know which way to go to get back to Sabitā and Gopīnāth. Her mouth was dry with anxiety as she strained her eyes to look all around. Sitting on a bench outside a shop, she peered into the faces of people passing by. The cruel feet of time tramped over her, and she began to imagine things—things that made her burn with jealousy and vengeful feelings. Now her eyes were dry and her temperature rose.

"There . . . here's sister sitting happily . . . and we were looking for her over there!"

Shāntī looked up at them in irritation; they were both red in the face with excitement. Sabitā put her hand into her bag.

"Look! Brother-in-law's bought you some oil for your hair, and I've got some wool for a sweater, and cream, and powder. When we get home I'll show you, alright?"

"Yes. Haven't you had enough now? We've looked at everything." Shāntī looked strangely at Gopīnāth.

"Right, right, let's go home. We've been here for ages."

On the way home, Sabitā showed Shāntī her wool. "Sister, shall I knit brother-in-law a sweater?"

"I don't know! Why ask me? Ask the one you're knitting it for!" Shāntī's response was tinged with anger.

Sabitā became so engrossed in her knitting, she didn't even notice the days going by. As the sweater neared completion, her face shone more and more brightly with success and satisfaction. She held it up in front of her to inspect it, delighted with its embroidered flowers.

Sweater in hand, Sabitā was on her way to measure brother-in-law, like she did almost every day, when she met Shāntī on the stairs.

"Look sister! His sweater's nearly finished. I'm just going to check that it fits. I think the sides might be a little too small. What do you think? Will it suit him? It will, won't it?" Sabitā spoke as if she had no time for anything else.

Shāntī swallowed hard and put on a smile. "Those flowers won't suit him; they'd look better on a woman. Give it to me instead, and I'll knit him another one."

"Oh, what a joke! After all this trouble for brother-in-law?" Sabitā laughed, ignoring Shāntī's comment, and ran into brother-in-law's room. Shāntī watched her go. When she saw Sabitā going into his room to measure him day after day, a doubt arose in her mind. She had spent several sleepless nights trying to suppress her suspicions.

So Shāntī couldn't sleep that night either. She got up three or four times to drink water. At last, she looked at her watch; it was half past two. In the silence of the night she rose smartly and went to Sabitā's bedside. Sabitā's contented breathing offended her; it was as if Sabitā had robbed her of sleep. Her mood changed dramatically, and her nails went toward Sabitā's throat. But the mood could not last for long.

She noticed the sweater hanging from the head of the bed, and she pulled it slowly toward her. Sabitā had started sewing the back and the front together. Shāntī guessed that it would probably be finished by the following evening. Sabitā's obsession with her task seemed to involve some kind of vow, some kind of powerful penance. Her austerities had not wearied her, however; on the contrary, they had made her more healthy and energetic. Shāntī thought some more. Tomorrow night, when Gopīnāth put the sweater on, she would lose all her rights, all her authority, in this house. He would be so delighted with this lovely, warm sweater, he wouldn't want to take it off. She was sure, too, that she would know no peace of mind so long as it remained on his body. It seemed to Shāntī that a curtain was rising on some dreadful game and that the sound of the bell that announced its commencement was making her shake all over.

Then it was as if her hopes and fears all came into a knot. She held the sweater tightly in her hands. They say prevention is better than cure, so why shouldn't she burn it before it reached him, now that it was in her control? But she was not totally unfeeling toward Sabitā, and her jealousy soon took another form. Slowly, she began unpicking the threads. Then her actions increased so much in speed that it was as if some machine were rapidly unraveling the sweater, and the loose wool piled up quickly beside her. In her hurry to complete the job, she accidentally struck Sabitā on the back, and Sabitā woke up. She looked at her sister in amazement, then asked in a small voice that trembled with fear, "What's the matter, sister? Why are you unpicking it?"

Shāntī stopped what she was doing. "A sweater like this won't suit him," she said firmly. "I'm going to knit him a different one."

Sabitā's face grew red with surprise. "It's not for brother-in-law!" she blurted out. "It's for you! I gave him *his* sweater last night. He put it on straightaway and went to bed in it. Go and see how nice it looks!"

(from P. Pāṇḍé [1964] 1982; also included in *Sājhā Kathā* [1968] 1979 and *Nepālī Kathā Sangraha* [1973] 1988, vol. 1)

Tāriṇī Prasād Koirālā (1922–1974)

Born in India and educated at Banāras and Calcutta, Koirālā was the author of a novel entitled *Snakebite* (*Sarpadaṃsha*, 1968), a startlingly Freudian tale of child psychology. Not a prolific writer, Koirālā published a few stories in *Shāradā* between 1939 and 1942, and the rest appeared after 1950. "It Depends upon Your Point of View" is still a very popular story. Koirālā's stories can be found in the collection *Rāto Svetar* (Red Sweater, 1981).

IT DEPENDS UPON YOUR POINT OF VIEW (*DRISHṬIKOṆ*)

Professor Niranjan got up later that day than he had ever done before. The red morning sun had already begun to fade. As soon as he got up he felt tired. He had gone to bed very late the night before, and he had not had enough sleep. His lassitude and weariness made him unwilling to leave his bed. How sour his mouth tasted, how heavy his head!

As he got up he remembered the previous evening. Each and every second of it danced before his eyes. What a terrible thing he had done. How low he had sunk through his sexual desire. His weakness had brought down his soul—the soul he had held in check for a very long time.

What if someone found out? This was his greatest fear. The honor and status he had preserved for so long would be completely wiped out. He would never be able to show his face again. What would they say to him at the college? How could he ever stand in front of his students? Because of one momentary, commonplace error, the professor, who had always been highly respected by his students, would henceforth be considered base and immoral. The college girls held him in particularly high esteem. They placed the greatest faith and trust in him because of his supposedly flawless character. But now? If they found out about last night, would they still behave in the same way? Those young women who came in groups to Professor Niranjan's offices to ask him about things they didn't understand—and sat reading for hours, unworried and sure of their safety, in a corner of his lonely room—would they still believe in him when they found out about this? Would they sit calm and trusting like that, reading alone in his office?

No, of course they would not. They would keep their distance and whisper among themselves. On the streets, people would point at him and whisper to one another, "That's the professor who . . . you know, with the daughter of the shopkeeper who rents the house below his."

Oh, the professor was anxious! Even the morning sunlight scared him, so he hid his face under his quilt.

Such a terrible misdemeanor, caused by such a mundane mistake! If he had returned from his friend's house just one minute earlier or later last night, he would not have had to endure such burning remorse. The difference of one minute had caused a terrible misdeed. Now the stain it left would not wash away, even in a lifetime. As he left, his friend's wife had tried to persuade him to stay for one more cup of coffee. If he had just agreed to that trivial thing, he would have gone straight to his room—the encounter on his doorstep, the whole episode, none of it would have taken place. Or if he had left ten minutes earlier, when he first stood up to go, such a terrible thing would never have happened. Such a tiny random chance can destroy a lifetime's happiness. He felt despair as he thought this. Man depends on such slender chances for his joy and sorrow, his excitement, remorse, and regrets, thought the professor, and he began to feel hatred for the world's precision.

The more he tried to console himself by belittling the ways of the world to hide the sin he had himself committed, the more his soul shrank down in size. He began to taunt and curse himself.

As he lay there in his agitation, he began to repent the mistake of the previous day. He imagined walking down the street. Some of the people were grinning at him; others pointed at him from a distance and whispered. The college boys would spread rumors about him; the girls would be afraid even to come near him. If this thing assumed larger proportions, the news of his immoral act would spread throughout the city, and seeing a blow to the college's good reputation, the legislative committee would expell him from his post as professor, stating, "The legislative committee of this college has expelled Professor Niranjan Kumār Sharmā on charges of immorality." What a disgrace! What infamy!

The professor could think of no solution. His desperation made him choke; he could not even weep. His hopelessness made his brain go blank.

He was weak and exhausted with remorse. He could not even get out of his bed. What was the point, after all? Whatever he did now, last night's deed was done. Last night, he must have thought that all the world's happiness would be his, that his immoral act was going to bring him lifelong satisfaction. He cursed himself. They said he was a great scholar. But such a stupid fool could not foresee the outcome. Great scholar, indeed! How highly the education department had regarded this unintelligent man! They said that there was no one in the whole city, let alone in the college, who could match his intellect. Was it a measure of his intellect that he could not foresee the result of such an ordinary thing?

A flame of regret was trying to burst from his throat—that was the terrible state the professor was in.

"But couldn't it be kept secret?"—the thought flashed into his mind like lightning amid black clouds of despair.

After all, he thought, she is not the type to go around spreading rumors. She surely has a woman's modesty, and this is a matter of shame for her, too. Surely she would try to hide it as strenuously as he would! Other than the two of them, no one knew anything about it. He himself was prepared to forget it, as if it had never happened. His only fear was the girl. But after all, what could she gain from telling others about it?

What could she gain? He was startled as it came to him that she could certainly benefit from it! Was it an ordinary matter for a common shopkeeper's daughter to make a respected professor her husband? If she realized her luck, she'd go around telling the whole world. She'd tell the police, and they would take him to their office for questioning. He would walk down the street between two policemen, hanging his head in shame. Oh, what a disgrace that would be, what a shameful thing! People would turn around to watch, whispering to each other. Some of them might even crack jokes, making sure he heard them. Nor would the earth break open or the sky tear asunder. The world would watch the spectacle, and he . . .

Terrified, Professor Niranjan hid his face once more. He was engrossed in his emotional turmoil when someone creaked the door open. With a shout, he sat bolt upright. A multitude of fears came all at once into his timorous mind. The wretched girl had informed the police, he thought; they were at the door all ready to seize him. What could he do? There was not even time to drown himself. In just a moment now, the professor would be led out by the police to walk out onto the crowded street, his head bent in shame. . . .

But a servant came in with some tea.

A gentle heavenly hand picked up the man who had been drowning in a deep flooded river, gasping, screaming, and helpless, and set him on the river bank—his fears had been quite groundless. If a domestic servant had no inkling of what had happened, what could outsiders know?

The professor decided that the shopkeeper's daughter had not said anything to anyone. An involuntary feeling of sympathy for that fair-skinned, round-faced Newār girl entered his still drowsy mind. What did it matter if she was poor and uneducated? Man's humanity and tenderness, and the sensitivity that is in him, are a natural virtue in all people. For that, wealth is unnecessary, and so are education, civilization, culture.

When the servant had gone, he sat silently drinking his tea and thinking all manner of things. Certainly, his spirits were lighter, but various doubts began creeping back. No, she won't have told anyone anything yet. But then, she won't have had a chance to, all through the night. When she left the professor's room it was already one in the morning. Her mother and father would have been asleep by then. Once she got up in the morning she would think about whether anything could be gained from mentioning last night or whether it would cause disaster. If the daughter of a man who can hardly provide two meals a day managed to get a professor for a husband, there'd be no talk of disaster! She would be thinking that she could hardly imagine getting a better husband than him. If she wanted to take advantage of what happened last night, and told of it, her life would fruit and flower. And so, the professor decided, she would think about it for an hour or two, then tell her mother and father, and they would make use of it like a long-sought opportunity.

Oppressed by all the world's remorse and worry, he paced aimlessly up and down the room. He hung his head as a great storm raged in his brain. He looked up into the mirror. His face seemed to have changed completely overnight. His hair was rumpled and uncombed, his manner had lost its firmness, his eyes were sunken, his face was white and drained—but, above all, his face was declaring his immoral crime. It was perfectly obvious that he had done something base and that he was trying to hide it.

He was in such despair that life itself seemed an intolerable burden. The sin of a single night was going to weigh down on him for the rest of his life. His whole body was weak with hopelessness. He wanted relief—mental relief. If he sat quietly, his mind became still more restless; his brain tried to burst with uproar. He would have to go to work to take his mind off all this. He took a bath, and as the cold water touched his body he relaxed for a moment, but the water pouring down on his head could not cleanse his brain. His mind did not cool down. He sluiced himself with gallons of water, as if he was washing off filth. But the stain was deep inside him, hidden behind the mirror of his flesh and bones. The more he tried, the cleaner the mirror became, but the stain stayed just the same.

Food was beyond him; he simply pretended to eat, then prepared to go to college. But did Niranjan, who had done that evil thing last night, have the courage to go outside? He was at least secure here behind the walls of his house. Could the guilty professor go out and walk down the open street in front of a thousand eyes? How could he go to college? What if people already knew? After all, she was only a common shopkeeper's daughter; she would surely tell. Perhaps she had told already. . . .

The professor made a great effort and left his house. His face was a sight to behold: cowed and fearful, ready to step up to the gallows. Glancing apprehensively from side to side like a thief coming out of a house, he had hardly stepped out of the gate when a youth on his way to college said, "Hello, professor."

Deep in his thoughts, the professor was startled, and he jumped as if someone had pulled out a knife. He did not even look at the student, nor did he return his greeting. Had it been offered with any expectation of a response from him? Should he make himself even more of a figure of fun by replying to a contemptuous, sarcastic greeting, offered only to provoke him? With head bent low and eyes fixed straight ahead, he went only a few steps further before peering at the shop below his home. His gaze fell upon the wicked girl who had plunged his life into darkness. Then he heard her father's voice calling him from somewhere—"Hey, sir!"

The professor gasped, as if his heart was about to stop. He walked on, looking down at the ground. It seemed to him that the ground was shifting and slipping away. When he heard the old trader's challenge, he held his breath and began to walk quickly, pretending not to have heard at all.

"Hey, sir!" The trader came out of his shop. Now he would run after the professor, grab him by the arm and shout, "Where do you think you're going, sir, now that you've ravaged my daughter?"

Should the professor run, run away? Run away and disappear without trace? Should he run as fast as he could? Pretending not to see or hear, he walked away so fast, with his head bent low, that from a distance he seemed to be running.

Turning a corner a little way off, he heaved a long sigh, but he kept his head down, engrossed in his unclean thoughts, and kept on walking.

"Hello, professor!" He heard the sweet voice of a young girl.

The professor hesitated, then said, "Hello," and hurried on with his head down. Suddenly he felt angry and he fumed to himself, thinking, after all there is a limit even to mockery. After all, is anyone as pure and sacred as a rock in the Gangā? After all, who has not done wrong once or twice in his life? And there is a thing called forgiveness.

"Hello, professor!" He didn't even look to see who mocked him this time.

As long as no one sees their sins, people remain as pure as gods. What a ridiculous anomaly of the world! If man did not do wrong, would rocks and logs do it? After all, what is life based upon? Is this population walking the street not the result of mistakes made by men and women? Can one call them mistakes? Once one is married, one gets a licence for doing wrong. Is marriage not society's acceptance of prostitution? And is *this* humanity—to accept the wrongs of a society based on this dishonest foundation and to allow oneself to flow along in its polluted stream? Is *this* manhood? Is *this* courage?

He suddenly felt heartened. He felt that he had done nothing wrong the night before. On the contrary, those who considered him guilty were the ones who did wrong. Was it human to follow the path of mean, selfish people who set out to do wrong? If this was bad, then why not oppose it? Why not try to make a separate path and lead the world along that? Were his intellect, learning, and brilliance merely a worldly anomaly? Was manhood only cowardice? Why should he fall when he had not been corrupted by the ways of the world?

He moved on more confidently.

"Hello, professor!" another girl greeted him. He glanced at her—it was Reṇu, on her way to college with two exercise books.

The professor was irritated. Sternly he said, "What do you want to say?"

Reṇu was speechless. She had never imagined hearing such harsh words from her beloved professor. She stared at him, amazed and stunned.

"Go on, what do you have to say to me?" the professor said more forcefully. "Why don't you say something? Speak openly, won't you! What are you afraid of? Go on, beat the drum and proclaim the news to everyone!"

Reṇu was struck dumb. She looked unblinkingly at the professor and automatically pulled her scarf onto her shoulder. "Please forgive me, professor!" she begged, in an innocent, tremulous voice.

The professor walked on angrily. What kind of civilized behavior was this that once one had made some commonplace mistake one should discard all hope of forgiveness and strip oneself bare to reveal one's immorality? And then, what had the professor done wrong? Wasn't the world's very existence based on relations between men and women? After all, what kept the world alive? The relationship between a man and a woman was such a common and inevitable thing that wasn't it mankind's mistake to consider it an error? But as soon as one puts on the clothes of the law. . . .

"Hello professor!"

"Learn some manners, Keshar, learn some manners," said the professor, gritting his teeth. "Just attending lectures is not enough."

Keshar was put out by this unexpected reply and he stared at the professor in amazement.

The professor said determinedly, "However much you stare at me, you'll find I'm still a human being!"

Unable to understand any of this, Keshar asked the professor for his forgiveness. He took leave of him without further ado, thinking that scholarly, virtuous, dear Professor Niranjan sometimes behaved oddly because on occasion his brain was unable to accommodate all the profound learning it was required to hold. Keshar experienced a feeling of deep reverence for the professor, and gathering up all the love he felt for him he prayed with great emotion, "Lord, if you are there, make our professor well."

Professor Niranjan's anger was growing. His heart became harder and harder. He became so indomitable that he felt no power could lay him low.

As soon as they saw him, the crowd of students at the college gates crowded round him, like they always did, and said, "Hello, professor."

He did not stand there smiling as he usually did; his mood became even worse.

"Good morning, professor"—there was sweetness in the young girl's voice and deep reverence, respect, and love, too.

Chewing on his anger, the stern professor said sarcastically, "Good morning, lady!"

The girl was dumbfounded. When the bell rang and the professor entered, the whole class of one hundred and fifty boys and girls was as silent as the funeral ground. They lacked the liveliness they usually had, and they all stared disconsolately at the professor's unnaturally severe face.

On the table lay a thick book entitled *The Theories of Freud.* He went to pick it up, then changed his mind. Then he began to teach: "The basis of all creation is life, and the foundation of life is the union of man and woman. This is the very nucleus of life. The distorted view that we human beings take of this in our ignorance . . .

The students listened, stupefied, to Professor Niranjan's lecture.

(first published in *Bihāna* magazine 1964;
from *Pachchīs Varshakā Nepālī Kathā* 1982)

Premā Shāh

Premā Shāh first came to the attention of Nepali readers with the publication of "A Husband," which probably surpassed the many other stories on the subject of widowhood. A second influential story is "The Yellow Rose" (*Pahenlo Gulāph*), the diary of a woman who is dying from tuberculosis and observing her husband from her hospital bed. Premā Shāh is also a noted poet. Premā Shāh's stories are collected in *Pahenlo Gulāph* (Yellow Rose, 1966) and *Vishayāntara* (Digressions, 1971).

A HUSBAND (*LOGNÉ*)

Nirmalā, who had just finished mourning for her late husband, came home for her younger sister's wedding. She was soon involved in making up her sister's face, although she herself looked pale and tired and approached the task halfheartedly. The whole affair seemed quite unreal: cream, powder, lipstick, rouge . . . where should she put this spot of mascara, on her cheekbones or on her chin? Oh, who wore such cheap stuff, anyway! It was like making up a mask. Nirmalā didn't feel like putting it on; it was so old-fashioned to wear such things on one's cheeks. And her sister's face was pretty enough—why overdo the makeup?

Nirmalā was trying hard to smooth out and hide the threads from her past that still scratched away inside her. But somehow the reflection of her and her sister in that big mirror simply reminded her of her feelings. The mirror stood just where it had two years before, when Nirmalā herself had gone from this house. It was still intact, its silver untarnished, but she felt she had changed completely and aged terribly.

Her mascara-rimmed eyes were too tired to dance here and there with the liveliness they'd once had, and there was no longer any zest for life in her heart.

When she had finished, Nirmalā turned her sister's face to the mirror. She felt so fond of that face. Although the makeup had been her own work, she felt like holding and kissing it. But she could not do that: she felt too shy and too proud as well. For she was just as pretty, prettier than her sister, even now. "Nirmalā's prettier than Urmilā"—everyone said the same, but she still felt that her beauty was fading in front of her sister. She had really made her look vividly beautiful, but she was not pleased by her skill. Indeed, it was envy she felt: if only she could make herself look like this!

The young man in the next room who had come to see Urmilā was a new friend of her elder brother's, from Birāṭnagar.[1] He was perhaps a professor, but Nirmalā wasn't sure. The two sisters could hear them talking quietly. Nirmalā pricked up her ears and narrowed her eyes; she noticed Urmilā smiling softly as she looked in the mirror. The rosy pinkness of her blush made her even prettier. Then their brother laughed at something, and they heard someone else laughing, too, in a soft, low voice. Nirmalā tensed. Although Urmilā turned and smiled at her, she felt stung by her sister's total beauty. Everything froze to ice inside her. Urmilā was still gazing into the mirror when Nirmalā suddenly plucked the flower from her hair and tore it to shreds. Urmilā was shocked.

"Why did you do that, sister?"

Nirmalā's fair, slender face broke into a sweat. She stared wildly at Urmilā, and then, without thinking, she plucked the *ṭīkā* from her sister's brow. Now Urmilā was really scared; avoiding her sister, she ran out of the room. Nirmalā was amused as she watched her escaping, and she smiled to herself in the empty room. But even as she smiled, she began to cry as well. Her heart seemed to shrink. She put her head on her knees and breathed slowly; then she coughed quietly. Her throat was dry—was it from thirst? No, she wasn't thirsty. But she picked up a glass from the table and drank a little water just to wet her throat. Her tears were still clouding her eyes, but she sensed that someone had lifted the curtain in the doorway and was peering in at her, so she turned around. It was Urmilā, who ran away as soon as her sister saw her, letting the curtain fall.

"Are you spying on me?" Nirmalā felt a sudden anger. "What do you think I would do if you came in? I wasn't going to pull out your hair.

1. Birāṭnagar is a large town in the Tarāī.

You've become very proud since your marriage was fixed. Do you think I've come to be your co-wife? Why else would you be spying on me?"

She clearly heard the sound of laughter coming from the next room, and she listened hard. It was that man again, that professor. What a pleasant voice he had. He was probably a nice man, too. An honest face, really fair, just the right height . . .

"Nirmalā, child, we need the key from the drawer in there!" called Godāvarī, unable to step in through the door.[2] But then she saw what Nirmalā was up to.

"Mother! Nirmalā, child, what's this you're doing?"

Nirmalā jumped, and the lipstick she had been running along her lips fell from her hand. In the mirror she saw Godāvarī standing in the doorway. And she saw herself, made up like a butterfly. She felt shaken—she did not know what on earth she could have been thinking of to make herself up like this. Crushed by the enormity of her deed, she stared fixedly into the mirror as Godāvarī confronted her.

"I see, Nirmalā, my child! So you're making yourself up as well, are you? And look—you're wearing a *ṭīkā*, too! You, a woman with no husband!"[3]

Yes. Yes . . . of course. . . . Her husband had died in an air crash just one year ago. That man in the next room . . . he was Urmilā's prospective husband. He had come to see Urmilā. . . . Nirmalā poured out the rest of the water from the glass and hurriedly rubbed the makeup from her face. Godāvarī made to leave with the key, but Nirmalā blocked her path.

"Godāvarī, I beg you, don't tell anyone! Please don't tell anyone!"

"Would I talk about your private affairs?" Godāvarī went out, smiling.

Nirmalā felt thoroughly ashamed of her weakness. She hadn't been able to hide it from Godāvarī. What would Godāvarī tell everyone now? She'd exaggerate the whole affair. Nirmalā's face turned red, and she wiped away the rest of the rouge and powder with her handkerchief.

"If mother or elder brother had seen me made up like this. . . ! Or Urmilā . . . !"

Just then, Godāvarī came back. "Nirmalā, child, your mother says you must come and help sort out your sister's clothes."

"I'm coming. Go away."

"Come quickly then, won't you!" Godāvarī turned to leave.

But Nirmalā stayed where she was. "So I have to go and help her dress, do I? She's getting a husband, but she's still a child!"

Mother led Urmilā into the room. "Why are you still in here? I called

2. Godāvarī, one assumes, is an old house servant.

3. A widow may not wear the vermilion *ṭīkā*, which is a sign of marriage.

you to help dress poor Urmilā. She's never worn such a dress before. She just wrapped it around her any old how. Just look at her now . . ."

Nirmalā looked her sister up and down. The sārī looked fine on her.

"Is she still a child, then? Her bridegroom's come to see her, you know!" Urmilā looked lovely in green. There was no doubt about it—the boy would surely like her.

"Come on then, Nirmalā. You must take Urmilā to him now."

"No, mother, I won't go. You will be with her, after all."

Nirmalā's mother looked aghast. "What disobedient daughters I have! Is it like this when there's work to be done?"

"I have a terrible headache, or else I would come. But I can't even raise my head."

"Right, come on then, Urmilā!" Mother stormed out of the room.

But Urmilā ignored her. "*Please* come, too, sister," she pleaded with all her might.

"He's come to see you, not me. What's the point?"

"I'll feel shy in there all on my own. How can I sit there all on my own?" Urmilā was close to tears.

"Why should you feel shy? He'll be your man one day, you know! How will you manage once you're married if you behave like this?" Nirmalā tried to smile, but Urmilā was solemn. Elder brother came in and fetched Urmilā away. Then Nirmalā's conscience pricked her and she followed them. They all went into the next room, except Nirmalā, who stood outside the door holding up the curtain.

Inside, elder brother introduced Urmilā. "Urmilā, my youngest sister. She passed matriculation this year." Then he gestured toward the door, "This is the middle one. Come in, won't you, Nirmalā?"

The man might have heard, but he did not even give Nirmalā so much as a glance. He seemed a gentleman; his gaze remained fixed on Urmilā's green chiffon sārī. Nirmalā didn't feel like staying, so she went out onto the balcony. Outside, the sun was fierce. She felt even more depressed by the sight of the dust blowing around on both sides of the road and by the deafening roar of the horrible trucks that went past the house one after another.

A new jeep was parked outside the gate; perhaps it belonged to Urmilā's young man. A man in a dirty white shirt and dark glasses sat hugging the steering wheel: his driver, she assumed. He started to whistle when he saw Nirmalā; this she disliked, and so she returned to her room. But there she found the man who had come to see Urmilā, sitting all alone reading a newspaper. She was startled: this wasn't her room; it was her brother's. Why had she come in here? She didn't know—but she could hardly walk straight out again. What would he think if she did? And what would he say if she just stood there doing nothing? She felt extremely awkward. The man looked up just once from his newspaper, and then he started to read it again. Nirmalā tried to move, but she was rooted to the spot. The man did not utter a word for ages—he never even asked her to sit down; he seemed too absorbed in his newspaper. His hair was untidy, and a slight smell of Colgate rose from him. Nirmalā looked at his round face as he bent over the paper. She forgot her surroundings, and the scene grew dim.

"Sit down, won't you? How long have you been standing there?" He smiled at her at last.

She did not sit down but trembled all over. The man shifted his seat until he was much closer to her. "Sit down for a minute, won't you?" He tugged gently at the edge of her veil, and she offered no resistance. After a moment, he took hold of her hands and set her down close beside him. There she sat, nonplussed. The warmth of his touch consoled her a little. She began reassembling her fragmented dreams. . . . Gardens full of flowers, a sky full of flowers, a road covered with flowers . . .

Then the long dream was shattered again, as she felt a sharp pain in her left cheek. She put her hand to her face and felt that it was hot and red. She stood up so quickly it made her feel giddy, and the man laughed unkindly. She looked at him distrustfully. But he stood up carelessly and, without a word, walked over to the window that looked out over the street. She felt like telling him that he was unfaithful and slapping him back in the face. But she didn't raise a hand. Who was he to her? He was Urmilā's man. . . . She felt chilled. Then she rushed out of the room and met Urmilā in the hallway.

"What happened, sister? What happened to your face?" Nirmalā's eyes were red as she looked at her, and Urmilā was frightened. "What happened? Tell me!"

Nirmalā shoved her against the wall. "Your husband's all alone. Go in there, why don't you?"

On her way across the hall, Nirmalā bumped into Rāmé the water carrier. Rāmé had found his chance: he smiled and pulled out a piece of folded paper from the inside pocket of his shirt. As he hurried past, he handed it to Nirmalā. "The master in the house next door asked me to slip this to you in secret," he told her.

Back in her own room, she slammed the door shut. Her soul was rustling and swaying like a bamboo grove in the heat of midday. The scarf over her shoulder felt like a serpent clinging to her. Quickly, she pulled off her dress and rolled onto her bed. But still she felt uneasy. She slapped her own face a couple of times, but it brought her no peace of mind. Her heart banged away like a window left open in a gale. She clutched at her breast, but her misery wrung her even more. She thought of the jeep driver whistling rudely at her . . . the letter from that scoundrel next door that Rāmé had passed her . . . and . . . Nirmalā couldn't remember.

She took two sleeping tablets from the bottle on her table and gulped them down. Then she laid her head on her pillow and let out the sobs that were hiding inside her.

(from Shāh [1966] 1972; also included in *Sājhā Kathā* [1968] 1979)

Parashu Pradhān (b. 1943)

Parashu Pradhān was born in Bhojpur district and gained an M.A. in Nepali literature and politics. He began to write short stories in 1962 and has also published two novels. Pradhān's main themes are social contradictions and human relations, and he is admired for the poetic and symbolistic quality of his prose. Recently, he has begun to include foreigners, particularly Americans, in his stories, but he has been accused of trying to depict a society of which he has little knowledge. Pradhān remains a significant and original Nepali writer, however, and is perhaps somewhat underrated by his peers. Pradhān's stories are collected in six volumes: *Vakrarekhā* (Curved Line, 1968), *Pheri Ākramaṇ* (Another Attack, 1968), *Yauṭā Arko Dantyakathā* (Another Folktale, 1971), *Asambaddh* (Disjointed, 1975), *Samudramā Astāune Sūrya* (The Setting Sun on the Sea, 1978), and *Parashu Pradhānkā Pratinidhi Kathāharū* (Representative Stories of Parashu Pradhān, 1984).

THE TELEGRAM ON THE TABLE
(*TEBALMĀTHIKO TYAS ĀKĀSHVĀṆĪ*)

Once more he read the telegram that lay on the table. Or rather, his eyes went along its lines once again. He suddenly felt happy, although he knew that he was very tired. All day he had been out relating the entire history of the country to tourists and answering their multicolored questions. Now it seemed that some life had returned to his flagging ambitions. He smiled. A tragedy like this should have made him weep. But none of it touched him at all. It felt as ordinary as his everyday life: getting up at dawn, hurriedly rinsing out his mouth, pulling on jacket and trousers, tying a knot in his tie, then smiling at strange faces as if he knew them well.

A few days before he had met a friend, one of his best friends from his village, who had also come to the city and become trapped in some menial job. This friend knew about his tragic event and had uttered words of sympathy: "I am very sorry, Krishna. You have my heartfelt sympathy."

But this sympathy had not touched him at all. It had seemed meant for someone else. To observe convention, he had smiled nonetheless and simply said, "Thank you."

That telegram had been lying there for weeks. He always came home from the hotel in the middle of the night, and he was always tired like this. He would have been caught by a pair of blue eyes or immersed in Western music. His eyes always shone when he looked at the telegram. Perhaps he had needed to receive it before he could really achieve what he aimed for. Now that he had received it, perhaps he was happy. Very, very happy indeed.

He had always tried to speak English since he was a child. He had dreamed in English and considered English his all. It had brought him a new wave of happiness. Now he explained the culture and customs in his own way: how the *kumārī* was chosen, how the *kumārī* was worshipped, what the horse festival was like.[1] He thought of the foreigners staring straight at him and of Judiths and Jennies amazed by his words. His life was most enjoyable. Often he dreamed of New York skyscrapers and awoke from his dreams amazed by the Goddess of Liberty there. Or else he would imagine lying beside the ocean, playing a tape of Nepali folk songs. Sometimes he dreamed sentimentally; then he became practical again. For it was quite certain that one day Krishna would follow a tourist girl far across the skies. Unfamiliar voices were calling him from distant lands. "Come to us just once," they seemed to be saying. "We will be your guides. We will welcome you. We love you."

But then there was that telegram, which he would rather not have received. It took him back to earlier times and forced him to think about things he would prefer not to consider. The person it concerned had never meant much to him. He had never felt the need to pay much attention to her. He still lived in the city, just as he had ten years before, trying to make his seedling dreams grow. The telegram should have made him weep, but it didn't. He should have felt regret, but he didn't. He should have fasted for a while, but he didn't. That telegram should

1. The *kumārī* is the so-called living goddess of Kathmandu. The horse festival (*ghoḍe-jātrā*) is celebrated on the Tuṇḍikhel each year and involves horse races and other equestrian events.

have affected him; it should have elicited some response. But the wires inside Krishna were strange. No current ran along them. Nothing ever touched him. No grief could shake his heart.

He put it out of his mind and tried to sleep. He turned the radio on low and switched off the light, but sleep would not come. All that afternoon's tourists came before him, asking, "How old is this piece of art?" "What's the importance of this?" "Is woodcarving a new tradition?" And so on and so on. He forgot them and thought about his lodgings. He paid a high rent, but there were few amenities. If he got up too late, there was no water. If he kept his light on for too long, everyone complained. All sorts of houses had been built on the empty fields in front. The open sky was a long way off. He thought he would like to move somewhere else. Then he could invite that Miss Pāṇḍé from the travel service home for dinner. But the room he rented was bad, and soon even that mundane wish dwindled away.

Then he thought of the distant hills of his home. He had not visited for many years. It would be good to go home every Dasain, he thought, to join in the dancing and dispel the emptiness of the city. He would gladly swap places with someone there, even if it were only for a few days. Or he could brag to the idle young folk. "If you've no work, come with me," he could say. "I'll fix you up with a job." But as he thought of the hill country, that woman came into his mind again—the woman he did not want to define. He did not want to accept her or identify her. But a telegram had come, and there it was written, "Your wife died yesterday." There could be no doubt about what it told him. Your wife died yesterday, it said; your wife died yesterday.

It would not allow him to sleep. He pressed a switch, and the room lit up. He went to the table and read it again, forcing himself to concentrate. Your wife died yesterday, it said. Your wife died; your wife died. . . . For weeks he had slept there within sight of that message, but tonight for some reason his mind was filled with desired and unwanted connections, thoughts of the present and the past, all of them in discord. Why couldn't he sleep tonight? Why couldn't he make sense of it and weep? Having lived alone for so long in the city, had he become like a stone? Was he incapable of thought? Suddenly angry with himself, he tore it to shreds and burst into tears. He cried and cried, he knew not how long.

(first published 1975; from P. Pradhān 1984)

A RELATIONSHIP (*SAMBANDHA*)

Time itself becomes lost in the mists: that's what winter is like. Gyānchā looks from tired eyes—it's that woman again. Everyone calls her "crazy

Kānchī," but he knows her as Gangā, and he recognizes her from the glass dot on her forehead and her dirty, tangled hair.

Once one morning he had caught hold of her by her hair and said, "Gangā, Gangā, the sun is on the temple roofs, and you're not up yet!" Gangā had slept on, as cold as a stone. Gyānchā had tried to rouse her by pulling her ear and pinching her cheek, but still she'd lain there, and so he'd been angry. "Hey Kānchī, you crazy mule, get up! Your husband's here!"

"You're mad, Gyānchā," Gangā had told him. "Leave me alone. I haven't slept all night, and now you come bothering me so early in the morning, you bastard!"

Bastard? Gyānchā's heart hardened. The sun had been shining, and trust had bloomed between them. Gyānchā touched its flower and vowed, "Truly I love you, you crazy woman. Why do you always elude me? Idiot! Am I some kind of monster?"

Gangā was still as cold as the dawn; like the rest of the town, she slept on. He was on his way out to wake up the city, to sweep its streets and alleyways clean. But his Gangā hadn't got up, so he just gave up trying. "If you don't get up, I'll never come back, understand? I'll never come back, not even if you die."

Then she smiled rather cruelly—"Gyānchā, why are you angry?" she seemed to say. Her face was gray, her eyes were sunken, and he felt sorry for her. "Didn't you eat yesterday?" he asked but was puzzled by her silence. "Not even a cup of tea?" Gangā shook her head. "Why, oh why didn't you come to me?" He felt like spitting in her face, like grabbing her by her matted hair and throwing her to the ground. But Gyānchā symbolized weakness; he was hopelessness embodied. His weakness had driven him down to Asan: in front of Kāl Bhairav he had clasped his hands.[2]

At Ratna Park once, they sat in a corner. He had whispered, "Gangā, come and live with me."

"In your house, you bastard?"

"Yes, of course, where else?"

"Could you look after a woman?" she'd said, challenging his manhood.

Gyānchā had thought of the smelly rooms of his house and recalled the silence and the loneliness there on that frightful evening when he first stood alone: all alone in the great wide world. He had held out his arms and begged then for a mother's embrace, a father's affection. But all he had been given was a sweeping brush, and now after all these long

2. Asan is the old market quarter of Kathmandu. Kāl Bhairav is a famous statue of a ferocious deity in the city's main square.

years he still went on accepting it. In summer and winter he wandered aimlessly through the great city. . . .

Then the atmosphere changed; time moved on, and the sun crossed over the mountains. I shall marry you, Gangā, he'd thought. And with a big celebration at Bhadrakālī, too![3]

The same porters' platform, the same woman, Gangā, the same kind of pitiless morning. For two or three years she'd disappeared. But now here she is, lying prone on the platform. Gyānchā sees that her teeth are revolting and her hair is tousled. She sleeps curled up like a dog. He feels like saying, "You crazy woman! I told you to get up at once! The sun is high in the sky!" He will shake her awake, he thinks, then embrace her and say, "I shan't go out sweeping today. Let the inspector do his worst! Now that I've met you again in the cold . . . "

Now the sun is shining down on the platform. A small crowd has gathered, and its mood is changing. Gyānchā is rooted to the spot; there are many more streets for him to sweep, but he is unable to leave. A voice comes out of the crowd, "She has no relations; inform the city council." Slowly, Gyānchā accepts the fact that Gangā is dead. She is just a corpse without heirs. A great palace of dreams collapses. "Gangā cannot die," he shouts silently. "She can go mad, for sure, but that's all. . . . "

"The police must be told"—another voice from the crowd. Gyānchā opens his eyes, alarmed. He feels as if he is far away. He is at Pashupati temple, perhaps, or by the Buddha of Swyambhū or the waters of the Bāgmati. Once, Gangā washed her feet there. "Hey Gyānchā," she had cried. "If I died, would you light my pyre for me? I need a man to do that, not a husband who causes me sorrow. Not a husband who drinks all night, then beats me black and blue." She smiled then, as if she were ashamed. Another evening, she was weeping: "My husband died, I became a widow. My son died, now I'm all alone. The house, the land—it all went to the moneylenders."

How could her body be taken to the Bāgmati? The Bishṇumati was far enough.[4] And what about her funeral rites? Gyānchā felt desperate: he couldn't perform these duties. He couldn't grant her only wish. There was nothing he could do for her, nothing at all. . . .

"Will anyone take responsibility for this body?" asks a policeman. A hush falls on the crowd, the silence of death. Then it turns into whispers.

"It must be removed from here. There's nobody here to take it, is there?"

Gyānchā imagines climbing a mountain, clutching at trees for support. He sees the clouds and the wide blue sky. The sun appears and he goes

3. Bhadrakālī is the name of a temple to a fearsome aspect of the goddess Durgā.

4. The Bishṇumati River runs through the western sector of Kathmandu; the holier Bāgmati is somewhat farther away.

on; his arms and legs are not tired at all. He arrives at the top, beneath a vast lovely sky—Gangā is there before him. When she sees him, she covers her mouth and smiles. Gyānchā reaches out to her; he gathers her up in his arms, caresses and kisses her: Gangā, Gangā . . . but she runs away. He hears her voice in the distance: "You may not touch me, not even when I am dead."

He feels anxious; he would like to say to the policeman, "Please go. I beg you. I will send her soul on its way." There are a couple of bank notes in his belt; perhaps he could afford the rites. . . .

But then the policeman roars at him, "Hey, were you something to her? You over there, the one sitting quiet! Why don't you say something?"

Gyānchā didn't know what to say. What was Gangā to him? Could he say that she was his wife? No, they had never married. His lover? No, they had never loved. What, then? There was really no relationship between himself and Gangā. She meant nothing at all to him.

"Is she your wife?" Another question—Gyānchā looks up. Everyone's eyes are on him, filled with curiosity. He breaks into a sweat, and it is as if he has suddenly lost his voice. As he stares, bearers pick the body up. "May the name of Rāma be truth," they chant, as they carry it away to the river.[5] The crowds do not disperse, and Gyānchā lingers there for a while, wondering what it really was that linked him with Gangā, with crazy Kānchī. How was he involved in her death? Because he could not join the bearers, what did he have in common with the people left behind?

He had nothing to do with them really, he thought. Gangā's was just one more anonymous death at the platform. He, Gyānchā, lived amid such deaths. He would be a death one day, too. Other than this, he was nothing.

He walks away and notices that sunshine is filling the street. "The inspector will give me the sack today," he thinks, and hurries off down the alley.

(first published 1970; from P. Pradhān 1984; also included in *Pachchīs Varshakā Nepālī Kathā* 1982)

5. This is the traditional chant of corpse bearers all over Hindu South Asia.

Dhruba Chandra Gautam (b. 1944)

Gautam is known chiefly for the five highly accomplished novels he has published since 1969, but he has also played an important role in the development of the short story in Nepali. A prolific writer with at least sixty stories to his credit, Gautam deals almost exclusively with contemporary social issues and has developed a unique narrative style. Gautam's stories are collected in *Andhyāro Dipmā* (On a Dark Island, 1978) and *Gautamkā Kehī Pratinidhi Kathāharū* (Some of Gautam's Representative Stories, 1987).

THE FIRE (*ĀGLĀGĪ*)

The boss of our squad had a habit that caused us great tribulation. While talking, make a decision, arriving at a conclusion, or, sometimes, laughing, he would suddenly stop to await a sneeze. To smile and sneeze at the same time is difficult, and so he would yawn and twitch his nose up and down, just like an ordinary man, and in a sense make a joke of the time it was taking. Sometimes the wait would last a whole minute or even two. We did not care whether he sneezed or not; the problem for us was that he would stop like this even while we were discussing some extremely important matter, so that we had to pause in the middle of our advice. Then his face would become red and pitiable, and we would feel as if we were all assembled there to wait for the same thing—for his deliverance from his bond, for him to be put out of this misery so that the conversation could proceed.

The squad was made up of the boss, me, and Rām Prasād. Rām Prasād and I were at the same grade. I did not know Rām Prasād very well.

We'd had no way of getting to know one another before, but we became good friends during these few days. Rām Prasād often slandered the boss behind his back. We had to be out of earshot before he could do this, but we found plenty of opportunities. The boss himself did not seem inclined to socialize with us very much: he probably thought that it was more convenient and beneficial for him to maintain a certain distance from us. But on occasions we had to laugh at his weak old jokes when he did the worthy deed of obliging us with his company. This was why Rām Prasād detested him. Waiting for his sneezes was a custom Rām Prasād found particularly intolerable. Sometimes he would leave the boss waiting for his sneeze and go outside to smoke a cigarette, although there was in fact no need to go outside to smoke in that office.

The remote village we had to visit was 10 miles away from where we set out. The boss mounted a horse, but Rām Prasād had never ridden. He told me later that he was frightened of horses.

"I have a scar where a horse kicked me when I was a child," he said.

"So do you believe that every horse is going to kick you?" I asked him.

"Do you need to believe something in order to be afraid?" he replied, without even looking at me.

There was nothing I could say to that, so I walked, too, because of Rām Prasād. The journey was dull and wearisome, but Rām Prasād made full use of every chance he found to mock our boss on his horse and so the trip was not without its amusements.

A part of the village had been destroyed by a fire: that was why we were instructed to go there from the center. To look at our task, you might think that we were going to have to rush about like firemen, but actually our duty was to prove that the fire had happened, rather than to put it out. Our orders were to establish the cause of the fire, to gather evidence for it, and to give a sum of money to the most needy family. But "most needy family"—what did that mean? There was another order—from among the families affected by the fire, we were to pick out the ten poorest and give 500 to each of them.

The boss had all the money allotted to us for this act of generosity, but we had our TADA,[1] and our fervent wish was to save something from it. If you added them up, it turned out that our joint expenses came to equal the sum of money we were going to hand out.

The man who was going to lead us to the village had already been picked for us. He was from that village but not from the part that had burned down. The information he gave us about the fire was detailed

1. TADA is the acronym for travel and daily allowances.

and interesting. Because his own house had not been damaged, he did not have the look of despair that would be on the faces of a family who had been badly affected. Because of this, there was one useful thing: he related events with complete objectivity, which perhaps would not have been possible in other circumstances.

As we approached the village, the fire seemed to make itself felt. Rām Prasād pointed to a bamboo grove adjoining the village and said, "Look, there's the fire." In fact, there was no fire there, but we did see burned bamboos and scorched leaves.

Next to the grove there was a pool, which was in a sense inside the village. As we came near to it, we saw that it was no longer really a pool at all. That is, there was no water, but there was plenty of mud. Actually, a little water remained in some small depressions (although the pool itself was little more than a depression), but these puddles were muddy, dirty, and shallow.

One enjoyable thing there was that Rām Prasād made fun of the boss: "It's like the boss," he said, in a satirical tone I suppose, "half dried up!" Rām Prasād made the journey pass by finishing everything he said with some rude remark about the boss. Now his insults were becoming poetic. The funny thing was that Rām Prasād went on as if he were the only educated man in the world to have passed all his exams without answering a single question on poetry.

Another thing we saw there was a number of village children sifting with their feet through the mud and dirty water. There were small children, stark naked, as well as a few young girls who had just reached the age when some modesty is required.

"What are they doing there?" we asked the villager who accompanied us.

"Fishing, sir." He had a habit of clasping his hands together when he spoke.

"Is this pool always dry like this?"

"No sir, it's been dry since the fire."

"Did the heat of the fire dry it up?" Rām Prasād's question was juvenile.

The villager laughed. "Could a pool be dried up by the heat of a fire? No, there wasn't much water in it before. They filled buckets from it to put out the fire. The fire didn't go out, but the pool's been like this ever since!"

When we reached the damaged part of the village, we discovered that the fire was still not completely out, although it had died right down. The people were no longer distraught; they were resigned by now. We realized that the fire was not out as we walked up and felt its warmth there. The heat was coming from mounds of ash that had once been houses of straw. In some places, small huts had burned down, and their ruins had been cleared away, but black marks could still be seen measuring out squares where living homes had once stood. Quite a big house must have stood in one particular place: some scorched hardwood pillars still remained, but there was no sign of anything else. Wisps of smoke still rose from some of the mounds: the fire still smouldered inside them.

What emerged from all this was that the people had given up putting out fires and had resigned themselves to their fate. Most of them lay on string beds under the open sky or on the ground. They looked up at the sky, remembering their homes.

A baby caught hold of a nipple and sucked, let go of it and cried, then suddenly found it and began to suck again, but his mother seemed oblivious to him. Surrounded by smoke, she stared right past him. We saw children gamboling happily as they roasted fish in houses where the fire was still burning. They were evidently excited by the fire, and this was what had inspired them to sift and dig through the pool. The fire was all around us. But perhaps they were making the best use of it, tossing their catch down somewhere and then looking at it after a moment to find a ready-cooked fish.

Our boss was influenced less by all this than by the opportunity it presented for him to carry out his duty. His opinion was that duty always ranked higher than sentiment. The very next day after we arrived, he set up his task like a column in the middle of the burned-out section of the village and began to explain it to the villagers. When a large number of them had gathered, he asked, "Who are the poorest people in this quarter?"

The villagers may not have understood him, or perhaps the boss realized that he had phrased his question wrongly. It was difficult to put a very clear interpretation on it. So he clarified the question, "Who among you is extremely poor?"

Henceforth, the villagers' difficulties were reduced at a stroke, but our problems increased greatly. What happened was that seventeen people lined up in front of us. More people would certainly have come, but our boss had begun to look rather *nervous*. So I stood up and prevented any more of the poor from coming forward.

Meanwhile, Rām Prasād sat in silence, observing the villagers' poverty. He actually seemed quite uninterested and had even stopped slandering the boss quite so much. A brief summary of the boss's foolishness and selfishness still entered my ears, nonetheless.

Our troubles really began at this point. How were we going to share out the money? But that problem would come later. First, how were we going to select the ten poorest families? Poverty is not some race in which first and second place can be clearly decided on the spot. All the families that surrounded us looked like worthy and presentable specimens of poverty. Compared to them, we seemed so well-off, especially me and Rām Prasād, that we felt uneasy. The boss, on the other hand, habitually lived a low-class life at the center.

The boss questioned the first man: "How will you prove that you're the poorest?"

Rām Prasād was annoyed by this. "Is poverty something that can be proved? Why don't you assess them yourself? Even some people who are comfortably off will declare themselves poor because it can't be proved!"

"What else can I do? This is the job we have to do," said the boss.

"Sir, it's ages since we ate rice," said the man.

"Then you've probably got diabetes, sugar sickness. I'm sure you eat bread, however, don't you?" This was the boss's question.

Then the second man spoke. "Master, I don't even eat bread."

"What *do* you eat, then?"

"Oh, sometimes this, sometimes that." The boss did not look very satisfied. He was about to ask another question when a young man spoke up, "Sir, this man owned a half *bighā* of land."[2]

The man with a half *bighā* jumped in alarm. This was a big impediment if he was to prove himself poor.

"Only until last year, master!" he said. "Last year it was all sold, and since then I've been destitute."

"But *I* didn't have that piece of land handed down to me by *my* forefathers," said the first man to the second, "so which of us is poorer?" This made the boss's dilemma even worse, not to mention the second pauper's. But he went on making it worse still as he questioned a third, then a fourth, then a fifth. . . . The more questions he asked, the more of a mess he got himself into. His perplexity and indecision began to show clearly in his face.

"You have to give *your* opinions, too, you know! Which seven families should be disqualified?" The boss looked at us, totally at a loss. He was usually arrogant when it came to making decisions, and showed more self-confidence than was needed.

"We've already cut the numbers down as far as we can," said Rām Prasād. "But then, are all the other people *really* less poor than these seventeen?"

"What can we do?" said the boss, "It's as if every one of them is just born poor!"

2. A *bighā* is equivalent to about five-eighths of an acre.

"If there's enough money," I suggested, "why don't we just share it out among all of them?"

"That's not possible," said the boss. "An order's an order. It can't be changed now. And anyway, if you're going to share it out like that, why give it to only seventeen families? You'd have to give some to everyone else, too, and then they'd only get a tiny amount each!" He began to be sarcastic.

"Right then, let's do it like this," said Rām Prasād. "Everybody's poor in this place, so you could say there's no one who isn't. In the report, let's write that we couldn't find the ten poorest families."

Now the boss became more animated. His brow furrowed, and he raised his eyebrows a couple of times. Then he asked, "What's the point of such a report?"

"It would make the country seem rich. Isn't that worth doing? If we can't find ten poor families in a village where everything's been reduced to ashes, what brilliant progress there has been! Let's not underestimate it!"

Rām Prasād was clearly teasing the boss, but the boss sat there digesting all this and said nothing.

We were sitting on a bed under a big banyan tree. The villagers were beginning to look rather fed up with queuing in the hot sunshine. Those who had been excluded were standing behind them. There were others, too, watching us and our work with curiosity.

We had not suspected that we would have to do all this pointless work just to dole out 5,000 rupees to a village or that we would have to give such thought to rules and methods. It felt as if we'd been trapped.

Then I remembered a custom. "Sir, shall I run a lottery? I could write out ten winning tickets and make all the others losers. We're down to seventeen; now we have to cut it down further. I think there's some sense in picking the ten out like this. This would be the best way."

The boss's face brightened, but Rām Prasād laughed. "So now we're going to judge poverty in a lottery, are we?"

I shut him up. "Rām Prasādjī, be practical. If we don't do it like this, no one will get anything. So isn't this better? However they get it, and whoever they are, ten poor people will at least gain something."

Rām Prasād did shut up, but I wasn't sure that he was reconciled to the idea. The boss, on the other hand, looked as if he had discovered a medicine that would uproot poverty once and for all.

The tickets were prepared. Ten scraps of paper had "500" written on them; twelve more had "0." There were twelve losing tickets because the boss generously gave five more families permission to take part when he discovered the lottery method.

The boss shuffled the tickets, and he was about to throw them out on the ground when his expression showed that a sneeze was coming. Rām Prasād grimaced, and the villagers laughed at the boss. This time the boss did not sit down to wait; straightaway he pulled a rag from his pocket, held it to his nose, and began to walk around. Then with a terrific noise that startled even the birds, he sneezed "Aaa-choo!"—and, to tell the truth, the pieces of paper fell out of his hand as he did so and were scattered all over the ground. He had intended to keep shuffling them for a little longer to heighten the suspense. But at least he had been put out of his misery quickly.

As soon as this happened, the villagers began to push and shove one another and descended upon the tickets. For a while, none of them even managed to pick one up; they were trying too hard to prevent each other, and they were too afraid of ending up with nothing. Such scenes were described in the tale of Swasthānī, when men and women ran around in terror during storms or tempests.[3]

Our boss was watching with amusement. This was the first time he had ever been seen so amused, for which we had the villagers to thank. They had proved that a little humor could be produced in the boss on occasion. And it was true that the deperate expression on the villagers' faces when the tickets were released might have been considered entertaining.

Anyway, we found the ten we needed. But what was the last thing the boss did? He had begun to worry that his TADA would run out halfway home. So he decided to give each family 400 instead of 500.

"Four hundred or 500, it makes no difference to them," he said. "But if we reduce each one by 100 it will make a great difference to us. We'll get home more easily . . ."

"But how will we account for the missing 1,000?" I asked him.

"Oh, they'll sign for 500, these people." Then, as we were starting out, the boss slipped 250 into each of our pockets as extra travel expenses.

On our way, Rām Prasād said, "You see our boss, how skillful he is? He even pays attention to rank when it comes to the size of a bribe! Just you watch—I'll bring this money down on his head."

As Rām Prasād was saying this to me, the sun was setting, and only a little of it could be seen. We were close to the pool again. There seemed to be more children searching for fish there now, and several older women were involved in the hunt, too. That was the only change we could see in two days. Their legs, their arms, even their faces were mud-

3. Swasthānī is a goddess to whom women take vows in order to bear children. The tale of Swasthānī is a popular story that is read aloud as a part of such rituals, particularly among the Newārs of the Kathmandu Valley.

dy, and the mud could not dry because they were sweating. They didn't appear to have found any fish for a long time.

Our boss had already set off on his horse. For a couple of minutes we stood and stared at the pool and the setting sun.

(first published in *Sāngrilā* magazine, 1982; from Gautam 1987; also included in *Samsāmayik Sājhā Kathā* 1984)

Manu Brājākī (b. 1942)

Brājākī's first published story appeared in a Janakpur magazine in 1962, but he is still regarded as a writer whose work reflects contemporary trends. Brājākī has published two collections to date: *Avamūlyan* (Devaluation, 1981) and *Ākāshko Phal* (Fruits of the Sky, 1986).

A SMALL FISH SQUATS BY THE DHOBĪ KHOLĀ (*SĀNO MĀCHHĀ DHOBĪ KHOLĀKO BAGARMĀ*[1])

Today he saw that the ugly iron Aligarh padlock[2] was still hanging on the outside of the lavatory door. Its paint and polish had all washed away. He stared at the locked lavatory, deep in thought. Someone had chalked a picture on its outer wall of a betel leaf pierced by an arrow. It seemed incongruous to him; this was no place to be wounded by love.

He remembered the strangeness of his landlady, Bajai Āmā.[3] Stranger still was the sight of this lavatory bolted shut with an ugly iron padlock since eight o'clock in the morning. He looked at his watch: it was half past eight. Outside, a light summer shower was falling. How many more times could he go running over to use Hari's? Hari had a landlord, too—what was he going to say? It was Hari who'd told him teasingly, "This is what you've been looking for! You won't find a better room than this

1. The Dhobī Kholā, or "Washerman's Stream," is a small river that flows through Kathmandu.

2. Aligarh is a large town in northern India, presumably the place of the padlock's manufacture.

3. Her name is a combination of *bajai*, "grandmother," and *āmā*, "mother."

anywhere for 50 rupees. After all, they *were* going to ask seventy or eighty for it."

Realizing that he had little choice in the matter, he swallowed his pride, picked up his umbrella, and went out of the room. On the stairs he met Bimlā. Bimlā looked coyly at him. Her lips did not smile, but her whole face, her eyes, were laughing. He felt her face showed sympathy, not mockery. And some slight sense, too, of a betel leaf pierced by a barb. After an awkward moment when they jostled on the stairs, they each went their own way. Bimlā's long skirt swayed on up the stairs. He wondered, did Bimlā have the key to the padlock? Who knows? She might not. And could he really bring up the subject of a lavatory in his first conversation with such an educated young woman? He pulled out a cigarette and struck a match. Perhaps because of the match light, the ugly iron lock appeared again before his eyes. He hurried irritably down the stairs.

At the door, he came face to face with Bajai Āmā, the landlord's wife: a yellow face full of creases and wrinkles, a sandalwood spot on her brow, some ritual materials in one hand, a lady's umbrella in the other.

"You're up very late, young sir. Where are you going?"

"Just off to buy some vegetables . . ."

She laughed, as people often do, and their conversation ended. Was there sarcasm in her voice or kindliness? He did not know. There was no time for him to know either. But as he hurried away he felt as if that wrinkled old face was shouting back at him, "Are you off to squat by the Dhobī Kholā? You should get up earlier in the morning!"

He strode off anxiously to Hari's house.

A month ago, he had come here with Hari, looking for a place to stay. They had wandered around for hours, and they were completely disheartened. The house was as historic as Kathmandu itself. That is, it looked however you wanted it to look: to a rich man it seemed derelict; for a poor man it was fine. Hari introduced him.

"Hello."

"Hello."

"You'll have looked at the room?"

"Yes, it's fine. I'm on my own; one room is enough."

"Have you no family then?"

Bajai Āmā looked keenly at him, and he felt uneasy. This "because of your family" business had already stopped him getting any further in several other places.

"Not at the moment."

Hari glanced at him; his statement was true. To tell the whole truth, he should really have said, "My family is in my village. I will bring them here soon." But the fish had already escaped, and he just sat wringing his hands in silence like a fool. The old woman talked about this and that but mainly about her own domestic affairs. She pointed to a photograph on the wall, "That is the father of Bimlā here."

Even as she spoke, they both turned around to look at "Bimlā here." An ordinary-looking young girl in a dress embroidered with silk looked back at them with curiosity. Then they resumed listening to Bajai Āmā.

". . . But now he's gone. What to do? That's the way fate has it."

"Ohhh . . ." They were both silent for a moment. Bajai Āmā sat in silence, too, remembering her husband.

The room where they sat was spacious. To one side, several mattresses were piled on a bedstead and covered by a cheap bedspread. Two thick quilts lay folded on top of the bed. Some flowers and wood apples were scattered across a three-foot bolster pillow. Bajai Āmā was sitting on a mat beneath the bedstead, and the two men sat before her, leaning on a wide, low table that was plain and old-fashioned. This table had a mirror in which there was a framed photograph of some unidentified saint or deity. The figure in the picture had been rendered quite unrecognizable by the stains of flowers, rice grains, vermilion, and sandalwood powders offered to it. A ceremonial spoon and cup, a bell, an incense burner, and a pot stood on the table, together with an old Coca Cola bottle containing a bunch of summer flowers. There were no chairs to go with the table at all.

Deciding that it was no good just sitting there saying nothing, Hari asked, "What did he do?"

"He was a poet, sir."

"A poet!" Hari thought that he had discovered a way of getting the room cheaply. Humbly he said to Bajai Āmā, "My friend here is a poet, too."

"A poet?" Her wrinkled face creased tighter, and an odd expression came over it. He and Hari both looked back and forth between Bajai Āmā and her husband's photograph. It was an impressive picture: a face with full round cheeks and an exceedingly well-tended moustache, topped by a neatly wound turban. When they looked at his eyes, they felt as if he was just about to roar out a poem about great heroism.

"This poetry has destroyed everything, sir."

This time she turned her gaze on Hari. The fish had already escaped, so Hari could only sit there looking blank and squeezing his hands. His friend had never even hummed a tune, let alone written a poem. As far as an interest in literature was concerned, he had read only the essential poets—Lekhnāth, Devkoṭā, Sama. And then it was only to pass an exam. To try to set things right, he declared, "Oh, it was only while I was studying, at school and at college. Then I used to scribble a few lines. But now I have to work for my keep. So what use is poetry to me?"

"Yes, that's right. It's no good getting involved in this poetry stuff. Your children will starve to death. Heaven and earth will mock you. You may be clever yourself, but if your children don't get to study, they'll turn out dumb idiots."

"He doesn't write any more. He hardly ever did, and now he has no time at all. All day at the office, studying mornings and evenings—the poor man doesn't even have time for his prayers." Hari told lie upon lie. He felt shocked by Hari's words. If he got the room tomorrow, who was he going to pray to, after all? At college, he had worshipped a "goddess" and even run to the temple several times because of her. But one day the goddess's minions had decided to worship her properly, and he'd completely forgotten the way to the temple. He had also begun to ignore beautiful flowers, moonlit nights, and the season of spring.

Hari and Bajai Āmā had begun to discuss the rent. He looked at the wall, where Hemā Mālinī was bending prettily to dance in a calendar advertising garam masālā.[4] He thought of turning around to look at Bimlā, but he could not. So he just stared into the corner.

The oddest things were scattered all over the room: *thānkā* paintings; alloy, copper, and brass idols both large and small; tattered old Hindu and Buddhist books; rosaries and beads; and all sorts of other things that he could not identify.

Looking at Bajai Āmā, he pointed into the corner, "What are these?"

She glanced where he was pointing and said, hardly pausing in the conversation she was holding with Hari, "Sir, those belong to my son; he collects all sorts of things. I don't know what they are. He sells them. . . . And the rent won't go lower than 50 rupees."

Hari glanced over at him, wearing a look that said, "Fifty is the lowest she'll go—what do you say?"

He indicated his assent and put an advance payment of 50 rupees straight into Bajai Āmā's hand. As they went down the stairs, Bimlā stood by the door. He thought she might have smiled, but he was not at all sure of it.

"Those things in the corner . . . " he began to say as they came out into the street.

"He'll be smuggling images and things, I expect," Hari cut in. "Bimlā was smiling at you, wasn't she, my lad?"

"Don't talk such rubbish, idiot!"

4. Hemā Mālinī is a popular Bombay film actress. Garam masālā is a mixture of cooking spices.

Who could say whether she had smiled or not? He didn't think any more about it.

Today he arrived at Hari's house, only to find him locking his door and on his way out. He hung back and saw Hari's landlord watching him with a frown. This was the tenth time he had run over here. The poor man would be getting angry.

Hari finished locking his door and turned around. He was surprised to see him.

"Hey, where are you off to, Ganesh?"

"I just came to visit you."

"I'm going to Binod's place. He's invited me over. I'm eating there, too."

"Are you leaving right now?"

Hari paused for a moment; then he laughed. "The same problem again, my lad?" He glanced at the landlord's window. The whole window was frowning by this time.

"Come on, let's go."

Out in the street, Hari said, "Sorry, my friend. But what can I do?"

"It doesn't matter. I'll be off." He felt as if he had a rock in the pit of his stomach.

"Are you angry? What's the matter?"

"Why should I be angry? It's not your fault. Didn't you see the old man at the window?"

"It's hardly my landlord's fault that you're having all this trouble. You're a fool—just ask Bimlā for the key, won't you? This will go on forever if you don't say something."

"She's a serious sort of girl. I never see her talking to anyone. Mother and daughter live together upstairs. And as for her brother, I never know about his comings and goings."

"You said she watches you from the window."

"Yes, certainly she watches me."

"Right, that's it then, you thickhead. Have a chat with her on the pretext of asking for the key. With *laḍḍus* in both hands.[5] Right, I'm off now." Hari set off from the crossroads for Binod's house. Ganesh couldn't follow Hari there because he did not know Binod.

He walked back to his lodgings, remembering Hari's remark about "*laḍḍus* in both hands." It was still raining slightly. He wondered, Had his blunder really been so great that it justified a transfer from the district to the center? He had never informed on anyone's corruption. He had taken bribes, for sure, but he had done the world's work, too. To take

5. A *laḍḍu* is a spherical Indian sweetmeat. What Hari means is that Ganesh should "sweeten her up" with a gift or with flattery. In the following passage, *laḍḍus* clearly symbolize bribes.

bribes and *not* to work—that was *real* corruption. But the traditions of corruption required that he should fall, and so he fell. The big fish got away. He was just a small fish: a paltry little hook could catch him, so how could he escape the net?

He was not of sufficiently high status to come with *laḍḍus* in both hands. He had eaten only one *laḍḍu*, and now in this summer rain he had to run from house to house. Otherwise, he, too, might have been squatting in a bathroom sucking hard on a Yak cigarette. The thought made his heart and mind burn.

Walking along beside the gutter, he arrived at his lodgings to see Bimlā sitting at the bottom of the stairs. Pleased, he approached her and said softly, "Is Bajai Āmā at her prayers?"

She seemed to smile, but she gave him no reply. He was at a loss—how should he broach the subject? The laws of nature say that you must labor hard, swallow your pride, and lay down your sorrows.

"Do you have the key? I got up late today."

Bimlā made a strange sound and pointed upstairs. Shocked, he stared at her in stunned silence. The poor girl was mute! From her serious face and fashionable clothes, he had assumed her to be an educated girl. But in a family where the son hasn't studied, a dumb daughter hardly would! Slowly it dawned on him: her eyes always smiled because without a voice her perception was particularly sharp. But what to do now? It would never do to show a dumb girl the lavatory and gesture at the lock and key. That would be most indelicate. It would soon become quite ridiculous.

Seeing him staring at her, Bimlā turned and went upstairs. He looked at that ugly lock on the lavatory door, then at the picture chalked on the wall. An arrow piercing a betel leaf! There would be no point in calling Bajai Āmā, so he went outside. I'll have to begin seeking new rooms tomorrow, he thought. The rock in his stomach had moved lower down.

He made haste for the Dhobī Kholā.

(first published in *Madhupark* magazine 1983;
from *Samsāmayik Sājhā Kathā* 1984)

Kishor Pahāḍī (b. 1956)

Pahāḍī is a "new" writer whose first story was published in 1971. Pahāḍī's stories are collected in *Bānchnu ra Bānchekāharū* (To Live and the Living, 1980), *Ghar-Khaṇḍahar* (Ruins of Houses, 1980), and *Vishudāī* (Vishudāī [a woman's name], 1988).

A LIVING DEATH (*MRITAJĪVĪ*)

Devayānī. Do you like that name? I liked it, too, when I heard it first. In fact, it was because of her name that I first employed Devayānī. After I had taken her on, I changed her name to "Kānchī": servants' names are always changed once they are employed.

"What jobs can you do?" I'd asked her.

"I can do whatever Bajyai tells me to," she'd answered. "Cooking, scouring pots, washing clothes, looking after children: I do everything."

I was rather relieved to hear this. It's hard when you have to keep finding jobs for someone else, day in and day out. I'd told my husband so many times to get a servant, but he'd taken no notice. *I* had to cook, *I* had to clean the hearth, *I* had to do the washing—there was so much work, I tell you! And so I was delighted when a woman came to the door to become my servant.

"How much do you want each month?"

"Let Bajyai give what she decides. I am not greedy for money. All I need is a refuge." Her voice was tragic, but I hardly noticed it. I should make it clear that I am not an especially sensitive woman. I hardly have time for my own children, so what interest did I have in Devayānī, a woman I'd only just met?

Anyway, the terms were agreed.

From her very first day, my work load lightened. In fact, I had nothing to do! Devayānī did everything, from making the tea first thing in the morning to washing the pots and cleaning the hearth in the evening. And she did not seem in the least unhappy about having to do all this work. She was always in a cheerful mood. Often she would happily declare, "What a fine refuge I've found in Bajyai's house!"

I was not of an age to be a grandmother really; she called me Bajyai out of respect because I am a Brāhmaṇ. There's a belief that women lie about their ages, but I'm not lying. She only called me Bajyai because I am a Brāhmaṇ. And because I am a Brāhmaṇ, I should not have eaten what Devayānī cooked; but both my husband and I keep well clear of such customs, and we don't care at all.

One morning, at about ten o'clock, I was feeding my little daughter when Devayānī came running in.

"Bajyai! I'm going to plant cauliflowers in the garden today, alright?"

Behind our house there is a small piece of garden. It had been empty for ages. Who was there to do the work, after all? Because of his office work he had no time to spare, and it was the same for me with the housework! Her idea surprised me.

"Do you know how to, Kānchī?" I asked.

She laughed and replied, "Why, is it so hard? I certainly know full well how to do it. It's better to plant something than just leaving it lying barren like that. I'll plant potatoes, spinach, and cauliflowers. Then you won't have to worry about vegetables. Just think how expensive they are nowadays!"

If someone does work that interests them, they are happy, and so Devayānī was happy as she planted the vegetables in that garden. It seemed to me that she had been born for hard work and accomplishment.

Every single person is born once and dies once—the history of the world is founded on this. History is the unfortunate things that take place between birth and dying. Some are dying as they live in this history; some are living as they die. But I, like Devayānī, am not among these; I just go on with my story.

One day, Devayānī pointed out a man and asked, "Do you know that man, Bajyai, the one on the motorcycle?"

"Who, that one with the dark face?"

"Yes."

"No, I don't."

"I do, Bajyai."

"So what?" I asked, but for some strange reason my question made Devayānī anxious. Without another word she ran inside to her room.

It seemed as if there was some kind of deep secret in this. Indeed, there was: Devayānī's nervousness did hold a secret. Devayānī told me about it one day, and I knew. But that was much later.

From that day on, I began to see that dark man on his motorcycle almost every day near our house. He may well have been there before, but I had not noticed him. Once Devayānī had pointed him out, I realized that he came up to the front of the house most evenings and parked his motorcycle there. He would look all around as if searching for something. This was while he bought cigarettes from a shop. For a few moments he would stand there; then he would go back to start his engine.

I saw this happen four days in a row. On the fifth day I saw something new: Devayānī was peering out through a chink in the curtains. The dark motorcyclist was on the street. I stared at Devayānī for a moment. She was peeping out with great excitement and did not know I was there. I was sure she was staring at that dark man, and I let her go on staring. I thought she was in love with him. But the dark man, what did he want? I felt apprehensive.

Next day I was at my window, having sent Devayānī out to buy oranges. The same man came and stopped outside the house. He had always come in the evening before, but today he came in the afternoon. He parked the motorcycle and looked all around.

So I sat and waited to see what would happen.

Very soon, Devayānī came back with the oranges in her hand. The motorcyclist saw her at once. Devayānī saw him, too, but she walked straight on. The motorcyclist seemed to call her, and Devayānī turned toward him.

I was still watching from my window.

The two of them began to talk. From the way they talked, they seemed well acquainted. But I began to feel suspicious and fearful: what destructive thing was Devayānī doing here? To ask me first whether I knew the man, then to peer out at him from her window, and then to spend so much time talking to him . . . what conspiracy was being planned?

They went on talking for ages; then they seemed to disagree. The dark motorcyclist started his engine and went slowly back the same way he had come. Devayānī approached the house and saw me in the window. She'd probably been unaware of my presence until then.

She came straight up the stairs. At the top, she could not raise her head to look at me. I stood there intending to tell her off. Then she looked at me, and what was this? Her eyes were streaming with tears.

"Bajyai, I am leaving this house right now!"

She's intending to run away with that man, I thought. Rather sternly, I asked, "Where are you going? Are you thinking of flying away on that motorcycle, or what?"

"No, Bajyai! It's the motorcyclist I'm running from!"

"Why? What happened?"

This made her cry all the more. I took the bag of oranges from her, took one out, and began to peel it. I am certainly not such a sensitive woman.

She wiped her eyes and looked at me. "I'm going now, Bajyai."

"Where are you going, Kānchī?"

"I don't know. Wherever. But away from this area."

"Why?" I remembered how much work I'd have if she left.

She was silent for a moment. I sat there eating my orange. "When I'm leaving I'll tell you why."

"Alright then, tell me, tell me." I went on chewing my orange. There was no interest at all in my voice.

"I am the daughter of a poor farmer's family, Bajyai. And that motorcyclist's my husband . . ."

It was as if someone had pricked my ears, and I jumped in alarm. Perhaps I had misheard. "Go on, go on, what did you say?"

"It's true, Bajyai. That motorcyclist is my husband . . ."

The last segment of the orange remained in my hand. I put it straight down with the peel on the floor.

"When we married, he was as poor as me," said Devayānī. "We had to struggle hard just to survive. His grandmother, mother, sister, brother, he, and I, we all lived off a tiny piece of land. It didn't provide three months' food a year. And he didn't even have a job either; he was studying at college. His brother and sister were small, and there was no father. His mother and I worked other people's fields, and his mother did most of the housework. I was the only one who did jobs like planting paddy in other people's fields, carrying bricks and sand on building sites, and so on. That was the money that kept him at college. I really suffered, Bajyai! I haven't worked even a quarter as hard in Bajyai's house! It was really tough to work outside all day, then to come home to fetch water morning and night, scour pots, clean the hearth, cook the food . . ."

Devayānī put on a pained expression, and I saw the past in her face. Even I felt wounded somehow. She went on with her story,

"I was exhausted, and I used to fall ill from time to time. But I said nothing to anyone. I just kept on working. I didn't even take any medicine—I said nothing about it. Who would buy me medicine, anyway? But illness is a marvelous thing, Bajyai! If you don't treat it, it gets better."

I was fascinated by Devayānī. Although she was much younger than me, I considered her far more experienced. Compared to her, what had I experienced?

"Kānchī, why did you come and wash pots for other people like this?"

She laughed at my question. "To change from Devayānī to Kānchī!

I'm not really a Kānchī! I've studied up to fifth grade. That was when I got married. What chance was there for any more education then? Although I'm poor, I've studied a lot. What a strange life this is!"

He had gone to the office; the children had gone to school. We had the house to ourselves. She told me her story as if it were an amusing tale.

"Didn't you have any children?" I asked.

"I don't know; the Lord didn't give us any." Devayānī spoke despairingly. "Sometimes I wonder if that's the Lord's job—to go on giving further misery to those who are unhappy. I suffered so much, you know? Later, when he'd finished his studies and left college, he became an overseer. He got an office job. I was astonished, Bajyai. I really was. I thought he would tell me that from then on, having suffered so much, I wouldn't have to work so hard; I wouldn't have to work for others. But no, Bajyai, he didn't say anything of the sort. His mother and grandmother did not speak up against him. They wanted me to be as unhappy as possible. However hard I worked, he would insult me and beat me. I had no one to turn to at home: my mother was all I had, and she died seven months after my wedding."

Devayānī paused, but I could not contain my curiosity. "Tell me then, what happened?"

"He kept on earning more and more money. I felt a kind of pride that my husband had become an important man. Once a man becomes important, so does his wife—that's what I thought. But more and more unpleasant things began to happen, things I'd never imagined. One day he came straight out with it. 'Get out of my house,' he said. This was while he was beating me, thrashing me."

"What had you done for him to beat you?"

"I told you, didn't I? Horrible things like that kept on happening. I didn't have to do anything, Bajyai, he just used to hit me for no reason. Then he was promoted a little; that might have been why he became totally indifferent to me. He had turned from a rural hill student into a cultured, senior *hakīm*, but I was still the same uncultured peasant. Perhaps that was why his family all showed such contempt for me. They all forgot how much a girl called Devayānī Maharjan had suffered for their family. So I was alone in the world, and I was miserable."

Now I could see the tears streaming down her cheeks. She quickly wiped her eyes and said, "One day, the office gave him a motorcycle—the same one he rides now. And the very next day he brought a form and told me to sign it. It was a form for a divorce. I was terrified. He said he was going to throw me out and get an overseer's wife. Why did such things happen to me? I had committed no sin! I told him, 'If we're divorced, where shall I go?' But he looked at me with wide eyes, 'Go where you like!' he said. 'What use are you, a wife who can't have children?' But that was just an excuse for getting rid of me. I said, 'But we didn't *want* children all these years.' His answer was to grab hold of my hair and start hitting me. After every blow, he told me to sign the form. I kept on refusing. His whole family gathered round and threatened me. 'We'll pour paraffin over you and set you alight!' they said. I started to weep and wail: one part of me felt that I shouldn't leave the house, even if they burned me alive. But something else told me to go, and so I ran away and came to work here. Then he found out where I lived and caught me today. He's already got his overseer's wife. He told me he'd bring the form right away and that if I didn't sign it he'd drag me off. That's why I'm leaving now. . . . But when the vegetables are ready, I'll be back to eat them, Bajyai."

When she had finished, Devayānī sighed wearily. Even this insensitive woman found tears coming to her eyes.

"You needn't be afraid, Kānchī," I told her. "If he comes, I'll be here, won't I? We'll do what has to be done. You don't have to leave. Where would you go? He'd easily find you again."

Devayānī was not convinced. "I don't want to get honest people like you involved," she said. "How many other women there must be living tragic lives in this world. How many of them can you save?"

And she left me and went away.

She said she would be back when the vegetables had grown, but they all died in the ground. She should have returned when they sprouted, but it's eighteen months now since Devayānī left this house, and she has never come back.

Now the garden is bare.

(first published in *Rūprekhā* magazine 1984;
from *Samsāmayik Sājhā Kathā* 1984)

GLOSSARY

Ādināth	a name of Shiva, or of an aspect of the Buddha worshipped at a particular temple in Chobhār village to the south of Kathmandu
Āmā	mother
Amshuvarmān	a Nepali king from the Lichhavī period
Anna	one-sixteenth of 1 rupee in old Indian and Nepali currency
Annapūrṇa	the goddess of plenty, whose name means "filled with grain"
Arjuṇ	the warrior on the battlefield at Kurukshetra during the war described in the Mahābhārata epic to whom Krishna delivered the famous sermon on dharma, which is preserved in the Bhagavad Gītā
Bāgmati	a holy river in the Kathmandu Valley that flows past the temple of Pashupatināth
Bāhun	(colloquial) Brāhmaṇ
Bajai/Bajyai	grandmother
Bajiyā	a serf or bonded laborer; sometimes used as a term of abuse
Banyan	a tree, *Ficus indica*
Baṛā Hakīm	"big officer"—a title given to a senior official in government service
Betel	the leaf of the piper betel tree (see pān)
Bhadrakālī	the name of a temple to the fearsome aspect of the goddess Durgā in Kathmandu

Bhairav	a fearsome aspect of Shiva that appears frequently in Newār iconography
Bhālu	bear
Bhanjyāng	a pass or col
Bhavānī	a name of the spouse of the Hindu god Shiva
Bhrikuṭī	daughter of the king Amshuvarmān, who was sent to Tibet to marry King Songsten Gampo during the seventh century
Bighā	a measurement of area, approximately five-eighths of an acre
Birtā	a grant of land made by the central government to one of its officers or as a reward for services rendered
Bishnumati	a river that flows through the western quarter of Kathmandu
Bodhisattva	a being who has achieved nirvāṇa, "enlightenment," but has returned to the world to work for the spiritual deliverance of others
Brahmā	the third great deity in the trinity of Shiva, Vishnu, and Brahmā; the creator of the universe
Brāhmaṇ	the priestly caste at the apex of the traditional Hindu hierarchy
Carram board	a popular game played with counters on a wooden board
Chautārā	a stepped brick platform built around the base of a tree (usually a *pīpal* or a banyan) where travelers may rest
Chi!	an expression of disgust or contempt
Chilāuné	a particular species of tree whose bark causes itching and irritation if touched
Chiurā	pounded dry rice husks; a common staple in Nepal
Chobhār	a village to the south of Kathmandu near the gorge through which the Bāgmati River makes its exit from the central valley
Dāl	lentils
Damai	the name of an artisan caste of tailors who rank fairly low in the caste hierarchy

Dasain — a great annual festival held on the tenth day of the light fortnight of the month of Ashvin (September–October) in honor of the goddess Durgā. Thousands of buffaloes and other animals are ritually slaughtered, and their meat is distributed. Dasain continues for several days, and Nepalis traditionally return to their ancestral villages during the holiday to visit their families.

Dharamshālā — a simple hostel for Hindu pilgrims

Dhobī — washerman

Didī — "elder sister," but often appended to the name of a woman who is older than the speaker, although not old enough to merit the titles *āmā* or *bajai* (q.v.)

Dwāré — a village official who can arrest offenders and try petty cases

Gāndharva — a celestial musician

Gaṇesh — the elephant-headed god, a son of Shiva, who removes obstacles to new ventures and brings good luck

Gangā — the sacred river Ganges of northern India

Garam masālā — a blend of various spices used in North Indian cuisine

Gautam Buddha — the historical Buddha Shākyamuṇi

Ghee — a cooking oil derived from butter

Gurkha — a Nepali who serves, or has served, in the army or, more particularly, in the armies of Britain or India; a word derived from the name of the central Nepali town of Gorkhā

Guru — a teacher or religious mentor

Hakīm — an officer or boss

Jogī — see *yogī*

Joginī — a female yogī or jogī; a female ascetic; a nun

Kānchī — a relationship term, "youngest girl," used to address or refer to any young woman who is significantly junior to oneself or to a servant girl

Kasāī — a caste of butchers

Kāsṭhamaṇḍapa — a large temple in the center of old Kathmandu (The name "Kathmandu" was probably derived from the name of this temple, which is said to be the oldest in the city and to have been built from the wood of a single tree.)

Kholā — a river or stream

Khukurī	the curved hunting knife carried by many Nepalis that has become an emblem of the Gurkhas
Kumārī	the "living goddess" of the Newārs: a young girl who is selected to represent the goddess Taleju and dwells in her own temple-house until reaching puberty
Laḍḍu	a particular kind of Indian sweet
Lakshmī	the goddess of wealth and good fortune
Magar	a Tibeto-Burman speaking ethnic group from southern central Nepal that is closely related to the Gurung
Māgh	the month of the Hindu calendar that corresponds with the second half of January and the first half of February
Māghé Sankrānti	an important festival on the first of Māgh (January–February) during which fairs are held throughout Nepal and northern India. These fairs are often occasions for courtship between young unmarried men and women.
Mahābhārata	the great Hindu epic that describes the war between the Pāṇḍavas and the Kauravas
Mānā	a measure of weight equivalent to one-half a seer, or approximately one pound
Manjushrī	the great bodhisattva from Tibet who, according to Buddhist mythology, drained the Kathmandu Valley of its lake
Mārunī	a male dancer who dresses in women's clothing
Mo-mo	steamed meat dumplings: a Tibetan delicacy
Mugalān	"the land of the Mughals": an archaic name for India
Mukhiyā	an officer of the third rank or a chief or village headman
Nārāyaṇ	a name for the great Hindu deity Vishnu
New Road	the main commercial street of Kathmandu; also called Juddha Saḍak
Newār	an ethnic group with the best claim to be indigenous to the Kathmandu Valley; the Newārs built the great cities of Kathmandu, Lalitpur, and Bhaktapur and have their own language and rich literary tradition. The Newārs are still somewhat despised by their Nepali-speaking conquerors.
Paddy	unhusked rice or rice that has yet to be reaped
Paisā	one-hundredth of 1 rupee

Pān	a mixture of pungent nuts and fragrant spices wrapped in a betel leaf that is chewed by many people in South Asia as an aid to digestion and to sweeten the breath
Paṇḍit	a scholar or priest
Pashupati/Pashupatināth	"Lord of the animals": a name of Shiva under which he is worshipped at the great temple just outside Kathmandu
Pāthī	a measure of capacity: 8 *mānā*
Pīpal	a particular kind of fig tree, *Ficus religiosa*, often planted beside a banyan to provide shade for travelers in the hills
Poḍé	a lowly and ritually unclean caste of Newār streetsweepers
Prayer flag	a cloth flag bearing Tibetan Buddhist mantras that is hung out in the wind
Purāṇa	a sacred book; one of a class of Sanskrit works containing history and traditional lore
Rāhu	a demon who seizes the sun and moon to devour them and thus causes eclipses
Raksī	an alcoholic drink distilled from barley, rice, millet, and so on
Rāmāyaṇa	the epic work of Hindu scripture that tells the story of Rām, the princely incarnation of Vishnu
Rāṇā	a name assumed by a group of families who usurped the authority of the monarch in the mid-nineteenth century and governed Nepal until 1951
Rānī Sāheb	the title given to the senior wife of a high Rāṇā official
Ropanī	a measure of area: 5,625 square feet
Samyak	a philosophical term meaning "complete" or "total"
Sānī	a pet name for a little girl
Sārī	the ubiquitous dress of the Hindu woman, of which there are many regional variations
Seer	a measure of weight: approximately 2 pounds
Shiva	the great ascetic god of Hinduism, conceived of as a *jogī* who lives on the Himalayan peak of Kailāsh. Shiva is the object of karma yoga, the "way of action," as distinct from bhakti yoga, the "way of devotion." With his cosmic dance, he constantly destroys and recreates the universe.

Stūpa	a dome-shaped Buddhist monument topped with a spire onto which there is often painted a pair of eyes with an enigmatic question mark between them. *Stūpas* may have originated as reliquaries for the remains of saints or holy books. The *stūpas* of Swyambhū and Bauddha are two of Kathmandu's most famous landmarks.
Subbā	a government official one rank higher than a *mukhiyā*
Sukā	25 paisā; one-quarter of 1 rupee
Sūrya/Sūrje	the deity who personifies the sun
Swasthānī	a goddess to whom women make vows in order to bear children. Originally a Newār deity, her popularity has spread throughout Hindu Nepal.
Swyambhūnāth	the great and ancient *stūpa* on a hill to the west of Kathmandu. Its name means "self-created lord" and refers to the flame that manifested itself on the waters of the lake that once filled the central valley and that prompted Manjushrī to come down from Tibet to drain its waters away.
Tarāī	the lowland area of Nepal that borders on India to the south
Thānkā	a heavily stylized and iconographic Tibetan religious picture painted on cloth
Tīkā	a dab of paste, or a small plastic disc, that is applied to the forehead for religious or cosmetic purposes
Tongā	a horse-drawn trap
Tuṇḍīkhel	a large open, grassy area in Kathmandu used for military parades on national occasions and by the people of the city as a park for the rest of the year. Also the scene of several notorious executions of political activists during the last years of the Rāṇā regime.
Virāṭaparva	a chapter of the Mahābhārata epic
Vishnu	one of the three great gods of Hinduism, whose incarnations include Rāma and Krishna. Vishnu is the preserver of order who has rescued humankind from evil throughout history. He is usually worshipped in the form of one of his ten incarnations, and these inspire *bhakti*, "devotion."
Yamarāj	the lord of the underworld, the god of death
Yogī	a wandering ascetic who has renounced the world and all material possessions

BIBLIOGRAPHY

Ādhunik Nepālī Kavitā (Modern Nepali Poetry). 1971. Kathmandu: Royal Nepal Academy.

Akādemī Nibandhāvalī (The Academy Collection of Essays). 1976. Edited by Lakkhīdevī Sundās. Darjeeling: Nepali Academy.

Bāburām Āchārya. 1972. *Purānā Kavi ra Kavitā* (Old Poets and Poetry). Kathmandu: Sājhā Prakāshan.

Ballabh, Ìshwar. 1981. *Samāntara* (Parallels). Poems. Kathmandu: Sājhā Prakāshan.

———. 1985. *Kasmai Devāya* (Oath of the Gods). Poems. Kathmandu: Sājhā Prakāshan.

Bandhu, Chūḍā Maṇi. 1979. *Devkoṭā*. Kathmandu: Sājhā Prakāshan.

Barāl, Ìshwar. 1974. "Balkrishna Sama." *Kailash* (Kathmandu) 2, no. 3, pp. 189–197.

———. 1968. Special Devkoṭā issue 5, no. 12.

Bhānu (Kathmandu). 1966. Special Lekhnāth issue 3, no. 8.

Bhāratīya Nepālī Kathā (Indian Nepali Stories). 1982. Edited by Dayārām Shreshṭha. Kathmandu: Royal Nepal Academy.

Bhaṭṭa, Ānandadeva. [1968] 1977. "Kavi Siddhicharaṇ Shreshṭhajyūmā Krāntikāritā" (Political Rebelliousness in the Poet Siddhicharaṇ Shreshṭha). In *Sājhā Samālochanā*, pp. 175–185.

Bhaṭṭa, Motīrām. [1891] 1964. *Kavi Bhānubhaktāchāryako Jīvan-Charitra* (Biography of the Poet Bhānubhakta Āchārya). Edited by Indra Bahādur Rāī. 4th ed. Darjeeling: Nepālī Sāhitya Sammelan.

Bhaṭṭarāī, Harshanāth Sharmā. 1976. "Nepālī Bhāshāko Kānūnī Prishṭhabhūmi" (The Legal Status of the Nepali Language). In *Nepālī* (Lalitpur) 73.

Bhaṭṭarāy, Chūḍanāth. 1961. *Taruṇa Tapasī Mimānsā* (Analysis of Lekhnāth's *Taruṇa Tapasī*). Lalitpur: Jagdambā Prakāshan.

———. 1962. *Kavi, Kavitā, ra Kavitāko Siddhānta* (Poets, Poetry, and Poetic Theory). Kathmandu: Smt. Bhaṭṭarāy.

Bhikshu, Bhavānī. 1960a. *Gunakesharī.* Stories. Kathmandu: Royal Nepal Academy.

———. 1960b. *Maiyāsāheb.* Stories. Kathmandu: Royal Nepal Academy.

Bikal, Ramesh. [1962] 1977. *Nayā Saḍakko Gīt* (The Song of New Road). Stories. 3rd ed. Kathmandu: Sājhā Prakāshan.

Brough, John. 1968. *Poems from the Sanskrit.* Harmondsworth, England: Penguin Books.

Datta, Chiranjīvi. 1973. *Kehī Nepālī Kāvyaharūko Samīkshā* (An Analysis of Some Nepali Poems). Kathmandu: Ratna Pustak Bhaṇḍār.

Devkoṭā, Grīshmabahādur. 1960. *Nepālko Rājnītik Darpaṇa* (A Political Mirror on Nepal). Kathmandu: Keshavprasād Lamsāl.

———. 1967. *Nepālko Chāpākhānā ra Patra-Patrikāko Itihās* (History of the Printers and Journals of Nepal). Kathmandu: Keshavprasād Lamsāl.

Devkoṭā, Lakshmīprasād. 1945. *Lakshmī Nibandh Sangraha* (Collection of "Lakshmī's" Essays). Kathmandu: Nepālī Bhāshā Prakāshinī Samiti.

———. 1976. *Lakshmī-Kavitā-Sangraha* (Collection of "Lakshmi's" Poems). Kathmandu: Sājhā Prakāshan.

———. 1981. "The Literature We Should Produce." *Literature* (Kathmandu) 1, pp. 1–5.

———. [1936] 1986. *Munā-Madan* (Munā and Madan). Poem. 18th ed. Kathmandu: Sājhā Prakāshan.

———. [1959] 1988. *Bhikhārī* (The Beggar). Poems. 11th ed. Kathmandu: Sājhā Prakāshan.

Dhungānā, Rām Chandra. 1972. "Nepālī Bhāshāko Mādhyam" (Nepali Language Medium). *Nepālī* (Lalitpur) 52, pp. 23–29.

Dīkshit, Rām Maṇi Āchārya. 1972. *Purānā Samjhanā* (Old Memories). Kathmandu: Nālinī Devī Āchārya.

Dowson, John. [1879] 1968. *A Classical Dictionary of Hindu Mythology and Religion, Geography, History and Literature.* 11th ed. London: Routledge and Kegan Paul.

Eliot, T. S. 1963. *Collected Poems 1909–1962.* London: Faber and Faber.

Gautam, Dhruba Chandra. 1987. *Gautamkā Kehī Pratinidhi Kathāharū* (Some of Gautam's Representative Stories). Kathmandu: Sājhā Prakāshan.

Gerow, Edwin. 1971. *A Glossary of Indian Figures of Speech.* The Hague: Mouton.

Giri, Agamsingh. 1976. "Nepālī Kavitā-Sāhityamā Nayāṃ Prayog" (New Experiments in Nepali Poetry). In *Akādemī Nibandhāvalī.*

Giri, Bānīrā. 1974. *Euṭā Euṭā Jiundo Jang Bahādur* (Each One a Living Jang Bahādur). Poems. Kathmandu: Pushkar Giri.

Giri, Krishna, and Pariyār, Kumār. 1977. *Dārjīlingkā Kehī Nepālī Sāhityik Pratibhāharū* (Some Nepali Literary Luminaries of Darjeeling). Interviews. Darjeeling: Nepālī Sāhitya Sanchayikā.

"Goṭhālé," Govind Bahādur Malla. 1959. *Kathai-Kathā* (Nothing But Stories). Kathmandu: Royal Nepal Academy.

Himāl Chulī (Himalayan Peak). 1969. Edited by Ìshwar Barāl. 2nd ed. Birāṭnagar: Pūrvānchal Pustak Bhaṇḍār.

Hutt, Michael. 1984. "Neon Lights and Vedic Caves: European Influences on the Nepali Writer." *South Asia Research* (London) 4, no. 2, pp. 124–138.

———. 1988a. *Nepali: A National Language and Its Literature*. London: School of Oriental and African Studies.
———. 1988b. "Four Poems by Mohan Koirālā." *Himalayan Research Bulletin* (New York) 8, no. 3, pp. 1–7.
———. 1989a. "A Hero or a Traitor? The Gurkha Soldier in Nepali Literature." *South Asia Research* (London) 9, no. 1, pp. 21–32.
———. 1989b. "Reflections of Political Change in Nepali Literature Since 1940." *Kailash* (Kathmandu) 15, nos. 3–4, pp. 135–156.
———. 1990. "The Blowing of the April Wind: Writers and Democracy in Nepal." *Index on Censorship* 19, no. 8, pp. 5–9.
Jain, M. S. 1972. *Emergence of a New Aristocracy in Nepal*. Agra: Sri Ram Mehra.
Jain, Narendra. 1982. *Nepālī Kavitā* (Nepali Poetry). Kathmandu: Indian Embassy.
Jhyālbāṭa (From a Window). 1949. Stories. Edited by Ìshwar Barāl. Banāras: Narendraprasād Regmī.
Joshī, Kumārbahādur. 1974. *Mahākavi Devkoṭā ra unkā Mahākāvya* (The Great Poet Devkoṭā and His Epic Poems). Kathmandu: Sahayogī Prakāshan.
Joshī, Ratnadhwaja. 1968. *Nepālī Kathāko Kathā* (The Story of the Nepali Story). Kathmandu: Sājhā Prakāshan.
———. 1975. *Sāhitya-Chintana* (Literary Contemplations). Kathmandu: Sahayogī Prakāshan.
———. [1968] 1977. "Kavishiromaṇi Lekhnāth: Bhāshāshailī" (The Poet Laureate Lekhnāth: Language Style). In *Sājhā Samālochanā*, pp. 24–35.
Kāinlā, Bairāgī. 1974. *Bairāgī Kāinlākā Kavitāharū* (The Poems of Bairāgī Kāinlā). Kathmandu: Sājhā Prakāshan.
Kane, P. V. 1971. *History of Sanskrit Poetics*. 4th ed. Delhi: Motilal Banarsidass.
Kathā Kusum (Story Flower). [1938] 1981. Stories. 11th ed. Darjeeling: Nepālī Sāhitya Sammelan.
Kaṭuvāl, Haribhakta. 1972. *Yo Jindagī Khai Ke Jindagī!* (This Life, What Life Is This?). Poems. Kathmandu: Ratna Pustak Bhaṇḍār.
Kavitā (Kathmandu). 1986. Combined issue, nos. 18–19.
Khanāl, Yadu Nāth. 1977. *Nepal: Transition from Isolationism*. Kathmandu: Sājhā Prakāshan.
Koirālā, Bishweshwar Prasād. [1949] 1968. *Doshī Chashmā* (Faulty Glasses). Stories. 4th ed. Nepal: Pratinidhi Sāhitya Prakāshan.
Koirālā, Mohan. 1973. *Mohan Koirālākā Kavitā* (The Poems of Mohan Koirālā). Edited by Ìshwar Barāl. Kathmandu: Sājhā Prakāshan.
———. 1978a. *Himchuli Raktim Cha* (The Snow Peak's Blood-Red). Poems. Kathmandu: Royal Nepal Academy.
———. 1978b. *Kavitābāre Kehī Charchā* (Some Comments on Poetry). Kathmandu: Royal Nepal Academy.
Kunwar, Uttam. 1966. *Shrashṭā ra Sāhitya* (Creators and Literature: Interviews with Nepali Writers). Kathmandu: Rūpāyan Prakāshan.
Larousse Encyclopedia of Mythology. [1959] 1983. 17th ed. London: Hamlyn.
Macdonald, Alexander W. 1975. *Essays on the Ethnology of Nepal and South Asia*. Kathmandu: Ratna Pustak Bhandar.

Madhupark (Kathmandu). 1981. Special poetry issue 14, nos. 6–7.

Mainālī, Guruprasād. [1969] 1986. *Nāso* (The Ward). Edited by Tānāsarmā. Stories. 10th ed. Kathmandu: Rājendra Prasād Mainālī.

Malla, Bijay. 1977. *Parevā ra Kaidī* (The Prisoner and the Dove). Stories. Kathmandu: Sājhā Prakāshan.

Matthews, David. 1984. *A Course in Nepali*. London: School of Oriental and African Studies.

Modern Nepali Poems (English translation of *Ādhunik Nepālī Kavitā*). 1972. Kathmandu: Royal Nepal Academy.

Mukherji, Amulyadan. 1976. *Sanskrit Prosody: Its Evolution*. Calcutta: Saraswat Library.

Nepālī Kathā Sangraha (Anthology of Nepali Stories). [1973] 1988. Edited by Tārāprasād Joshī. 2 vols., 11th ed. Kathmandu: Mohan Prasād.

Nepālī Kavitā Sangraha (Anthology of Nepali Poetry). [1973] 1988. Edited by Tārāprasād Joshī. 2 vols., 4th ed. Kathmandu: Mohan Prasād.

Nepālī Padya-Sangraha (Collection of Nepali Verse). 1949. Edited by Pushkar Shamsher Rāṇā. Kathmandu: Nepālī Bhāshā Prakāshinī Samiti.

Pachchīs Varshakā Khaṇḍa Kāvya (Twenty-five Years of Nepali Episodic Poetry). 1982. Edited by Mādhavprasād Ghimire. Kathmandu: Royal Nepal Academy.

Pachchīs Varshakā Nepālī Kathā (Twenty-five Years of Nepali Stories). 1982. Edited by Dayārām Shreshṭha. Kathmandu: Royal Nepal Academy.

Pachchīs Varshakā Nepālī Kavitā (Twenty-five Years of Nepali Poetry). 1982. Edited by Abhi Subedī. Kathmandu: Royal Nepal Academy.

Pāṇḍé, Nityarāja. 1960. *Mahākavi Devkoṭā* (The Great Poet Devkoṭā). Lalitpur: Madan Puraskār Guṭhī.

Pāṇḍé, Poshaṇ. [1964] 1982. *Ānkhījhyāl* (Lattice Window). Stories. 3rd ed. Kathmandu: Sājhā Prakāshan.

Pārijāt. 1972. *Blue Mimosa*. Translated by Tanka Vilas Varya and Sondra Zeidenstein. Kathmandu: Sondra Zeidenstein.

———. 1987. *Pārijātkā Kavitā* (The Poems of Pārijāt). Edited by Ìshwar Barāl. Kathmandu: Sājhā Prakāshan.

———. 1988. *Euṭā Chitramaya Shuruāt* (A Beginning of Pictures). Kathmandu: Pratibhā Prakāshan.

———. [1964] 1989. *Shirīshko Phūl* (The Mimosa Flower). 6th ed. Kathmandu: Sājhā Prakāshan.

Pauḍyāl, Lekhnāth. [1916] 1934. *Ritu Vichāra* (Contemplation of the Seasons). Poem. Kathmandu: Jorgaṇesh Chāpākhānā.

———. 1953. *Taruṇa Tapasī* (The Young Ascetic). Poem. Kathmandu: Anantanāth Pauḍyālaya.

———. 1967, 1968. *Lālitya* (Delicacy). Poems. 2 vols. Birāṭnagar: Pustak Saṃsār.

Pradhān, Hriday Chandra Singh. 1964. *Nepālī Kāvya ra uskā Pratinidhi Kavi* (Nepali Poetry and Its Representative Poets). Kathmandu: Ratna Pustak Bhaṇḍār.

Pradhan, Kumar. 1984. *A History of Nepali Literature*. New Delhi: Sahitya Akademi.

Pradhan, Paras Mani. 1978. *Mahākavi Laxmi Prasad Deokoṭā* (The Great Poet Laxmi Prasad Deokoṭā). Kalimpong: Bhāgya Lakshmī Prakāshan. (In English.)

———. 1979a. *Ādikavi Bhānubhakta Āchārya* (Founder Poet Bhānubhakta Āchārya). Kalimpong: Bhāgya Lakshmī Prakāshan. (In English.)

———. 1979b. *Kavishiromaṇi Lekhnāth Pauḍyāl* (Poet Laureate Lekhnāth Pauḍyāl). Kalimpong: Bhāgya Lakshmī Prakāshan. (In English.)

———. 1980. *Bālakrishna Sama*. Kalimpong: Bhāgya Lakshmī Prakāshan. (In English.)

Pradhān, Parashu. 1984. *Parashu Pradhānkā Pratinidhi Kathāharū* (Parashu Pradhān's Representative Stories). Kathmandu: Om Prakāsh Agravāl.

Prāngan (Kathmandu). 1981. *Sama Smriti-Ank* (Memorial issue) 3, nos. 3–4.

Prasāī, Ganeshbahādur. [1968] 1977. "Kavi Vyathit: Ek Parichayātmak Lekh" (The Poet Vyathit: An Introductory Article). In *Sājhā Samālochanā*, pp. 151–163.

Premchand. [1936] 1961. *Godān* (The Gift of a Cow). Novel. Allahabad: Saraswatī Press.

———. 1988. *Deliverance and Other Stories*. Translated by David Rubin. New York: Penguin Books.

Rāī, Indra Bahādur. 1960. *Bipana Katipaya* (Many Awakenings). Stories. Darjeeling: Shyām Brothers.

Raj, Prakash A. 1979. *A Nepalese Discovers His Country*. Kathmandu: Sājhā Prakāshan.

Rākesh, Rāmdayāl. 1987. *Nepālī Kavitā: Vibhinna Āyām* (Nepali Poetry: Varied Dimensions). Kathmandu: Sājhā Prakāshan.

Riccardi, Theodore. 1988. "Four Nepali Short Stories." *Himalayan Research Bulletin* (New York) 8, no. 1, pp. 1–24.

Rimāl, Gopālprasād. [1962] 1983. *Āmāko Sapnā* (A Mother's Dream). Poems. 3rd ed. Kathmandu: Sājhā Prakāshan.

Risāl, Rām Maṇi. 1974. *Nepālī Kāvya ra Kavi* (Nepali Poetry and Poets). Kathmandu: Sājhā Prakāshan.

The Rising Nepal (daily newspaper in English). January 17, 1984.

Rossabi, Morris. 1988. *Khubilai Khan: His Life and Times*. Berkeley: University of California Press.

Royal Nepal Academy. 1975. *Seven Poets*. Poems. Kathmandu: Royal Nepal Academy.

———. 1983. *Nepālī Brihat Shabda-Kosha* (Nepali Dictionary). Kathmandu: Royal Nepal Academy.

Rubin, David. 1980. *Nepali Visions, Nepali Dreams: The Poetry of Laxmiprasad Devkota*. New York: Columbia University Press.

Sājhā Kathā (Sājhā Stories). [1968] 1979. Edited by Bhairav Aryāl. 3rd ed. Kathmandu: Sājhā Prakāshan.

Sājhā Kavitā (Sājhā Poetry). 1967. Edited by Chūḍā Maṇi Bandhu. Kathmandu: Sājhā Prakāshan.

Sājhā Samālochanā (Sājhā criticism). [1968] 1977. Edited by Krishna Chandra Singh Pradhān. Kathmandu: Sājhā Prakāshan.

Sama, Bālkrishna. 1954. *Āgo ra Pānī*. (Fire and Water) Poem. Kathmandu: Nayapāla Rājyalakshmī Shāh.

———. 1966, 1972. *Mero Kavitāko Ārādhana* (My Worship of Poetry: Autobiography). Vol. 1. Kathmandu: Royal Nepal Academy. Vol. 2. Kathmandu: Sājhā Prakāshan.

———. 1981. *Bālkrishna Samakā Kavitā* (The Poems of Bālkrishna Sama). Kathmandu: Sājhā Prakāshan.

———. 1972. *Expression After Death*. Kathmandu: Sājhā Prakāshan.

Samsāmayik Sājhā Kathā (Contemporary Sājhā Stories). 1984. Edited by Mohanrāj Sharmā and Rājendra Subedī. Kathmandu: Sājhā Prakāshan.

Samsāmayik Sājhā Kavitā (Contemporary Sājhā Poetry). 1983. Edited by Tārānāth Sharmā. Kathmandu: Sājhā Prakāshan.

Shāh, Premā. [1966] 1972. *Pahenlo Gulāph* (The Yellow Rose). Stories. Kathmandu: Ratna Pustak Bhaṇḍār.

Sharmā, Mohanrāj. 1978. *Kathāko Vikās-Prakrīyā* (The Development of the Short Story). Kathmandu: Sājhā Prakāshan.

Sharmā, Nagendra. 1976. *Folk-Tales of Nepal*. New Delhi: Sterling.

Sharmā, Tārānāth. 1982. *Nepālī Sāhityako Itihās* (History of Nepali Literature). 2nd ed., rev. Kathmandu: Sankalpa Prakāshan. (For first edition, see Tānāsarmā 1970.)

Sherchan, Bhūpi. [1969] 1984. *Ghumne Mechmāthi Andho Mānche* (A Blind Man on a Revolving Chair). Poems. 4th ed. Kathmandu: Sājhā Prakāshan.

Shreshṭha, Bishwabimohan. 1987. *Bishwabimohankā Kehī Kavitāharū* (Some Poems by Bishwabimohan Shreshṭha). Kathmandu: Royal Nepal Academy.

Shreshṭha, Dayārām. 1975. *Nepālī Sāhityakā Kehī Prishṭha* (Some Pages from Nepali Literature). Kathmandu: Sājhā Prakāshan.

———. 1976. "Munā-Madanko Srota tathā Preraṇā" (The Sources and Inspiration of Munā-Madan). *Rachanā* (Kathmandu) 14, no. 4, pp. 28–37.

———. 1982. "Ādhunik Nepālī Kathā: Prishṭhabhūmi ra Pravritti" (The Modern Nepali Short Story: Background and Trends). In *Pachchīs Varshakā Nepālī Kathā*, pp. 1–32.

———, (ed.). 1987. *Pushkar Shamsherkā Kathāharū* (The Stories of Pushkar Shamsher). Kathmandu: Royal Nepal Academy.

Shreshṭha, Dayārām, and Sharmā, Mohanrāja. 1977. *Nepālī Sāhityako Sankshipta Itihās* (A Concise History of Nepali Literature). Kathmandu: Royal Nepal Academy.

Shreshtha, Keshab. 1979. *A Field Guide to Nepali Names for Plants*. Kathmandu: Natural History Museum.

Shreshṭha, Siddhicharaṇ. [1964] 1978. *Mero Pratibimba* (My Reflection). Poems. 3rd ed. Kathmandu: Sājhā Prakāshan.

Subedī, Abhi. 1970. "The Movements in Nepali Poetry of This Decade." *Flow* (Kathmandu) 1, no. 2, pp. 65–70.

———. 1978. *Nepali Literature: Background and History*. Kathmandu: Sājhā Prakāshan.

———. 1981. *Sirjanā ra Mulyānkan* (Creation and Evaluation: Critical Essays). Kathmandu: Sājhā Prakāshan.

Sūkti-Sindhu (Pheri) (Ocean of Aphorisms). [1917] 1967. Poems. Edited by Shyāmjīprasād Aryāl and Kamal Dīkshit. Lalitpur: Jagdambā Prakāshan.

Swatantratā (Freedom). 1979. (Kathmandu) 2, no. 12.

Tānāsarmā. 1970. *Nepālī Sāhityako Itihās* (History of Nepali Literature). Kathmandu: Sahayogī Prakāshan. (For 2nd, revised edition, see Sharmā 1982.)

———. [1977] 1979. *Bhanubhaktadekhi Tesro Āyāmsamma* (From Bhānubhakta to the Tesro Āyām: Critical Essays). Kathmandu: Sājhā Prakāshan.

Thākur, Madhusudan. 1975. *Nepal, a Miscellany*. Kathmandu: Uttam Kunwar.

Tripāṭhī, Vāsudeva. 1977. *Lekhnāth Pauḍyālko Kavitvako Vishleshaṇ tathā Mūlyānkan* (An Analysis and Evaluation of the Poetry of Lekhnāth Pauḍyāl). Kirtipur: Tribhuvan University.

———. 1980. "Bahumukhī Pratibhā Bālkrishna Sama" (Sama: a Multifaceted Genius). *Vāṇmay* (Kirtipur) 1, no. 1, pp. 56–62.

Turner, Ralph Lilley. [1931] 1980. *A Comparative and Etymological Dictionary of the Nepali Language*. 1st Indian reprint. Delhi: Allied Publishers.

Upādhyāya, Keshavprasād. 1975. *Rimāl: Vyakti ra Kriti* (Rimāl: The Man and His Works). Kathmandu: Sājhā Prakāshan.

———. [1968] 1977. "Gopālprasād Rimāl ra Āmāko Sapnā" (Rimāl and "A Mother's Dream"). In *Sājhā Samālochanā*, pp. 118–131.

Vermā, Yugeshwar P. 1980. *Nepal: Progress and Problems*. Kathmandu: Pratibhā Vermā.

———. 1981. "Contemporary Nepali Poetry" (unpublished seminar paper).

Vettam Mani. 1975. *Puranic Encyclopedia*. Delhi: Motilal Banarasidass.

"Vyathit," Kedār Mān. [1952] 1962. *Sangam* (Confluence). Poems. 3rd ed. Kathmandu: Ratna Pustak Bhaṇḍār.

———. [1958] 1968a. *Ek Din* (One Day). Poems. 3rd ed. Kathmandu: Ratna Pustak Bhaṇḍār.

———. 1968b. *Nārī: Rasa, Mādhurya, Ālok* (Woman: Flavor, Sweetness, Brightness). Poem. Kathmandu: Nepālī Sāhitya Sansthān.

———. [1958] 1971. *Sanchayitā* (The Hoarder). Poems. Kathmandu: Ratna Pustak Bhaṇḍār.

Whelpton, John. 1983. *Jang Bahadur in Europe*. Kathmandu: Sahayogi Press.

INDEX

Text:	10/12 Baskerville
Display:	Baskerville
Compositor:	J. Jarrett Engineering, Inc.
Printer:	Bookcrafters, Inc.
Binder:	Bookcrafters, Inc.

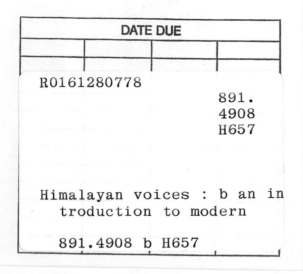